Stanford Studies in Jewish History and Culture
Edited by Aron Rodrigue and Steven J. Zipperstein

The Sultan's Jew

The Sultan's Jew

Morocco and the Sephardi World

Daniel J. Schroeter

Stanford University Press

Stanford, California 2002

Stanford University Press
Stanford, California

© 2002 by the Board of Trustees of the
Leland Stanford Junior University

Printed in the United States of America
on acid-free, archival-quality paper

ISBN 0-8047-3777-0 (cloth : alk. paper)

Original Printing 2002

Last figure below indicates year of this printing:
11   10   09   08   07   06   05   04   03   02

Typeset by James P. Brommer in 10/12 Galliard

To my parents

Contents

Illustrations

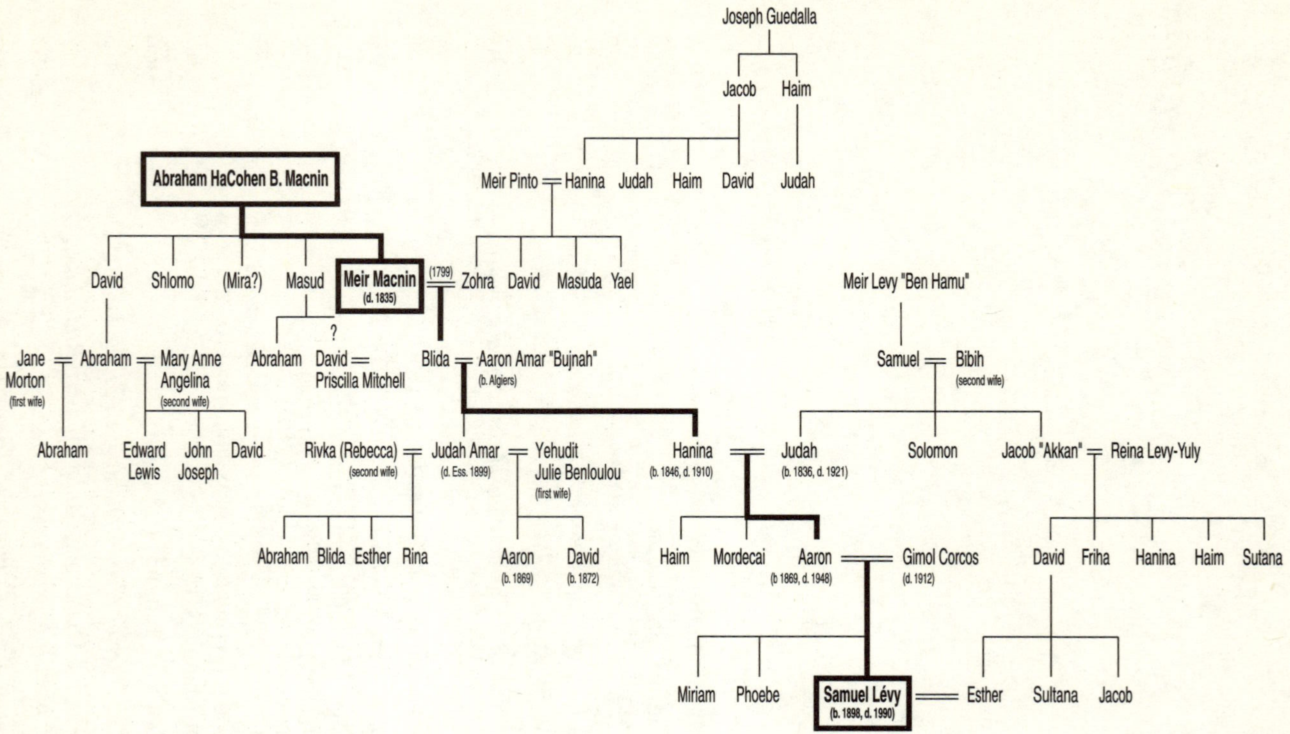

FIGURE 1. Macnin family tree, showing links to the Lévy family.

Preface

An unusual discovery by Professor Joseph Chetrit of a private collection of documents in Paris in 1985 initiated me into the project that has resulted in this book. The setting for this extraordinary archive was not what one would generally associate with great finds. It was not a château belonging to a descendant of the aristocracy tucked away in the countryside, or an elegant Parisian residence of a noted bourgeois family, but rather a modest high-rise apartment in a rather nondescript neighborhood. The owner of the archive, the late M. Samuel Lévy-Corcos—at the time, an ailing man in his nineties—preserved a legacy of documents, photographs, and memories of his family that spanned the entire history of his native Moroccan town of Essaouira, known to Europeans as Mogador.

The collection preserves the record of the Macnin family and their descendants. The Macnins were among the most famous Jewish merchant families of late eighteenth- and early nineteenth-century Morocco. Natives of Marrakesh, they were one of the first important merchant families that settled in the newly constructed town of Essaouira in the 1770s. Established by the ʿAlawid sultan, Sidi Muhammad b. ʿAbdallah, in 1764 as a royal seaport where all of Morocco's European trade was to be concentrated, the new town enhanced the traditional role of Marrakesh's Jewish merchant families as intermediaries between Morocco and Europe. Though we know nothing about how the family became prominent in Marrakesh and later in Essaouira, it is clear that they benefited from the policies of several sultans in relying on Jews and links between their empire and the Christian world. This was certainly the case with the family's most famous member, Meir Macnin.

FIGURE 2. Samuel Lévy-Corcos in his apartment in Paris. Photo by the author.

Meir Macnin was frequently the most important intermediary between the Moroccan state and the European powers during the first three decades of the nineteenth century, above all under the rule of Sultan Mawlay Sulayman. He began a long residence in London in 1800 at the time of the great bubonic plague in Morocco. For over a decade prior to his departure, he had been closely associated with the governor of Essaouira, and was referred to by the Europeans as the "governor's Jew." During his residence in London, Macnin was periodically commissioned to perform certain tasks as agent of the sultan. He would present his credentials as the Moroccan diplomatic representative, and in Mawlay Sulayman's correspondence with the foreign powers, he was referred to as "our Jew."

During the first two decades of the nineteenth century, Meir Macnin traded both for his own account and for the account of Sultan Mawlay Sulayman. Among European merchants with dealings in Morocco, Macnin had the reputation of a disreputable scoundrel who, through his brother and the close-knit coterie of Sephardi merchants in Essaouira, accumulated major debts in the financial centers of Europe. During the Napoleonic Wars, London boomed as a financial center, and commercial speculation was rife. Despite Macnin's notoriety in Europe, he was still able to make deals with merchants who considered him an indispensable gatekeeper to the centers of power in Morocco.

With his quasi-monopoly in trade, Macnin was the essential intermediary between Morocco and Britain. Sometimes acting as the sultan's agent in London, he secured ships, arms, and munitions for Morocco. He endeavored to keep a high profile at the Court of St. James, presenting exotic gifts, such as Moroccan lions, to the king of England from the sultan.

Meir Macnin had either the acumen or the luck to cultivate close ties with Mawlay Sulayman's successor, Mawlay ʿAbd al-Rahman. Upon the death of Sultan Sulayman in 1822, Macnin returned to Morocco. He acquired monopolies on exports of various items, and was granted the financial control of most of Morocco's seaports. He became the chief intermediary between the Moroccan court and the consular representatives in Tangier. In 1827 he was sent as ambassador at large to Europe, but the British refused to recognize his diplomatic credentials because of his scandalous debts, and he was threatened with arrest upon landing on British soil. It was an empty threat, and he was able to resettle in London for a period of time. He returned to Morocco in about 1833, and died in Marrakesh, the city of his birth, in 1835.

Despite the importance of Meir Macnin to the Moroccan state, no trace of his existence has been found in its archives. This may be due in part to the state of organization of the royal palace archives at the time of my research, but more important is the fact that records from before 1830 are extremely sparse. Few archives have survived from the reign of Mawlay Sulayman, which can in part be attributed to the very limited bureaucracy of the Moroccan court. One reason for this was that the bubonic plagues of 1799–1800 and 1817 decimated the officials of the royal court. The importance of Macnin's position, however, is evidenced both by the letters and *dahir*s (decrees) of the sultans preserved in the family archives, and by the frequent correspondence concerning Macnin between European diplomats and the Moroccan government, preserved in the records of the British Foreign Office and the French Ministère des Affaires Etrangères.

Among Moroccan Jews, the Macnins and the family name have mostly been erased from memory. Early on in my research, I was asked by a number of Moroccan Jews and specialists on Moroccan Jewry if perhaps I was confusing the family name with "Waqnin," a much more common Jewish name in Morocco. But for Anglo-Jewry, at least for those with some antiquarian interests, the name of Macnin is permanently etched in the historical memory, and is repeated in the various histories of the community. Meir Macnin even appears in the diary of Lady Montefiore, wife of the most famous leader of Anglo-Jewry in the nineteenth century. The first "history" that mentions the Macnins that I have found was written by E. H. Lindo in 1838 and updated to 1860 (*A Jewish Calendar*). This short work contains tables of the Jewish calendar and "a chronological table, forming a summary of Jewish history from the Flood to the present time." One of the entries for 1813 is "Masahod C. Macnin, Esq., appointed Envoy from Muley Soliman, Emperor of Morocco, to the British Government"; and one of three entries for 1827 is "Meir Macnin, Esq., appointed Envoy from the Emperor of Morocco, Muley Abda-rahman, to the Court of St. James." That Meir Macnin failed to receive an audience from the king and was spurned by the Foreign Office is not mentioned, or perhaps was not even known to the author: so enamored was Anglo-Jewry of Jews in Gentile politics!

Given Meir Macnin's obvious importance and the limited documentation about him, Chetrit's discovery of the Macnin family papers was an important find. Monsieur Lévy-Corcos was aware that his ancestors were among the mercantile elite of Mogador, and was proud of this history. He seemed flattered by our interest in his family. Understandably he was unwilling to let the documents be removed from his house for photocopying. But he was not at all adverse to the idea of our photographing the documents; quite to the contrary, he was happy to have our company. For about two weeks we returned nearly every day to photograph the material, and he told us what he knew about his family and his life in Morocco before moving to France. One year before his death in 1989, he allowed Joseph Chetrit to photocopy the collection.

I had encountered Meir Macnin in the Foreign Office archives in the Public Record Office in London and in the archives of the Ministère des Affaires Etrangères in Paris prior to our discovery, and had taken notes with some interest. The discovery of the family archive suggested to me the value of trying to bring to life aspects of history through reconstructing aspects of Macnin's life story. It has now been some years that I have been fascinated with Macnin. Some might call it an obsession. I have traveled back repeatedly to the British and French archives to try to find additional pieces in the puzzle of his mysterious and controversial life. Yet after all my efforts, he remains somewhat of an enigma. In the Lévy-Corcos collection and in the various archives consulted, hardly an echo of Macnin's own voice is heard. There are plenty of notarial documents pertaining to commerce and real estate, and letters sent to him from the Moroccan government (Makhzan). His relations with Europeans in the capacity of merchant or agent of the sultan are reported in detail in the European archives. Generally the diplomatic correspondence refers to Meir Macnin's unpaid debts, and according to the European accounts, his disreputable dealings.

In the absence of memoirs or personal correspondence, I can only guess what his personality was like. Since he rarely speaks in the documents, he is my invented informant around whom I attempt to imagine the world in which he lived. On the surface, his life seems to reveal the perennial negative stereotype of both Jew and Oriental: a cosmopolitan polyglot traveler; a schemer and scoundrel; a venal manipulator of other people's fortunes; a seeker of wealth, honor, and prestige. To European merchants and diplomatic agents in Morocco, Meir Macnin appeared to combine the arrogant self-righteousness of the Jews and the moral depravity of the East. Despite his notoriety and history of unpaid debts, he was still able to operate and outmaneuver his detractors, flaunting his sometimes dubious status as Jewish agent of the Moroccan sultan.

The family archives do not help us understand Meir Macnin's personality, nor do they overturn the negative image of his character represented in the foreign archives. If anything, the numerous deeds and records of transfers of property preserved in the family archives are evidence against both Meir Macnin and the Moroccan government's claims that the family had no assets from which he could repay his debts. But the family archives do illuminate the milieu in which prominent Moroccan Jewish merchants lived. The picture that emerges is one of considerable complexity, raising an array of interesting questions about Moroccan Jewry and the Sephardi world at a critical conjuncture of history. Moving back and forth between Morocco and England, Meir Macnin's story reflects an era in which relations between different parts of the Jewish world were rapidly changing. The Lévy-Corcos papers also continue after Meir Macnin's death, and encompass the lives of Macnin's descendants well into the twentieth century. The transformation of the Moroccan Jewish community is the subject of ongoing collaborative research with Joseph Chetrit, in part based on the papers, and a future book. *The Sultan's Jew* is the first part of the story.

This book eschews easy compartmentalization. It bridges together a number of fields that have often been treated separately. The effort to make these connections reflects my own background and training in Middle Eastern studies, my teaching of Jewish history, and my reaction against the artificial institutional boundaries often imposed by the academy between different fields of area studies. The Maghreb (generally encompassing Morocco, Algeria, Tunisia, and Libya) often falls between the cracks of both African and Middle Eastern history. Moreover, it is fashionable today to reject area studies altogether, especially when the area pertains to the formerly colonized world. Jewish history, for its part, has been dominated by the German tradition of Jewish historiography that originated in the nineteenth century. While the Jews in "classical" Islam or Muslim Spain received considerable attention from historians, the modern period has been considered somewhat irrelevant until relatively recently. Many who have studied the modern history of the Middle East and North Africa have been caught in the Western European mode of interpretation, which focuses on the familiar trajectory of modern Jewish history: from emancipation to assimilation, from anti-Semitism to Zionism. Non-Western Jews became defined already in the nineteenth century as "Oriental," and if their history was to be studied at all, it was a history that was solely shaped by the influence of the West. Western European Jewish questions are asked for the "Oriental" Jewish communities, which experienced a very different history.

The consequence of this kind of compartmentalization and marginalization is that many aspects of cross-cultural interaction escape historical interpretation. In this book, I would like to offer a broader cross-cultural analysis of areas often analyzed separately: Jewish and Muslim, Ashkenazi and Sephardi, Middle Eastern and European. There is perhaps a particular contemporary relevance and poignancy to the story of Meir Macnin: as part of a Diaspora culture, a traveler who went back and forth between different countries and cultural milieus, he demonstrates the historical depth of the multicultural world in which we now live.

Acknowledgments

I have thought about Meir Macnin for many years, and am grateful to friends and colleagues who have not lost interest in this project. This book would not have been possible without the collaboration of Joseph Chetrit of Haifa University, who originally discovered the personal archives that became the foundation of this book. Without his linguistic skills in nineteenth-century Moroccan Judeo-Arabic and Hebrew and his help in reading the texts, I would not have finished the manuscript. I am indebted to the late Samuel Lévy-Corcos, who with an open mind, allowed a couple of strangers to spend many hours with him photographing his family archives and asking him all kinds of questions. The Macnin family name has practically disappeared, but I was fortunate to have been contacted by Miss Audrey Macnin, a descendant of the family living in England, who was researching her family's history. I am grateful for her sharing with me information about the Macnin family in England. Barbara Barnett and Sarah Orkin of London, whose ancestors were connected in some way to the Macnins, also shared with me their family history or traditions for which I am thankful. I am grateful to Claire Manson and George Goldstein for their friendship and hospitality during my many stays in London.

Miss M. Rodrigues-Pereira, Honorary Archivist of the Spanish & Portuguese Jews' Congregation, was extremely helpful each time I visited the synagogue's archives, and always willing to answer my queries by correspondence, even long after my visits. I am particularly indebted to Pascal Even and the archivists at the Ministère des Affaires Etrangères in Nantes not only for their general helpfulness, but especially for opening the doors of the archives after hours.

I am grateful to my research assistants at the University of Florida for their help during the early phases of research for this book: especially to Randy Kaufman, Jan Shetler, and Larry Odzak. A research fellowship from the National Endowment for the Humanities enabled me to embark on this project. Collaborative work with Joseph Chetrit was assisted by a grant from the Israel–United States Binational Science Foundation. I am indebted to Lucette Valensi, Mohamed El Mansour, Harvey Goldberg, Khalid Ben Srhir, Susan G. Miller, and Emily Gottreich for their helpful criticisms of and comments on the manuscript. I am especially grateful to Gavin Lewis, whose skillful editing and many insights and suggestions, on both small details and large historical questions, immeasurably improved the quality of this book. I am grateful for the assistance I received in the final stages of producing this book and especially thank the following individuals: Marc Kanda for help in creating the Macnin family tree; Amelia Lyons for skillfully preparing the index and assisting me in proofreading; Dorothy Schroeter for taking the time and initiative to carefully read the proofs; and Anna Eberhard Friedlander, at Stanford University Press, for guiding the manuscript through the production process with skill and wisdom. To Jessica, I am forever grateful for her support and patience on a project that I sometimes thought would never conclude.

Note on Transliteration, Spelling, and Usage

This work draws from sources in many languages and from various time periods. As a consequence, proper names and terms appear in variant spellings and systems of transliteration in the different original texts. It therefore makes little sense to impose one system of spelling and transliteration, and the most that the author can aspire for is to maintain at least a certain degree of uniformity.

For transliteration of Arabic, I have dispensed with most diacritical marks; the ayn is written with ʿ; and the hamza with ʾ. Hebrew spelling follows the Library of Congress system of transliteration, with the exception of omitting "h" for the Hebrew letter "hé" when it comes at the end of a proper name. When the same name appears in Arabic and Hebrew, Arabic transliteration is used for Muslims and Hebrew transliteration for Jews (unless there is no known Arabic or Hebrew equivalent).

For those people who adopted or were known by European spellings, I use a romanized spelling of their names even when I am referring to an Arabic or Hebrew text (e.g., Macnin instead of Maqnin or Maknin), and English spelling over that of other European languages, unless the name concerned appears primarily in a language other than English.

During the colonial period, names and terms were most frequently rendered from colloquial Arabic and the Berber dialects into French, rather than from a standard system of transliteration of classical Arabic. A number of words and place names commonly found in the literature of the period will appear in their French forms (e.g., *dahir* instead of *zahir*), unless commonly known in English or appearing in scholarly works in English (e.g.,

Maghrib instead of Maghreb, Marrakesh instead of Marrakech, Fez instead of Fès). Preference will be given to present Moroccan usage for place names (e.g., Essaouira instead of Mogador, El Jadida instead of Mazagan).

The term *sultan* is not used as a title of the Moroccan rulers in the Arabic texts, but I have translated *mawlana* or *sayyidna* (both literally "our master"), as "sultan" in accordance with common English usage. However, I sometimes use the title *Mawlay*, or the colloquial *Sidi*, when used as part of the sultan's title. In the middle of a name, Ibn (from Arabic) and Ben (from Hebrew), literally "son of," are both abbreviated with "b"; the Berber equivalent is left as "U."

Note on Coins and Currency

The monetary system in Morocco in the late eighteenth and nineteenth centuries is a complicated matter, with constant changes affecting the meaning of terms found in sources of the period. Primary and secondary sources refer to the same coins found in Morocco by different names and in various languages. In this period, foreign silver coins dominated the Moroccan market, especially the Spanish real, from which the Arabic term *riyal* is derived, and which was both a silver coin and a money of account.

One of the major categories of Spanish coins in circulation at this period was what was known in English as the "Spanish hard dollar" or piastre, and in Arabic as the *riyal kabir*. In Spanish it had many names: the *peso fuerte*, the piastre, the *peso duro*, the *duro*, or (since it was equivalent at this time to eight silver reals) the *real à ocho*. The Spanish silver coin had become in this period the standard coin used in foreign exchange and the reference currency for the Moroccan monetary system.

The French silver five-franc piece also became increasingly common in the nineteenth century. The Arabic term *riyal* was used for a variety of silver coins in circulation, and in the latter half of the nineteenth century also referred to an accounting currency. The *dirham* was a Moroccan silver coin (and the word is used today as the name of the standard currency in Morocco). The *ducat* was a gold coin. The *mithqal* had been at various times either a gold or a silver coin, but during the period of this study, it was only an accounting currency. There were ten *uqiya* per *mithqal*. For detailed studies of Moroccan numismatics and the monetary system, see Daniel Eustache, *Corpus des monnaies ʿAlawites*, 3 vols. (Rabat: Banque du Maroc,

1984); ʿUmar Afa, *Masʾalat al-nuqud fi tarikh al-Maghrib fi al-qarn al-tasiʿ ʿashar (Sus 1822–1906)* (Agadir: Jamiʿat al-Qadi ʿIyad, Manshurat Kulliyat al-Adab wa-al-ʿUlum al-Insaniya bi-Agadir, 1988); idem, *al-Nuqud al-Maghribiya fi al-qarn al-thamin ʿashar: inzamitiha wa-awzaniha fi mintaqa Sus* (Rabat: Manshurat Kulliyat al-Adab wa-al-ʿUlum al-Insaniya bi-al-Rabat, 1993); Thomas K. Park, "Inflation and Economic Policy in 19th Century Morocco: The Compromise Solution," *Maghreb Review* 10, nos. 2–3 (1985): 51–56.

The Sultan's Jew

Introduction: Court Jews and Muslim-Jewish Relations in Morocco

Meir Macnin's career as a merchant and courtier was not a new phenomenon in Moroccan history.[1] He followed a long tradition of "court Jews": individuals who served in the courts of rulers as intermediaries between royal authority and the population, and in domestic politics or foreign diplomacy. Jewish families have been closely tied to the ruler throughout most of the history of the Moroccan monarchy. This is no revelation to students of Jewish history, for throughout the Islamic as well as the Christian worlds, Jewish courtiers have often been prominent, and much has been written about them. Yet few studies are based on extant sources from the families of court Jews themselves. Most rely on Jewish literary sources, Muslim polemics, or secondary descriptions. They tell us more about perceptions, mentalities, or even literary genres than about the actual social and economic conditions that enabled these families to remain in a position of influence.

Since time immemorial there have been anecdotes and traditions relating to the meteoric rise to power of the court Jews followed by their rapid demise, and these stories have been told and recast in various forms. German-Jewish historians of the nineteenth century were particularly enamored of the powerful and influential court Jews of medieval Spain. Jewish Spain's "Golden Age," as Jews have called this period since the last century, is represented by these illustrious Jews, whose positions are equated with that of Jewish society as a whole.[2] "To some extent," writes Jane S. Gerber in a recent history of Sephardi Jews, "the history of the Jews in Muslim Spain is indeed a history of the forceful, versatile personalities who charismatically dominated the Jewish communities while at the same time managing to negotiate their way in Gentile society."[3] Usually the court Jews have been depicted positively: they not only excelled in their diplomatic or financial tasks, but were often patrons of scholarship and supported the public welfare of the Jewish communities.[4]

While nineteenth-century historians often focused on Jewish courtiers in the Golden Age of Hispano-Jewry, historians during this century have followed this path in depicting court Jews elsewhere in the Jewish Diaspora,[5] emphasizing their "nonpolitical" or "outsider" status, coupled with their important role as merchants and intermediaries. Rulers often found it less risky to employ court Jews than members of the majority religion. Court Jews were simultaneously empowered and vulnerable. Their position of power depended on their ability to maneuver adroitly so to remain in favor with the sovereign; but if they were seen as acquiring too much power and influence, thereby alienating too large a sector of the non-Jewish population, they could outlive their utility to the ruler who could dismiss them or even have them executed. Sometimes popular hostility toward the court Jews turned into popular uprisings against the Jewish community as a whole.

In the Muslim world, political fragmentation and the emergence of competing states and dynasties gave opportunities to Jews whose services could help rulers gain a competitive edge over their rivals. Sephardi Jews, dispersed throughout the Mediterranean world, found many opportunities in the service of various rulers. The Ottoman sultans relied on Jewish physicians, tax collectors, and administrators in their efforts to assert control of the Middle East. But perhaps nowhere in the Islamic world were Jewish courtiers so important as in Morocco—even more than in the Ottoman Empire where indigenous Christians might compete for positions.[6] The Berber Marinid dynasty, which established control in Fez in the thirteenth century, constantly faced hostility from the Muslim inhabitants of the capital, and therefore often recruited Jews and other outsiders to its service. The employment of Jews was driven less by a benevolent attitude to the Jews than by necessity, for when the hostility of the population toward Jews in the service of the rulers intensified, or when relations with the prominent Muslim leaders of Fez improved, the positions of the court Jews were jeopardized.[7]

Court Jews maintained their prominence in Christian Spain as well until the expulsion of 1492, as the rulers continued to employ them in the administrative system which they largely took over from the Muslims.[8] The court Jew may have reached the pinnacle of influence in Central Europe in the age of absolutism from the mid-seventeenth to the mid-eighteenth century—not because the so-called *Hofjude* was so unique in terms of his essential characteristics as Selma Stern argued in her classic study, for many of these characteristics are found among court Jews in other times and places. What was distinctive about the age of absolutism, as Stern also shows, was that because of the preponderance of money in the expansion of state-sponsored mercantilism, an unprecedented level of opportunities awaited the enterprising Jewish merchant and financier. In the quest of the rulers to amass wealth, often unavailable in the coffers of the states of central Europe in the wake of wars, they permitted the Jews to play a central role in finance and commerce. As outsiders who were removed from the entrenched interests of urban elites and landowners, and as merchants with a network of financial and commercial connections, the court Jews were both dependent on the rulers and invaluable sources for accumulating wealth.[9] Yet, despite their position, the power and influence of the court Jews during this period proved to be a transitional phenomenon that declined with the weakening of royal authority and the expansion of a capitalist economy.

Under the ʿAlawid dynasty, corresponding to the same period that the *Hofjude* gained so much influence, more Jews served the sultans than perhaps at any earlier time in Moroccan history.[10] The ʿAlawids wrested control of Morocco in the mid-seventeenth century, and as with the Saʿdians who preceded them, the ruler was considered to be a descendant of the Prophet Muhammad, a *sharif* (plural, *shurafaʾ*). In a departure from the practice of the Berber dynasties that preceded them, sharifian descent was a legitimating principle of the Arab dynasties of the Saʿdians and ʿAlawids. The "sharifian" rulers, as they represented themselves, relied heavily on Jews for conducting foreign trade. In the latter half of the eighteenth century, Jewish royal merchants were also instrumental in the efforts of the state to consolidate its power based on trade, especially through the port of Essaouira where the Macnin family settled. But the important role of the court Jews in Morocco declined in the nineteenth century, not because of the development of capitalism, nor because new sources of state power were to emerge domestically in Morocco, but because the ability of the sultans to rule was undermined by foreign intervention. After Meir Macnin's death in 1835, Jews continued to play important roles in the royal court, but times had changed. Between 1830 and the beginning of colonial rule in 1912, Moroccan sovereignty was challenged by European intervention at an increasingly accelerated pace. The Jewish elite, although still tied to the sovereign, also became increasingly linked to the European powers; some of the most important Jewish families became protégés or even consular agents of European or American states, often at the same time that they fulfilled important functions for the sultans. In a sense, just as they emblematized *dhimmi*s (literally "protected persons") of the sultans—in accordance with the Islamic legal theory and practice that guaranteed the protection of the Islamic state to non-Muslims in exchange for their recognized inferiority—they now became simultaneously like *dhimmi*s of European states, which offered their protection and jurisdiction in accordance with treaty arrangements often imposed on Morocco by the threat of force. The Moroccan sultans, as a result, no longer had the same level of control over the Jewish courtiers. Macnin lived during this period of transition—one in which, because of the limited importance of Morocco to the European powers, the sharifian court was able to maintain the illusion of parity. Macnin's role as the intermediary of the sultan needs to be understood in this context. In some ways, he was the last great court Jew in Moroccan history; his life story symbolizes the changing power relationship between Morocco and Europe.

The study of Meir Macnin's life also raises some important questions about Muslim-Jewish relations in Morocco. For some historians, the study of the court Jew becomes the symbol of the relationship between Muslims and Jews as a whole. Moroccan Jewish history is often recounted through the biographies of prominent court Jews, almost to the exclusion of any other history.[11] While the court Jews have often been represented positively, their vulnerability is often stressed. In some instances, the fall of a Jewish courtier—often corresponding to the overthrow of his non-Jewish patron— is followed by the massacre of the Jewish community. The vicissitudes of the vulnerable court Jews are linked to the history of the Jewish community as a whole.

From this perspective, general conclusions are reached on the underlying precariousness of the Jewish position in Morocco. Unlike the rather positive picture painted of the condition of the Jewish communities in the Golden Age of Spain, the position of Moroccan Jewry is depicted in a more negative light. The disabilities of the *dhimmi*s, as defined by the so-called "Pact of ʿUmar" (to be discussed below) are stressed. This approach suggests a bleak picture of Jewish life in Morocco.[12]

A recent generation of Moroccan historians has taken exception to this negative portrait of Jewish life in Morocco. At the same time, they link Jewish to dynastic history. However, the emphasis moves away from the rise and fall of the court Jew toward a more general analysis of the status of the Jew in the state. By extension, an assessment of the overall relationship of Muslims and Jews in Morocco is offered. The general thrust of their argument is that the Jew was protected by the Makhzan, and that this tended to overshadow the disabilities associated with the Pact of ʿUmar (i.e., the protective connotation of *dhimma*—the contract obligating the Islamic state to protect its non-Muslim subjects—is stressed).[13] In this paradigm, the benevolent relationship between the Jew and the state, and consequently, between Muslims and Jews generally, was only undermined by foreign interference, especially through the granting of consular protection to native Jews. The

Jews henceforth became either the unwitting victims of foreign powers which greedily withdrew a portion of the population from the jurisdiction of the Makhzan, or guilty of abusing the new system of protection that had emerged.[14] Implicit in these arguments is that the Jews, as a consequence, were to play an extremely small role in the modern nationalist movement, and instead, tended to identify themselves with the colonial regime.

There has been considerable debate in recent years on the status and position of the "Jews of Islam."[15] But what in fact is meant by this term? Does it refer to the theoretical position of Jews in the Islamic religion, to the relationship of the Jews to the Islamic state or states throughout history, or to Muslim-Jewish relations in general? Can generalizations be made, based on how Islam defines its theological relationship to the Jews, on the Jewish experience in the Islamic world throughout history? Confusion between the theory of the relationship of the Muslim community with non-Muslims, and the historical circumstances that shaped this relationship in various settings, has clouded interpretation.

Furthermore, historical analysis has been guided by the political preoccupations of the times. In the nineteenth century, central European Jewish scholars were among the pioneers in the study of Islam, and they generally emphasized the more tolerant nature of the Islamic world (at least in the classical period). It was in the nineteenth century that the notion of the "Golden Age of Spain" was invented—especially referring to Muslim Spain—which could serve as a model of interconfessional tolerance in stark contrast to the history of anti-Semitism in medieval Christendom. The Turks as well were seen by Jews in a positive light, since it was the Ottomans who had welcomed the Spanish Jews when they were expelled in 1492, while much of Christian Europe still excluded the unwanted refugees. The image of a climate of enlightened tolerance in Islam could also serve as a model for an emancipated Jewry seeking acceptance in a society where modern anti-Semitism was beginning to emerge.[16]

In this century, the notion of symbiosis, borrowed from biology and applied to the cultural intermingling between Jews and non-Jews, gained currency among German-Jewish scholars. If the Holocaust cast doubt on the notion of a German-Jewish symbiosis, the idea continued to be applied to Jewish history elsewhere in the world. It was S. D. Goitein who firmly established the idea of "creative symbiosis" for the Jews of the Islamic world, and this characterization has been followed by most scholars ever since.[17] Goitein based his conclusions on a diverse collection of documents dating from the tenth through the thirteenth century that were discovered in the Geniza of Fustat (Old Cairo today). (A *geniza* is a repository of discarded documents, resulting from a Jewish practice of burying rather than destroying writings that might bear the name of God.)[18] Goitein undertook a massive study of these documents, and produced a voluminous portrait of Jewish life in the Muslim Mediterranean world during this period. In Goitein's view, this period of creative symbiosis lasted until 1300, which is about when his Geniza material ends. The Geniza people are out of the picture. "Arabs faded out from world history, and Oriental Jews from Jewish history," he states.[19] Goitein in the 1950s was following the conventional model of Orientalists who depicted the later Middle Ages as a time when Islamic civilization was in decline.

Bernard Lewis follows Goitein's model closely, painting a picture of a shared cultural tradition between Jews and Muslims, which he dubs "Judaeo-Islamic." Lewis compares this symbiosis to the modern Western European and American experience. Echoing Goitein, he depicts the emergence of a kind of cosmopolitan "bourgeoisie," characterized by freedom of movement and international trade, which in this period of decentralized government fostered greater tolerance.[20] Goitein saw parallels to the laissez-faire, free enterprise system of the United States.[21] Lewis also sees the later Middle Ages as a time when the Muslim-Jewish symbiosis was in decline, and although during the Ottoman heyday of the fifteenth and sixteenth centuries there was a cultural resurgence, in all the following periods the "Jews of Islam" were in decline.[22]

Haïm Zafrani, a Moroccan Jewish scholar who pioneered the study of the history and culture of Moroccan Jewry, agrees with this image of decline as it pertains to Morocco. For Zafrani, the high point was the "Hispano-Maghribi" Golden Age, followed by a period of impoverishment, isolation, and stagnation. Yet it is precisely on these centuries of stagnation that Zafrani's œuvre concentrates,[23] belying the decline theory that he argues. Unlike Goitein, whose period of symbiosis ended in the Middle Ages, Zafrani depicts an uninterrupted history of symbiosis between Muslims and Jews in Morocco. He writes idealistically of "privileged meeting places where, in the closeness of language and similar mentalities, true symbiosis was expressed." Symbiosis was achieved in daily life, social imagination, and popular culture. In these privileged spaces of convergence, religious and "national" frontiers collapsed; Moroccan Jews remained an integral part of the "sociocultural and linguistic landscape of the Muslim West and the old Hispano-Maghribi world."[24]

This image of cultural symbiosis and coexistence has in this century been somewhat overshadowed by another image, created in part because of the intractable Arab-Israeli conflict; the twentieth-century political history of Palestine and Israel is seen as intrinsic to the Arab world as a whole for all places and times. Instead of focusing on the acceptance and tolerance of Islam, the persecution of Oriental Jewry in Arab lands is emphasized. Such a depiction seeks to offer an explanation for the emigration of most of Asian and African Jewry to Israel. The argument made is that like Ashkenazi Jews, Oriental Jewry also suffered from "anti-Semitism," or were victims of pogroms.[25] These contrasting images, indeed myths, of the condition of Jews of the Islamic world have generated a lively debate on the actual conditions that shaped the Jewish experience among Arabs.[26]

For critics of Zionism seeking a "diasporized identity,"[27] Goitein's world of creative symbiosis presents a much more palatable model of diasporic multiculturalism than the existing polarities between Jewish and Arab cultures in Israel. In an invocation of Goitein's world, Ammiel Alcalay recasts Goitein's Mediterranean into a model for interpreting the contemporary world of Levantine culture, where Jews are seen as integrally woven into the cultural fabric of the Arab world.[28] "As reclaimed in Alcalay's book," writes James Clifford, "the Sephardi strand offers a specific counterhistory of Arab/Jewish coexistence and crossover."[29] In this idealistic "counterhistory," the same "Levantine" culture that was so disparaged by Israel's Ashkenazi establishment suggests the possibility of peaceful coexistence in a postnational world; interconfessional tensions and conflict are minimized, and medieval and modern history are compressed into a single, essentialized Levantine world.

The theory itself of non-Muslim status within the Islamic polity gives rise to often diametrically opposed generalizations on the Jewish position in the Muslim world. Nascent Islam, in defining its relationship to the older religions from which it sprung, assigned a position of inferiority to Judaism and Christianity. Jews and Christians (and sometimes other religious groups as well) became, within the Islamic polity, *ahl al-dhimma*— literally, "people of protection"). Jews and Christians were regarded as "people of the book" (*ahl al-kitab*), because it was believed that they had received divine revelations embodied in their sacred texts. Thus, the Jew and the Christian as *dhimmi*s were guaranteed the protection of the state. This protection, however, came at a price. Having rejected the final truth, as revealed to the prophet Muhammad, that corrected their imperfections, Jews and Christians were consigned to an inferior status. This status was defined by the Pact of ʿUmar, a document attributed to the second caliph of Islam, ʿUmar b. al-Khattab (634–44), which extended the protection of the state to the defeated Christians, but stipulated specific disabilities that were to reflect the inferiority of non-Muslims. The document is probably not authentic, and the stipulations of the Pact of ʿUmar were probably defined in a somewhat later period. Regardless of when the pact was formulated, however, it served as a model for the status of both Christians and Jews—and sometimes other religions were included as well. The stipulations of the Pact of ʿUmar were meant to place Jews and Christians in an inferior and humble status. Among other disabilities, *dhimmi*s were not to build new churches or synagogues nor repair old ones; their clothing was to be distinct from Muslims; and they were not to mount animals that were taller, nor build houses that were higher than those of Muslims. Most important was the annual poll tax, known as the *jizya*, that every adult male *dhimmi* had to pay.[30]

The development of the Islamic religion was inseparable from the formation of the Islamic state. Consequently, not only was the separation of church and state that prevailed in Western Christendom absent, but there was a kind of theoretical uniformity in the status of non-Muslims within the Islamic polity. What this also meant was that the legitimacy of the ruler of the state was based on his function as upholder of Islamic law, the *shariᶜa*. This law, however, pertained to Muslims, and apart from the Pact of ᶜUmar and certain other requirements of the state, Jews were to conduct their lives according to their own law. Just as Muslims were to conduct themselves on the basis of the *shariᶜa*, derived from the Quran and the traditions of the prophet (*hadith*), Jews were permitted to practice their religion and live their lives according to their law, the *halakhah*, based on the written and the oral Torah, the divine revelations to Moses. The oral Torah, attributed to Moses was passed down to the rabbis, and together with the written Torah formed the basis for extensive rabbinical discussions and writings that were compiled in the voluminous source of *halakhic* authority, the Talmud. The arrangement with the Islamic state by which Jews were allowed to practice their religion and follow their law gave them a large measure of self-government. It should be emphasized as well that even though the Islamic world was soon fragmented into separate and often antagonistic states, the religious law of Muslims and Jews transcended political frontiers.[31] A Jew, for instance, who acquitted himself of his annual poll tax in one Muslim state would in theory not have to pay again that year if he moved to another state. The same Jewish law also would apply across political boundaries.

In a certain sense, therefore, one can talk about the "Jews of Islam," because until modern times, government was by definition Islamic, guided by the principles that defined the status of non-Muslims in the state. In nineteenth-century Morocco, *dhimmi* status was invoked when it appeared as if the Jews were attempting to overstep the bounds of their station defined by the Islamic state.[32] This, however, did not mean that the conditions of Jews were uniform throughout the Islamic world, nor were all the stipulations of the Pact of ᶜUmar applied with the same rigor. Some of the prohibitions, such as that on building new houses of worship, proved to be impractical as Jews were often an indispensable part of Muslim colonization in new regions. During certain periods, many of the prohibitions were ignored, arousing the consternation of Muslim jurists. The *jizya*, the most important symbol of the superiority of Islam over the inferior religions, was not abandoned until the modern period, but the method of collection and the amount assessed could greatly vary.

These variations have suggested opposing generalizations about the condition of the Jews in Islam. Furthermore, there was a kind of duality in the relationship of the state and the Jews, since the former on the one hand offered the Jews its protection and allowed them a large measure of autonomy, but on the other hand, imposed certain disabilities. Thus, drawing from the same traditions, different conclusions are reached, depending on whether one wishes to emphasize the disabilities (Jews as second-class citizens) or the benefits of protection offered by the state. Yet each approach asks essentially the same thing that is part of the nationalist discourse: Was the state good or bad for the Jews? Depending on the answer to this question, conclusions are reached about Muslim-Jewish relations in general.

These considerations have guided assessments of Morocco. Jewish history in Morocco, on the one hand, is reconstructed by a narrative that links incidents of anti-Jewish violence, especially during interregnums. Often the history of the Jews is taken out of the more general context of Moroccan history. On the other hand, nationalist discourse in Morocco stresses the historic coexistence of Muslims and Jews, and the state is seen as the guarantor of this benevolent relationship. This latter approach places too much emphasis on the pernicious effects of imperialism by ignoring the deeply embedded preexisting differences and tensions between Muslims and Jews in Morocco.

In one sense, however, both interpretations of Jewish history in Morocco are correct: it was in the interest of the state to protect the Jews. In Morocco, the Jews were the only *dhimmi*s, because no indigenous Christians had lived in the Maghrib (in contrast to Egypt and elsewhere in the Middle East) since the Middle Ages.[33] Therefore, the lower status of the Jews was evidence of the superiority of Islam. In other words, the inferiority of the Jew helped to legitimize the Islamic state. Yet implicit in this pact of protection was that protection came at a price: Jews were to be subservient, and consequently at times more vulnerable to attack.

It is equally important to emphasize that few generalizations about Muslim-Jewish relations as a whole can be reached solely on the basis of dynastic history. Muslim-Jewish relations were not static in Morocco, and there were great variations in these relations in different periods and regional settings.[34] How best to characterize Muslim-Jewish relations in Morocco remains a subject of dispute. Lawrence Rosen insists that ethnic identity has not created barriers precluding close social ties between Muslims and Jews in Morocco. "For the Muslims," Rosen argues, "the Jew stands neither as an exception nor as a contradiction to a social order founded on networks of dyadically contracted personal bonds linking people whose inherent membership in any particular group or category serves only to establish a baseline for interaction with others rather than as an all-pervasive typification."[35] Henry Munson argues that Rosen does not pay adequate attention to the structural constraints on individual ties between Muslims and Jews. "The existence of cordial and even intimate relationships between individuals of generally hostile collectivities does not mean that the society in which such relationships occur is best seen in terms of individuals rather than groups."[36]

Whether one judges that Muslim-Jewish relations were shaped more by individual ties or collective structures, most scholars would agree on the interdependency between the two communities. Jewish middlemen played a vital role as merchants, and on a smaller scale, as peddlers between town and country.[37] The court Jew is symbolic, indeed, an extension of the interdependency between Muslims and Jews in Morocco. The position of Jews as intermediaries in society was built on reliance, yet at the same time tension, stemming from the fact that the two religious communities lived lives at once both together and apart. Though foreign interference accentuated tensions between Muslims and Jews, it was able to do so because tensions and differences were an inherent part of the system itself.

The prevalence of court Jews in the sharifian court was also closely connected to the relationship of the Islamic state to the Christian powers. The paradigmatic ruler of the Islamic state was not only responsible for upholding the *shariʿa*, and maintaining order within the country, but protecting the Muslim community from violations of its territory from outside the realm of Islam (*Dar al-Islam*). The just heir to Islamic government was also bound by duty to conduct *jihad*, or "struggle" against the unbelievers. At the same time, Muslim jurists recognized the need to maintain trading relations with the Christian states, and this was accepted, provided the purpose of the trade was to strengthen the position of Muslims. This contradiction—on the one hand, the requirement of *jihad* against the Christians, and on the other, the necessity for peaceful commercial relations—often needed to be reconciled and to find legal justification.[38]

The dilemma of simultaneously fighting and trading with the Christian powers was a factor that ensured the centrality of Jewish courtiers in the sharifian state. The legitimization of the Moroccan state, from the rise of the sharifian dynasty of the Saʿdians in the sixteenth century, depended on the formal struggle against Christians on Moroccan territory. As the legitimate Muslim ruler, the sultan was committed to fighting against the encroachments of Christian Europe and, in the sixteenth and seventeenth centuries, Spanish and Portuguese incursions into Morocco were a major threat to the territorial integrity of the state. The requirement of *jihad*, as the duty of the just heir to the throne, was reinforced by the ideology of sharifian descent (i.e., descent from the prophet Muhammad). This ideology of royal power became well entrenched during Saᶜdian rule, and after a struggle between sharifian lineages, continued under the ᶜAlawids who took control of Morocco in the seventeenth century and remain the ruling dynasty today.[39] The expression of legitimate rule was symbolized by the caliphal title, *amir al-muᵓminin*, the commander of the believers, whose duty was to conduct *jihad* against the unbelievers.

At the same time, the growing military and commercial power of Europe compelled Morocco to acquire arms from and engage in trade with the Christian powers. These concomitant aims—of *jihad* and commercial dealing with Europeans—were ideologically incompatible. One of the important ways in which the Moroccan state dealt with this contradiction was by concentrating much of the trade and diplomacy with the Christian powers in the hands of Jewish merchants closely attached to the court of the sultans. By employing Jews as royal merchants in the Moroccan ports and as emissaries in Europe, the Muslim rulers avoided direct contact with Christians which could potentially compromise the ideological underpinnings of the state. Quite simply put, Jews were already considered unbelievers and therefore the state was not concerned with the corruption of their souls. Moreover, the sultans were less willing to rely on Muslims who might use the profits accruing from trade, and the firearms obtained from Europeans, to establish an independent base of power which could undermine the authority of the dynasty.[40] Jews, however, posed no such threat since they lacked a political base of power. As a consequence, each new generation of rulers had prominent Jews closely associated with the palace. From the Palaches in the sixteenth and seventeenth centuries, to Sumbal, Benider, and Buzaglo in the eighteenth, Jews were the indispensable intermediaries for both the Saᶜdian and ᶜAlawid dynasties. It is into this long line of court Jews, closely linked to the sultan, that Meir Macnin falls.[41]

The sultan's power depended on the alliance of the palace with often disparate tribes and urban groups. The unifying factor that transcended tribal and other corporate affiliations was the ideology of the sultan being a *sharif*, a descendant of the Prophet. While there were frequently revolts against the sultan's efforts to collect taxes, it was rarely the sharifian ideology itself that was questioned. The religious authority of the sultan was recognized by virtue of his holy lineage. Rebellions to depose the sultan were therefore often led by ᶜAlawid pretenders who could base their legitimacy on their own sharifian claims.[42]

In a paradoxical way, a personal relationship between the sultan and the Jew was formed by each one's social separation from society, and in this sense, Meir Macnin's relationship to the sultan was similar to the relationship of court Jews to sovereigns in Europe in the age of absolutism.[43] Unlike other sectors of the population, Jews, as *dhimmi*s, were by definition under the protection of the ruler. It was incumbent on the sultan, as the protector of the Islamic state, to guarantee the security of the Jews. Failure to protect the Jews challenged the polity itself. As Sultan ʿAbd al-Rahman wrote to the governor of Tetuan in 1825, "The Jews' [*ahl al-dhimma*] protection is inviolable; as [our Prophet Muhammad] said (God bless Him and grant Him salvation), 'whoever ill-treats them will be accountable to me on the Day of Judgment.'"[44]

Jews were therefore the only group in Morocco whose status was based exclusively on the personal protection guaranteed by the sultan himself. This basic concept is reflected in the sultan's relationship to his Jewish agents. In letters to government officials or foreign powers, the sultans and their entourage often refer to their courtiers and merchants as "our Jews,"[45] or even "our chattel."[46] This does not mean, however, that these Jews were exactly the same as property, and could be bought or sold in the same manner as slaves.[47] Only non-Muslims who refused to submit to Muslim rule could be enslaved. Jews and other *dhimmi* groups who submitted to Islamic governance, together with converts to Islam, were considered by jurists to be free.[48] This patrimonial designation conferred upon the Jews by the rulers also did not mean that the Jews were powerless, lacking the ability to negotiate their position and relationship with the sultan. Perhaps we can accept David Biale's generalization that "the Jews possessed an extraordinary ability to maneuver between the extremes of a quest for full sovereignty and a state of political passivity."[49] Jews who served the ruler did so also because they were individuals with ambitions who were willing to take risks to acquire wealth and achieve power within their own communities. But there was, nevertheless, a very large measure of possession in this relationship, comparable in some ways to the status of Jews in medieval Christian Europe. In many places in Europe, Jews received special protection as "serfs of the chamber," implying that their property, goods, and money belonged to the ruler or the church.[50] While the church condemned usury, the right of Jews to collect interest, provided that it was "moderate," was defended.[51] Moneylending was seen as a necessary evil practiced by Jews, justified by the belief that they were already sinners.[52] The church sometimes justified the practice of rulers protecting Jewish moneylenders with the theory that the Jews' possessions belonged to them and therefore the money accrued from usury could be taken for the general welfare of society. The Muslim world was even more unequivocal in its condemnation of usury, and taking interest was not allowed. But there is still a comparison to be made with the Christian world of the Middle Ages in that the protection of the Jews was in both cases linked to their profitability. As a collectivity, the protected status of Jews was linked to the payment of *jizya*; for individual Jewish merchants and courtiers, their royal protection was directly attributed to and justified by their profitability to the Makhzan, and by extension, the welfare of the Muslim community.[53] Thus the court Jews, as influential agents of the sultans, were mediators between the Jewish community and the state since their very ability to gain revenue for the state legitimized the position of Jews in society as a whole. Furthermore, the sultans' Jewish agents could help raise money for the Makhzan from the Jewish community—sometimes a Jewish community as a collectivity would be obligated to loan money[54]—and to mobilize their network of connections within Morocco or abroad. Since the Jewish community as a whole was dependent on the ruler for the protection of its members, the court Jews' ability to build up a base of power that could threaten the authority of the sultans was greatly limited. To the extent that they were able to break away from the grasp of the sultan, they had to align themselves with another powerful Muslim potentate, such as a prince seeking to gain control of the country during a period when the succession was contested. Only when European intervention began to challenge the sovereignty of the Moroccan government did some prominent Jews, now closely linked to foreign power, begin to break away from their close dependency on the ruler.

In the second half of the eighteenth century, during the reign of Sultan Sidi Muhammad b. ʿAbdallah, Morocco began to open its doors to European trade. Numerous commercial treaties were concluded with foreign powers, and the port of Essaouira was built. This reorientation toward Europe appeared to be reversed under the reign of Mawlay Sulayman (1792–1822). To outside observers, the sultan was one of the most enigmatic rulers of the Islamic world in the late eighteenth and early nineteenth century. In the age of European commercial expansion, Morocco appeared to be closing its doors to Europe. The sultan was undoubtedly preoccupied with defending Islam from foreign encroachments. He was perhaps the only Muslim ruler outside Arabia to embrace, or at least sympathize with, the Islamic reformist doctrine espoused by Muhammad b. ʿAbd al-Wahhab. The attraction of Sultan Sulayman to Wahhabism explains in part his attempts to curb what he viewed as the heterodox practices of the Sufi orders (mystical orders that were numerous and widespread in Morocco). This policy, which aimed at strengthening the Islamic state from within, failed to make any major inroads in Morocco where the culture of the Sufi orders was too well entrenched. The sultan's control of the country was limited because of his commitment to ideological priorities that ran against the grain of traditional Moroccan society.[55]

This disregard of tradition is also reflected in the sultan's administrative policy. In place of delegating responsibilities to traditional notables and tribal chiefs, the sultan made some unsuccessful attempts to install a limited number of his own personal appointees over a highly fragmented country. Mistrustful of both urban and rural notables, Mawlay Sulayman maintained an extremely reduced administrative apparatus, employing individuals who could be easily controlled.[56] The sultan also relied almost exclusively on Jews in trade and diplomacy. By employing Jews as merchants, tax farmers, and diplomatic agents, the sultan could count on the support of a segment of society whose position was totally dependent on his protection. His almost complete reliance on Macnin for foreign affairs can be understood in this context.

The disparity in power between the Islamic world and Europe became much more apparent in the period in which Macnin lived. Napoleon's invasion of Egypt sent shock waves throughout the Islamic world, and Morocco was no exception. Mawlay Sulayman sought to strengthen the base of society by turning to the puritanical Wahhabi movement which sprang from Arabia in the latter half of the eighteenth century, and which sought to purge Islam of extraneous influences that were believed to have weakened the Islamic polity.[57]

By employing Meir Macnin as a key intermediary, and guaranteeing his protection in Europe, Mawlay Sulayman was legitimizing his role as Islamic ruler in his relationship to the *dhimmi*s. The ability of the state to protect the Jew measured the strength of the Islamic polity itself. Yet the very reliance on Macnin underlined the weakness of the Moroccan state. This dependency on Jews in the age of aggressive European expansion opened the door for foreign interference in Moroccan affairs. How much so could not possibly have been prophesied in the decades before the invasion of Egypt, when Moroccan trade and contacts with Europe were increasing, and Jewish merchant families such as the Macnins were benefiting from the Makhzan's reliance on them to increase in status, wealth, and power.

CHAPTER TWO

The Rise of the Macnins

Meir Macnin was born in Marrakesh probably in the late 1760s.[1] His full Hebrew name was Meir Ben Abraham Cohen—Meir the son of Abraham Cohen. But Meir's father was known as "Macnin," the word in Moroccan Arabic for "goldfinch." The bird is found in parts of North Africa, and is known in Morocco for its melodious song. It therefore seems likely that Meir's father was called Macnin because of his beautiful voice. In any case, the name was passed down to the children. In Arabic documents, Meir and his siblings were called "Awlad Macnin," the children of Macnin—a family name that was practically unknown, perhaps even unique, in Morocco. Once he had lived in London for some time, Meir became known simply by his anglicized name, Meir Macnin, or sometimes as Meir Cohen Macnin.

Remarkably little is known about Marrakesh and its Jewish community in the eighteenth century, despite the fact that Jews were more numerous there than in any other city in Morocco with the exception of Fez. Estimates for the number of Jews in Marrakesh in the eighteenth century are lacking; accounts by European travelers dating from the 1830s estimate about five thousand Jews out of a total population of fifty to ninety thousand.[2] The number may actually have been somewhat higher, for as a British traveler observed in 1836: "There are here about five thousand Jews, exclusive of the children, who are very numerous."[3]

Marrakesh was founded in 1062 as the capital of the Berber dynasty known to Europe as the Almoravids (*al-Murabitun*), builders of an extensive empire that ruled over the Maghrib and Spain. Forbidden to reside in

FIGURE 3. *Marocco* (*Meraksce*) (Marrakesh). From Jacopo Gråberg di Hemsö, *Specchio geografico e statistico dell'impero di Marocco* (Genoa: Dalla Tipografia Pellas, 1834).

the new capital, Jews lived in Aghmat about forty kilometers southeast of Marrakesh, though they undoubtedly were able to come to the city for business. It is unclear if Jews actually lived in Marrakesh at the time that the Almohads, the dynasty that succeeded the Almoravids, conquered the city in 1147.[4] The Almohads were intolerant of non-Muslims, and the Jews were subjected to persecution and forced conversion. Many Jews may have continued to practice Judaism secretly, and there were periods even during the Almohads during which Jews could practice Judaism openly, such as the reign of al-Maʾmun (1227–32), when Jews are found living in Marrakesh.[5] There were Jews living in Marrakesh during the period of the Marinid dynasty in the mid-thirteenth century[6] and in all subsequent periods, they were allowed to practice Judaism.

A major influx of Jewish refugees from Spain in the late fourteenth and fifteenth centuries must have augmented Marrakesh's Jewish community.[7] Although Marrakesh's political role was eclipsed by Fez, which had become the Marinid capital in the thirteenth century,[8] the prominence of Marrakesh was renewed in the sixteenth century when the Saʿdian dynasty restored Marrakesh as their principal capital. Jews became more numerous in the city, and the new rulers built a Jewish quarter (*mellah*) between 1553 and

1573 where all the Jews of the city were required to live. The term *mellah* (lit. *mallāḥ*) was derived from the name of the district in Fez where in the fifteenth century Jews were first compelled to live in a quarter enclosed by a wall. It came to mean all the Jewish quarters in Morocco, and by extension, the Jewish community of a given town. Morocco's second *mellah* was in Marrakesh.[9] Not only were demographic pressures caused by an increased number and visibility of Jews a probable cause for the creation of a *mellah*, but as part of the Saᶜdian effort to assert their control of the southern capital, an enclosed Jewish quarter, as already existed in Fez, may have helped legitimate the new dynasty's claim to royal authority: protecting *dhimmi*s was an important obligation of the Islamic ruler.[10] The *mellah* of Marrakesh was where Meir Macnin grew up.

Little is known, too, about the origins of the Macnin family, or of how they became prominent in Marrakesh or subsequently in Essaouira. What we do know is that the family played an important role in the early development of the commercial life of the new seaport. Essaouira was to become Morocco's principal port of trade, where all the consulates and merchants trading with Europe were to be concentrated. A tradition of the Jewish community of Essaouira relates that in 1766 representatives of ten of the most important Jewish families of Morocco were chosen by the principal Jewish diplomatic agent and secretary of the sharifian court of that era, Samuel Sumbal, to conduct the new town's trade. The sultan conferred special privileges upon these Jewish merchants. Whether or not it was Sumbal who actually chose specific Jewish merchant families to inhabit the new town is uncertain, but his official connections with Essaouira are confirmed by later evidence.[11] In 1768, the French consul in Rabat, Louis Chénier, wrote from Marrakesh that Sumbal was assembling merchants from Essaouira and Agadir: "The motive for this gathering is unknown," he remarked, "but perhaps its purpose is the farming of ports."[12] Typically, the Makhzan leased Moroccan ports to Jews, who paid for the exclusive privilege of collecting customs. Such was the case for the ports of Tetuan and Agadir in this period.[13] Jews also were typically leased ports for the exclusive export of specified items, such as coral.[14] But Sultan Muhammad b. ᶜAbdallah had more in mind when he founded Essaouira in 1764: he wished to attract all the principal merchants, European and Moroccan, to the town. Essaouira soon became the most active Moroccan seaport. European, Muslim, and Jewish merchants built houses there, attracted by promises that customs duties would be relaxed.[15]

Apparently, it was not among the first group of ten elite Jewish families that Abraham Hacohen b. Macnin of Marrakesh arrived in Essaouira with his four sons, Shlomo, Masud, Meir, and David (he also had at least two daughters of whom less is known), but the Macnin family likely arrived in the 1770s, or early 1780s.[16] Meir Macnin's prominence in the town dates from the late 1780s, and it is at that time that the sources begin referring to his activities. By that time, Jews had become numerous in Essaouira, as noticed by a British traveler, Colonel Keatinge, on a mission to Marrakesh. After denouncing the maltreatment of the Jews by the governor during the arrival of a Swedish embassy, who "without a moment's warning, turned a rich Jew merchant and his family out of house and home, to accommodate some of the Swedish gentlemen," he was quick to add: "yet Jews do build houses here!"[17]

The Macnin brothers joined the ranks of the most privileged families, trading on considerable sums of money advanced by the sultan. Islamic law prohibited interest on loans, but unlike medieval Christianity with its negative attitude toward acquisition, Islam regarded profit positively, as the normal outcome of commercial activity.[18] Thus, the sultan's merchants were expected to supply the palace with luxury goods and weapons, and to generate revenue for the Makhzan through customs charged on the goods they imported and exported. When trade slackened and the Makhzan became hard pressed for cash, repayment of some of their outstanding loans was demanded. Such was the case in July 1789, for Tahir Fannish, a corsair, merchant, governor, and diplomatic agent for the sultan.[19] Similar orders were sent "for the Governor's Jew, Meyer Mecknin [*sic*] and the sheikh of the Jews, Moseh Taperro; the Kaid Omar answered for the former, the latter is still in irons."[20]

Thus, Macnin's position, was sufficiently strong that he had obtained the protection of the governor, ʿUmar b. al-Daʾudi, unlike the shaykh (or "elder") of the Jews who was the chief intermediary between the Muslim authorities and the Jewish community. The power and authority of the Jewish shaykh (in Arabic, *shaykh al-Yahud*; in Hebrew, *nagid*), varied from place to place, though as a rule he was in charge of collecting taxes, policing the Jewish community, and sometimes enforcing the decisions of the community and rabbinical court.[21] The *nagid* was often in a precarious position because Muslim potentates regarded him more as an individual who could be squeezed for money than as a representative of the Jewish community. Consequently, *nagid*s such as Tapiero were constantly at risk of having arbitrary actions taken against them by the authorities.[22] As a merchant, Meir Macnin was also potentially vulnerable, but less so than the *nagid*. As official representatives of the sultan, the local authorities were more circumspect in their treatment of the merchants. The *nagid*s in Essaouira never appeared to have come from the wealthy and powerful merchant families, who must have regarded the position as highly undesirable.

It is curious that the Macnins do not appear in *Massaʾ Baʿrav*, the vivid account of Moroccan Jewish life by the Italian Jewish writer, Samuel Romanelli.[23] Romanelli traveled to many of the larger Jewish communities in Morocco, and was living in Essaouira at the end of the reign of Sidi Muhammad b. ʿAbdallah and the beginning of the reign of Mawlay Sulayman, employed as a secretary by the Guedallas, the leading merchants of the town, who were heavily involved in trade with London. Romanelli characterized the founder of the mercantile family as "the richest man in all Morocco."[24] According to tradition, his wealth inspired the jealousy of Sultan Mawlay al-Yazid.[25] Most of the other principal families of the merchant elite are mentioned, so it is entirely possible that Meir Macnin was in Europe during Romanelli's stay in Essaouira. Romanelli describes a circumcision celebration in the home of Abraham de Lara, a merchant from Amsterdam who married into the Guedalla family, later to be closely associated with the Macnins in Essaouira and London. Also included in the gathering of the town's elite described by Romanelli were members of a number of other families: Abudarham of Gibraltar, Akrish of Livorno, and Pinto "who though a Moroccan, was also splendidly dressed in our style."[26] Most probably, Romanelli is referring to the merchant Meir Pinto, married to a Guedalla and the future father-in-law of Meir Macnin.[27] Among the privileges rewarded to the elite Jewish merchants was their right to wear Western clothing, later a cause of dispute between the Makhzan and a few Jewish merchants of Essaouira.

In the 1780s the most active Moroccan merchants in the port of Essaouira were Jews: Solomon Sebag, Haim Guedalla, and Mordecai De La Mar. These Moroccan Jewish merchants were included in the corps of "European" merchants in Essaouira, as we learn from a petition of the foreign merchant corps of the town, known as *il Commercio*. The merchants were protesting the imposition of a tax of one *mithqal* per quintal on merchandise exported from the port to replace an anchorage fee that the captains of vessels had been required to pay.[28] In the merchant community there were "about thirty houses of different nations of Europe, whose inmates live in an intercourse of amity and hospitality, uninfluenced and unbroken by the squabbles of the parent states."[29] The governor of Essaouira was also clearly chosen for his experience with Europeans:

The present governor here had been ambassador in various parts of the world—to England, to Vienna, to Constantinople. He received his visitors, sitting cross-legged on cushions, at the upper end of a small room, with some principal officers in his company, to whom he appeared to have been reading; though probably the book was merely kept in hand, as we see at home frequently on such occasions, not to appear *désœuvré*. He was well acquainted with the rules of politeness and the intercourse of life; paid many compliments to the British nation, and inquired particularly for such distinguished persons he had known; amongst other, by name, for lords North, Suffolk and Rochfort. Chairs were brought for the Europeans, and tea was served round.[30]

FIGURE 4. *A View of the Arsenal at Mogador*. From G. Beauclerk, *Journey to Morocco* (London: Printed for Poole and Edwards, etc., 1828).

The elite Jews were part of this cosmopolitan society of foreign commerce, well acquainted with Europe. The Jewish merchants who traded with Amsterdam, Livorno, London, and Marseilles often had members of their families in these European ports.[31] For example, Mordecai De La Mar's brother Masahod (Masud) resided in Amsterdam and dispatched ships to his brother in Essaouira or El Jadida.[32]

Equally important for this network of trade were the numerous connections with the interior of Morocco. Jews profited from the ransoming of shipwrecked European captives whose ships, en route to West African ports or fishing along the coast, often ran aground along the treacherous coast south of Agadir at Wad Nun (Oued Noun, in its French form) and the Saharan littoral.[33] Seized by the indigenous inhabitants of the region, they were often brought to the interior markets, as described by the British merchant in Essaouira, James Grey Jackson:

After traveling three days to one market, five to another, nay sometimes fourteen, they at length become objects of commercial speculation, and the itinerant Jew traders, who wander about from Wedinon to sell their wares, find means to barter for them tobacco, salt, a cloth garment, or any other thing, just as a combination of circumstances may offer, and then return to Wedinoon with the purchase. If the Jew have a correspondent at Mogodor, he writes to him, that a ship had been wrecked, mentioning the flag or nation she belonged to, and requests him to inform the

FIGURE 5. Wreck of the *Sophia*. From Charles Cochelet, *Narrative of the Shipwreck of the Sophia, on the 30th of May, 1819, on the Western Coast of Africa, and the Captivity of a Part of the Crew in the Desert of the Sahara* (London: Printed for Sir Richard Phillips & Co., 1822).

agent, or consul, of the nation of which the captain is a subject; in the mean time flattering the poor men, that they will shortly be liberated and sent to Mogodor where they will meet their countrymen: a long and tedious servitude, however, generally follows, for want of a regular fund at Mogodor for the redemption of these people.[34]

Many of the captives disappeared, converted to Islam, and others remained enslaved for several years before a suitable offer was negotiated. The trials and tribulations of these enslaved seamen in "Barbary" inspired a popular literature in Europe and the United States. Jackson estimated that between 1790 and 1806 about thirty vessels, mostly British, were shipwrecked along this coast, and an estimated eighty sailors were ransomed via Essaouira.[35] A French captain who was shipwrecked and ransomed in 1785 wrote: "If ever the French government, or any other, receive information of the loss of a vessel in these latitudes, it would be advisable for its agents, either at Mogador, or Tangier, to address themselves to a Jew of the name of Aaron, who resides at Gouadnum [*sic*]. This Jew sends his emissaries to the different parts of Africa, to reclaim the crews of shipwrecked vessels."[36] The principal Jewish merchants in the port of Essaouira, for example Mordecai De

La Mar, were involved in the ransoming of Christian slaves in the south of Morocco.[37] The Jewish network of trade relations with their coreligionists in southwestern Morocco in places such as Iligh and Goulimim (in Wad Nun), where the captives were often held by the local chieftains until the ransom was secured,[38] facilitated the preponderance of Jews in this enterprise. An account by an American sailor who was shipwrecked and held in captivity in Wad Nun in 1799–1800, reveals the intricate negotiations that went on between the consuls and the Jews of Essaouira, and their connections with coreligionists and competing Muslim chiefs in the south:

One of the strangers asserted that the English Consul was unable to buy so many of us; and that if we were carried to Elie [Iligh], the Jews there would buy us all. Others objected to that plan, and said that the plague still raged in Elie, for which reason we should not fetch anything there, or at most, according to the last accounts, not above thirteen dollars each. Again, there were some of them who thought it best to divide us into two separate companies, and carry one part of us to Elie and the rest to Swearah [Essaouira]; alleging, that the younger ones especially would go off best at the Elie market. They broke up at last, without coming to any settled determination respecting the manner of disposing of us.[39]

The almost exclusive reliance of Sidi Muhammad b. ʿAbdallah on Jewish merchants to conduct his trade with Europe was also closely related to the fact that the Jews did not constitute a political risk, as did Muslim potentates. One of the reasons for the sultan's creation of Essaouira was to secure state control of the southern trade, which often had been appropriated by dissident political powers in the southwestern Sous region of Morocco that conducted trade with Europeans independent of the Makhzan. In particular, a governor appointed to the port of Agadir, al-Talib Salih, had rebelled against the sultan and appropriated the profits of trade for himself in the early years of Sidi Muhammad b. ʿAbdallah's reign.[40] Within a decade of Essaouira's construction, Agadir was closed to foreign commerce, and many of its inhabitants were forced to move to the new royal port.[41] In Essaouira, the concentration of commerce in the hands of Jewish merchants, who were granted trade advantages by the sultan, thus helped ensure that the profits accruing from foreign trade would be appropriated by the state, rather than ending up in the hands of rebellious provincial dissidents.

Not only did Jews act as crucial intermediaries between the state and the foreign merchants that populated the new town, but many, with a string of family members stationed in Europe, were also dispatched on diplomatic missions abroad. Mordecai De La Mar of Essaouira and his brother Masahod (Masud) in Amsterdam were closely linked to the sultan, and were often charged with diplomatic missions. Masahod was appointed by the sultan to go to Britain from Amsterdam to restore diplomatic relations following a dispute between the sultan and the British consul in 1782.[42] Masahod, it seems, stayed in London for a number of years, claiming that he had been appointed as "*chargé d'affaires* in Europe," and is referred to by the British consul in Tangier as "the Emperor's Jew." In London, he stayed with the prominent Sephardi Jew, Mendes de Costa.[43]

These elite Jewish merchants of Essaouira, together with the European traders in the town, periodically made the three- to four-day journey to Marrakesh to the court of the sultan when he was present in the southern capital, bringing with them presents and often receiving in return advantages such as a reduction in duties.[44] Gifts were therefore carefully selected to please the sharifian monarch. The visit in Marrakesh could last a couple of weeks, and according to Jackson, the merchants were received three times: at a reception upon arrival, at a business meeting, and at a final audience of departure.[45]

Some of these merchants received special privileges from Sultan Muhammad, such as the right to export grain. Trade in wheat with Europe was generally not allowed and required special government authorization. Its export often aroused popular opposition and the objections of ulama because of the belief that it resulted in shortages and rising food prices. In 1789, Meir Pinto and Haim Guedalla were granted permission to export wheat from El Jadida.[46] The two merchants, with their close ties with London, were also involved in importing munitions.[47] The prominent court Jews Eliahu Levi (also Elijah and Elias in the sources), a competitor of Sumbal,[48] and Jacob Attal were also involved in the wheat trade from El Jadida, which was renewed by the sultan shortly before his death.[49]

The story of such merchants as these is emblematic of the few Jewish courtier families who were able to attain status through their links to the state. The Jewish merchants and agents of the Makhzan needed to maneuver adroitly and with cunning, and sometimes ruthlessly, to obtain and maintain positions of preeminence.[50] Under Sultan Sidi Muhammad, numerous Jews, as well as a number of Christians, had been employed at the royal court: Eliahu Levi, Jacob Attal, Mordecai De La Mar, David and Isaac Cordoso, and Francesco Chiappe were among the principal courtiers in the latter part of the sultan's reign.[51] For many years, Samuel Sumbal, who had had a French education in Marseilles, was the preeminent figure in foreign relations in the courts of Mawlay ʿAbdallah and Sidi Muhammad b. ʿAbdallah. He served as an adroit negotiator, interpreter, and secretary for both sultans until 1782, when he fell out of favor. Sumbal, like other Jewish agents of the sultan, also attempted to win favor from the foreign powers and received money from them in exchange for services. This enabled him to purchase considerable property. Individuals were allegedly forced to sell him property out of fear, giving rise to cases before the rabbinical courts, in one instance thirty years after the sale of a house and after both parties were deceased. Sumbal's access to the sharifian monarch was at times indispensable for the foreign representatives, but they could easily be frustrated by his frequent failure to communicate letters. He allegedly transferred his property to Genoa in 1780, and then attempted to escape the country. Georg Høst, agent for the Danish African Company, recounted that being fined by the Sultan several thousand piastres, he departed for Guinea with a "well-filled casket," dressed like a Muslim, but he was betrayed by Muslims who wanted to steal his belongings and he was brought to Essaouira in chains. From there he was led to Marrakesh, imprisoned for four months, and transferred to Salé. After paying a fine of six thousand piastres, he was pardoned by the sultan and reinstated in his position as first secretary. Ultimately he died from poisoning in Tangier in 1782. Høst describes the aging sultan, troubled by issues of succession, as feeling the loss of Sumbal: "The death of Samuel Sumbal frequently plunged him in a state of disarray; he missed him much and did not find anyone who could take care of his affairs with the same diligence and intelligence as this Jew."[52]

Romanelli describes one of the principal Jewish intermediaries under Sidi Muhammad b. ʿAbdallah, Eliahu Levi, as a particularly vicious abuser of power,[53] who seemed constantly to get embroiled in disputes, competing for favors with the sultan.[54] At the same time, he served Sidi Muhammad as an important diplomatic agent and intermediary with the foreign powers, especially after the death of Samuel Sumbal.[55] He continued to serve under Mawlay al-Yazid and, according to several sources, converted to Islam.[56] Romanelli wrote that he died shortly thereafter because "the multitude of his tribulations and his abominable deeds that had collected in his heart haunted and tormented him, and he died a few days later bitter and depressed, tainted with Cardozo's blood and besmirched by his own detestable acts."[57] In fact, another source suggests that he did not die, but left Morocco, probably for England, with one of his two wives (where he probably returned to Judaism).[58] Another well-connected Jew who managed to maneuver his way in and out of favor was Mordecai De La Mar, who served as one of Sidi Muhammad's principal Jewish secretaries, and managed to survive the reign of Mawlay al-Yazid. He was imprisoned in 1793 in Safi, accused of passing on a falsified receipt,[59] though clearly he did not remain incarcerated for long, and continued to trade from Safi, which at the time was controlled by the dissident Ibn Nasir.

The European powers accepted the diplomatic services of Jews rather grudgingly. Christians were not allowed to reside in some centers of trade, such as Tetuan, and therefore Jewish agents were indispensable.[60] The British consul general in Morocco wrote in 1770: "I acknowledge that his Majesty's service in the Dominions of the Emperor of Morocco, at present cannot be executed without the assistance of Jews," adding that "the Jews are known to carry on the chief business of the whole country, and it seems necessary to employ those by whom His Majesty's affairs can be executed." The consul did suggest that British youth should come to be raised in Morocco to obviate this reliance on the Jews,[61] an unrealistic proposal in light of the marginal interest the British had in Moroccan affairs.

Jews also served as interpreters when foreigners obtained an audience with the sultan. Europeans were mistrustful of their Jewish interlocutors, as described by Jackson:

What expectations can be indulged of terminating successfully negotiations with a prince, in conversing with whom some ignorant illiterate interpreter, generally a Jew, and a devoted subject of the Emperor, must be made the confidential servant of the party treating? Besides, every one acquainted with the nature of the government, and political principles of the Court of Marocco, is well aware, that, even supposing it possible to procure a Jew, capable of interpreting accurately the English into Arabic, and vice versa, yet there are many expressions necessary for an Envoy to use to the Emperor, which no Jew in the country would dare to utter in the imperial presence on pain of losing his head: the generally garrulity of these people, moreover, is such, that they are perhaps unworthy of being entrusted with any secret wherein the interest of a nation is concerned.[62]

A British traveler in 1785, who accompanied a British embassy to Marrakesh, echoes Jackson: "an envoy here is liable to very awkward consequences, from the system of interpretation, of which, be its effects or defects what they may, he is obliged to avail himself without resource. The office is usually performed by a Jew; and when the state of that people here is considered, it will readily be judged how little they are competent to deliver a meaning which they consider as not acceptable to the higher powers."[63]

During the interregnum after the death of Mawlay al-Yazid, when power was being contested by several of the sons of Sidi Muhammad b. ʿAbdallah, the Jewish courtiers were in a precarious position since their financial support was solicited by the different aspiring pretenders to the throne and their backers. Many of the important Jewish traders under Sidi Muhammad b. ʿAbdallah found themselves in areas under the control of Mawlay Hisham and his supporter, Ibn Nasir (Marrakesh and the Atlantic coast were under their control), and few believed that Mawlay Sulayman was going to succeed in gaining control of the sharifian dynasty. Pretenders to the throne would compete for the support of Jewish financial backers and merchants involved in the European trade, placing them in a very vulnerable position. Further complicating their situation was the fact that a number of them during this period accepted consular posts from Spain (despite the fact that since 1492 Jews were not legally allowed in Spain, and the Inquisition was still in force),[64] which linked them with a European power that had cultivated close ties with Mawlay Sulayman's rivals.[65] Mawlay Sulayman, it seems harbored resentments against the merchants of Essaouira for having maintained connections with Ibn Nasir.[66]

The most successful Jewish courtiers would make themselves indispensable in commerce, administration, and diplomacy. Yet undoubtedly they needed to have some base of power from which to begin their careers. Unlike members of the Muslim elite, whose power could rely on their religious status or tribal affiliation, the primary basis of Jewish power in the wider society was wealth and the ability to use it. Yet we know very little about the nature of Jewish wealth. The emergence of a capitalist class of Jewish merchants has been linked in some studies to the era of European penetration in Morocco following Meir Macnin's times. With foreign commerce, and foreign protection, Moroccan Jews allegedly had the means to purchase land at home and invest abroad. But this does not explain how Jewish merchants built their commercial empires in earlier periods.[67]

The wealth of Jews was precarious. In the absence of banks, the opportunities for investment were limited, and profits were often reinvested back into commerce. In the late eighteenth century, very few Jewish merchants were investing their money in Europe, where opportunities were only beginning to open for foreign Jews. Jews might invest in movable property, or in valuables such as jewels and other precious items — a fact well known to the Muslim population who could prey on this form of wealth during times of disorder, such as that which began with the death of Sultan Sidi Muhammad b. ʿAbdallah on 11 April 1790.

Sultan Sidi Muhammad b. ʿAbdallah was succeeded by Mawlay al-Yazid,[68] during whose short and violent reign Morocco was in turmoil. According to a tradition of the Jewish community of Fez, the sultan gave the order to exterminate all the Jews in his kingdom, but was persuaded instead to pillage them, stripping them of all their belongings.[69] But in fact Mawlay al-Yazid's reign of terror was a bloodbath, a violation of the Islamic ruler's obligation to protect the Jews. Such occasions of government-sanctioned violence against Jews were practically unheard of in Morocco, but when it was perceived that Jews had acquired too much power or overstepped the bounds of their subordinate positions as *dhimmi*s, then popular hostility could be aroused and violence sometimes ensued. They were most vulnerable during dynastic power struggles since prominent Jews of the court owed their elite positions to the sultan, with no other basis of political power.[70] It should be remarked, however, that it was not only Jews who were the objects of the sultan's wrath. Muslims as well were massacred; tribes and several whole towns fell victim to the sultan's bloody rise to power.

Though the causes of the violence were complex, one of the sultan's aims was undoubtedly to eliminate individuals and groups on whom his predecessor had depended, and to rid himself of other ʿAlawid pretenders to the throne. A number of the prominent Jewish courtiers, who had served the previous sultan, were executed. The brutal execution of Jacob Attal made a particular impression: "The emperor's Jewish and favourite secretary, had more influence with his royal master, and did more mischief by his intrigues and address, than all the other ministers put together," wrote one European observer.[71] Having spent several years in Gibraltar, Attal was known for his pro-English leanings and his hostility to the Spanish. The British consul general in Tangier lamented, upon his execution, that "being cut in four and burnt, was by far the mildest part of his treatment. On this occasion I lost the most faithful, and most useful agent I ever had in the country."[72] Other Jews who were members of the elite managed to escape abroad.

General pillaging of the Jewish quarters (known as *mellahs*) was encouraged by the sultan. As one historian of the period, al-Duʿayyif, wrote with some relish: "And he [the Sultan] ordered that the Jews be plundered wherever they be found and in every *mellah* in every town of Morocco, because he [the sultan]—may God save him—hated Jews and Christians."[73] The most detailed accounts of violence against Jews in Morocco deal with the events in Tetuan where Attal was executed. The sultan ordered the foreign consular agents living in Tangier to come to Tetuan to bring him presents. They arrived in the aftermath of the pillaging of the *mellah*, and witnessed further plundering by men from the surrounding countryside. A number of people were killed and numerous Jewish women were raped. Muslim houses adjacent to the *mellah* were also not spared.[74] Violence and plunder against Jewish residents in Fez, Meknes, Tangier, Taza, and al-Qsar also occurred. In Fez, Jewish homes and synagogues were destroyed and the Jews themselves were chased out of the *mellah*. In Meknes the *mellah* was plundered by the sultan's *udaya* troops (from one of the government-created "tribes" that did military service in return for land rights).[75] These men, together with the ʿabid (a unit of hereditary slave soldiers), formed the sultan's corps of professional soldiers created by Mawlay Ismaʿil in the later part of the seventeenth century. In Tangier, and probably in other cities as well, the Jews were forced to go barefoot.[76]

Some of the worst atrocities occurred in Marrakesh. The people of Hawz, the region surrounding Marrakesh, and a number of other tribes abandoned the sultan in favor of his brother, Mawlay Hisham, to whom the people of Marrakesh declared their allegiance (*bayʿa*).[77] Sultan al-Yazid routed the tribes, entered Marrakesh, and allowed it to be pillaged. Thousands of the inhabitants were killed, and the elite of the city were systematically executed by decapitation. After the city was plundered by the sultan's troops, numerous Jews were allegedly robbed and murdered and women raped, and according to al-Duᶜayyif, Mawlay al-Yazid

ordered them [the troops] to the *mellah* which they plundered and razed, and in it they found about four hundred thousand *mithqals*, not counting the merchandise, jewels, and gold; and when they informed the sultan what they had found in it [the *mellah*], he responded by saying: "no Jew will be seen except without money and with empty sacks; the face of one of them bruised and the other one cut." And he ordered the Jews out of Bab Dukkala barefoot and naked to live in the street.[78]

Essaouira was in a state of terror, but was spared calamity because of the death of Mawlay al-Yazid in Marrakesh on 16 February 1792. The sultan had demanded a huge sum of money from the Jews of Essaouira, and according to Romanelli, had all the Jews imprisoned except for the influential merchants.[79] The sultan also ordered the execution of several dozen of Essaouira's elite, as listed by one contemporary source: "There were three Christian houses to fall; those of Messrs Siccard and Barr, Leyton [*sic*], & Co; of Messrs Chiappe, brothers, & Co; of Messrs Jackson, Court, & Co: and with these the governor and forty of his friends; ten Festes [people from Fez], the rest of the Agaderies; and the family of the Jew De La Mar."[80] The sultan's orders are corroborated by the Dutch consular agent who gives a slightly different list of those destined to be executed: Joseph Chiappe, Layton, Sicard, Barre, Dⁿ Pedro, Jacob Guedalla, Meir Pinto, Abudurham, Mordecai Zagury, Maimon Corcos, Ben Sassi, Solomon Sebag, the wife of Tapiero, and the widow of Bagha (Macnin, it should be noted, is conspicuously absent from this list). The governor and his friends were to be led to Marrakesh in chains. The consul wrote with considerable emotion shortly after the death of Mawlay al-Yazid: "This event has rescued us from the terrible blow which would have befallen us if the monarch had remained living for just one more day, but God has saved us by his great mercy and did not allow innocent blood to be shed by a massacre that would have been perpetrated against us according to the orders sent by the monarch to be put into effect."[81]

Those chosen to be executed had all been accused of conspiring with ᶜAbd al-Rahman b. Nasir, the governor of Safi and the Abda tribe who, supplied with Spanish firearms, had rebelled against Mawlay al-Yazid and given his support to Mawlay Hisham.[82] The Jews, it seems, were compelled to support the rebellious *qaᵓid*, who upon his arrival outside of Essaouira in November of 1790, exacted payments from the Jewish merchants and forced some Jews to follow him back to Safi.[83] The sultan's list of those to be executed seems to have been derived from denunciations by a number of local officials in Essaouira and by ᶜAbdallah Fannish, who was a trader in Essaouira (the brother of Tahir Fannish, recently appointed governor of Tangier),[84] and from the machinations of Eliahu Levi. Levi, who had fallen into disfavor under Sidi Muhammad, managed to exonerate himself and then sought to rid himself of his rival, Mordecai De La Mar, who as we have seen, was one of the former sultan's principal agents.[85] De La Mar, while he was resident in Safi, had previously been imprisoned by Mawlay al-Yazid, but had then been freed and allowed to export wheat.[86]

Despite Mawlay al-Yazid's aversion to Christians and Jews, probably part of a popular reaction against the policies of his predecessor Sidi Muham-mad,[87] he continued to employ Jews and conduct commercial relations with Europe. If the Guedallas were later included on the list of the sultan's vic-tims, Mawlay al-Yazid earlier considered them extremely valuable, as he wrote to them in October 1791: "Know that of the *ahl al-dhimma* they [the Guedallas] are among our most loyal servants as they were under the reign of our late father. We shall keep them in the same rank in commercial affairs with the countries of Europe and in our empire."[88] Meir Macnin still served the governor of Essaouira during Mawlay al-Yazid's reign.[89] Privileges were granted to certain Jewish merchants, including Mordecai De La Mar, who received the exclusive privilege to export wax from all the ports.[90] The Ge-noese merchant Francesco Chiappe, who had been appointed by Sidi Mu-hammad b. ʿAbdallah in 1784 as secretary for foreign relations,[91] continued to serve under Mawlay al-Yazid.[92] The port of Agadir was to be opened again, and the merchants of Essaouira who had formerly resided in the town were ordered to return.[93] Special privileges were to be granted to the Dutch, as the British merchant Jackson wrote: "The emperor has consented to the proposition of the Dutch government, to open the port of Agadeer, or Santa Cruz, in the province of Suse, to the commerce of that nation, and I have finally resolved to establish a house there, so soon as the Sultan Yezzid's or-der respecting that port shall reach the hands of Alkaid Oumer ben Daudy, the governor of this port." Jackson predicted that commerce from the port of Essaouira would be diverted to Santa Cruz, the gateway to the Sudan (sub-Saharan Africa) as he explains: "The merchants of Fas also, who have their establishment and connections at Timbuctoo, and in other parts of Sudan, will resort to Santa Cruz in preference to Mogador, for all European articles calculated for the markets of Sudan, the former port being in the neighbourhood of the desert, or Sahara, and at a convenient distance from Akka in Lower Suse, the general rendezvous of the akkaba, (or accumulated caravans,) destined for the interior regions of Africa or Sudan."[94] Jackson moved to Agadir shortly thereafter, appointed as agent for Holland by the Dutch consul general in Tangier, Webster Blount.[95]

Shortly after the death of the sultan, the merchants of Essaouira, the governor, ʿUmar b. al-Daʾudi, the captain of the port, ʿAbdallah ʿAntari, and ʿAbdallah Fannish went to Marrakesh to attend the royal court.[96] At the time, it appeared from Essaouira that the prince (*khalifa*) Mawlay Hisham would succeed in his claim to succession to the sharifian dynasty. Mawlay Hisham depended on the backing of the merchants of Essaouira, and consequently offered them a reduction in duties, apparently in exchange for a cash advance. Furthermore, his claim to rule was recognized by the virtually independent potentate ʿAbd al-Rahman b. Nasir, who was still receiving the support of Spain. A number of merchants from Essaouira moved to Safi, which was controlled by Ibn Nasir.[97] As the de facto ruler of Marrakesh, Mawlay Hisham controlled that capital and the area extending to the Atlantic coast. Therefore, Essaouira came under his authority.

Despite considerable unrest in the provinces, commerce continued in Essaouira at a normal pace. Several months after receiving the merchants in Marrakesh, Mawlay Hisham arrived in Essaouira and summoned all the consuls and merchants. In October, a number of ships were reported in the harbor of Essaouira: five English ships consigned to Leonardi, Meir Pinto, Layton, Guedalla, and Lee; two Dutch ones for Chiappe, Sicard Barre & Cie, three French ships for Sicard Barre & Cie, Guedalla, and Meir Pinto; and an American ship for Chiappe. Mawlay Hisham arrived in Essaouira and received all the consuls and merchants.[98] But according to British reports, "his conduct at Mogador was far from laudable, his whole time being given to women and liquor, and to procure the former, his violence was equal to that of his brother Yezid's."[99]

The vice-regent Mawlay Sulayman, who preferred studying religion to politics, was proclaimed sultan in Fez in 1792. It took him several years to wrest control of the country from Mawlay Hisham, first contesting power with Mawlay Maslama in the north. Essaouira and the Haha (the region adjacent to Essaouira to the south) had been controlled by Ibn Nasir, with Abu Marwan ʿAbd al-Malik b. Bihi al-Hahi, recognized leader of the Haha, as governor. In late 1794, Essaouira proclaimed its loyalty to Mawlay Sulayman, and al-Hajj Muhammad b. ʿAbd al-Sadiq, commander of the ʿabid of the town, was named governor.[100] The foreign merchants of Essaouira were urged not to trade with Safi and El Jadida, which were still controlled by the dissidents, especially Ibn Nasir. Commerce suffered from an almost continuous blockade, while those merchants from Essaouira trading in Safi paid considerably reduced duties under Ibn Nasir. It was not until 1797 that Mawlay Hisham abdicated (for the second time), and Ibn Nasir placed himself under Mawlay Sulayman's authority.[101] Only in 1799 was Mawlay Sulayman securely recognized as successor to the sharifian throne.[102]

Already before the crisis, Meir Macnin, together with his brother Shlomo, had joined the ranks of the most active traders in Essaouira.[103] Although Meir's protector ʿUmar b. al-Daʾudi was replaced as governor of the town, Macnin maintained close ties to the new governor, ʿAbd al-Sadiq. His connections to the authorities served him well. In the mid-1790s, the Macnins were involved in a renewed effort to revive the trade in the port of Agadir. Mawlay al-Yazid's interest in Agadir was continued by Mawlay Hisham while he was in control of Marrakesh. Among the prominent Jewish merchants of Essaouira to settle in the reopened port were Haim Guedalla (the Guedallas were originally from Agadir), Meir Pinto, Moses De Lara, and Cardozo. The British merchant James Jackson remained there for several years as both merchant and Dutch consular representative.[104] Now, Meir Macnin was to be the instrument for Mawlay Sulayman's effort to control trade in Agadir, as we learn from a letter to the sultan's nephew Mawlay ʿAbd al-Malik al-Zayzun, the governor of Agadir.[105] "We order you to provide him with a house that he can live in and fill with commerce because he [the sultan] wishes commerce in Agadir to be represented by the merchant Zuzab [?], his [Macnin's] associate. He [Macnin] should be given favor and privilege over the other Jews there since he is our *dhimmi* and our chattel (*mataʿuna*)."[106] Already, Meir Macnin was climbing the ladder to become one of the state's principal Jewish merchants, with the conditions of both power and subservience that such a position entailed. Soon his brother Shlomo appears as one of the active traders in Agadir, exporting goods on Spanish and Portuguese ships. Export duties were assessed at 4,518 *mithqals*, but the Makhzan consented to reduce his debt considerably so that he only owed 693 *mithqals*.[107]

The sultan was unable to control the renewed trade at Agadir, and it seems probable that ʿAbd al-Malik began to operate in Agadir quite independent of central authority. When Mawlay Sulayman was consolidating his position in the south, he recalled his nephew to Marrakesh where he was chastised for the costly attire that he wore in audience with the sultan. ʿAbd al-Malik was then exiled to Tafilalt, the patrimonial region from where the ʿAlawid *shurafa* originated; subsequently he was sent to Fez. The sultan then closed down the port of Agadir,[108] and all the merchants and Jews were required to leave the city. Other towns were also closed to foreign commerce: Safi, Tit, and Dar al-Bayda (Casablanca), ports where European and Jewish merchants had received special trading privileges. The income generated from uncontrolled trade had helped precipitate the resistance to Mawlay Sulayman's efforts to secure control of the country. Trade concessions granted to the Spanish were abrogated as well. Shlomo Macnin was one of the last merchants allowed to remain in Agadir after all the others were required to leave in 1798.[109]

With the Moroccan trade again almost wholly concentrated in Essaouira, Meir Macnin became the preeminent merchant trading for the Makhzan. Not only were his ties to the authorities essential for his position, but so was his network of relations with the other prominent Jewish merchants.

One of the most important ways to achieve status in the elite was through marital ties, and many of the Jewish merchants engaged in the European trade were related to each other. Marital decisions were very much a business strategy among the merchant elite in premodern Jewish society in Morocco and elsewhere.[110] At the end of 1796, the Dutch consular agent wrote:

The Jewish nation is prospering these days, and Mier Mackniel [*sic*] is one of the foremost entrepreneurs in the grain trade, sending ships that come here with cargoes to Cadix and Lisbon, in which he is helped by my neighbor, but I believe that the head of our city without naming him is the most interested in it. It is being said that this Jew is going to marry one of the daughters of Mr. Mier [*sic*] Pinto, but he is finding much opposition from the Guedallays [*sic*] who are against it.[111]

Meir Macnin clearly combined business with nuptial strategies. As we have seen, Meir Pinto, together with his brother-in-law Haim Guedalla, was involved in the most important commercial activities of the port of Essaouira in the 1780s and 1790s, receiving special privileges from the sultans and pretenders to the throne, such as reestablishing commerce in Agadir and Safi, and the rights to import cannons and export wheat.[112]

The reasons for the Guedallas' objection to the marriage are not disclosed. The family was, however, related to the Pinto family, since Meir Pinto was married to Hanina *née* Guedalla, sister of Judah and Haim. The opposition of the Guedallas may have been a reason for the protracted betrothal, for it was nearly three years later that Meir and Zohra were married in an elaborate wedding: "The youngest daughter of Mr. Mier Pinto got married to the merchant Meir Macknin, and great celebrations took place on this occasion. He gave a magnificent meal for all the gentlemen consuls and merchants, but the ladies did not come."[113] Jewish weddings in Morocco, where the ceremonies continued for two to three weeks,[114] made a great impression on Europeans, for it was one of the few rituals which foreigners were invited to attend.[115] And an impression is exactly what the Macnin, Guedalla, and Pinto families wanted to make on the "gentlemen" (i.e., European) merchants and consuls. For it was through alliances with the foreign community that business deals were made. The elite Jewish merchants often competed for favors and advantages, but were almost all linked by marital ties. Whatever differences the Guedallas had with the Macnins were overcome, for the two families were subsequently enmeshed in a web of business ties. With the Macnin marital links firmly established, nothing barred Meir and Shlomo from rising to the position of the leading trading house in Essaouira in the first decade of the nineteenth century.

The Macnins' most important form of investment, besides reinvestment in trade, was in urban real estate in Marrakesh and Essaouira.[116] The acquisition of land in the countryside was generally not possible for Jews before the mid-nineteenth century, since rural landownership was linked to tribal affiliations or saintly lineage, from which Jews were excluded. Thus, most of the investments of the Jewish elite were in urban property.

Meir Macnin began purchasing property in Essaouira early in his career. We do not have a complete list of his real estate, but the scattered documents in the family collection indicate the degree to which he was an important property holder. In 1787, the "young man" ("*bahur*"—the term probably was used to indicate his unmarried status) Meir engaged in what may have been his first speculation in land when he purchased a plot jointly owned by Barukh Bukis, Moshe Ben Simhon, and Zako b. Aharon Ben Shabbat for only ten *mithqal*s. According to the formulaic language of the document—the earliest deed in the family archive—the property was purchased "according to law, religion, fairness, and *halakhah*," and recognizing the possibility of property being acquired through arbitrary means, the document typically states that the transaction took place "without any trace of force and coercion whatsoever . . . "[117]

Meir Macnin and his brothers continued to speculate in real estate in Essaouira in the 1790s. In 1795, Meir and Shlomo purchased a house in the casbah, the former residence of Catholic priests, from Yaᶜkov Ben Sassi, who had previously bought the house in 1787 for 381 *riyal*s. It was sold to the Macnin brothers for 850 *riyal*s.[118] In 1796, Meir Macnin attempted without success to purchase the Dutch consular residence in Essaouira (now that the Netherlands had become, under French occupation, the Republique Batave) for one thousand *riyal*s ("hard piastres," in the language of the document), a price lower than the amount it was valued at by the vice consul. He assured the consular agent that he would willingly cede the upstairs rooms if he were sold the house, since his main intention was only to make use of the storerooms.[119] In the following year, Meir Macnin purchased the Portuguese consular house.[120] That same year he purchased half a house in the casbah from Muhammad b. al-Ghazwani al-Sarghini, and another half of a house next to his own house for 885 *riyal*s from al-Hajj ᶜAbd al-Malik al-Ribuh al-Asfi, who had lived there for fifteen years.[121] His brother Masud purchased a house in Essaouira in 1798 for 600 *riyal*s, and the same year received another house as mortgage for a debt owed to him.[122] Even after his departure from Essaouira, Meir preferred to invest his money back in property in Morocco, probably executing the transfers during business trips to Essaouira. Thus in 1800 Meir purchased one-third of a house from Saᶜada, daughter of Shalom Cohen of Rabat, outside the casbah.[123]

No doubt as well, the many houses purchased by Meir's brother and business partner Shlomo reflect the profits made from their lucrative royal patronage. As major creditors to both Muslims and Jews, the Macnin brothers often obtained mortgages for urban property. These properties were often commercial premises, and the Macnins held them in usufruct. Islam prohibited interest, so acquisition of property from their many debtors was really a kind of concealed form of interest since the value of the property held as collateral often appreciated considerably, even though the amount of the loans remained the same. The Macnins loaned money to Jews and Muslims alike.[124]

The ability of the Macnins to accumulate wealth and property was not only the result of royal patronage. Their trading network linking Europe with southern Morocco was also essential. In fact, royal patronage to the Jews of Essaouira and the southern trade were interrelated, for it should be recalled that one of the major reasons for the foundation of the town was the sultan's desire to closely control this trade, which was often diverted by dissidents in the southern port of Agadir. The Macnins were closely connected to brokers in southern Morocco. For example, only a few months prior to his departure for England in 1799, Meir Macnin loaned some 664 *doro*s to a Jew of Iligh, Moshe b. Mashisha.[125]

The *murabit* (a title indicating descent from a revered holy man) of Iligh, Hashim b. ʿAli, ruler of the sharifian house of Abu Damiʿa since 1790, was reasserting the power of this once notable lineage, and in the power vacuum that emerged after the death of the sultan Sidi Muhammad, was once again turning the seasonal pilgrimage (*mawsim*) to the shrine of Sidi Ahmad U Musa into the most important commercial emporium for the Saharan and trans-Saharan trade.[126] A British sailor, Robert Adams, who was shipwrecked on the southern coast of Morocco in 1810 and ransomed in Essaouira, passed through Iligh and learned that Hashim had an army of about six hundred blacks and appeared to be very rich, "having numerous camels, goats, sheep, and horned cattle, and abundance of piece goods of various kinds, as also shoes and other manufactures which were exposed for sale in shops kept by Jews."[127] He saw a large quantity of silver dollars and remarked that Hashim was at war with the sultan.[128] Adams was present at the *mawsim* of Sidi Ahmad U Musa and observed at least four thousand people present. The British consular representative in Essaouira, who arranged Adams's ransom, noted that "this chief has lately opened an extensive trade with Soudan, for gums, cottons, and ostrich feathers, ivory, gold-dust, and slaves, which are sold by his agents at the great annual market of *Hamet a Moussa*. The traders from Southern Barbary resort to this market in great numbers."[129] Jews were the key intermediaries for Hashim's trade,[130] and the Macnins, it seems, quickly established their ties with this community.

By the end of the 1790s, the Macnins had considerable assets, close connections to the local government of Morocco's most important port, a network of relations with southern Morocco, and numerous debtors with considerable obligations to their commercial establishment.

As a result, when Meir Macnin embarked for London in 1799, he already had the wealth, standing, and contacts to become in a short time Morocco's indispensable agent in Europe. But most likely, he left the country not in search of wider opportunities, but in fear of death from a disease that still infested North Africa at the turn of the nineteenth century: the bubonic plague.

CHAPTER THREE

The Plague and the
World of Mediterranean Jewry

The plague of 1799–1800, known to survivors as "the big plague" (*al-taᶜun al-kabir*) as distinct from other pestilences,[1] was the most lethal epidemic since the Black Death of the fourteenth century.[2] There are no reliable estimates of the mortality rate since no one knows what Morocco's population was before and after the plague. But foreign sources agree on the extent of the devastation. A reasonable, though imprecise, estimate would suggest that one-fourth of the population at large perished, while urban losses tended to be greater: anywhere between one-half to two-thirds succumbed to the pestilence.[3]

The plague came from the east, and seems to have been first reported in Fez in February.[4] British concern that ships spread contagion was not misplaced, though they did not understand the cause of the plague. Boats that plied the Mediterranean ports, transporting infected passengers and cargoes, were often the primary culprits in pandemics of the plague.[5] Alexandria, Istanbul, Izmir, Saida, and Tunis were among the principal locations where ships had originally become infected, spreading the contagion to other ports in the Mediterranean basin.[6] From the ports the plague spread inland, and its dissemination was usually rapid. Already in April, it was reported by a contemporary historian that in Fez and the area, "so many died that only God (may He be exalted) could count their number."[7] A crop failure the preceding year and the privations that this caused may have made the population more susceptible to the epidemic. Drought continued in 1799 after the outbreak of the plague.[8] The plague was probably spread further by the

FIGURE 6. *A New and Correct Map of the Empire of Morocco.* From William Lempriere, *A Tour from Gibraltar to Tangier, Salle, Mogadore, Santa Cruz, Tarudant; and Thence over Mount Atlas to Morocco: Including a Particular Account of the Royal Harem &C.*, 3d ed. (London: Printed for L. J. Higham, 1804).

movement of the sultan's troops, which marched from Fez to Rabat in April, continuing south across the Atlantic plains, and reaching Safi and Marrakesh in May and June.[9] The pestilence was soon raging in Marrakesh. The consular representatives in Essaouira urged the governor of the town to take precautions by closing the gates of the city. The governor responded that he could not do so without the sultan's orders, though he would prevent persons and merchandise from entering the city.[10] But precisely at this period of time, a large detachment of the sharifian army from Marrakesh, clearly infected with the plague, encamped near Essaouira. At the beginning of July the plague was reported in the town. One month later, deaths had reached over one hundred a day. In September, the contagion diminished appreciably, and by October it was believed to have ceased. But apparently it still lingered until March or April before it finally disappeared.[11]

A seasoned British merchant in Essaouira, James Grey Jackson, estimated that forty-five hundred died in Essaouira, and that in the neighboring village of Diabet to the south of the town, one hundred perished out of a population of 133.[12] His estimate for Essaouira is probably somewhat high; if one calculates according to the number of daily deaths given, then Jackson's estimate needs to be reduced by about one thousand. Nonetheless, this was a heavy toll of human life, amounting to over a third of the town's population.

The plague not only killed a large percentage of the Moroccan population, but it also was responsible for diminishing the size of the Makhzan. Apparently, many officials died in the epidemic, which must have damaged the mechanisms of government. Provincial governors, officials in the capital cities, and many members of the sharifian family perished, including four brothers of Mawlay Sulayman.[13] The bureaucratic apparatus also seems to have been decimated, and probably as a consequence, few records remain for the period. It was reported also that "the majority of the [Islamic] jurists of Meknes, Fez, and elsewhere died."[14]

The plague in Morocco also led to chaos in the military, and probably government officials abandoned their duties. The governor of Essaouira sent for troops from Agadir to guard the town.[15] The French vice-consul at Essaouira writes apprehensively that "the prejudices of the Moors are such that one fears in the case that the disease will come to carry away several of their chiefs, then anarchy will reign everywhere and we will be exposed to pillaging by the black soldiers" (a reference to the corps of black soldiers created by Mawlay Ismaᶜil in the seventeenth century).[16]

With local authority collapsing, there would have been little effort to prevent those who wanted from seeking to escape—especially from the towns, where the plague raged most fiercely.

The spread of the disease in the towns led to pandemonium almost everywhere. Masses of people would leave the stifling confines of the walled-in cities to seek refuge in the surrounding countryside, a type of collective behavior that was also characteristic of preindustrial Europe.[17] This was the case with both Muslim and Jewish families in Essaouira. Jewish families who sought refuge in Essaouira were not allowed within the walls and "died in misery in the sand."[18] Only when it appeared that the plague had subsided would the town residents return. The wealthy elite's reaction to the plague differed little from that of the poor masses, except that they had greater means to escape. And both rich and poor, if they were Jewish, might also escape overseas. In doing so, they made use of the long-standing network of Sephardi commercial and cultural contacts that spread right across the Mediterranean, linking the Levant with the Atlantic, and Christian Europe with Muslim North Africa.

The center of this network was Livorno, known to the English as Leghorn. In the 1590s, the grand duke of Tuscany, Ferdinand I, encouraged foreigners to settle in the town by granting special fiscal privileges to merchants. Livorno developed as a free port, neutral and detached from the disputes of the great powers.[19] The grand duke liberalized his own Jewish policy to help expand the trade of the new port, and in 1593 granted the Jews privileges to settle and trade there in a charter called the *Livornina*, referred to by a number of commentators as the Magna Carta of the Jews of Livorno.[20] Ferdinand was specifically interested in the North African trade, a fact reflected in the *Livornina*, which invites settlement by "Ebrei, Turchi, Mori." In a subsequent edict in 1595, the grand duke referred to "Moreschi, Barbareschi, Ebrei." The *Livornina* specifies that the residents of Livorno would be free to trade with the Levant, Barbary, and Alexandria.[21]

Jews in particular found haven in the growing port. They were protected from the papal inquisitors and were not compelled to live in ghettos as did most of Italian Jewry. Livorno became a place of refuge for Marranos from the Iberian peninsula and from other Italian communities. By 1655, about three thousand Jews lived in Livorno, constituting about 20 percent of the population. Livorno thus had the highest Jewish-to-Christian ratio of any major town in Western Europe. By the mid-seventeenth century, Livornese Jews were to be found throughout the Mediterranean basin, and Livorno served as the main entrepôt for the Dutch and English Mediterranean trade. Livorno and the Sephardi community of Amsterdam and later London developed close ties.[22]

Livorno was also distinguished in the field of rabbinic scholarship and publishing, becoming the most important center for learning and culture in the eighteenth-century Sephardi world. Rabbis throughout the Levant and Maghrib often had their books published by the Hebrew printing presses of Livorno.[23] What particularly distinguished Livorno was its Sephardi culture. Jews of Spanish and Portuguese descent, especially the Marranos, rather than Italians, were the dominant element in the community. The formal, hierarchical and authoritarian communal structure of Spanish Jewry was reproduced within the self-governing Jewish community of Livorno.[24] In the late eighteenth century, the "administrators" of the "Jewish Nation," an oligarchy of sixty men, were predominantly from the Sephardi merchant aristocracy involved in international commerce.[25]

With the considerable privileges and freedom accorded and protected by the Grand Duke of Tuscany, numerous Jewish immigrants poured into the port. Through residence in the town, Jews were able to become naturalized as subjects of the Grand Duke of Tuscany by a procedure called *ballottazione*, according protection of their persons and property under the law. Those naturalized through *ballottazione* were generally the merchants and businessmen, and especially those who needed protection against foreign creditors in Tuscany. Many other, less prosperous immigrants never went through this naturalization procedure, but were nevertheless allowed to remain in Livorno and, provided that they did not cause trouble, benefited from the protection of their lives and property.[26] Once having become "Livornese," some went to live in other cities of the Mediterranean, but still tenaciously maintained their identity and newfound culture, with European dress and customs, and the Italian language. Livornese Jews were important throughout the Mediterranean basin, sometimes establishing "colonies" that kept their distinctive identities, though they were known by a variety of names: Italians, Portuguese, and "Franks" (*Francos*). Important Jewish commercial establishments from Livorno were found in Alexandria, Cairo, Rosetta, Aleppo, Salonica, Izmir, Sidon, Algiers, Gibraltar, Essaouira, Tetuan, Safi, and most importantly, in Tunis.[27] Throughout the Levant, Livornese Jews sought and obtained the status of French protégés. Such an arrangement was of mutual benefit for both the French and the Jews. The French, competing with other foreign powers, were reliant on the Livornese Jewish merchants and their network of ties as well as the consular taxes they paid. The Jews, for their part, needed the protection of a foreign power and the extraterritorial rights that their status of protégés offered.[28]

The principle of extraterritorial rights was based on agreements between the Ottoman Empire and the European powers, known as the Capitulations, that allowed the consulates jurisdiction over their subjects and protégés. Capitulations were granted by the Ottoman state to France in 1535, which placed all foreign merchants living in the empire under French consular protection. The British and Dutch also concluded their own capitulatory agreements. However, the Tunisian Beylicate was only nominally a part of the Ottoman Empire, and really had its own foreign policy. Therefore, France often concluded its own commercial and diplomatic agreements with Tunis. While French merchants in Tunis paid only a 3 percent customs rate, the Livornese Jews were obligated to pay 10 percent, as did the native merchants. Consequently, Livornese Jewish merchants often used the names of French merchants to avoid paying the higher rate and in order to extend their trade to the lucrative port of Marseilles, where foreign merchants were still barred.[29]

The degree of integration between the Livornese Jews and the native Jewish inhabitants varied. In Tunis they were an important element of the

Jewish population, known as the "Grana," and distinguished themselves from the native Jews, who were called the "Twansa." By 1685 they constituted some forty-nine merchants. In 1710, the Livornese Jews of Tunis broke away from the authochthonous Arabic-speaking Jews to form a separate synagogue. By 1741 the rupture with the native Twansa was complete: henceforth the Grana maintained their own autonomous Beit Din and burial grounds.[30]

North African Jews, especially, were attracted to the port of Livorno. This migration, which began in the second half of the seventeenth century, increased significantly throughout the eighteenth century. From the list of *ballottati* spanning from 1753 to 1807, we learn that about 29 percent of the immigrants came from North Africa.[31] By the end of the eighteenth century they constituted about 13 percent of the Jewish community of Livorno, and Jewish merchants of North African origin played a preponderant role in international commerce. From a register of "patents" in 1809, listing the amounts that merchant firms had to pay during the Napoleonic period, it appears that about 43 percent of the Jewish merchant firms were of North African origin.[32] In the 1790s, several representatives of the major Moroccan merchant families, predominantly from Essaouira, are listed among Livorno's immigrants: Abudurham, Ben Attar, De La Mar, Akrish, and Delevante.[33] This emigration coincided with the period of political turmoil in Morocco when trade greatly slackened. Some of the North African Jews arriving in Livorno at the end of the eighteenth and beginning of the nineteenth century had little trouble integrating themselves within the community, often marrying into the native families, buying rural estates, and serving among the leaders of the "Jewish nation." Often, however, the intention of the Maghribi Jews was not to remain for a long period of time in Livorno. Jews of North African origin, also, often maintained their distinctive identity, continuing to use Judeo-Arabic even after a relatively long residence in Livorno.[34] This seems to reflect the increased number of North African Jews in the town, who had now become a more important element among the Sephardi population there.

The Jewish merchants of Livorno, together with their coreligionists in the Maghribi ports, formed an extensive trading network and a web of associations and familial ties that dominated the North African trade in the eighteenth century.[35] Between 1765 and 1790 Livornese Jews had a quasi-monopoly: the proportion of Jews to non-Jews exporting to North African ports was usually over 90 percent.[36] The flow back and forth of merchants from Tunis, Algiers, Tripoli, Tetuan, Essaouira, and Gibraltar was constant. Particularly important were the Livornese Jews of Tunis and Algiers. Some of their most important activities in the seventeenth and eighteenth centuries were business operations connected to the corsair trade, upon which the Tunisian and Algerian states depended. Their role in ransoming North African Jewish captives was essential; it was they who executed the necessary monetary transactions in Tunis and Livorno. The Jewish community of Livorno had a fund to rescue captives that was established in 1606 and continued to exist until 1799. Livornese Jews also financed shipping and were involved in the grain trade.[37]

Some North African Jews would often stay in Livorno for a relatively short period of time, receive Tuscan citizenship, and return to their native country with a new "Livornese" identity. During the French occupation, Jews were considered French citizens, and in a decree of 1811, even those Jewish *ballottati* who had been naturalized prior to the French occupation were to be accorded French citizenship. Exception was made because it was "just to maintain the advantages of those who acquired them before the union [annexation], and of those, for the most part, who are at the head of the principal merchant houses of the city of Livorno."[38] French consulates in North Africa began to complain of the growing number of unemployed French nationals coming from Livorno who seemed to acquire French nationality too easily.[39]

The ports of Morocco were very much a part of the Livornese network of trade and scholarship. In the eighteenth century, Livorno was one of Morocco's principal trading partners.[40] The Jewish community of Tetuan especially had close connections with Livorno, and the majority of Moroccan Jews who settled there came from Tetuan, usually with an intermediary stop in Gibraltar.[41] From the 1770s, when Essaouira became Morocco's principal port of trade, the movement back and forth between the new port and Livorno was frequent. Jews from Livorno, such as members of the Akrish family, settled in the Tuscan port; likewise, Essaouira sent some of its merchants to Livorno.[42] Not only merchants but emigrants in more modest occupations, such as domestic servants, moved to Livorno from Morocco.[43]

At the beginning of the nineteenth century, Livorno was under French occupation and Europe was at war. The trade of Livorno diminished significantly when the port was subjected to a maritime blockade. But instead of ending the flow of Jewish emigration between Livorno and the Maghrib, the crisis simply reversed it. Livornese Jews seeking a livelihood now arrived on the North African coast with their recently acquired French nationality.[44]

The constant flow of merchants between Morocco and Livorno often went together with the exchange of rabbis and rabbinical scholarship. Morocco was a part of the scholarly and publishing circuit for which Livorno served as a nucleus. In the late eighteenth and early nineteenth centuries, a noted *dayyan* from Tetuan, Abraham Coriat, the author of *Zekhut Avot*,[45] became a leading rabbi in the young community of Essaouira, and then spent time in Gibraltar and Livorno.[46] Since Morocco had no printing presses,

Moroccan rabbis would frequently publish their religious texts in Livorno, likely staying for extended periods of time in the Tuscan port.[47]

Marital ties helped strengthen commercial relations between Essaouira and Livorno. The Macnins had close commercial ties with Livorno, dispatching cargoes and receiving shipments from that port. Meir Macnin's daughter, Blida, married Aaron Amar, who came from a family of Algerian "Livornese" Jews. Samuel Levy Bensusan of the Jewish elite of Essaouira pledged to marry Stella Amar (possibly a daughter of Aaron) in Livorno in 1820.[48] After the Napoleonic Wars, when trade between Livorno and the Maghrib again began to increase, Aaron Amar moved to Livorno, where he became associated with the one of the two leading merchant families of Algiers and Livorno: Bujnah (also spelled Busnach).[49] The Bujnah family of Livorno established itself in Algiers in 1723 and 1724, while the Bacri arrived in Algiers around 1770. The two families of Bujnah and Bacri, who entered into partnership at the end of the eighteenth century, became the principal grain exporting firms and community leaders in Algiers. From their branches in Algiers, Livorno, and Marseilles their commercial network extended throughout the Mediterranean basin and Europe. Especially important were their wheat exports to France and to Napoleon's army in Italy and Egypt.[50] These exporting activities later caused them to become embroiled in a sordid dispute over unsettled debts and claims that ultimately led to the famous incident in 1827 when the French consul of Algiers struck the dey with a fan. This precipitated a break in diplomatic relations and, three years later, France invaded Algeria.[51]

David Bujnah, together with his relative Salomon Cohen Bacri, represented the firm in Livorno. Bacri arrived in Livorno from Algiers about 1787, while Bujnah arrived about 1786, according to their own testimony.[52] It was with David Bujnah, the head of the family in Livorno, that Aaron Amar "Bujnah" was apparently connected. There is a contract in the Levy family collection, notarized in Livorno in 1822, in which David Bujnah chartered a brig flying the Russian flag, under a Captain Stellato, for shipment to and from Essaouira.[53] In 1838, it was probably the same Stellato who became involved in a dispute with Aaron Amar's son, Leon.[54] Aaron Amar began shipping to Essaouira, and then settled there permanently as the agent of the Bujnah firm. He himself became known as "Bujnah," and was considered, by one observer, to be the most "opulent" merchant of the town.[55]

Besides Livorno, Gibraltar had become an important destination for Moroccan Jews during the eighteenth century. Soon after the British occupation of Gibraltar began in 1704 and well before the treaty with Spain was concluded, many Jews, mainly from North Africa, had joined the ranks of Gibraltar's residents, to the chagrin of the British authorities, who claimed that they occupied the best houses in town and were driving up prices. In the Treaty of Utrecht concluded with Spain in 1713, the British agreed to prohibit Jews and Moors from residing in Gibraltar. At the time about 150 Jews, of whom two-thirds were from North Africa, lived in Gibraltar. The Jews were required to leave, but it is likely that a number of Jewish merchants remained and others soon came since their services were considered indispensable. In 1717 it became apparent that about 300 Jews were residing in the town. Allegedly, Lieutenant Governor Cotton had received bribes from them. Again the Jews were forced to leave Gibraltar, only to return a few years later. A treaty with Morocco in 1721 guaranteed the Jews rights to be judged by Jews in domestic disputes, and those residing in Gibraltar "shall be esteemed as his [Majesty's] natural-born subjects," despite the Treaty of Utrecht. From this time on, Jewish settlement in Gibraltar was firmly established. In the wake of the settlement of affluent Jewish merchants came Moroccan Jews of more modest means: shopkeepers, workers, porters, peddlers, and craftsmen. It was also perceived by the British authorities in Gibraltar that they could manipulate the network of ties between the Jews of London, Gibraltar, and Morocco for conducting peaceful relations between England and Morocco. A treaty concluded between Britain and Morocco in 1729 allowed Moroccan Jews or Muslims to freely trade in Gibraltar for a period of thirty days, but not to reside there. This restriction was quickly ignored.[56]

The population of Gibraltar began to grow, and Jews remained an important element. In 1725, there were 111 Jews out of a population of 732 (about 15 percent); of those about 77 percent came from the Maghrib.[57] In 1754, there were 604 Jews out of a total population of 1,810. In 1777, Jews numbered some 863, or 27 percent of the civilian population.[58] In 1826, Gibraltar had a population of 15,503, out of which 1,203 were listed as "native" Jews and 456 as "Barbary" Jews.[59] The number of "Barbary" Jews was in fact much higher, considering that most of the "native" Jews of Gibraltar were of North African descent.

Gibraltar was not only a destination in itself, but also a stepping stone to a number of other European destinations, in the Mediterranean and elsewhere. Spain was still out of bounds for the Jews, with the Inquisition still in force: a man was still denounced by the Inquisition of Seville for heretical Judaizing practices in 1799. It was not until the mid-nineteenth century that Jews were allowed entry; most of the Jewish immigrants to Spain in this period, though few in number, were from Morocco.[60] In Portugal as well, the Inquisition had been in force since the end of the fifteenth century, and Jewish settlement was barred. However, Jews began trickling into Lisbon from Gibraltar and North Africa, at least from the early nineteenth century, and in 1816 the Portuguese government allowed Jews to openly prac-

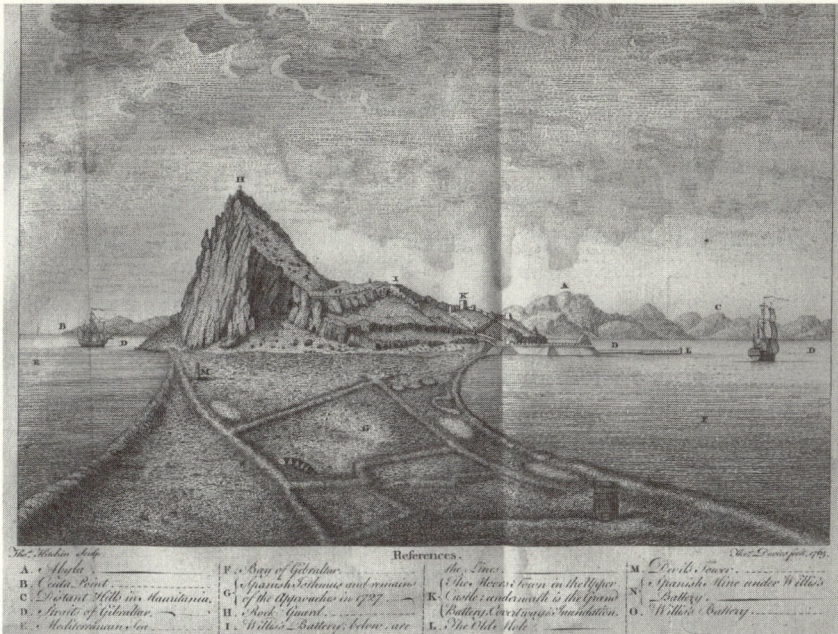

FIGURE 7. Gibraltar, 1763. From Thomas James, *The History of the Herculean Straits, Now Called the Straits of Gibraltar* (London: Charles Rivington, 1771).

tice their religion.[61] By 1825, about five or six hundred Jews were reportedly living in Lisbon, with three synagogues.[62] A significant proportion of the new, openly Jewish community of Lisbon came from Essaouira, helping establish commercial ties between Portugal and Morocco.[63] A virulently anti-Semitic Christian missionary from this period commented on the Jews of Lisbon: "I found them a vile, infamous rabble, about two hundred in number. With a few exceptions, they consist of escapados from the Barbary shore, from Tetuan, from Tangier, but principally from Mogadore; fellows who have fled to a foreign land from the punishment of their misdeeds."[64] Meir Macnin made use of the newly formed community, and established commercial relations with Lisbon.[65]

While some Jews of North African origin moved between Gibraltar and Lisbon, even more important was their migration to Britain, to which Gibraltar was also, of course, a convenient stepping stone—above all to London, which became increasingly attractive to Moroccan Jews in the latter part of the eighteenth century.[66] In earlier periods, Sephardi Jews were instrumental in the Dutch-Moroccan trade. Trade between Holland and Morocco was conducted by Jewish merchant firms, which maintained an extensive network of relatives and agents in Amsterdam and in Moroccan cities and seaports.[67] In the latter part of the eighteenth century, London's importance in the Moroccan trade superseded Amsterdam's, and increasingly the former city was seen as a place of opportunity for Moroccan Jews. Already the largest city in Europe in the eighteenth century, during the Revolutionary and Napoleonic Wars London became the most important financial center of the world, taking the preeminent position formerly held by Amsterdam.[68]

After the outbreak of the naval war with France in 1793, the French Mediterranean trade declined, and hence, the demand for English goods grew. The subsequent French occupation of much of western Europe crippled the Mediterranean trade of the Dutch and the Italians, Morocco's other principal trading partners.[69] Following Napoleon's invasion of Egypt in 1798 and the subsequent victory of the British fleet under Nelson, England's domination of the Mediterranean trade became complete. England for a period of time became practically Morocco's only European trading partner, while French commerce with the port of Essaouira declined precipitously.[70] Not surprisingly, growing numbers of Moroccan Jews began to settle in England. Nor is it surprising that England was Meir Macnin's destination when he left Morocco in 1799.

On 26 July 1799, Meir Macnin set sail for London on board the ship *Aurora*.[71] The ship had originated in London, sailed to Gibraltar, and from there continued to Essaouira where it had arrived on June 1, remained for nearly two months, and spent most of July loading its cargo. The cargo was a typical one, containing the standard exports in the Moroccan trade: calf and goat skins, almonds, and gum arabic.

The reasons for Meir Macnin's departure in 1799 for London are nowhere disclosed in the sources at hand, apart from the fact that he had been employed by the governor of Essaouira to trade with his money.[72] But it is reasonable to surmise that Meir Macnin's commercial ties with London would have made it relatively easy to establish himself there. London was Morocco's principal trading partner in 1799. Traffic between Morocco and Europe had dwindled over the past ten years, and apart from Tangier, where the foreign diplomatic corps resided and which shipped supplies to the British in Gibraltar, Essaouira was the only port that still carried on any significant foreign commerce.[73] Of the handful of Moroccan and foreign merchants there who carried on a rather limited trade, the two most important merchant houses were Guedalla and Macnin, and both had close commercial ties with London. In fact, it would be fair to say that most of Morocco's trade with Europe was conducted by these two merchant houses.[74]

In addition, Macnin was following in the footsteps of other prominent Jewish merchants from Morocco who settled in England. Soon after the establishment of the royal port of Essaouira in 1764, Moroccan Jewish merchants began traveling to Europe. Their sojourns in European ports were often prolonged and it was not long before some merchants began taking up permanent residence in London. The timing of Macnin's departure suggests the possibility that he was seizing the opportunity to accompany his large and valuable shipment of goods, which was assessed at £5,375 (some 39 percent of the value of the cargo on the *Aurora*), just as the plague made its approach to Essaouira. Although we do not have any individual testimony on Meir Macnin's motives, the French consular agent reported on others who had set sail for England about the same time in another ship, the *Lark*, to escape the contagion.[75] Members of the Guedalla family had already left for London in May: "two brothers of Messrs Guedallay & Co. left for London where I believe they will remain, namely Juda & David Guedallay, sons of the two deceased Guedallay brothers," wrote the Dutch consular agent.[76] Aboard the three ships that left Essaouira a couple of months later in the summer of 1799 were some of the leading merchants of Essaouira. Apart from Meir Macnin, members of two other families related to him by marriage were aboard the *Aurora*: Abraham and Solomon Sebag, and Abraham and David Pinto. Members of other Jewish merchant families included M. Cohen de Lara, Judah Coriat, Joseph Abensur, Nina Aflalo, and Mordecai Afriat. A representative of the leading Muslim merchant family, Elhaban (?) Buhillal, was also on board.[77] The two De Lara brothers left later in September, one for London and the other for Gibraltar.[78] Under normal circumstances, special authorization was needed to travel abroad, and often only after agreement was reached and signed on the amount of deposit to be pledged as security.[79] This was because the Moroccan merchants in Essaouira traded with money from the royal treasury, and were in theory indebted to the sultan.

Some of the wealthy merchants of Essaouira remained in Morocco. Members of the Guedalla and Pinto families took refuge in the gardens of the town. Others just shut themselves inside their houses.[80] Meir Macnin left behind his bride, Zohra, daughter of one of the prominent merchants in the town, Meir Pinto. Unless intending to permanently leave the country, merchants would generally leave their wives and families in Morocco. Sometimes as well, the authorities would prevent those merchants who were trading on the sultan's credit from traveling abroad with their families, keeping them in Morocco as "collateral."

Meir's departure before the onslaught of the plague may have helped him escape the fate of some members of the Jewish elite. Many who remained in Essaouira died in the epidemic, including Meir's father-in-law.

Mier [*sic*] Pinto died the first of October in a most pitiable state of the plague and his wife and eldest daughter are very ill; people speak of this house as entirely lost.

Mr. Foxcroft lost his twin daughters, owing to the cruelty of the Jewish wetnurses who left them and have received their reward since the two are now dead. The Guedallay family are also almost all sick and no one from that family has left their house; at the death of Mr. Pinto the daughter that Mier Mackniel [*sic*] had married has lost her mind, just think what a state this poor woman must be in.[81]

We know nothing about Meir Macnin's reaction to the loss of his father-in-law and to the emotional state of his wife, whom he had recently married. We also have no knowledge of when he received news of Meir Pinto's demise or what he heard of his wife's mental health. In any case, there is no indication that he returned to grieve with his family in Morocco. Was it because he was a hard-hearted and selfish individual? Can we simply state that this apparent negligence was deplorably the typical response of powerful and ambitious male merchants who were willing to abandon their families in times of distress? Or perhaps there were other prevailing circumstances about which we simply do not know.

Whether or not Macnin left Morocco on account of the plague, the epidemic certainly made it difficult for him to arrive at his destination, on account of the stringent British quarantine precautions. On August 27, the *Aurora* anchored at Stangate Creek at the main quarantine station on the River Medway, a waterway that maritime ships entered en route to London; and two other ships from Essaouira reached Stangate Creek in mid- to late October. The British consul general in Tangier, James Matra, reported that the captain of one of the other ships, the *Lark*, had died of the plague at Essaouira and he warned the Foreign Office of the danger of the ship approaching the British coast.[82]

The British quarantine committee looked into the matter and recommended that the ships and their cargoes be destroyed. The members of the Privy Council (the king's advisory body) were not satisfied with such an immediate and drastic step, but the committee insisted that prudence was of the utmost importance, in light of the level of the plague in Essaouira at the time that the cargoes were being loaded. Among other things, the committee pointed to

the peculiar susceptibility of infection, and liability to retain infection, attached to the articles forming a principal part of the cargoes of those vessels, especially the goat skins, which are entire, with the hair turned inside: and the great difficulty, if not impracticability, of such airing and expurgation thereof, as would be sufficient security against the danger of contagion: having regard as well to the nature and form of the article itself, as to the circumstances of the time and place when the articles were brought into, lodged in warehouses at, handled and packed, and carried on board the vessels from Mogador; in which process the natives, many of whom were supposed to have died of the plague, appear to have been concerned.[83]

The report added that there were inadequate quarantine facilities, and although the passengers and crew were not sick, "the committee cannot but entertain apprehensions of the possibility of lurking and dormant infection being retained in articles thus susceptible, and unapt for the application of the ordinary and efficacious methods of purification."[84]

With regard to the *Aurora*, it was argued that although the ship had departed shortly before the outbreak of the plague in Essaouira, the hides had been collected and transported over some two to three hundred miles, and therefore could have been infected prior to reaching the port. It was pointed out as well that none of the passengers or crew were sick, but it was felt that the plague still might remain dormant.

On 7 January 1800 the Privy Council ordered that the crews and passengers be taken on board other vessels at Stangate Creek and placed under quarantine for fourteen days. On January 18, the three ships were taken out to sea, burned, and sunk in deep water.[85] The value of the ships, cargoes, and personal effects was assessed so that all interested parties could be compensated for their losses. Meir Macnin and his fellow passengers would have been aboard the ship for nearly six months.

This lengthy delay was the result of a long-standing British policy, influenced by medical theories of the late seventeenth and early eighteenth centuries, of seeking to cut the country off from foreign outbreaks of the bubonic plague. British quarantine policies had been initiated in 1709, by orders in council, during an outbreak of the plague in the Baltic Hanseatic ports. In 1710, a royal proclamation was issued, which enacted quarantine into law. According to the proclamation, ships from the Baltic had to keep forty days of quarantine, and this was to take place at Stangate Creek for ships bound for the Thames.[86] These policies were based on the ideas and recommendations of a London physician, Richard Mead, a contagionist who believed that the plague was spread by diseased persons or goods from infected places, but he also reconciled these views with those of the more classical miasmatists who attributed the spread of disease to the corrupted state of air.[87] Throughout the eighteenth century, new statutes were enacted to further regulate the standards of quarantine. A statute of 1788 required the quarantine officer "to demand of the master, in addition to the obligations already specified, whether his ship had touched at Rhodes, Morea, the coast of Africa, and Magadore [Essaouira], whether any member of the ship's company or passengers had had any contact whatever with a ship touching these places, and whether any person had been sick and with what."[88]

British medicine was quite proud of what many but not all investigators believed to be the result of this policy: the fact that the plague had not struck London, in particular, since the 1665 epidemic that was portrayed in lurid detail in Daniel Defoe's famous *Journal of the Plague Year*. Various reasons were given for London's apparent immunity from the plague: the sulphurous quality of the coal that was mainly used, the strictness of the quarantine laws, and the advanced state of hygiene. One author rejected the notion that quarantine defended the city against the plague, but attributed it instead to London's healthier conditions: "the more recent occurrences of plague in some of the larger cities of Europe, are fairly attributable to their defective conditions in respect of those particulars to which the present salubrity of London is so largely indebted."[89]

While some doctors considered the plague to be essentially the result of miasma, many others saw the disease as the result of contagion.[90] The raging controversy in the late eighteenth and early nineteenth centuries between contagionists and miasmatists clearly had economic consequences since it impinged on the wisdom of imposing quarantines, which disrupted commercial intercourse between foreign countries.[91] An authoritative early nineteenth-century investigator, Thomas Hancock, took a middle road, arguing that an African contagion was necessary to produce the plague, but a "pestilential constitution of the air" was what caused it to spread.[92] Another medical authority argued that the plague was caused by the influence of atmospheric change, assisted by a person's mental disposition. Why, this author asked, was pestilence less frequent in northern than in southern Europe?

The nations of the North generally have been advancing in cultivation, while those of the Levant have been retrograding; some of them, however, have either been stationary, or made less progress than others; and accordingly we find the provinces of Spain, some parts of Italy, the old Venetian provinces of Dalmatia, Istria, &c., many parts of Poland, and the Eastern frontiers of the Austrian dominions, as Hungary and Transylvania, little less liable to epidemic diseases than formerly; not because they are adjacent to Turkey, as has been inferred in conformity with belief in contagion, but because they are in so backward a state of cultivation.[93]

The contrast between what appeared to be London's immunity from the plague and the state of health in the East was most glaring even though European and Muslim notions about medicine were not as far apart at the turn of the nineteenth century as most western Europeans believed.[94] Although the British had no idea about the bacterial causes of the bubonic plague (the correlation between rats and fleas in the dissemination of the epidemic was only made at the turn of the twentieth century), the orderly fashion in which the problem was dealt with at home seemed to the British to underscore the disparity between the West and the Orient, or in this case Barbary. To the British, the spread of the epidemic was due to the negligence of the native population and their total lack of understanding about the way the contagion spread; for some, their level of civilization was the chief cause of pestilence. The pandemic in Barbary was not only attributed to the ignorance of the natives, but was also caused by their unyielding belief in predestination.[95] A typical example of this perception is found in an account of one European traveler to Morocco: "The Mussulman knows not how to defend himself against the plague and the leprosy, and he does not wish to know. By the letter of the Koran—or rather by the unintelligible interpretation of it which has been given by the Moorish doctors—it is an offence against Heaven to avert the misfortunes and scourges which it sends to the true believers."[96] The plague, therefore, is a blessing from God to purge the world of sin, and therefore there is no way to cure it or prevent it from happening.[97] (In fact, measures such as shutting the gates of the cities were taken in Muslim countries to prevent the spread of the epidemic.) In another sense, the outbreak of such a devastating plague symbolized to eighteenth- and nineteenth-century English observers a kind of moral depravity in Barbary, contrasting with the orderliness and decency of British civic society.

Just as the plague led Britain to restrict contacts with Morocco, it may also help to explain why, in the foreign reports from the period, the Sultan Mawlay Sulayman is seen as turning inward, discouraging any commerce with foreigners. It has been suggested that one reason that the sultan restricted trade with Europe was that he was no longer in need of revenue from maritime trade since the royal treasury acquired considerable property from the numerous people who died without heirs.[98]

The sultan was also well aware of events to the east.[99] In the year before the plague, Napoleon had invaded Egypt, causing alarm throughout the Islamic world. Ripples of fear undoubtedly shook the Muslim state of Morocco. The sultan of Turkey wrote an appeal to the Moroccan sultan to come to the aid of Egypt and the defense of Islam.[100] Mediterranean commerce was also hampered, not only by the departure of European merchants during the plague and the resulting cessation of trade, but by the consequences of the Napoleonic Wars in Europe as well. Morocco had not been so isolated in decades and the foreign threat loomed large.

Yet if the Moroccan government was to maintain its army and its dwindling navy in order to consolidate its authority from within, it still needed military hardware and other supplies from Europe. In 1801 and 1802, the sultan was attempting to assert his authority in the southern regions of the country,[101] and was under pressure to obtain arms and cash. With continued unrest in the south, merchants in Essaouira were required to advance money to the governor for the army, and to import goods for the sultan.[102] A few Moroccan Jewish merchants, with their already established network in Europe, were the solution. Meir Macnin, now living in London, was well positioned to become Morocco's preeminent agent in Europe. A scandalous affair of 1801 and 1802 that involved him suggests that he was closely associated with royal power in Morocco, and already began to play the role of mediator between Morocco and Europe in these early years of his career in England.

In 1801 and 1802, the British consul in Tangier sent a series of reports to the British Foreign Office concerning Meir Macnin of London. As the pages of the diplomatic correspondence unfold, we learn of a dispute involving two ships in the seaport of Mogador (Essaouira) that were detained by the Moroccan sultan, Mawlay Sulayman. The sultan had confiscated the cargo of these ships, which amounted to an estimated two hundred thousand Spanish hard dollars (also called piastres, and in Arabic, *riyals*) or about thirty thousand pounds sterling. Macnin had purchased the cargo at long credit from several dozen London traders. The correspondence soon divulges that Macnin was also trading on the credit of the Makhzan. The governor of Essaouira had advanced money to Macnin and sent him to London. From there, Meir had dispatched cargoes to his brother, Shlomo (referred to sometimes as Shalom and in English documents as Solomon), and to Essaouira's leading merchant, Haim Guedalla. The governor, Muhammad b. ʿAbd al-Sadiq, the *qadi*, customs officials (*umanaʾ*), and Shlomo Macnin were summoned to Marrakesh and arrested during the sultan's visit to the area from Marrakesh.[103] The governor was released after two days, but was removed from office. Shlomo Macnin was also apparently released shortly thereafter. Some half a million dollars of Makhzan funds were missing, used by the governor for commerce through the two Macnin brothers.[104]

Macnin claimed bankruptcy, and the sultan sequestered the goods since Macnin was trading at the expense of the Makzhan. The Foreign Office's interest in what would otherwise have been of no concern to it was due to pressure from about fifty British creditors of Macnin, who had advanced goods in considerable quantities that were on these ships, and who had petitioned British intercession for restitution of the money owing to them.[105] The creditors also petitioned Sultan Sulayman:

Whatever be the cause of Macnin and his unfortunate Family having incurred your Royal displeasure must be left to your Majesty's wisdom and mercy, but in no instance whatever ought the innocent to suffer for those either suspected or guilty, such may it please your Majesty, would be the hardship of your Memorialists as said Meir Macnin is suddenly plunged into a state of distress, and having in consequence of his formal abandonment, relinquished his Right and Title to both the said cargoes, whether attended with profit or loss for the benefit of Us his creditors.[106]

Consul Matra had little hope for success in retrieving the debts owing to the British creditors.[107] His reaction to the incident typified European attitudes toward the Jew from the Maghrib — or Barbary, as the region was known to the British. The "Barbary Jew" is seen as duplicitous and untrustworthy.

I hope, Sir, that our merchants will not lose so much as they fear they shall do. It is not very probable that a stranger and a Barbary Jew could obtain credit in London to the amount of the two cargoes, nor, considering the funds that he certainly carried with him could he stand in need of such credit. When he heard of the seizure of the two ships in Barbary he had I am told three rich cargoes coming out which were stopped; one from London, the others from Amsterdam and Leghorn; the two last I take for granted were not bought on trust and may enable him to satisfy his English creditors: but Sir I believe that the Jew is not in such extreme penury as by his letters to the country he pleads, and so far from intending to satisfy his creditors has formed a plan to dupe many more.[108]

Macnin applied to the sultan, through the offices of the British consulate in Tangier, to grant his safe return to Morocco, have his property restored, and allow him to continue his business. He also requested a letter from the sultan stating that whatever property was entrusted to him be placed under the protection of the sharifian sovereign. In exchange for this favor, he offered a considerable amount of gunpowder and other supplies. Sums of money were offered to Mawlay ʿAbd al-Salam, brother of the sultan, and to the governor of Essaouira. The consul expresses his surprise, considering that as someone

born and brought up in this country he must know that if he had five hundred letters of protection they would not save one ounce of any cargo he brings with him, nor do I believe that he means it; he also knows that the emperor has still a demand against him for two hundred thousand mexicos: he will make his peace here by what he can procure in Europe. He doubtless will obtain all the papers he asks from the Emperor, and in a city abounding in commercial speculators like London, may find many to rely on Barbary faith.[109]

Diplomatic efforts to recover the goods for the British merchants were to no avail, "because independent of H.I.M. disinclination to part with what has once been received, he has in that cause what to an African Prince must appear as a substantial right."[110] With growing annoyance, the British consul general gave his interpretation of the sultan's intentions:

The proceedings with the Commerce of Mogador continue as injudiciously vexatious as ever: my time from one week's end to another is completely taken by eternal complaints from that quarter: in the smaller points even where the Treasury is concerned I succeed, but in any thing of real consequence I am heated as I am in Macnin's cause left without an answer. One unpleasant consequence to me is that it obliges me to be constantly hearing the Emperor when in all things in the world is what he most dislikes [*sic*]. I know most perfectly the wish of his heart is to oblige by repeated imposition all Christian traders to quit the south, to confine his foreign commerce to his own Jews, whom he can manage as he pleases without being annoyed by remonstrances.[111]

The British consul had a clear understanding of the situation. The sultan was indeed interested in limiting foreign trade to a small number of Jews who could be closely controlled. In response to the British efforts to recover the merchants' debts, the Makhzan essentially asserted that Macnin himself was the property of the sultan: "Be it known to you," wrote the governor of Tangier, Muhammad b. ʿAbd al-Salam al-Salawi, "that Meir ben Macknin [*sic*] is our Jew, & all the funds with which he trades was money belonging to the Moorish Treasury in Mogador."[112] Despite the petition to the Foreign Office by Macnin's creditors, the British government was clearly unwilling to act, apart from sending a few formal protests to the Makhzan.[113] Meanwhile, Macnin's request for pardon was accorded, as the consul complained: "H.I.M. declares it impossible for any man to believe that a stranger Jew should suddenly get such credit in London; that he has only seized what belonged to his Treasury, and now having no further demands against the Jews, he pardons him; he may return here and trade, or he may remain in London and trade to the country, for his person and property are safe."[114] Matra, nevertheless, pursued Macnin's claims against the Makhzan, even after he was allegedly offered and turned down a bribe by Macnin.[115] Macnin's claim through the offices of the Foreign Office, it seems, was probably a ruse to deflect the demands of the British creditors.

The Moroccan trade was too insignificant for the British to pay much attention to such a minor matter. But for the Moroccans, it was of major consequence. Macnin had become the Makhzan's foremost merchant conducting trade with Europe. The sultan may have been irritated by the behavior of Macnin and his brother, and wanted to ensure that Meir would avoid taking such independent actions in the future. It may have been also that the sultan was willing to let Macnin off the hook only after the latter gave assurances that he would send considerable quantities of arms, munitions, and various provisions. Shortly after the arrest of the governor and the sequestration of Macnin's goods, the sultan had visited the town and upon receiving the corps of merchants, announced his intention to put an end to the problem.[116] The governor continued to serve the Makhzan and was reinstated in Essaouira in 1803.[117] Perhaps the whole incident was some sort of smokescreen; at any rate, whatever trouble he had got into with the Makhzan soon passed, and made no difference to his prominence as an intermediary between Morocco and Europe. Likewise, whatever trouble he had got into with his creditors in England, it made no difference to his establishing himself as a person of high standing within the Sephardi elite of Anglo-Jewry.

CHAPTER FOUR

The 'Berberiscos' of London

In May of 1802, Meir Macnin was made a denizen in England.[1] Endenization was a partial solution for a limited number of privileged foreign Jews who were able to obtain letters patent from the king. As a denizen, a person was "in a kind of middle state between an alien and a natural-born subject,"[2] since it did not entail exemption from alien duties, and children born before endenization could not inherit real property. Naturalization was still not an option for new Jewish immigrants, though it was certainly hoped by the Sephardim of London that it would become possible. A "Jew Bill" was introduced in Parliament in 1753, through the urging of Joseph Salvador and other prominent Sephardi merchants, that would have allowed for personal naturalization. But after it initially passed the Commons, a surprising vociferous public clamor led to its hasty repeal. It was in fact not until 1826 that Parliament passed a bill abolishing the requirement to take the Anglican sacrament as a condition of naturalization, which effectively enabled Jews to become naturalized.[3]

The Jews of England were on the threshold of a new era in the period Meir Macnin lived in London. Although the Jews were not fully freed from legal disabilities as were their coreligionists in revolutionary France, from the time of Cromwell when they were allowed to resettle in England, their status had been different from that throughout the rest of Europe. Many of the medieval disabilities that Jews endured in much of Europe were absent in Great Britain. England was the first European country in which Jews, once admitted, were legally able to settle anywhere they pleased. In con-

trast, in most of Europe until the nineteenth century Jews had no right of
residence and had to secure charters from the local or state authorities specifying the conditions and duration of residence in a given city or locale.
Prior to the French Revolution and emancipation, Macnin would have enjoyed much more freedom of movement in Morocco than in much of Europe. In Morocco and elsewhere in the Muslim world, Jews, together with
other religious groups, were in theory free to move anywhere subject to the
same rights and disabilities everywhere. Moreover, Jews experienced far
fewer impediments in the Muslim world to practicing different trades than
in pre-emancipation Europe, even if they tended to concentrate in specific
professions.[4]

England was the exception prior to the age of Emancipation, because of
both the freedom of movement that Jews enjoyed, and the relatively few
restrictions that existed on the professions that Jews could enter (though
they were excluded from the House of Commons, the Inns of Court, and
universities). Jews paid no special taxes, duties, or tolls as was often the case
in pre-emancipation Continental Europe.[5] One noted nineteenth-century
observer of Anglo-Jewish life wrote:

Though the position of the Jews in England was not in itself especially brilliant or
enviable, Great Britain was to the Jewish race a very Garden of Eden as compared
with many other countries. What if they possessed neither civil nor political rights;
if they were usually regarded by the mass of the population with a mixture of contempt, suspicion and aversion; if they had to endure slights and rebuffs with smil-
ing lip and cringing step! At least they enjoyed under the British flag a certain
amount of material prosperity. Their lives and limbs and property were safe; and
above all they were permitted openly to follow the practices of their religion and to
worship the Lord of their forefathers.[6]

Perhaps even more important was the degree to which many Jews were
becoming acculturated in English society. Jews were starting to be accepted
in Gentile social circles. Political and social conditions were favorable to integration, and as a result, the ties of Sephardi Jews to Judaism, especially
among the wealthy but also probably among the less well-to-do, were
weakened considerably in the eighteenth and nineteenth centuries. As Todd
Endelman argues: "The radical assimilation of scores of Sephardim in
eighteenth- and early nineteenth-century England has no parallel in the
Jewish communities of Europe at the time."[7] To be sure, prejudices remained, even among those who advocated the removal of all remaining disabilities. Conversion to Christianity was the path to full assimilation for
many Sephardim. Those Jews who were ambitious and wished to become
fully identified with English upper-class society, or those who simply wished
to eliminate any social impediments standing in the way of their advance-
ment in society, found entering the Church of England an easy option. A

grandnephew of Meir Macnin, Abraham, was baptized in a London church in 1817; Meir's nephew, David, married a non-Jew.[8]

Attitudes in general were changing toward the Jews. Philo-Semitism had become fashionable among educated non-Jews, reversing to a certain degree the negative stereotypes which had so pervaded the mentality of medieval Christians.[9] Changing attitudes of society toward the Jews are reflected in the career of a once popular English playwright, Richard Cumberland.[10] Cumberland achieved a certain renown for his philo-Semitic drama, *The Jew*, which opened in 1794 at the Drury Lane, one of London's principal theaters. The play hardly does away with the negative stereotype of the miserly Jew so ingrained in the English consciousness, but does justify Jewish miserliness in its portrayal of the main character, Sheva, a moneylender who demonstrates great charity. Cumberland revived this theme in a far less successful comic musical farce, *The Jew of Mogadore: A Comic Opera in Three Acts*, which received scathing reviews when it opened at Drury Lane in 1808.[11] Wrote one reviewer: "Mr. Cumberland, who used to imitate Fielding and Milton, has now, with a sort of anticipation of future admirers, imitated himself. Nadab the Jew is a mere copy of Sheva the Jew; he is an old man overflowing with money and benevolence, a miser that others may be rich, a slave to poverty that he may release slaves."[12] The play closed down after three or four nights. What is of interest in *The Jew of Mogadore*, however, is clearly not its literary merits, but rather the possibility, suggested by the British consul in Tangier in 1823, that one of the main characters in the play was based on Meir Macnin. The consul was writing, with some dismay, about Meir Macnin's recently acquired powers under the new sultan, Mawlay ʿAbd al-Rahman.[13] There is no contemporary evidence proving that Cumberland was actually inspired by Macnin and his activities.[14] The play offers no details that actually correspond to known events in Macnin's life. Some of the audience, however, would have heard about Macnin since he had become a known and notorious figure in London's commercial circles. And for those to whom Macnin himself was unknown, the stereotype of the Barbary Jew was part of the literary imagination of the theatergoing public. More specifically, the figure of the Moroccan Jewish courtier and merchant was already well known in London's theater circles.

The story of Joseph Sumbal, a son of the famous court Jew Samuel Sumbal,[15] shows the fascination of the British public with exotic "Barbary," combined with the antipathy toward Jews. We learn about him from the memoirs of a famous actress, Mary Wells,[16] who married Joseph Sumbal in prison, where he had been incarcerated for debt. The father, it seems, was able to smuggle considerable property out of Morocco to Europe, where the family had spent time. For this he was imprisoned by the sultan, but he was able to escape to Gibraltar, where he had sent considerable supplies from Essaouira.

Finally, he allegedly died of poisoning through the sultan's intrigues. The sons of Sumbal went to claim their inheritance in France but were unable to reach a settlement. Joseph Sumbal went to Holland and then England, where, according to Wells, he was pursued by one of his brothers who had him arrested and confined to the Fleet, the famous debtors' prison in London: another account alleges that he was imprisoned for contempt of court for refusing to answer interrogatories concerning a large quantity of diamonds in his possession.[17] Meanwhile, as the actress tells us: "I was in the prison at this time: he came in with all the pomp and splendour of an eastern monarch, attended by a number of Moorish servants."[18] Wells, who had a reputation for eccentricity, accepted Sumbal's marriage proposal and converted to Judaism, changing her name to Leah. The *Morning Post and Gazetteer* reported on the wedding:

On Thursday evening last, the marriage ceremony, in the Jewish style, was performed in the Fleet, uniting Mrs. Wells, late of Covent-garden theatre, to Mr. Sumbel, a Moorish Jew, detained for debt in that prison. The ceremony was solemnised with all the Jewish magnificence. The bridegroom was richly dressed in white satin, and a splendid turban with a white feather: the bride, who is now converted to a Jewess, was also attired in white satin, and her head dressed in an elegant style, with a large plume of white feathers. Mr. Sumbel's brother assisted at the ceremony, dressed in pink satin, and a rich turban and feather. The apartment was brilliantly illuminated with variegated lamps, according to the customs of the Jews. The rest of the company who attended were Jews, in their common habiliments—as old-clothesmen.

But with the exception of the guests, every thing had the appearance of eastern grandeur, Mr. Sumbel, though confined for debt to a large amount, is possessed of property.[19]

The *Morning Herald* reported, with some bemusement, that "Mrs. Becky Wells, late of every theatre in this kingdom, has extended her *known good-nature* so far as to *marry a Moorish Jew!*" Sumbal protested in a letter to the *Morning Post and Gazetteer*, that "he is confined in Fleet not for debt, but contempt of court."[20] About a fortnight after their marriage, compromise was reached with his brother, and he was freed from prison. "After his emancipation," she wrote, "he took a house in Orchard-street, Portman-square, to be near the Turkish ambassador, with whom he was intimate, and often visited."[21]

Mrs. Sumbel offers us glimpses of her Orientalist imagination in depicting her husband's exotic customs:

The graces of his person were not visible in the European habits. This circumstance augmented his chagrin; and he did not recover any portion of his placidity till he sat cross-legged in all the magnificence of his Moorish paraphernalia. For this important metamorphosis, his trunks were at every stage unpacked, and I had the supreme felicity of seeing my *illustrious* partner, once, during every twelve hours, decked in the splendour of a second OTHELLO.[22]

Sumbal, it seems, planned to return to Morocco to become the sultan's court Jew, "and to make his visit the more acceptable, he laid out large sums of money in presents: among the items of which, there were £20,000 worth of brass cannon."[23] Not surprisingly, the marriage did not succeed, and Mrs. Sumbel escaped; the divorce was reported in the papers in 1798. She writes disparagingly of the Jews: "As all their ceremonies, whether of a domestic or religious nature, are regulated according to the Mosaic laws, they (with the low cunning so peculiar to the people of that nation) always pervert the meaning to answer their own purposes; for I firmly believe the Jewish faith is merely a quibble of words arising from interested motives."[24] This cunning is combined with an Oriental duplicity:

If the rest of the Moors are of his disposition, they must be a very unhappy people. As, in his own country, he was accustomed to have all his wants anticipated, so he expected it in every other: but, under such circumstances, the situation of both master and servant must be dreadful; for among them the attendant who commits an error (sometimes even of the slightest nature) is deprived of his existence; and the only means they have to guard against it, is to cut off the master either by the dagger or by poison; so that a fear of death constantly hangs over both.[25]

As will a scenario that will become familiar with Meir Macnin, the unfortunate Mrs. Sumbel was left with major debts and pursued by creditors after her former husband left the country. She writes: "I have since learned from a gentleman that he went to Altona in Denmark, where he built a large street at his own expense."[26] From another source, we learn that she may not have been exaggerating his largesse. David Corcos, who apparently was related to Sumbal, reportedly had documents in his collection that attested to Joseph consecrating religious endowments (*hekdesh*) to his Talmud-Torah school and synagogue in Altona. Joseph Sumbal died there in 1804.[27]

The depiction of Sumbal in these memoirs offers a kind of prototype for Meir Macnin, who arrived on the London scene just a few years after Sumbal. The image of the seductive, duplicitous, and exotic Oriental in his flamboyant garb, who is more comfortable in the company of the Turkish ambassador than with the English, is combined with that of the cunning Jew. The scenes of Oriental Jews in their splendor, and of a wedding in prison, are at once followed by the more familiar and prevalent stereotype of contemptible Jewish hawkers of old clothes, lest the reader forget from what people the Barbary Jew originated.[28] Conversely, though the Ashkenazi street peddler would have been a more familiar figure to Londoners, the stereotypical image of all Jews was that of a swarthy and sinister-looking Sephardi.[29] The popular travel literature of this period also often discovered that although different in external appearance, the Barbary Jew and the familiar Jew of London were part of the same "race." In a description of the Jewish quarter of Tetuan, a traveler in 1838 finds that you can

go where you please, the same characters always mark these sons of Israel and are so forcibly written on their external lineaments, that whether with the skullcap, embroidered vest, and sash of Barbary, or with old clothes' bags on their shoulders, in Monmouth Street, there is no mistaking them. In their prying and busy countenances are written the innermost thoughts of their souls—gain and filthy lucre. It is this, perhaps, which gives them that meanness of appearance, of which they are never divested.[30]

This negative image was not really dispelled in Cumberland's plays, though the audience was challenged to believe that the Jew was really virtuous. The Jews themselves were indifferent to Cumberland's good intentions, and uncomfortable with the way they were represented.[31] In addition, perhaps, most of the Jews preferred to distance themselves from the oriental image with which they were associated in Cumberland's play.

Philo-Semitism of the late eighteenth and early nineteenth centuries was ambivalent, as reflected in Cumberland's plays or even Leah Wells's marriage to Sumbel. At the same time that Jews were being accepted, somewhat grudgingly, into English bourgeois society, and as a result becoming rapidly assimilated, anti-Semitic stereotypes prevailed. For example, philo-Semites believed that Jews had a propensity for greed and unscrupulous commercial practices, but that these were the unfortunate consequences of discrimination against them by Gentile society. There were Gentiles, therefore, who advocated the removal of civil and political disabilities, yet often coupled this with a disparaging attitude, especially as the number of Jewish immigrants to England increased appreciably in the late eighteenth and early nineteenth centuries. Another concern besides removal of the civil disabilities of the Jews was the idea of assimilating them through conversion to Christianity. In 1808, the same year that Cumberland's play appeared, the London Society for Promoting Christianity among the Jews was established. The efforts of this missionary society, however, did not meet with the universal approval of Christians, not only because of the unscrupulous methods of gaining converts that it employed but also because of racist opposition to the conversion of Jews.[32]

Sephardi Jews in particular were one step ahead of the Ashkenazim on this road of acculturation, and even to a certain degree, secularization. In the mid-seventeenth century, the Sephardim were the first Jews to live in England, since none were allowed in the country from the time of the general expulsion in 1290. Even prior to the official acceptance of the right of Jews to live in England in 1656, a small number of Marranos, or crypto-Jews, began settling in London and Bristol during the sixteenth century.

"New Christians" had already established themselves in Amsterdam in the early seventeenth century, where they were able to openly profess their Judaism, and it was from there that the initiative to seek the readmission of the Jews in England was launched. The Sephardi rabbi, Menasseh ben Israel of Amsterdam, came to London in 1655, and although he believed that the Jewish return to England would expedite the scattering of the Jews to all corners of the earth as a harbinger of the messianic age, he also emphasized the economic contribution that the Jews would make. Interest in the Jews was also spurred by the religious turmoil of the Civil War period. Protestant notions about the ushering in of the Second Coming saw in the return of Jews to England the hastening of this apocryphal goal, though millenarian influence on the readmission of the Jews was probably less important than the disruption of traditional privileges brought by the Civil War. Cromwell convened the Whitehall Conference in 1655 to consider the readmission of the Jews, and, although failing to gain the approval of the delegates, he made it clear that the Marranos were free to practice their religion—thereby paving the way, without a formal decree of readmission, for the formation of a Jewish community in London.[33]

Marrano settlers continued to come to London, but these crypto-Jews were now able to openly profess their Judaism once they arrived in England. The dominant element came from Portugal. It should be recalled that a vast number of Spanish Jews moved to Portugal from Spain during the year of the mass expulsion in 1492. They, too, were forced to choose between conversion or expulsion just a few years later, but because they converted en masse under considerable duress, many maintained their corporate identity as crypto-Jews for centuries. With the political union of Portugal and Spain (1580–1640), many *Marranos* moved back to Spain to escape the Inquisition in Portugal, which was considered even more ferocious than in Spain. The term "Portuguese" in Spain came to be associated with "Jews," in other words, the descendants of Portuguese *conversos*. The language of the Sephardi immigrants in England was either Spanish or Portuguese, but Portuguese prevailed as the official language of the congregation. The term "Portuguese" came to refer to the Sephardi Jews generally in London, as it did in Italy and Holland.[34]

From the latter part of the seventeenth until the end of the eighteenth century the number of Sephardi Jews in England, and especially in London, increased. In the eighteenth century their numbers were outstripped by Ashkenazi immigrants, though the Sephardim remained wealthier as a whole.[35] By the middle of the eighteenth century, the Jewish population of England numbered seven to eight thousand, of which about two thousand were Sephardim. By 1800, the Sephardim in London numbered about four thousand, a fifth of all Jews of that community.[36] One of the reasons for the relatively small increase in the number of Sephardi Jews seems to have been that a proportion of them assimilated into English society and severed their ties with the Jewish community. In contrast to Ashkenazi Jews, Sephardim, descended from New Christians in Spain and Portugal, frequently had much greater exposure to Western, sometimes secular, culture. This may explain the propensity of Sephardi Jews to assimilate into English society, which often led to intermarriage and conversion. This process of intermarriage and conversion, not because of forced baptism as in the medieval period but because of acculturation, was more far-reaching than anywhere else in the Jewish world for this period. Even apart from this, acculturation often meant the abandoning of religious practice, infrequent synagogue attendance, and working on the Sabbath.[37]

Some of the Sephardim achieved prominence in the financial institutions of the City of London. Some became stockbrokers, merchants, and government loan contractors.[38] As men of wealth, they invested in property and country estates, establishing social ties with the Gentile landowning upper class. Their privileges were both protected and limited. At the Royal Exchange, the Jewish brokers gathered together under a colonnade between the Portuguese and Spanish merchants in a place known as the "Jew's walk."[39] The number of licensed "Jew brokers" at the Stock Exchange remained restricted to twelve until 1830, and because of this limitation, licenses changed hands at very high prices. Jews had to pay the Lord Mayor dearly to be nominated for a broker's medal when one of the few allocated places became vacant. There were, however, many unsworn brokers as well as an unrestricted number of "jobbers" who dealt in stocks on their own account rather than as intermediaries. The distinction between stockbrokers and stockjobbers was, in fact, not that clear, since various kinds of activities were frequently combined.[40] Although a minority of brokers were Jews, they were nevertheless disproportionately represented in the profession. Despite the limited number of licensed Jewish brokers, they appeared so prominent in the Stock Exchange, that to some observers, it seemed as if the profession was dominated by them.[41]

The Sephardim jealously guarded their privileged position, a status recognized by Gentile society. Although there were certainly wealthy Ashkenazi Jews and poor Sephardim, non-Jewish observers of the period made sharp distinctions between the elite Sephardi and poorer Ashkenazi Jews: "The praise which is due to the generality of the Portuguese relative to their manners and morals," according to one London observer in 1791, "cannot be bestowed upon the majority of the German Jews. They are great sticklers for their old tenets and usages; but they allow themselves great liberties in regard to their morals. I believe few burglaries, robberies, and false coinages are committed, in which some of them are not, in one shape or other, concerned."[42] Such views about the lower class of Ashkenazi Jews are echoed in Patrick Colquhoun's well-known book on crime in London:

A Class of Cheats of the Society of Jews, who are to be found in every street, lane and alley in and near the Metropolis, under the pretence of purchasing old cloaths, and metals of different sorts; Their chief business really is to prowl about the houses and stables of men of rank and fortune, for the purpose of holding out temptations to the servants to pilfer and steal small articles, not likely to be missed, which these Jews purchase at about one third of the real value. —It is supposed that upwards of fifteen hundred of these depraved people are employed in diurnal journies of this kind; by which, through the medium of bad money, and other fraudulent dealings, many of them acquire property, and then set up shops and become Receivers of Stolen Goods.

It is estimated that there are from fifteen to twenty thousand Jews in the city of London, besides, perhaps, about five or six thousand more in the great provincial and sea-port towns; (where there are at least twenty synagogues, besides six in the Metropolis;) most of the lower classes of those distinguished by the name of German or Dutch Jews, live chiefly by their wits, and establish a system of mischievous intercourse all over the country, the better to carry on their fraudulent designs in the circulation of base money, —the sale of stolen goods, and in the purchase of metals of various kinds; as well as other articles pilfered from the Dock-Yards, and stolen in the provincial towns, which they bring to the Metropolis to elude detection, —and *vice versá*.

Educated in idleness from their earliest infancy, they acquire every debauched and vicious principle which can fit them for the most complicated acts of fraud and deception; to which they seldom fail to add the crime of perjury, whenever it can be of use, in shielding themselves or their associates from the punishment of the law. —From the orange boy, and the retailer of seals, razors, glass, and other wares, in the public streets, to the shop-keeper, dealer in wearing apparel, or in silver and gold, the same principles of conduct too generally prevail.

The itinerants utter base money to enable them, by selling cheap, to dispose of their goods; while those that are stationary, with very few exceptions receive and purchase, at an under-price, whatever is brought them, without asking questions.[43]

The Sephardi Jews themselves regarded Colquhoun's book as an authoritative source on the condition of the Jews in London.[44] The Sephardim looked down upon their Ashkenazi coreligionists, as increasing numbers from Germany, Poland, and Russia began to join the Sephardi synagogue, *Saar Asamaim*, in the seventeenth century. The Sephardim, calling themselves *Nossa Nação*, "our nation" or "our people," sharply distinguished themselves from the Ashkenazim, whom they labeled *Tudescos*. This appellation, used by the Sephardim of Venice to refer to the Ashkenazim, derived from the Italian word for a "German," but had a Spanish and Portuguese plural form; and in fact the Ashkenazim, too, identified themselves as "Dutch" (that is, German—from *deutsch*) Jews.

The term *Tudesco* migrated to the Sephardi Jews of Amsterdam, whose community was influenced by Venice.[45] The Amsterdam Sephardi community looked down on the *Tudescos*, and resented having to give them charity. Despite the changing character of the Ashkenazi immigrant community, Sephardim of Amsterdam thought of the Ashkenazim as poor and prone to moral corruption. The Sephardi congregation in Amsterdam began to institutionalize discrimination by, for example, preventing the Ashkenazim from using the cemetery of their community, not allowing the Ashkenazim to slaughter meat, excluding new Ashkenazi students from the schools of the congregation, and barring Sephardim married to Ashkenazim from synagogue membership. In the 1630s, a fund was established by the Sephardi community to induce the Ashkenazim to emigrate.[46]

The Amsterdam community, in turn, had a significant influence on the Sephardim in England, and discrimination by London's Sephardi community against the Ashkenazim followed closely the pattern of Amsterdam. Tensions grew and in 1678–79, the elders of the synagogue, the *Mahamad* (lit., *maᶜamad*), passed an ordinance excluding the Ashkenazim from synagogue offices and from receiving honors such as being called to the Torah. As in Amsterdam, the Sephardim of London regarded the influx of Ashkenazim with some alarm, and in 1682 passed an ordinance stipulating that destitute Ashkenazim arriving in England should receive five shillings and then leave the country (often back to Amsterdam!) within four days. There was even a prohibition against Ashkenazim who could not afford to pay the Sephardi burial tax, interring their dead in the community's cemetery, and consequently, an Ashkenazi cemetery was created. Not surprisingly, in the last decade of the seventeenth century, the Ashkenazim broke away to form their own organized community. In 1701, the Sephardi congregation, for its part, having outgrown its original building on Creechurch Lane, which dated back to 1657, opened the Bevis Marks Synagogue (named from the neighborhood in the district of Aldgate, in the eastern part of the City of London, where it was located), which was modeled on the great Portuguese synagogue of Amsterdam.[47]

Although in the early stages of its history, the Sephardi community gave some assistance to Ashkenazim, as the numbers of Ashkenazi Jews far outstripped the Sephardim in the eighteenth and early nineteenth centuries the community emphasized that "the charitable institutions formed by the Spanish and Portuguese Jews were solely directed to assist their brethren who either fled from the alluded persecution or were reduced by other misfortunes, and not for the purpose of encouraging German, Dutch or Polish adventurers."[48] Representative committees of the two Jewish "nations" of "Portuguese" and "German" (or Ashkenazi) Jews did join together in 1760 to collectively represent Anglo-Jewry before the public in a body known as the Board of Deputies, still the formal representative today of British Jews.[49] But in 1802, apparently after the Ashkenazi committee had submitted to the House of Commons a petition in which both Jewish communities would be considered as one unit for the purpose of poor relief, the Sephardim of the Board of Deputies were quite explicit that they wanted to be regarded by the British government as a separate body. This was not only because of their distinctive customs and ceremonies, but also "because not having increased in number their establishments remain competent to their wants—whereas within the last fifty years the German Jews have increased prodigiously in number, coming from all parts of Germany, *and mostly of the poorer class*. So that their poor bears no proportion to the Portuguese poor, who have suitable establishments and are well provided for, while they have none and want for everything."[50]

While gaining status and respect, and even assimilating to a degree into Gentile society, the Sephardi Jews of London in the eighteenth century still did not have the full rights of citizens and were still regarded as a separate, corporate community: the "Portuguese Nation." At the very foundation of the Sephardi community in London, its bylaws (*ascamot*) solemnly declared that "experience has shown that it is a necessary thing in all states and nations to have statutes wherewith to be governed."[51] The Sephardi community considered itself a "nation" as, on the one hand, a separate and honored autonomous government, and on the other hand, superior and distinct from other Jews. There was a sense as well that this nation was a kind of supranational Diaspora community, transcending political boundaries between states. To a certain extent, the origins of this identity can be traced to the seventeenth century, when Amsterdam emerged as the epicenter for this "Portuguese" Marrano Diaspora corresponding to the preeminence of the Dutch in the Atlantic trade. Other Sephardi communities that emerged in this period, such as London, modeled themselves after the Amsterdam community.[52]

Affiliation to the Sephardi community meant, among other things, charity toward Sephardi immigrants, and assistance to Sephardim in distress in other parts of the world. For example, based on practices in Amsterdam and Venice, the Spanish and Portuguese Congregation of London established an office called *Parnas dos Cautivos*, or "Warden of the Captives," that ransomed Jews taken captive by Mediterranean corsairs.[53] Despite assimilation, the eighteenth-century London Sephardim were as much a part of the wider Sephardi world as they were English. This hybrid identity, on the one hand of aspiring to become an integral part of English society and to see the remaining legal disabilities removed, and on the other, of asserting an aristocratic pride of belonging to a special class of Jews, became increasingly untenable in the nineteenth century.

One of the causes of increased tension between a Sephardi and English identity was the changing character of the Sephardi community itself. In the past, the majority of the members had been former Marranos coming directly from Spain and Portugal. In the early years, the Spanish and Portuguese Jews were less discriminating in accepting those new arrivals who did not come directly from Spain, called *Berberiscos* (i.e., people from Barbary) and *Italianos*. Strictly speaking, many of the Jews coming from North Africa were not "Spanish," not having been descended from the Iberian refugee community. Some communities in Morocco were bitterly divided between the refugees, who were collectively known in Hebrew as *megorashim* (those expelled), and the *toshavim* (the native inhabitants). But almost everywhere in Morocco, Sephardi customs, rituals, and legal institutions exercised an influence over the "indigenous" Jews at the same time that the Spanish immigrants and their descendants were increasingly becoming acculturated, leading to a uniquely Moroccan cultural synthesis. And while distinctive customs and even separate synagogues and institutions remained, many Moroccan Jews came to identify themselves as Sephardi, even when their ancestors had not issued from the Iberian peninsula. Moreover, the concept of "Sephardi" was elastic, depending on the social context. A Jew might identify either with the Sephardi or with a local rite or *halakhic* tradition in Morocco, but almost certainly would assert a Sephardi identity in Europe, where belonging to the Sephardi community carried greater prestige than belonging to the Ashkenazi community.

The Sephardim in England regarded the "foreign" Sephardim with some disdain for their different practices and customs concerning religious and communal affairs. In 1710, the congregation ordered that newly arrived *Italianos* and *Berberiscos* in England should be given only modest provisions, but then be obliged to leave the country.[54] In the 1730s the *Mahamad* came up with the scheme to ship the community's poor off to a Sephardi community in the New World.[55] The Amsterdam Sephardi community, also confronted with the growing number of Sephardi poor, similarly paid the poor to migrate elsewhere in the Sephardi Diaspora, including Gibraltar, Essaouira, Tunis, Livorno, Istanbul, Hamburg, London, and the Dutch colonies of the New World. Ironically, it was to Amsterdam, Rotterdam, and Hamburg that the Sephardi community of London had dispatched the impoverished Ashkenazim in the latter part of the seventeenth century.[56]

As the number of poorer Jewish immigrants from the Mediterranean increased in the latter half of the eighteenth century, the antagonism of the older Sephardi residents toward them grew. The more Anglicized families of earlier Portuguese and Spanish Jews considered themselves citizens of the country, who had fought for their civil rights and who had entered into the liberal professions as a matter of choice, as against their more alien coreligionists, who for the most part were engaged in commerce.[57]

Despite the misgivings about the influx of Sephardim to London, the trend continued in the latter half of the eighteenth century, and by the time of Macnin's arrival in England the composition of the Sephardi congregation had been transformed. A significant proportion of the Jews arriving in England during the late eighteenth and early nineteenth centuries who became part of the Sephardi congregation were from North Africa, especially Morocco.

Other North African Jews reached London directly from the Maghrib. The 1803 aliens' register of the Bevis Marks Synagogue lists the countries of origin of members of the congregation arriving in the latter half of the eighteenth century: Holland, 41; Italy, 27; Morocco, Tunis, and Gibraltar, 22; Portugal, Spain, and Brazil, 17; Ottoman Empire, 12; Hamburg, Vienna, and Poland, 12; Bordeaux and Bayonne, 7.[58] This suggests that about 16 percent of the new arrivals came from the Maghrib or Gibraltar.

Although some of the Jews from North Africa, like Meir Macnin and most of his fellow passengers on board the *Aurora*, were prosperous merchants, many immigrants were of more modest means. Many came to seek opportunities in England as the economic position of much of the Sephardi Diaspora continued to deteriorate.

Immigration from North Africa and Gibraltar started in the 1770s, and most gravitated toward the Spanish and Portuguese Congregation, with which they already had ties. About 250 Gibraltarian Jews arrived in England after the evacuation of the population in 1781 due to French siege between June 1779 and February 1783. Most of them arrived destitute, placing a great burden on the Bevis Marks Synagogue, which formed a special committee and extended the congregation's support. Many of the refugees remained in England as permanent residents after peace was restored.[59]

The famous journalist Henry Mayhew, writing in 1851, offers a portrait of an elderly street-seller, whose itinerary was probably typical of the Moroccan Jewish emigrant at the turn of the nineteenth century. The street-seller said that his father, who had died when he was about ten years old, had been a tax-farmer in Essaouira, renting the whole market from the Makhzan and collecting tolls from sellers occupying stalls; as such, he had been neither rich nor poor. At about age eighteen, the street-seller left for Gibraltar, where he made a living selling handkerchiefs for about six years. He emigrated to England in 1811, eventually joining other Moroccan Jews, mainly from Essaouira, selling rhubarb and spices in the streets of London, an occupation that he had heard about as a child growing up in Morocco. After two years, he had saved enough money to open a shop in Exeter with three other Moroccan Jews. The business failed after about five years, and he returned to London, resuming his occupation as a rhubarb and spice seller, but never again prospering.[60]

FIGURE 8. *Moroccan Peddler in London*. Anonymous, c. 1800. The Jewish Museum, New York, Gift of Dr. Harry G. Friedman, F 5895. Photo © The Jewish Museum, New York/Photo: John Parnell.

Moroccan and other North African Jewish peddlers became a familiar part of the Anglo-Jewish landscape in the nineteenth century, noted for their Turkish-style dress, which included baggy trousers and a turban, their long beards, and for specializing in the sale of spices, rhubarb, and Moroccan slippers.[61] Learned Moroccan Jews were also an identifiable element in the Anglo-Jewish landscape in the early nineteenth century. An evangelist of the Unitarians noticed that among his audience of five hundred in Falmouth there were "two Jews, who are said to be men of considerable learning, especially one of them, who is from Morocco, and was in a Moorish dress."[62]

London, center of commerce during the Napoleonic Wars, was linked to the Mediterranean network of Jewish traders, and the Sephardi community of London was closely connected to Livorno. Sir Moses Montefiore, the most prominent member of England's Jewish elite in the nineteenth century, came from a Livornese family that moved to London in 1744 and made its fortune in the English-Italian trade. The Montefiores kept close connections with Livorno, where Moses was born in 1784.[63] The rabbinical leadership of the Spanish and Portuguese community of London also often came from Livorno. Such was the case with Raphael Meldola, appointed rabbi in 1805; and with his predecessors Rabbi David Nieto (appointed in 1700 and remaining until his death in 1728) and the latter's son Isaac Nieto (arrived in London in 1747, and temporarily appointed in 1751). Isaac Nieto was most famous for the translation of the Sephardi prayerbook into Spanish.[64]

Growing numbers of Jews joined the ranks of London merchants frequenting the coffeehouses of the City, where much business was transacted. With London's commercial expansion, middling merchants came to dominate the City and obtained political power. The growing importance and power of the commercial classes enabled more Jews to ascend the social ladder than ever before.

The newfound importance of those engaged in commerce was disconcerting to many. To conservative observers, commerce was undermining the very fabric of society: "The commercial system has long been undermining the distinction of ranks in society, and [is] introducing a worse distinction in its stead. Mushrooms are every day starting up from the dunghill of trade, nobody knows how, and family pride is therefore become a common subject of ridicule in England." Commerce in England, continued the same commentator, "poisons every thing:—literature, arts, religion, government are alike tainted, it is a *lues* which has got into the system of the country, and is rotting flesh and bone."[65] Commerce is seen as undermining both the aristocracy and the peasant small landowners; agriculture is becoming commercialized; the traditional gentry is in decline; and merchants, bankers, and contractors are ascending the social scale and by wealth reaching the ranks of the nobility. The ease by which money allowed people to be named baronets (the lowest rank of nobility) was disconcerting to many.

Macnin rapidly learned to take advantage of the commercial world of London and, despite his bad reputation among London's traders, found numerous opportunities to pursue his business. Macnin's first place of residence and business was within a few streets of the Spanish and Portuguese Synagogue on Haydon Square, formerly the place of the old lockup (the "Cage"), stocks, and engine house in the precinct of the Minories. The neighborhood was inhabited by many Jews, and the streets were filled with Jewish hawkers; in the evenings, the old clothes men gathered there in a market called the Rag Fair.[66] The vestry (the governing body of the parish), regarded these Jewish hucksters as a nuisance.[67] Eventually, however, in 1814, Macnin moved to New Broad Street, not far from the Bevis Marks Synagogue in Aldgate, which he had already joined in 1800.

FIGURE 9. Interior of the Bevis Marks Synagogue. I. M. Belisario, 1812. Courtesy of the Spanish & Portuguese Jews' Congregation, London.

The vicinity of the Bevis Marks Synagogue was a polyglot district. On this semineutral ground of international commerce, Moroccan Jews and Muslims mixed with Christians. Muslim merchants, upon arriving in London, resided with Jews. Take, for example, the case of al-Hajj ʿAbd al-Salam Buhillal from Tangier. The Buhillals were among the most prominent merchant families from Fez, whose mercantile interests stretched from Timbuktu to Europe.[68] In 1799, ʿAbd al-Salam Buhillal petitioned the duke of Portland, the British home secretary, concerning some lost cargo. On a commercial trip to Amsterdam, he had been captured by a French privateer, then freed after a British frigate recaptured the French ship. Buhillal claimed that the cargo, instead of being restored to his possession, was sold. Some thirteen years previously he had been in London, and presently he claimed that he was in the service of the sultan. Buhillal resided at 7 Castle Street, the residence of Abraham Benjamin, next to the Bevis Marks Synagogue.[69]

It was therefore natural for Meir Macnin to gravitate toward the Bevis Marks Synagogue. Like many other newcomers from Morocco who arrived in London in the late eighteenth and early nineteenth centuries with considerable wealth and status, he was able to find a prominent place in the Spanish and Portuguese Congregation. In the first two decades of the nine-

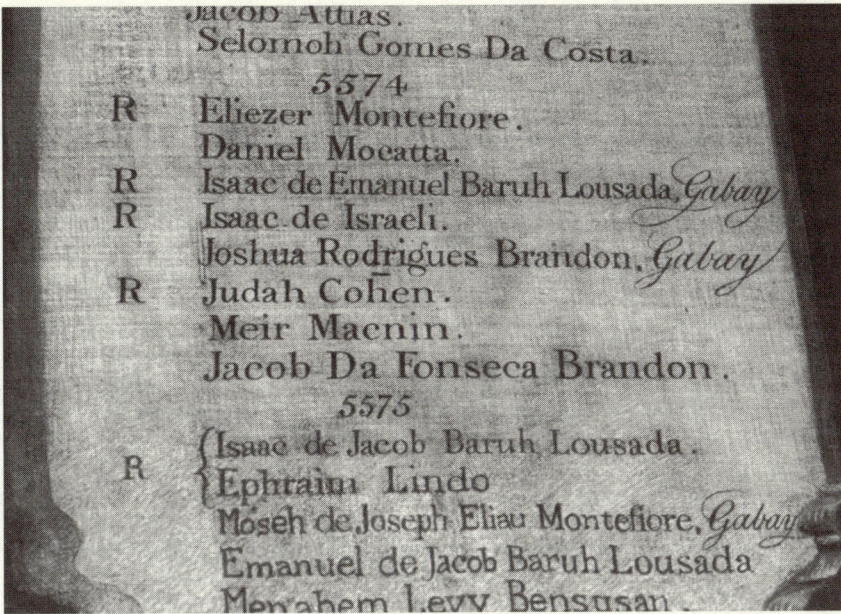

FIGURE 10. *Parnasim* board in Bevis Marks Synagogue, London, listing *Mahamad* members including Meir Macnin (5574 = 1813/14). Courtesy of the Spanish & Portuguese Jews' Congregation, London.

teenth century, representatives of some of the leading Moroccan families settled in London and became members: Abitbol, Afriat, De Lara, Massiah, Cohen Solal, Abecasis, Levy Bensusan, Sebag, Guedalla, Zagury, Aflalo, and Hadida, to mention some of the principal names. Many of these elite Moroccan Jewish merchants during this period married into some of the older and most prominent Sephardi families of London.[70]

On becoming a member of the synagogue, Macnin's annual tax (*finta*), assessed on the commercial operations of all individual privileged members (*yehidim*) and that supported the expenses of the synagogue, was fixed at six pounds (the maximum assessed at this time was about fifteen pounds). He was also assigned a prominent seat (*gaveta*) in the synagogue, in accordance with his rank.[71] A representative of the other most important merchant firm of Essaouira, Judah Guedalla, the son of Haim Guedalla, had become a new member of the synagogue in 1799, with a *finta* of five pounds. In 1801 Guedalla was elected a warden (*parnas*) of the *Mahamad*.[72] In subsequent years, the *finta* of both Judah Guedalla and Meir Macnin increased considerably.[73] In 1809, Judah Guedalla was elected *gabay* (treasurer),[74] with the chief administrative responsibility for the congregation. Eventually,

Macnin, too, became part of the oligarchic governing body that headed the congregation. In 1814, he was elected as *parnas* and the following year he became the *presidente* of the *Mahamad* (election was for one year).[75]

Once elected to the *Mahamad*, a former *parnas* often continued to play a leading role in the congregation. The moral authority of synagogue office was considered exceptionally high: "It is being highly essential for the good government of this *kaal*, that its *Mahamad* consist of persons of capacity and respectability, fearing God, it is equally necessary that the election of the four Parnasim and one Gabay of which the said *Mahamad* is to be composed, be made with all possible impartiality and solemnity."[76] In reality, an equally important qualification for office was wealth, considering that the *parnasim* had to deposit one hundred pounds to contribute to synagogue expenditure when elected to office, while the *gabay* was required to deposit six hundred pounds. These deposits were returned upon completing the term of office.[77] Furthermore, election to office in the congregation was not a matter of choice: anyone nominated was required to accept his duties or be subject to fine or other sanctions. This became a means which the synagogue used to raise money. Isaac D'Israeli, the father of the prominent parliamentarian and prime minister Benjamin Disraeli, declined the honor of his election as *parnas* in 1813 and refused to pay the fine of forty pounds. A few years later, after a lengthy correspondence, Isaac D'Israeli resigned from the synagogue, complaining of the attitude of "injudicious individuals" on the *Mahamad* including Meir Macnin, and later had his children baptized.[78] Abraham Cohen Macnin, a nephew of Meir's who was a member of the Stock Exchange, agreed to pay a fine of twenty-five pounds after declining the office of "Hatan Tora," the "bridegroom of the Torah," the reader of the final portion of the Torah on Simhat Torah.[79]

Thus, Meir Macnin rapidly became integrated into the upper echelons of the Sephardi elite of London, his wealth and status clearly overshadowing the disdain that some of the Sephardim had for the *Berberiscos*. Social and marital ties soon linked the newcomers with the Montefiores, the most famous name in nineteenth-century Anglo-Jewry. Eleven days after the marriage of Moses Montefiore (to Judith, the daughter of Levi Barent Cohen), the most prominent leader of Anglo-Jewry for much of the nineteenth century, Lady Montefiore wrote in her diary: "Mr. Macnin, Mr. Sebag and Mrs. Sebag (?) dined with us, and we spent a very agreeable evening."[80] "Mr. Sebag" was Solomon b. Masaod Sebag, a relative of Macnin's who was born in Essaouira in 1783 and arrived in England with him on the *Aurora*. His father was the son-in-law of Abraham Macnin, Meir Macnin's father. His petition for denizen status states that he is "Clerk to the Moorish Minister, Meir Cohen Macnin."[81] Lady Montefiore was correct to question the marital status of the woman accompanying Solomon Sebag, who was probably the latter's fiancée at the time, though in the following year, Moses Solomon Sebag married Moses Montefiore's sister, Sarah.[82] The Guedallas were also connected by marriage to Montefiore, as well as related to Meir Macnin: Judah Guedalla married a cousin of Moses Montefiore in 1811.[83] Judah's son Haim Guedalla, who became one of the most prominent Jews in England, completed the circle by marrying a daughter of Solomon Sebag.[84] Many of the prosperous Moroccan Jewish merchants became an integral part of the Sephardi oligarchy by marrying into the older Portuguese families.[85]

Marital ties in both England and Morocco were essential for entering the Sephardi upper class, and indeed, the *Mahamad* of the Spanish and Portuguese synagogue prohibited its male members from marrying below their social rank without permission. The *Mahamad* also placed impediments on marriages with Ashkenazim.[86]

Meir Macnin's status as royal merchant for the Moroccans, together with his wealth, explains his prominence in the Sephardi community of London. His foreign background did not bar him from entering the Sephardi elite of London. Despite the many years he spent in England, Macnin was never able to perfect his English. With the growing number of immigrants from Morocco or of Moroccan origin, Arabic was undoubtedly heard in certain social circles. Members of the Moroccan Jewish elite also usually knew Spanish, since many of them traced their origins to Spain and Portugal. Some, such as the Guedallas, corresponded in Judeo-Spanish, suggesting that Spanish was their principal spoken language. Though the Macnins were Arabic speakers, it is likely that they were equally fluent in Spanish.

The Moroccan Jewish immigrants in England also remained very much a part of the Sephardi network of Jewish learning. The congregation of Bevis Marks, especially, maintained relations with Sephardi communities in Europe, North Africa, and the New World.[87] By the late eighteenth century, London had clearly joined Amsterdam and Livorno as part of the Sephardi Mediterranean scholarly circuit. Gibraltar's chief rabbi, Isaac Almosnino of Tetuan, arrived in London during the siege of Gibraltar in 1781, and remained in England until his death in 1785.[88] The itinerary of the kabbalist and rabbi, Moshe b. Yitshak Edraʿi, is more unusual, but also somewhat reflects the Sephardi rabbinical circuit. He was born in Agadir in 1774, but when, as he wrote, "I was still suckling my mother's breasts," all the people of Agadir were expelled and went to Essaouira. After his father died when the boy was nine, he went to live and study in Rabat. He returned to Essaouira and then went to live in London in 1801/2, about the same time Meir Macnin settled there, and studied in the Beit Midrash of the Sephardi congregation. Apparently he traveled around Europe and then settled in Amsterdam, where he taught in the school of the Sephardi Congregation, and died in 1828/29. He published numerous books in Amsterdam and London, some of which cast

FIGURE 11. A Moroccan kabbalist and rabbi, Moshe Edraᶜi, originally from Agadir, who lived in London at the beginning of the nineteenth century. From Moshe b. Yitshak Edraᶜi, *An Historical Account of the Ten Tribes, Settled beyond the River Sambatyon in the East* (London, 1836).

doubt on his scholarly reputation.[89] Noted Moroccan sages from Marrakesh and Essaouira, such as the venerated Haim Pinto of Essaouira, corresponded on *halakhic* questions with the chief rabbi of London's Sephardim, the Haham Raphael Meldola, who was appointed in 1805, and with his son, David, who succeeded his father upon his death in 1828.[90] Moroccan Jewish rabbis published their scholarly works not only in Livorno, but also in London and Amsterdam.[91] It was often the wealthy merchants of the community who helped subsidize the publication of scholarly or spiritual books. For example,

Judah b. Haim Guedalla, Meir Macnin, and Solomon Sebag helped subsidize the publication in Amsterdam of the work of a noted Moroccan author of liturgical poetry (*piyyut*) from Meknes.[92] His poetry was famous and chanted throughout Morocco.[93]

In the Sephardi community of London at the beginning of the nineteenth century, knowledge of Spanish or Portuguese was more important than that of English for most communal and religious activities. Schools for Sephardi children were still taught in Spanish and Portuguese, and the records of the Spanish and Portuguese synagogue were kept in Portuguese until 1819. This, however, in some ways belies the fact that when Macnin began living in London, Anglo-Jewry was undergoing profound transformations. Already, most of the longtime Jewish residents spoke English, and increasingly Portuguese and Spanish were falling into disuse. In 1803, a noted member of the congregation, Isaac Mocatta, delivered a scathing address to the elders of the congregation on the spiritual decay of the community, on the neglect of education and the need for reform. English, he argued, needed to be used in education instead of Spanish.[94]

Mocatta's speech reflected the growing acculturation of many Sephardi Jews in English society. In many respects, also, the impact of Continental European ideas of emancipation began to be felt within London's Jewish community, and were translated into the idea of religious reform, especially by those who identified themselves as entirely English. Not surprisingly, sharp divisions developed within the Sephardi community, especially between the more recent arrivals and the older and more assimilated "Portuguese" families. An official history of the synagogue recounts a dispute that took place in 1822:

A small incident gave occasion for the latent animosity to break out in an acute form. Some of the new members, especially those who had come from Gibraltar and North Africa, had brought with them customs and traditions, which were not well known or not practised here. Thus in accordance with their tradition a certain number of them, among whom were the Benoliels, Abecasis, Guedallas, Aloofs, Pintos, &c., gathered together in order to read on the eve of the feast of Shebuouth a certain portion of the Bible and of the Zohar, at the close of which, after they had formed a Minyan, they read prayers, at the dawn of the day, without for a moment thinking that by so doing they were transgressing one of the most jealously guarded laws of the Community. They were acting against the famous Escama No. 1., which under the penalty of Berach, i.e., Herem or excommunication, forbade the holding of such a gathering within a radius of six miles from the Synagogue. The house in which the service was held was within one mile of the prohibited area.[95]

The first statute or "Ascama"(*Hebrew haskamah*) of forty-two Ascamot (*haskamot*) instituted by the Sephardi congregation *Saar Asamaim* in 1664, at the time of the formal reestablishment of the Jewish community in England, stipulated that no other synagogue could be established within London and its environs. This was a principle drawn from the Amsterdam Sephardi community. In general, London's regulations were based on Amsterdam's statutes, which were, in turn, drawn from Venice. The *Mahamad* of the Sephardi community in London, however, went even further in arrogating to itself censorship and control over the Jewish community.[96] But already, as we have seen, the Spanish and Portuguese Congregation was compelled to relinquish its control over the Ashkenazim. With the growing numbers and influence of the Moroccans in London, authoritarian control over the Sephardim was also becoming increasingly difficult. The North African Jews brought with them different customs, and inevitably, this led to rivalry and disputes. The "Portuguese" establishment, nonetheless, attempted to preserve its authority, and prohibited prayer outside the *Saar Asamaim* synagogue. Finally a *herem* was issued against those in the rebellious *minyan* who refused to comply, and the ruling was posted on the door of the synagogue for the members to see. When a child of the Abecasis family died, the child was not allowed to be buried in the cemetery. It took several years before a reconciliation was achieved.[97]

These divisions certainly existed at the time of Macnin's arrival but were not yet accentuated, and he was therefore able to join the ranks of London's elite Jewish merchants. Charged with a number of commissions by the Moroccan government, Meir Macnin was guaranteed a prominent place among London's merchants, despite the lingering misgivings of some of his creditors. Within the Sephardi community, he was among the elite.

Ironically, the growing importance of London as a center for the Sephardim came at a time when a significant number of Jews were assimilating into the mainstream of English society. It was the last period when it was still possible to speak of a kind of Sephardi "world order," whereby descendants of Spanish and Portuguese Jews maintained a network of connections and ties, sometimes through members of their families, in conducting the Mediterranean and Atlantic trade. It was the last period in which attachment to their Sephardi heritage transcended, in many respects, their attachment to the countries in which they lived.

CHAPTER FIVE

The Macnins in Morocco

Though Meir Macnin was an integral part of the Sephardi community with its growing number of Moroccans, he remained closely tied to Morocco. Many of the *Berberiscos* of London, such as the Guedalla family, gradually severed their ties with the Maghrib and became a part of the Anglicized Jewish community, but Macnin's high status, indeed preeminence, in the Sephardi congregation in London depended on his merchant firm in Morocco and his ties to the sultan. While some Moroccan merchants began to invest in London's financial markets, often as a prelude to their permanent installation in England, Macnin continued to invest his money in real estate in Morocco.

From the time of his arrival in London in 1800 and for the next two decades, Meir Macnin was frequently found at the center of London's trade with Morocco. He developed a reputation in London's merchant community for not honoring his debts. Periodic claims against him were still made, but it seems probable, in the absence of any contrary evidence, that he reached a settlement with the fifty creditors who had petitioned the Foreign Office to help them recover their money and goods. In any event, the controversy subsided, and after 1801, no further claims were made for a number of years, at least not via the Foreign Office. At the same time, his connections to Morocco were indispensable and those merchants who still wanted a part in this trade had no choice but to come to terms with Macnin.

Meir Macnin benefited from the very limited nature of foreign trade with Morocco, and the controls imposed on European commerce by Mawlay Sulayman. Powerless to compete in the expanding capitalist market of Europe, and fearful of seeing Morocco embroiled in the Mediterranean conflict during the Napoleonic Wars, Mawlay Sulayman implemented a policy of strict control by which he hoped to maximize profits for the Makhzan, and minimize involvement in European affairs. Europeans interested in expanding trade in Morocco found this policy, prudent in hindsight, irksome. James Jackson, one of two British merchants remaining in Essaouira in this period, offered the following reasons for the decline in foreign (i.e., European) trade. First, the sultan allowed European merchandise to enter via Algiers and Oran overland to Fez, where he received a 14 percent ad valorem duty. Furthermore, Europeans paid a 10 percent duty while the merchants from Fez paid only 5 percent, which placed Europeans at a disadvantage. Second, Muslims and Jews received credit, and the debts of Europeans needed to be attested before a *qadi*, to the disadvantage of Christians. Often Christians were unable to recover their debts. Third, no one in the sultan's entourage understood the "spirit of trade," and therefore trade was not encouraged. European houses in Essaouira were limited to six (or five, since Jackson included the house of Haim Guedalla & Co., connected to the firm of Judah and David Guedalla in London, in this category).[1] Other reports make clear that the export of various items, such as olive oil, sheep, dates, tallow, and honey, was periodically prohibited.[2] Mawlay Sulayman also tried to control the products imported into the country. Most of the limited trade between Morocco and England in the first decade of the nineteenth century was conducted by the firms of Guedalla and Macnin, with their establishments in both Essaouira and London.[3]

Political factors, and even demographic changes caused by the plague, were probably more important than the sultan's ideological aversion to trade during this period. Not only was Europe still in the throes of the Napoleonic Wars, but Mawlay Sulayman was struggling to assert his authority over both the mountainous interior and the coastal plains. These factors prevented the sultan from deriving much revenue from foreign trade. In 1798, prior to the plague, some sixty European trading vessels reached the port of Essaouira, but in 1812, this number had dwindled to twenty-four. Only four European trading firms engaged in commerce with Europe were to be found in Morocco's principal seaport.[4] James Riley, the shipwrecked American captain who was captured along the southern coast of Morocco and liberated in Essaouira in 1815, mentions "the four Jew merchants Ben Guidallas, Macnin, Abitbol, and Zagury" who "live in high style; are absolute in the Jews town, and manage nearly all the English trade at Mogadore."[5] Riley is correct in identifying these merchants: the only Jewish mercantile establishments in Essaouira involved in the European trade during these years in any significant way were those of Haim Guedalla, Shlomo Macnin, David Macnin, Salem Abitbol in partnership with Semtob Ben Attar (the former was known as the *Bel Capitain* because of his official position as appointed head of the corps of merchants at the port), Mordecai Zagury, and David Pinto.[6] All of these merchants had relatives in London who were active in Bevis Marks. Prior to the development of European steamship lines in the latter half of the nineteenth century,[7] members of the family would travel back and forth between London and Essaouira on cargo ships, frequently accompanying orders of goods, as Riley describes in 1815: "A schooner arrived from Gibraltar under the English flag, though a Genoese vessel, as the Barbary powers were at war with Genoa: she brought a cargo of dry goods, iron, steel, cotton, &c. to Ben Zagury, a Jew: one of his sons came passenger in the vessel; his name was Elio Zagury; he was a young Jew, was dressed in the European fashion, had been educated in England, and spoke the English language fluently."[8] During these years, the number of ships reaching Essaouira's harbor ranged from twenty to twenty-five, mostly English vessels.[9]

In the first two decades of the nineteenth century almost all of Morocco's trade with Europe was conducted by these few Jewish merchant firms. The sultan preferred Jewish to Christian merchants. Under Sidi Muhammad b. ᶜAbdallah, the principal merchants in Essaouira trading with Europe, both Christian and Jewish, negotiated terms of trade with the sultan jointly through *il Commercio*. The leading Jewish merchant, Haim Guedalla, was also then considered part of the "foreign" corps of merchants. But Mawlay Sulayman saw advantages in detaching the Jewish from the Christian merchants and giving the former trading privileges. Dealings with Christian merchants could always potentially lead to conflict with the foreign powers, while merchants who were *dhimmi*s could be better controlled by the sultan. There may well have been a rising tide of hostility toward Christian merchants in Morocco who were blamed for corrupting the morality of the Muslim population.[10] The policy of extending privileges to a few Jewish merchants may also have aimed at curtailing some of the commercial activities of Muslims engaged in foreign trade. When this policy was protested by the Muslim merchants, Mawlay Sulayman defended his policy of employing the Jews by citing Malik Ibn Anas, the founder of the Maliki rite, the prevalent school of jurisprudence in Morocco.[11] When some merchants from Fez attempted to prevent Jewish shoemakers from selling their products in the markets of Old Fez, Mawlay Sulayman invoked the *shariᶜa*, arguing against any effort to prevent the Jews from productive activities, which would cause general harm.[12]

The number of Jews directly connected to trade with Europe was disproportionately higher than that of Muslims in Morocco's coastal seaports. Muslim merchants tended to concentrate in the domestic and trans-Saharan trade, although Jews were heavily concentrated in these trading sectors throughout Morocco as well. There were also Muslim merchants in the import-export trade, especially in the interior capital of Fez, where Jewish merchants were less important.[13] A few of the prominent Muslim merchant families from Fez and Tetuan were also found in the Atlantic seaports, but their numbers were significantly smaller. The Jewish merchants in the ports relied on a network of both Muslim and Jewish traders and brokers in the port towns and in the interior to bring goods for export and to distribute imports to the domestic market.

The concentration of the European trade in the hands of a few Jewish merchants in Essaouira clearly worked to the Macnins' advantage. As Jackson indicated, little could be done to recover debts, and he may well have been referring in particular to the house of Macnin.[14] There were other ways also in which the efforts of European merchants to gain a foothold in the Moroccan commerce were frustrated by the house of Macnin. Customarily, the British consular agent in Essaouira, who was also one of the few European merchants in this period, would send a list of imports from England, supplied by the merchants. The Jews were reluctant to comply, and it was only after the vice consul brought Shlomo Macnin before the governor that he complied with the requirement to give accounts for the vessels he chartered. Macnin continued, however, to obstruct the efforts of the British consulate to obtain the information.[15] Although supposedly reprimanded by the governor, he seems to have been working in concert with the authorities to make commerce difficult for the European merchants. The consulate reported in 1814 that the European merchants in town were compelled to pay a levy of $118 "without any cause being assigned why or wherefore," and an additional amount was to be paid as a present "to the Prince Mulai Brahim at Morocco [Marrakesh]." Furthermore, the sultan had ordered that all the ships coming from London would have to bring with them one hundred pounds of loaf sugar and one thousand pounds of tea, and pay duties on these goods. The consular agent complained that such fees and expenses, though charged recently to the Jewish merchants, had never been required of Christians. The governor demanded that the consular agent pay the duties and supply the sugar and tea for a ship already in the port at the time the order was given: " . . . the governor told me I should pay said amount or I should not be permitted to load, which words he again repeated before the secretarys or clerks of the Customs House in presence of the Jew Merchants." Macnin later came to see the consular agent, and threatened that if he did not comply the governor would not only prohibit his loading the ship he had chartered, but would remove the protection accorded by the sultan. Consequently, the consul sent the sugar under protest, but did not send any tea, claiming he had none. "I have now to request you will please favor me as your representative with instructions

how far I may act & stand up as becomes my situation & my wishes to defend the rights of my fellow subjects & countrymen against encroaching
acts of oppression which I make no doubts is exercised against them at the
instigation of the Jews."[16]

Over the next several decades, the few Christian merchants who remained
in Morocco had to play by the Sultan's rules, and like the Moroccan merchants paid their respects with annual gifts to the royal palace. They entered
into a relationship of credit and debt, becoming merchants of the sharifian
monarch just like the Jewish and Muslim merchants.[17] These royal merchants received loans or credit on customs duties from the sultan, and repaid
the Makhzan in monthly installments. From 1814 to 1815, the Macnins paid
an average of two thousand *riyals* monthly to the Makhzan. Yet this was not
a matter of simply returning money loaned by the palace; rather, each
month Shlomo Macnin collected sums of money from Muslims and Jews
with whom he had dealings in order to send the installment. In effect, the
Macnins acted as commissioners of the royal palace, and just as they were required to make their monthly payments, they were undoubtedly delegated
by proxy to collect the funds owing to the Makhzan.

The few privileged Jewish merchants had enormous advantages over the
Christian merchants. As one of only a handful of Moroccan merchant firms
engaged in the European trade, the house of Macnin had numerous clients
and a wide network of relations. Business in Morocco knew no religious
boundaries: Jewish and Muslim traders both had extensive dealings with the
house of Macnin. Both Jews and Muslims received loans and both cash and
goods were advanced on credit.[18] More frequently than not, merchandise
was exchanged by barter, often through an elaborate network of exchange
and credit. Traveling with specie, in any event, was risky, and thus the bill
of exchange (*itra* in Judeo-Arabic, probably from the Spanish *letra*) was
commonly used. We learn, for example, that a bill of exchange was sent to
the Macnins' principal agents in Marrakesh, Mordekhai Miran and company, which was to be used to collect payment from Sidi Muhammad al-
cAbdi in new *dirhams* (Moroccan silver coins).[19] Another bill of exchange
was sent to Rabat to the merchant Maraji, ordering that he pay Sidi al-Talib
Sidi Muhammad an amount in new *mithqals* (an accounting currency).[20] Although a perennial problem for the Jewish authorities was abiding by the
Talmudic injunction not to litigate in non-Jewish courts, the Macnins had
no compunction about going to the Muslim legal authorities for settling
commercial claims, even when it involved other Jews. Thus we discover that
Yackov b. Avraham b. Jak testified before Muslim rather than Jewish authorities, that he was willing to drop all claims against Shlomo and Meir Macnin, and their mother, Blida.[21] This was not unusual, however, for where evidence exists from *sharica* courts elsewhere in the Islamic world, it can be

demonstrated that Jews often resorted to the Muslim legal authorities to settle disputes among themselves.[22]

The Macnin trading establishment kept daily records of its commercial transactions in the port of Essaouira. These account books were kept in Arabic. Unlike the language of literate Muslims, this was a colloquial dialect with the particular idiosyncrasies of the Jewish accent, and written in Hebrew characters.[23] This language, known as Judeo-Arabic, was commonly used by Jews for secular purposes throughout the Arabic-speaking world. It was thus a language well adapted for the purpose of commerce, absorbing into its lexicon various words from foreign languages, especially commercial terminology and names of products from Spanish, Italian, and English. Transactions were recorded in accordance with the Jewish calendar, unless they involved payments to the Makhzan which were dated according to the Muslim lunar calendar. In case of dispute, legal authorities could require that these written records be produced as evidence.

From these two surviving account books, the first belonging to Shlomo Macnin and the second to Meir Macnin, a window is opened on the world of the Moroccan-Jewish merchant in the early nineteenth century. The articles most in demand from Europe that the Macnins imported were manufactured textiles, the quintessential product of the Industrial Revolution. Other items included sugar, coffee, pepper, iron bars, steel, tin, alum, paper, knives, and various other manufactured goods. In later decades, green tea from China that reached Morocco via England was to become the drink of the masses and one of the major commodities imported by the Jewish merchants,[24] but during Macnin's time it was still regarded as a luxury item and imported in lesser quantities. In 1814 and 1815 most of the imports were shipped from England, where Meir Macnin resided. The first account book, dating from June 1814 to November 1815, recorded the transactions of Shlomo Macnin of Morocco. From London, we learn that goods were sent not only by Meir, but also by Isaac Afriat and Meir's nephews, David Cohen Macnin and Solomon Sebag. The goods imported were sold to both Muslim and Jewish brokers in Essaouira, given to auctioneers to sell in the market, or, most importantly, sent to the Macnins' many agents in the interior. The most important destination was Marrakesh, Morocco's southern royal capital and emporium of trade, but goods were sent to a wide variety of other locations: Imin Tanaʾute, Rabat, Miramir, Demnat, Dukalla, Wad Nun, Fez, Tarudant, Ida U Tanan, Iligh, Skura, and Tillin. Shlomo Macnin employed a Jewish agent, Mordekhai Miran, and his associates who brought the goods or monies to Marrakesh. Goods imported often went to the Macnins' principal Jewish agents in Marrakesh.

In exchange for imports, the Macnin house exported the whole array of commodities that were the mainstay of Morocco's foreign trade: goat and

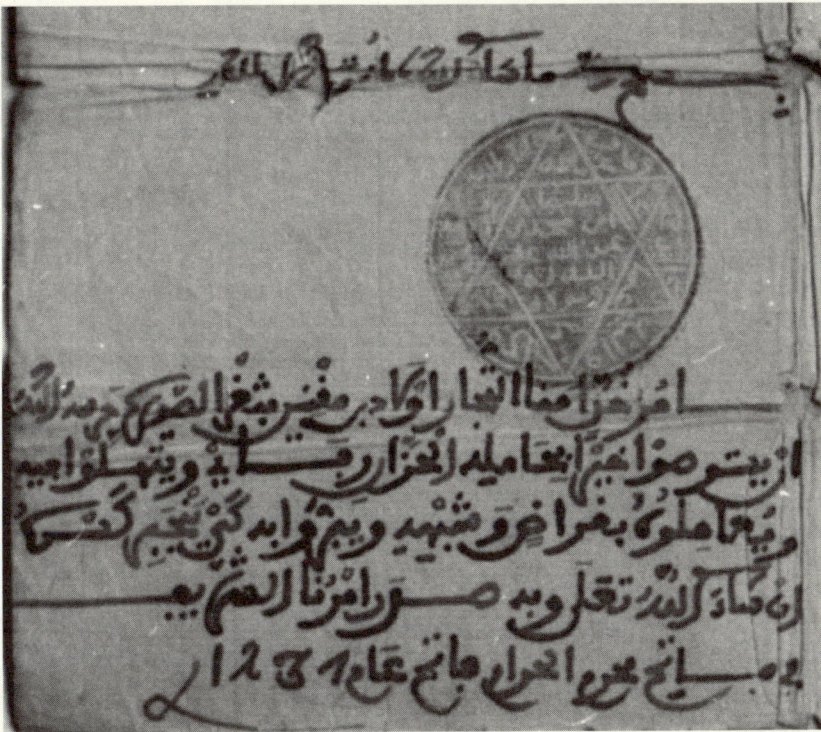

FIGURE 12. *Dahir* of Sultan Mawlay Sulayman to "the merchants, the sons of Macnin," ordering them to take charge of Rabbi Rafael and advance him a loan (1815).

calf skins, almonds, dates, gum arabic, gum sandarac, ostrich feathers, and wax. Some of the deals recorded in the account book were with the few other shippers of Essaouira, such as the company of Salem Abitbol and Semtob Ben Attar, from which export items such as almonds were purchased. Among the frequent Muslim customers of the Macnins were Mawlay ʿAbd al-Rahman al-Fasi, Sidi Mubarak b. Ahmad, Sidi al-Hajj Salih, Sidi al-Hajj Anba, and Sidi al-Hassan U Sulayman. These accounts, dating from the first two decades of the nineteenth century, demonstrate how enmeshed the Macnins were in Morocco's foreign trade, and with the principal merchants of Essaouira, Marrakesh, and southern regions of Morocco.

Shlomo engaged a variety of employees in Essaouira, who appear in his account book. When Shlomo was away on business, he employed Abraham Zafrani to buy all kinds of goods. In addition to domestic servants, he employed stevedores to load the merchandise on skiffs that went out to the ships in the harbor. When skins were brought, they were placed on the ground and he would pay Jews to sit and even to sleep on them in order to flatten them as well as to guard them prior to shipment.

The house of Macnin remained very much a family business. Shlomo's brother, Masud, who lived most of the time in Marrakesh, was entrusted with important dealings with the royal palace. Shlomo, who had more disposable capital, would pay his brother's debts to the Makhzan. In exchange for this service, Masud gave his brother goods. The brothers, including Meir, owned property jointly in Marrakesh, and income from these properties could be used to pay the remainder still owed to Shlomo.[25] Shlomo frequently traveled to Marrakesh, leaving a female member of the family, Mira (perhaps a sister), in charge of paying the monthly installment to the Makhzan in his absence. Masud, who lived most of the time in Marrakesh, sometimes came to Essaouira to run the business when Shlomo was in Marrakesh. Through his brother and relatives in London, Shlomo Macnin commanded the Moroccan import trade.

As we have seen, among the elite merchant families nuptial strategies and business concerns were closely linked. We do not know if Shlomo Macnin ever married. But in 1815, when he must have been at least fifty years old, he broke off an engagement to Mani, the widow of Mordekhai b. Shlomo b. Saʿadya al-Fasi.[26] As a result, he had to seek an annulment of the *ketubah*, or contract of betrothal, from the Jewish authorities. The *ketubah* established the amount of the dowry as well as additional amounts that the husband was to give to his future wife. If the husband died first or divorced, the amount in the *ketubah* reverted to the wife.[27] For wealthy merchants, marriage was an investment involving a large amount of money and property. Shlomo and Mani had committed to give to each other a large amount of property, some of which was to be held jointly, including a synagogue, houses, and stores. Shlomo testified that Mani had forced him into the engagement, and that the only reason he had agreed to marry her was because he feared that she would denounce him to the Muslim authorities if he refused. What would have been betrayed to the authorities is not disclosed in his affidavit, but his claim that he was threatened was accepted since he was allowed to annul all his obligations of property, goods, and money. The rabbis, however, did not take the breaking of a marriage contract lightly and stipulated that if he committed to a marriage in the future, then he would be obligated to carry it through unless, according to the stereotypical formula, "ten rabbis from the Land of Israel" would free him from his contract (a highly unlikely scenario).

Family ties alone were not enough to achieve high status in the society of merchants where the Macnins lived. The ambitious Macnins maintained their close connection with the sultan. In 1809, Sulayman decreed to the governor of Essaouira, Muhammad b. ʿAbd al-Sadiq, that Macnin's privileged position should be scrupulously safeguarded: "You should keep the merchant, the son of Ibn Macnin, in his customary position of respect and preferential treatment over other *ahl al-dhimma* so that he can perform his duties in our sharifian service. Grant to him what is necessary for this, and do not let anyone humiliate him."[28] It is unclear if the *dahir* referred to Shlomo or to Meir during a period when the latter was back in Morocco. But what is clear is that there was little that could stand in the way of the ambitions of the house of Macnin. The family invested heavily in maintaining their special connection to the government, sending presents to the Sultan at the time that they made their monthly installments, or bringing gifts to government officials.[29] In February 1815, shortly before the *mulud* festival celebrating the birth of the Prophet, Shlomo Macnin traveled to Marrakesh with some twenty boxes of presents for the Makhzan. Contained in these boxes, precisely recorded in his account book, were a variety of luxury items including velvet, satin, and other fine cloths and linens, some of which were embroidered, silk, fine tea, loaf sugar, fine porcelain, a silver platter, candles, medicine, and watches.[30]

Like all men of power—*qaᵓids* and wealthy merchants, Muslims and Jews—the Macnins participated in the rite of giving gifts to the sultan (*hadiyya*), reaffirming on the occasion of Muslim festivals their place in the social hierarchy and their relationship to royal power.[31] Their ability to present such an array of much sought-after luxuries established the Macnins' hierarchical position among other *tujjar-al-sultan* (royal merchants); gift offerings were, as Rahma Bourqia has called them "an investment for prestige."[32] The ceremonial giving and receiving of gifts took place in the royal court with much pomp and fanfare, a theatrical dramatization of social hierarchies with the sultan at the top of the pyramid. A Christian merchant of Essaouira in the early 1840s, one of the *tujjar*, recounted his experience of the gift-giving deputation of merchants.

The presentation of the merchants to the Emperor was conducted as follows: At nine in the morning, they were admitted into a garden in the presence of about two thousand imperial guards, all drawn up in file, looking extremely fierce. Passing these bearded warriors, they were conducted into a large square lined with buildings, where, after waiting about five minutes, the gate of the palace was suddenly thrown open, and the Emperor rode out superbly mounted on a white horse, followed on foot by a group of courtiers. His Imperial Highness was attended by the Governor of Mogador, who walked by his side. . . . The first persons presented to the Shereefian lord were the officials of Mogador, who were introduced by the Governor of Mogador; afterwards came some Moorish grandees; then the Christians were presented, and finally the Jewish merchants. The latter were introduced by the Governor of Mogador, the Jews taking off their shoes as they passed before the Emperor. One passed at a time, with his *cadeau* behind him, carried by an attendant Jew. As the merchants moved on, his Imperial Highness asked their names, and condescended to thank each of them separately for his offering.[33]

The Makhzan reciprocated with gifts, affirming its monopolization of the cult of prestige. Not only did the merchants receive trading privileges, but they also received presents of fine linens in return.[34] Once every few years, the merchants of Essaouira (including foreigners) would travel as a group to the sultan bringing with them considerable gifts and receiving credit on export duties in return.[35]

The connections of the Essaouira merchants with the royal family and the Makhzan were what assured their preeminent status in Morocco's foreign trade. Strengthening one's ties with the sultan enhanced one's power, and therefore, all those who maintained close ties with the royal household constantly exchanged gifts with him.[36] In Morocco, an independent and politically powerful merchant class did not exist. The sultan was in effect the preeminent merchant of the country.[37] In their semiofficial status as royal merchants the Macnins and other *tujjar* were given advantages (such as exemptions from customs duties) over foreign merchants.

Being a royal merchant was prestigious and profitable, but also meant a degree of servitude to the sultan. The *tujjar* were vulnerable, subject to unpredictable commercial actions by the sultan. Since they traded on the credit of the Makhzan they could not operate as free agents, and were often ordered arbitrarily by the government to undertake specific commissions. Since all the *tujjar* were indebted to the sultan, their goods and properties were subject to confiscation, something which occurred with relative frequency, especially since the sultan himself had limited liquid capital. Merchants could be ordered to import specific items. For example, in a letter to the merchant corps of Essaouira in 1807, the sultan wrote:

At this time I have found this place destitute of goods and of such merchandise as is wanted in the country and I observe the reason is because you do not bring goods which pay duty but you only bring hard cash which is no profit to me and ballast which is an encumbrance. I wish you to bring such goods as are necessary for the country . . . for which reason I now order Ben Abdesadack that whoever does not import goods to the benefit of the country and employment of the Port, but brings only ballast and empty ships, not to suffer such empty ships to remain in the harbour but to send them away.[38]

At other times, the sultan gave merchants goods that had lost their value and were difficult to sell, much to their detriment. Constant disputes between Europeans and Moroccans arose as a result since the Moroccan Jewish merchants also traded on the credit of European merchant firms. Goods or specie advanced on credit might be confiscated by the Makhzan, and frequently the Moroccan merchants were unable to honor their debts.

This relationship between the royal merchants and the Makhzan applied to Muslims as well as Jews. But for the Jews, there was an additional sense of dependency and vulnerability because of their status as *ahl al-dhimma*, as legally protected by the Islamic state. The Jewish royal merchants were thus protected both because of their status under Islamic law, and because they were the agents of the sultan, the supreme arbiter and protector of the Islamic state. But this protection was also legitimized by the idea of the *dhimmi*'s profitability. Jurists in Morocco, though differing on the degree to which Jews and Muslims should intermingle, recognized that the sultan could acquire funds needed for *jihad* against the infidels from the Jews.[39]

Not only could specie be arbitrarily confiscated, but property as well could be seized by the state. In Essaouira, the merchants of the casbah, the residential quarter of the ruling and mercantile elite, were leased houses at low rents by the Makhzan. It was in the casbah that the Macnins together with a small group of other merchants lived and intermingled with government officials—the ruling elite. And although, as we have seen, the Macnins and other merchants purchased private property in other parts of the city and in other towns, the fact that they lived in the government-owned Makhzan property made their choice of residence subject to governmental decision. Merchants could be moved involuntarily to a new location, as many were compelled to do when the port of Essaouira was developed as Morocco's main commercial entrepôt. Jews from the community of Tetuan were also compelled to settle in Chaouen when Sidi Muhammad b. ʿAbdallah was planning the conquest of Ceuta.[40] The merchants were allowed to travel outside of Morocco only with the sultan's authorization, and only after they pledged their property and goods as collateral. Often, they were also required to leave their wives behind, which was possibly the reason that Meir Macnin's wife did not go to London with him (though our sources reveal nothing of such personal matters).

The ambivalent position of control, manipulation, and protection by the sultan symbolized the relationship between the state and the Jewish masses. The violent reign of Mawlay al-Yazid can be seen as an aberration, a gross violation of the pact of protection guaranteed in Islam. In the tradition of the Moroccan Jewish community, Mawlay Sulayman is seen as a pious ruler whose treatment of the Jews was benign. In Fez, Sulayman was blessed as a king "who is deserving of blessing from the Lord of the kingdom."[41] Although irked by the sultan's restrictive trade policies, Europeans as well saw him as a just ruler: "He governs Barbary with discretion and moderation; in the distribution of justice, on rewarding his subjects, he is just and impartial; in his private conduct no less pious and exemplary, than, in his public capacity, firm and resolute, prompt and courageous."[42] Yet it was a period in which the Jews were not only being protected by the sultan, who scrupulously followed the law, but were also closely controlled.

Both Jews and the sultan were well aware of the risks involved in crossing certain boundaries that defined the symbolic subordination of Jews to

Muslims. Everywhere in Morocco Jews wore distinctive clothing, usually a black burnous (a hooded and sleeveless cloak); were obligated to take off their shoes when walking on a street where there was a mosque or other Muslim shrine; and in some towns had to walk barefoot outside the *mellah*.[43] A British army physician visiting Morocco in 1806 was somewhat surprised to see the British vice consul of Tetuan, a Moroccan Jew, remove his slippers and walk barefoot when passing by mosques.[44] When Jews paid their annual poll tax, the *jizya*, they frequently received a symbolic blow on the neck to mark their subordination. Even the elite Jews were not exempt from these requirements, and may well have understood that it was the outward signs of subordination that protected their position of superiority in wealth and property over most of the Muslim population.[45]

The growing exchange with Europe initiated by Sultan Muhammad b. ʿAbdallah gave a number of Jews the possibility to evade this symbolic boundary. Sultan Sulayman saw this as a threat to Moroccan sovereignty. Some native Moroccan Jews, who may have acquired foreign nationality or protection in Gibraltar or England, returned to Morocco wearing European attire. It was observed by a visitor in 1803 that the Jews in Essaouira "enjoy . . . more liberty than at any other place in the empire; they are even permitted to wear European dress, and to live like the merchants of the other nations."[46] The requirement stipulated in the Pact of ʿUmar that Jews had to wear humble clothing in distinction to Muslims was being violated.

One day, the Emperor seeing in the place of audience, at a great distance, a gentleman, apparently an European ambassador, ordered the master of the audience to go and see who he was, and what nation he represented; but it being discovered that he was a Marocco Jew, his scarlet and gold dress was torn from him, and a *burnose* (a large black cloak, the costume of the Jews of the lower order), was put over him, when he was buffeted and kicked out of the place of audience, the Emperor was exasperated at this circumstance, which he considered a vain deception: he ordered his secretary to write to all the ports in his dominions, to desire that Jews should wear the *burnose*, that Christians only should wear the European costume, and Moors and Arabs theirs; so that thus every individual might be known by their respective dress.[47]

This was in 1806. The intervention of the Foreign Office was sought by some Jews of Gibraltar, and consequently the order was annulled.[48] Conflict over Jews who were subjects of foreign countries wearing European clothing, however, was not really resolved. Riley left us an account of the ship he embarked on from Tangier on January 29, 1816: "This vessel had been hired by a certain Jew, named Torrel, to carry his family across to Gibraltar, which, with two or three other families of European Jews, who would not conform to the dress in which all Jews in Moorish Barbary had been ordered to appear, nor pay the tribute lately levied on them by the Sultan, were ordered to depart forthwith from his dominions." A crowd of other Jews, according to this report, escorted them to the port and were brutally beaten by the port authorities.[49]

Controversies arose periodically for a few more decades before all efforts to prohibit foreign Jews from wearing European clothing were abandoned. Clearly by the 1820s, during the reign of Mawlay ᶜAbd al-Rahman (1822–59), many Jews in Tangier were wearing European clothing. In 1824, the governor of Tangier prohibited Jews from leaving the city dressed in European clothing, under penalty of a two-hundred-*riyal* fine and two hundred strokes of the cane. Non-Moroccan subjects had to request an exemption from the prohibition.[50] The question was again renewed in 1831 by Sultan ᶜAbd al-Rahman, and only after negotiation with the British did the sultan agree that Jews coming from Gibraltar would be allowed to wear their foreign clothing, but for no longer than one month. Notions of citizenship did not exist in Morocco, and the sultan made clear that the distinction remained between the Jews as *dhimmi*s and Christian merchants living in the country whose status was defined by treaty relationships with their governments: "Be it known to you that the Nazerenes [*sic*—Christians] are with us in relation different from that of *clients under protection* [*dhimmi*s] because the Nazerenes have treaties with us and those said protected are under pledged conditions of security."[51] A number of other cases would arise before ultimately the question of foreign Jews wearing European clothing subsided.

Guedalla apparently was the only Jewish merchant who at least sometimes wore European attire in Essaouira before the 1820s. Riley mentions him as doing so, but also includes him with Shlomo Macnin among the four leading Jewish merchants of Essaouira, who "wore coloured silk handkerchiefs on their heads, covering their caps, and tied loosely under their chins: they also go bare legged, and wear black slippers on their feet, as the luxury of coloured slippers is forbidden them."[52] While the clothing of the wealthy was far superior to the poor, Shlomo still wore the distinguishing clothes of a *dhimmi*. This may have changed in the 1820s during the reign of ᶜAbd al-Rahman, when one visitor observed that "many of the richer Jews wear round hats, and some indeed frock coats; an affection borrowed from the Europeans." The privilege of wearing European hats, according to the same writer, "often costs them very dear. . . . I was informed that a Jew there had paid 8000 dollars for this privilege."[53] Jackson tells us how after the order was issued by Mawlay Sulayman that Jews should not wear European costume, "an opulent Hebrew merchant at Mogador felt so much the insults he was exposed to, from wearing the Jewish costume, that he actually paid several thousand dollars to obtain the privilege he had formerly enjoyed, which, in consequence of his being an opulent man, and a foreign merchant, was granted him." Jackson does not reveal the name "not to give umbrage to his family,"[54] but it is likely that he was referring to Guedalla.

The collection of the *jizya*, the annual poll tax incumbent on adult *dhimmi* males, was arguably the most important symbol of the subordination of non-Muslims to the Islamic state. It was the state that assessed the amount of tax that each community was to pay, while the community then figured out internally how to apportion the burden. Islamic jurists and theologians differed on the degree of harshness in the methods of collection. Often emphasized was the importance of each individual bringing his portion to receive a symbolic slap on the neck from the tax collector,[55] but the authorities were frequently content to receive the payment in one lump sum. Riley's account of Essaouira in 1815 suggests that Mawlay Sulayman preferred the harsher method. He describes how the Jewish community apportioned the burden by four classes of the community, and how each individual received a blow on the forehead when paying the tax. Despite the privileges conferred on Macnin and the few other Jewish royal merchants, they were not exempt from payment of the *jizya*.[56] They were sometimes able to escape the humiliation of receiving the blow by paying the lump sum—a privilege that the Jewish masses did not enjoy. But in 1844, we learn that even the merchants were not exempt from receiving their symbolic slap.[57] There is no echo in the sources of how the Jews reacted to the *jizya*, and whether members of the community rallied to support those unable to meet their obligation. Likely the tax was seen as an example of the Jewish experience in exile, but accepted as a part of the social order.[58] As disturbing as it may have been to European observers, the Jews long recognized the *jizya* as the price paid for protection by the state, and certainly accepted it in preference to the conditions of anarchy that reigned during Mawlay al-Yazid's time. Mawlay Sulayman clearly believed in the strict application of the law, and that included adherence to the conditions stipulated for the *dhimmi*s, but Jews could see him as a just and pious ruler who restored stability in the relationship between Jews and the government.

For this restored stability, Jews had to pay a very heavy price. In 1807, just one decade after the walls of the Italian ghettos were torn down with the Napoleonic conquests, Mawlay Sulayman decided to force Jews in a number of cities to move to newly founded Jewish quarters. At the turn of the nineteenth century, most cities did not have distinctly demarcated quarters where Jews were required to live, even though Jews tended to be concentrated in specific neighborhoods. Only in the large imperial capitals, Fez, Marrakesh, and Meknes, were Jews required to live within the walled-in confines of the *mellah*. Essaouira did not have a physically demarcated *mellah* where Jews were required to live prior to 1807, although the term itself was used to refer to the "Jewry" of the town. A deed by which Meir Macnin purchased a piece of property from Shalom Cohen in 1800 outside the casbah refers to the former as "from the Jews of the *mellah* of Essaouira."[59] After the *mellah* was completed, reference is still made to the "*dhimmi* Shlomo b. Macnin of the Jews of the *mellah* of Essaouira," even though he lived in the casbah. Thus, the term *mellah* here connotes not the physical space, but the communal space, of the Jews.

In 1807, however, Mawlay Sulayman dispatched orders to a number of cities that Jews who lived alongside Muslims should sell their homes to Muslims and move to *mellah*s that would be demarcated by the Makhzan. Among those cities included in this decree were Tetuan, Salé, Rabat, and Essaouira,[60] though in the case of Tetuan Jews already had a neighborhood to which they were confined.[61] During the course of the nineteenth century, additional *mellah*s were built.

There are different traditions regarding why Mawlay Sulayman decided to have new *mellah*s built in 1807. It should be remarked that there were conflicting ideas in Islam about confining *dhimmi*s to specific quarters. There were legal scholars who argued that Jews and Christians who bought houses in Muslim quarters should be obligated to resell them to Muslims. Some jurists were in favor of physical isolation, while others contended that increasing contact would be beneficial since such exposure would lead Jews to the true religion of Islam.[62] It is probable that Mawlay Sulayman, in his concern for the rigorous application of the *shariʿa*,[63] saw in the creation of *mellah*s an assertion of his moral authority over the country by, on the one hand, fulfilling his duty to protect *ahl al-dhimma* who were more vulnerable to attack during periods of rural rebellion and, on the other hand,[64] physically separating Muslims and Jews to avoid the possible negative consequences of too close contact.

Though it is clear that the creation of *mellah*s became a general policy of Mawlay Sulayman, each community maintained local traditions as to why the decision was made in their town. A tradition in Salé recounts that the sultan was impelled to build the *mellah* following the false accusation that Jews had intentionally broken a bottle of wine in front of a mosque near to where Jewish houses were located.[65] This tradition is similar to the legend that explains the reasons for the founding of the *mellah* of Fez in the fifteenth century. In Fez's tradition, disturbances broke out following rumors that Jews had poured wine into the mosque's lamp reservoirs, and thus, Jews were confined to a Jewish quarter next to the palace.[66] The tradition in Rabat tells the story of a Muslim woman falling in love with a handsome young Jewish man but leveling false accusations against him after being spurned, thereby provoking disturbances against his coreligionists. Consequently, the sultan built a *mellah* to give the Jews of Rabat protection from the Muslims.[67] In Tetuan, a tradition recounts how Muslim residents complained that the existing Jewish quarter was adjacent to the big mosque which was being reconstructed. It was the Jews who heard the call to prayer of the muezzin, so as a consequence, the new *mellah* was built.[68] The foundation of the *mellah* of Essaouira, according to a Jewish tradition, was the consequence of a request to the sultan from the "second class" of Jews living among the Muslims (i.e., not those in the casbah) that measures be taken to guarantee their safety because of the general insecurity of the period. The decision to establish the *mellah*, however, came as a bitter surprise.[69]

Although the foundation of the *mellah*s in 1807 may have been partly motivated by the sultan's desire to protect the Jewish communities, for the Jewish masses who were forced to move it caused great trauma. Al-Duᶜayyif reports that on 25 Shaᶜban 1223 (16 October 1808) the Jews left the old *mellah* of Rabat for the new one after the construction was completed; two days later more left "crying and wailing"; and their rabbi who had delayed leaving was struck by an official and imprisoned.[70] Some of the Jews of Rabat and Salé converted to Islam rather than move.[71] The Jews of Essaouira, according to the British consular agent, only succeeded in enraging the sultan when they sought a delay in moving to the *mellah*:

The Jews are ordered immediately to carry away their effects to the place allotted for a new Juderia. This new order has been (as I hear) principally caused by the impudence of the deputation sent to Morocco [Marrakesh] who at their first audience obtained leave for the Jews to retain their houses for two years, to give them time to build other houses, but they made a second and third application demanding more which so enraged H.I.M [His Imperial Majesty] that he sent orders for their immediately being turned out, but for the truth of this report, I cannot vouch.[72]

There can be little doubt that the Jews were compelled to leave the main part of the town (*madina*), although they were allowed to hold commercial premises and keep them open during daytime in other parts of the town.[73] From a letter from Essaouira published the following year in the *Gentleman's Magazine* in London, we learn the following:

Last year, the Jews were, by an order of the Emperor, turned out of the Inner Town; and so severely and instantaneously was this order executed, that women who had been brought to bed a few hours before, were not suffered to remain in their houses even until the next day. The Jews, many of whom owned excellent houses, were compelled to part with them to Government at a very low valuation, and they were ordered to remove to a sandy spot to the Northward, which was allotted to them for their future residence. Here they were exposed to a scorching sun, strong winds, and occasional heavy rains, until they could provide for themselves covering. They have now nearly completed their town; which is surrounded by a lofty wall, and at the gate are placed guards, to prevent any Moors going into the town, unless on some particular occasion.[74]

The Jews were to receive from the sultan the value of the homes they had to abandon. The amount was to be assessed according to the price that the

eventual Muslim buyers were to offer. However, apparently the local authorities assessed the property at a fraction of its value, and out of that assessment, the sultan took one-third. It is likely that the Makhzan paid the Jews a
minimum amount and then sold the property to Muslims at a profit.[75]

Exactly what was the status of the real estate allocated to the Jews in the
mellah is not entirely clear. From later sources, we know that a significant
number of dwellings were classified as Makhzan-, i.e., state-owned land.
These properties, in both the *mellah* and the *madina*, were let at a low rate.
In 1879, the total number of units in the "old *mellah*" (a new *mellah* had
since been built) was forty-four, less than the fifty in the old casbah. The
rent paid in the casbah was considerably higher.[76] A proportion of the
property in the *mellah*, however, had been purchased by individuals.

The Macnins and Guedallas were perhaps the only Jewish merchants not
required to move to the *mellah* with the common Jews, continuing instead
to live in the casbah quarter of the ruling elite; eventually, about twenty
other Jewish merchant households joined the ranks of the casbah elite.
Even some of the wealthier Jews had to live in the *mellah*. Zagury, for example, lived there, though he and Abitbol had their stores in the casbah.[77]
Riley mentions that in the casbah, the "*Guidallas* and *Macnin* are permitted
to reside and stay at night, by paying a handsome sum to government."[78] It
is doubtful that they paid money specifically for the privilege, since they
were already inextricably bound to the Makhzan through the services they
rendered. Being a royal merchant also brought benefits, and merchants paid
a low rent for their Makhzan property in the casbah.

While the forced move to a barren new quarter in Essaouira must have
been traumatic for Jewish commoners, wealthy Jewish merchants profited
from the building of the *mellah*. Riley's comment that the four wealthy Jewish merchants (Guedalla, Macnin, Abitbol, and Zagury) "are absolute in the
Jews' town," seems an apt description in the case of the Macnins. They did
not miss an opportunity, and began to purchase plots of land and houses in
the new *mellah* of Essaouira which they could rent or sell at a profit. In 1807
when the *mellah* was being constructed and several days after the sultan had
ordered the Jews to relocate there, Shlomo Macnin purchased from a Muslim, al-Hasan b. Bujamaᶜa, "all of the plot that is shoring up the wall being
built for the Jews (*ahl al-dhimma*)," at the inexpensive price of twenty-four
*mithqal*s and five *uqiya*s.[79] A few days later, Shlomo purchased a plot of land,
formerly owned by a Muslim, from a Jew known as Abu al-Jawwad.[80] Some
of the houses already built in the Bani ᶜAntar quarter may have been in-
corporated in the new *mellah* as is indicated in a deed from 1807 whereby
Shlomo Macnin purchased a house from al-Hasan b. Qadur and Zahra for
thirty *mithqal*s in gold coin.[81]

In addition to their private initiative, the Macnins also had the support of the sultan in their efforts to acquire property in the *mellah*. Already in 1809, Mawlay Sulayman issued the following decree:

We give permission to the *dhimmi* Shlomo ibn Macnin to open a mill that was owned by al-Tahir b. Sulayman and to purchase it from the proceeds of the sales that we have authorized him to make from his existing properties in the new *mellah* of the port of Essaouira (God protect it); and [from that which] he will gain as profit from the various assets: from rent, etc. From this time on, no one should prevent him from exercising the right to dispose of these assets whenever that may be. When he purchases it [the mill] from his money that was set aside for this purpose, whoever is in charge of our finances should do what is necessary for him and should not neglect him.[82]

With considerable surplus capital at their disposal, the Macnins were in a position to make loans, which according to Islamic law had to be interest-free. This, however, did not prevent profit: a debtor who defaulted might be required to put up his property as collateral, as we learn from the testimony of Shlomo Levi and his wife from the *mellah* of Essaouira, who received a loan in gold and money from Shlomo Macnin. When they were unable to meet their obligation, they gave their house in the *mellah* as collateral.[83] Undoubtedly this was another way that the Macnins increased their holdings in the *mellah*. The Macnins like other elite merchants became *mellah* landlords, and the rents from these family properties helped support Meir Macnin's descendants long past the time that the family ceased to have a profitable merchant establishment.

In the first three decades of the nineteenth century, however, the ability of the Macnins to acquire real estate was the result of their thriving business and the close connections they maintained with the sultan. Given the large amount of real estate that they purchased in this period, it can be assumed that the Macnins became major landlords in Essaouira. In 1803, with his brother Meir as guarantor, Shlomo Macnin purchased a house for 325 *mithqals* from Yitshak b. Moshe ᶜAttiya. The latter, in turn, had purchased the house the previous Jewish year for 290 *mithqals*.[84] In 1806, Shlomo and his brother bought half a house in the casbah from Yehuda b. Yosef Benzimra for three hundred Spanish *riyals*.[85] In 1818, Shlomo Macnin purchased half a house for 730 *mithqals* from Yitshak b. Masᶜud Benmellul in the *mellah* that "our lord the king (God protect him) gave to us."[86] Following his return to Essaouira in 1822, Meir Macnin was constantly buying boards for construction in his various *mellah* houses.[87] He also owned two bakeries in the *mellah*, one of which was newly built. He rented out the two bakeries, stipulating that the tenants do his baking for free, and mentioning bread, donuts, the Sabbath stew (*skhina*), and grilled meat; the tenants must send someone to fetch the dough from Meir's house and return with the bread when it was baked.[88]

The benefits that the Macnins derived from these investments were clearly diverse. They also purchased synagogues in Essaouira and Marrakesh, which not only increased their prestige in the community but could also be a good investment. In December 1804, for example, Shlomo Macnin purchased half a synagogue in the casbah from Shlomo b. Yehuda Sasportas for 320 Spanish *riyals*.[89] The sale of a synagogue between Jews could even be transacted through a Muslim deed, for example in the case of a synagogue sold in 1823 to Shlomo in Marrakesh, where the Macnins maintained both symbolic and commercial interests: "The *dhimmi* Shlomo b. Macnin of the Jews of the *mellah* of Essaouira, formerly resident in the *mellah* of *ahl al-dhimma* of Marrakesh, purchased from the seller, Hayyim b. al-Hazan [Rabbi] Shlomo Bihar of the Jews of the *mellah* of the *ahl al-dhimma* of Marrakesh, all of the three-quarters of the synagogue which is in the *mellah* of the *ahl al-dhimma* of Marrakesh."[90] Meir also purchased synagogues in both Essaouira and Marrakesh. Synagogues were thus considered to be private property which could be bought and sold, and like any other real estate, inherited or used as collateral for debts.

In addition to acquiring the premises of the synagogues, some of the deeds stipulate the books, Torah scrolls, income, and authority that the Macnins received in the transfer.[91] Besides the property itself, synagogues generated income (called *renta* in the Sephardi tradition) from the selling of *mitzvot*. A *mitzvah* was literally a religious "commandment," but in the sense that it is used here, it meant the purchase of the honor of performing certain religious rituals in the synagogue, most important of which was the right to go up to the pulpit during the reading of the Torah (*ʿaliyah*). *Mitzvot* were auctioned once or twice a year. Meir Macnin agreed to give a percentage of the money received to Avraham b. Saʿid Ben Shabbat, undoubtedly someone who either managed the synagogue or officiated at synagogue rites.[92] Revenue was also generated by donations given for circumcision and wedding ceremonies, and oil given for the lamps. These revenues were considered not inconsequential, as evidenced by the fact that Meir Macnin made claims against the son of Shlomo Sasportas regarding the profits of the synagogue that had accrued since the death of his father who had jointly owned the synagogue with Macnin. Soon thereafter, Meir Macnin purchased the other half of the synagogue from Sasportas.[93] Besides profiting from the income of synagogues, the Macnins, like other men of means, made donations to synagogues at the time of Jewish festivals. Shlomo donated some of the money he earned from trade, for example, to the synagogue of Rabbi Haim Pinto.[94] Pinto was the leading rabbi of Essaouira in the nineteenth century and was venerated throughout southern Morocco as a saint. His saintly status continued long after his death, and his picture is still hung in the homes of Moroccan Jews today. The Macnins had many dealings, both commercial and legal, with Haim Pinto—not surprising that they would contribute to the rabbi's synagogue.[95]

The opening of privately owned synagogues as opposed to those owned by the community had become increasingly common in the eighteenth century, and in the nineteenth century most synagogues in Morocco were owned by individuals. In earlier centuries, rabbinical authorities had been unequivocally opposed to the opening of private synagogues for a number of reasons: it threatened to deprive the rabbis of their income; it was potentially divisive in the community; and it could arouse the hostility of the Muslim population because of the Islamic injunction (usually overlooked) against opening new houses of worship. By the nineteenth century, however, the rabbis accepted the proliferation of private synagogues as a fait accompli. The custom in Fez and most of Morocco in previous centuries had been that a rabbi associated with a synagogue, after paying rent to a lay owner, was entitled to the income of the synagogue. The rabbis were opposed to the idea of profiting from *mitzvot*. However, the common practice in Marrakesh and southern Morocco (which would include Essaouira) had always been that a lay heir could keep the income of the synagogue for himself after paying the rabbi's salary.[96] The picture that emerges from the synagogues purchased by the Macnins is that they had almost total authority over the synagogues, only conceding a small portion of the income to those officiating there.

The acquisition of property in Morocco by the Macnins provided Meir, pursued as he frequently was by his European creditors, with a safe haven for the profits of his dealings in London. The real estate holdings were protected, provided that the family could stay in favor with the sultan; and accordingly, Meir Macnin arrogated for himself the position of official representative of the Moroccan government in London. It is doubtful that Mawlay Sulayman had issued him a carte blanche to act on behalf of the Makhzan. Nevertheless, Macnin acted in London not only on behalf of his coreligionists from Morocco, but also for Muslim merchants. For instance, in 1808 he writes to the secretary of war, Lord Castlereagh, on behalf of Sidi Mubarak Qasim of Marrakesh, asking that he be granted a passport to embark on a British ship.[97]

In 1804, in an effort to consolidate control of the coast, and possibly fearful of French expansion, Mawlay Sulayman began negotiating with the British for the purchase of two ships. ʿAbd al-Karim Ibn al-Talib, a prominent Muslim merchant, and ʿAbd al-Khalaq ʿAshʿash, from a family that figured among the ruling elite of Tetuan, were sent to London for that purpose. It seems, however, that no deal was made. The British were concerned that the credit that they were to extend for the sale of the ships would not be honored by the Moroccans.[98] Frustrated over British reticence, the sultan demanded in 1805 that the eight trading establishments of Essaouira provide him with forty carriages full of ammunition for his guns and mortars in that town and Agadir, otherwise they would have to leave the country.

Meir Macnin used his semiofficial status as Moroccan emissary in London to engage in some personal diplomacy, deploying symbols of exchange between the Moroccan and English royalty. Two lions were sent to England from Morocco, ostensibly as gifts from the sultan to King George III. However, the British determined that the lions were not a present from the sultan. "Mess[rs] Guedalla and Macnin to whom the lions belonged, sent a Jew named Salem, or as he is here called Shellam Ben Harbon, to attend to feed them on the voyage, and they were sent to Mess[rs] Judah Guedalla and Meir Macnin of London, each one, so that they were not a present from the Emperor to His Majesty." Ben Harbon, the vice consul remarked, was of no significance, "a poor obscure Jew" of Marrakesh.[99] The ship carrying the lions was captured by a French privateer, but then retaken by a British warship, but Salem was allegedly robbed by a British sailor and thrown overboard. The Foreign Office, though not able to ascertain the truth of the allegation, decided to compensate Salem: " . . . as however he is the subject of the Emperor of Morocco for whom His Majesty entertains the highest regard, His Majesty, as a mark of that regard, and in consideration of the Friendship which has so long subsisted between the two powers, has been pleased to order that this [Moor] should be repaid the Amount of his loss."[100] Another passenger on the ship, Benarroch, petitioned the Foreign Office that his nine doubloons had been taken and that he was penniless in London.[101]

Whether or not Macnin was able to impress the king with his presents is unknown—there is no echo of this semiprivate diplomatic venture in the London newspapers—but he did continue to command the Anglo-Moroccan trade, combining his sometimes official functions with his personal enterprises. For example, in May 1807 when Macnin chartered a British ship to carry cargo to Gibraltar and Essaouira and return with new merchandise, he was compelled to replace some of his cargo with a shipment of copper and oil belonging to the sultan, to be delivered to the captain of a Moroccan frigate in Lisbon. The ship departed for Lisbon in September, but was unable to find the Moroccan ship, and with the approach of the French army, the British ship departed for England. The British shippers made claims against the Moroccan government for the various expenses incurred.[102]

In March of 1808, Mawlay Sulayman renewed his efforts to obtain a ship from the British. The *qaᵓid* of Essaouira, ᶜAbd al-Sadiq, was ordered to write Macnin to purchase a brig cutter equipped with twelve brass cannons, stipulating that it should be delivered to Essaouira within three months.[103] It may

well have been that Mawlay Sulayman hoped the copper and oil shipped several months previously could defray the costs of the ship (though apparently
the oil had leaked out because of faulty barrels). With the recent French occupation of Portugal, the Moroccans were becoming increasingly alarmed.
The British agreed to the request.[104] A few months later Macnin repeated his
request to Castlereagh, enclosing copies of the governor's letter in translation, and informing the secretary of state "that the greatest impatience is expressed by His Majesty for the completion of this service." Concerned about
his own involvement in the deal, and undoubtedly under pressure from the
Makhzan, Macnin requested an answer, "so as no blame may be attached to
me."[105] Still not receiving a satisfactory response, he wrote again requesting
to inspect the ship at Portsmouth.[106] A few months later, Macnin began to
show his irritation at the British government: "I beg to say that by the last
letters from Mogadore, the said vessel was impatiently looked for by His
Majesty; I beg also to inform you, that I did not fail to minutely represent to
his said Majesty with what promptitude his wishes were executed by the
British Government." He requested that the ship be sent to Essaouira with a
British crew, and that the letters from the sultan and ʿAbd al-Sadiq be an-
swered when the vessel is sent. These would be delivered to the sultan by
Macnin's brother. The letter ends with a reminder that "the present oppor-
tunity is highly favorable for the British Government to obtain any favour of
His Majesty the Emperor."[107] It seems that finally in November 1808, the brig
Arthur was completed and due to be sent to Morocco.[108]

With the retreat of the French armies in the Iberian peninsula from 1808,
and their expulsion in 1813, Morocco seemed to be in less immediate peril.
Britain remained throughout this period Morocco's principal trading partner. The purchase of the brig in 1808 seems to have been Macnin's last official
commission for five years, and although he continued in the import-export
business with his brother Shlomo in Essaouira, the European-Moroccan
trade remained, as we have seen, extremely limited in these years.

For British merchants there were many risks involved in trade with Morocco during this period, and the major merchant establishments of London
found trade with other countries more profitable. Certainly one reason for
this was the degree to which trade was strictly limited and controlled by the
sultan. Yet despite the outrage of British merchants over what they saw as
the unscrupulous commercial practices of the Barbary Jews, the possibility
of profit continued to attract European speculators, whose only means of
penetrating the Moroccan market was through Moroccan Jewish brokers. In
1811, for example, the vice consul in Essaouira reported the arrival of a ship
from London for Mordechai Zagury, whose cargo amounted to seventy-
seven hundred pounds. "This is another proof of the credulity of our countrymen with regard to Barbary Jews," complained the vice consul.[109]

The Moroccan Jewish merchants, to be sure, used their positions as royal merchants to their own advantage, attracting private investors from European seaports. The British government, however, tended to be more circumspect in their dealings with, as they saw it, duplicitous "Barbary Jews" who flaunted their credentials as royal agents. Take, for example, the case of Moses Abitbol, the son of the appointed head of the corps of merchants in Essaouira, Salem Abitol. Moses, who represented the family's interests in London, petitioned "the Right Honourable Lords Commissioners of His Britannic Majesty's Board of Trade, praying as commercial agents to the Emperor of Morocco, for leave to export one hundred bails of gunpowder for use of His said Majesty the Emperor's service." Clearly, the Foreign Office questioned Abitbol's credentials as a true representative of the sultan, prompting him to write:

My father, Salem Abitbol of Mogador, has for some time past had the honor of being distinguished with peculiar marks of favor as a merchant by that monarch, in the course of which time the Emperor commanded him to order me to execute several orders in commercial matters, which I had the honor of accomplishing from time to time, as I can prove by several persons in this metropolis who manufactured such, as well as by other merchants who have generally known me in this country as a merchant trading to that part of the world for some years. From the nature of things in that country, it is not in my power to produce any documents to satisfy your Lordship on the subject of my agency as those documents remain with my father at Mogadore.

With a ship about to depart for Essaouira, Abitbol asks that his request be granted and that permission be given for the appropriate papers to be supplied subsequently.[110]

Despite the reluctance of the British to deal with Moroccan merchants, in light of the limited interest they had in the country, Morocco was in a strategic position during the Napoleonic Wars, a point well understood by Sultan Sulayman. The British bastion of Gibraltar in southern Spain was dependent on Morocco for provisions. With the British armies in Spain and Portugal, interest in the Moroccan trade was renewed. Sultan Sulayman was interested in responding to a British request to ship grain to the British forces on the Iberian peninsula, as long as this trade could be strictly controlled. Normally, the export of grain was prohibited, especially since it was a product that was subject to taxes prescribed by Islam, the tithing (*ushur*). The export of grain therefore often required the sanction of the Muslim legal establishment, the ulama, and usually needed to be justified as being for the purpose of defending Islamic territory.[111] Perhaps because of its questionable legitimacy, the export of grain was often consigned to Jews in Morocco and elsewhere in the Maghrib.

The "godlessness" of the French was well known to the Moroccan sultan since Napoleon's invasion of Egypt, which sent shock waves throughout the Islamic world. Mawlay Sulayman, scrupulous in his adherence to Islamic precepts in his dealings with foreigners, could justify the export of duty-free grain to the foreign armies only in terms of the defense of Islam. According to the governor of Essaouira, Muhammad b. ʿAbd al-Sadiq, in 1813 the sultan had agreed to allow fifty thousand quintals of grain to be exported to Lisbon free of duties to help the British armies in Spain and Portugal. A Jewish agent of the sultan, Isaac Israel, was sent to the port of Essaouira for that purpose. The governor learned that the British consul, instead of delivering the grain for the armies, sold it in Lisbon and elsewhere, dividing up the profits with his Jewish associates. The governor demanded a response from the Foreign Office as to whether or not the British consul in Tangier was actually instructed to ship the grain for the armies in the Iberian peninsula.[112] Meir Macnin was delegated with the responsibility of soliciting a response to the governor's letter, and sent a letter to Lord Castlereagh informing him of his official commission: "I beg leave to acquaint your Lordship, that my brother Mr. M. C. Macnin is arrived in this country, officially charged by his Excellency Hadge Mohamed Ben Abedsedek, one of His Majesty the Emperor of Morocco's Ministers (and Governor of the province of Mogadore and its Dependencies) with a letter which his said Excellency desired my brother to deliver, thro' any means to his Britannic Majesty's government." No doubt in order to increase the chances of receiving a reply, the governor of Essaouira was referred to as one of the sultan's "ministers,"[113] a position he did not in fact hold.

The letter was left with a Mr. Chapman, who according to Macnin, had promised to respond in the matter. Over a month later, Meir Macnin wrote another letter with a more impatient tone, concerned that the request had not been brought to the attention of Lord Bathurst, the foreign secretary: "As my brother Mr. M. C. Macnin's mission to this country is solely on account of said letter and I am yet not favored with your promised communication on the subject, I beg you will have the goodness to inform me whether the same has been laid before his Lordship."[114] A response was still not forthcoming, and ten days later Macnin again wrote to the Foreign Office.[115] Finally he received some response, and was requested to translate the letter from the governor.[116]

How this mission of Meir's brother Masud actually ended is unclear, but the translation that Meir produced is of interest.

Jews were as a rule not literate in classical Arabic, so clearly Macnin found a Moroccan Muslim translator. The translation was hardly an accurate rendition, altering and embellishing the classical formulas and clichés for the titles and positions of both the English and Moroccan sovereigns, as well as the *qaʾid* of Essaouira. In the English version the governor (the author of the original letter) is referred to, as in Macnin's letter to Castlereagh, as "Governor and Captain General of the Province of Mogadore and its Dependencies" though it could be better translated as "governor of the port of Essaouira and commander of its glorious army" (*qaᵓid thaghr al-Sawira wa-nazir jayshihi al-saᶜid*). Furthermore, the term *thaghr* signified not only a seaport, but often implied a site of *jihad*. The sultan is called "our Sovereign Lord and Master His Most Gracious Majesty Seedna Mulay Soliman (whom God Protect) the most Glorious Mighty and Noble Emperor of Africa and of Morocco, King of Fez, Taphilet, Suz, Sahra, and all the Algarbe, and its Territories in Africa, Grand Shariff, &c. &c. &c. &c. —" All the Arabic refers to is "the sovereign exalted by God" (*al-maqam al-ᶜali bi-llah*).[117] As for the recipient of the letter, the translation renders him as "our Good and Worthy Friend, the Noble Great and Wise Minister of His Most Excellent Majesty, the King of Great Britain." A version closer to the original would read, "to our friend, the renowned minister of the ruler of the English state" (*sahibina al-wazir al-shahir mudabbir amr al-dawlat al-Injliziya*). Macnin's manipulation of the translation, embellishing the position of the sultan and *qaᵓid*, as well as the position of the British minister and his sovereign, and de-emphasizing the potential military aspect of the relationship, demonstrated his nuanced understanding of diplomacy from both the Moroccan and British perspective.

A few years later Macnin and Guedalla, still operating out of London, were given new commissions from the Makhzan. In 1816 and 1817, Judah Guedalla was entrusted by Sultan Sulayman with procuring ammunition for the defenses of Essaouira.[118] The ammunition was delivered to Essaouira sometime between 1816 and 1818, but disputes over payment continued for years. Arrangements for payment were made through Tangier, where duties on shipments of provisions to Gibraltar were to be used to remit payments. But payment was suspended when the plague struck Morocco in 1818. Only in 1821 did commercial intercourse resume with Gibraltar.[119]

The British at this stage began pressing Macnin to pay off a debt he owed for the brig that he had built and armed for the sultan in 1808. Some £10,256 of an account dating from 1809 remained unpaid. Meir Macnin's nephew, D. C. Macnin of 35 New Broad Street, London, requested in September that a new arrangement be made. Meir was in Livorno at the time, and his nephew (David Macnin) requested that he complete half the payment and that the other half be paid by J. and D. Guedalla of Finsbury Square, who were awaiting further instructions from Essaouira. Macnin, according to his nephew, was undergoing some commercial difficulties, and asked that the Foreign Office delay communication with the sultan until advice and remittance arrived. "The proposed communication to the Emperor would most probably be followed by his displeasure at Mr. Macnin's

not having *immediately* obeyed his orders without reference to Mr. Macnin's circumstances, as such displeasure would be highly detrimental to his
family and interests in Morocco (the bulk of his property lying there)."[120]
The order from the sultan had directed Macnin in London to pay the
British "immediately," and the governor of Essaouira was to pay his brother
for that amount.[121] Numerous other letters were exchanged on this matter,
with Meir stalling for time by offering to meet the payment in *riyals* at the
exchange rate of the time of the transaction. The Makhzan wrote to the
British vice consul, explaining that the Macnins had sufficient sums in their
possession from the duties on goods shipped from Essaouira, and that they
did not refuse payment but were awaiting orders on whether to pay according to the exchange rate at the time the ship was built or at the current
rates. The Makhzan ordered them to pay according to the previous rate of
exchange, but rather vaguely added at the end of the letter: "if you are not
satisfied and wish [payment] at the current rate of exchange and if you do
not want the lawful [amount of the payment] then we shall pay you, by the
power of God, that which you wish."[122] The British, not surprisingly, demanded that interest be paid.[123] Though making an excuse for Macnin, one
Makhzan official still wrote him a harsh and threatening letter:

To the Jew Meir Macnin, residing in London. How dare you, you low, mean, fellow, when an order from my Master was presented to you among Europeans to pay
part of the money which you owe him, having much more than that, in your possession, to refuse complying with it, even if it was for more than you are worth, you
ought to pay, and obey the supreme order. Even if you were obliged to pawn your
own person, my master would condemn you afterwards, and now you will pay to
the English Minister, what he asks either at the Exchange of the day or at the time
the vessel was built without the delay of a minute.[124]

Payment was finally remitted for the brig by Judah Guedalla and David Macnin in early 1817, through the assistance of a British creditor, Robert Burchall,
who some ten years later was still attempting to recover his money.[125] Shlomo
and Meir were in any event assisted by the sultan who in the following year
ordered the governor of Essaouira, ʿAbd al-Khaliq ʿAshʿash, to ensure that
the customs duties owed in the various ports by Shalom Corcos and Wild
[son of] al-Hazan (probably Haim Guedalla) be deducted from their debt
for the amount paid for the ship, some 14,176 *riyals*.[126] David Macnin claimed
over two years later that he had never been reimbursed by Shlomo for the
half he paid the British government for the ship: "although he has been paid
the amount by the Emperor, he had delayed remitting me the same under
the most frivolous pretexts and to my very great loss & inconvenience."[127]
Close family ties helped facilitate business deals, but did not prevent disputes
between family members. The Foreign Office refused to intervene on David
Macnin's behalf.

It seems quite possible that Meir Macnin absconded from England about this time in order to defer settling accounts with David. We know, in any event, that in 1818 Meir Macnin was no longer in England from a petition to the Foreign Office by one Yosef Ben Ribuh asking the British government to help him pay for his passage from London to Livorno, where he had relatives; the petitioner mentioned that he had worked for Macnin, until the latter left the country.[128] It was David Macnin who now represented the Macnin interests in London, in close association with Judah Guedalla. In 1818 both wrote to Earl Bathurst regarding some letters transmitted from the sultan through their houses in Essaouira.[129] How David's dispute with Shlomo Macnin over the reimbursement of his funds ended is not disclosed.

Creditors of Meir Macnin who advanced sums for the purchase of the brig *Arthur* and other articles sent in 1817 were still seeking the restitution of their debts, giving John Simpson of Tangier, British vice consul, power of attorney. Simpson sent a letter in Arabic, presumably for transmittal to Mawlay Sulayman, to the British consul general in Tangier, James Douglas, and requested that Douglas obtain an order from the sultan for Macnin to repay the sum via the British vice consul in Essaouira. "It might perhaps be well," wrote Simpson, "if you mentioned that such unjust proceedings as Mr. Meir Macnin has been guilty of at the present instance cannot but influence more or less His Majesty's credit."[130] Douglas and Simpson began an exchange of letters from which it is clear that they were irritated with each other over this affair. Simpson reiterated the facts of the case, stressing that "the justice of the demand [be] forcibly impressed upon the emperor's mind. It is not a matter of a few pounds, it is a claim no less than £7391 sterling. I can only say that in the event of a refusal on your part I shall feel it my duty to solemnly protest against such refusal." Douglas wrote Simpson that he had produced no document to prove that Macnin had refused payment of the debt, and shrugged off his threatened protest. Simpson then clearly provided him with further documentation, to which Douglas replied:

As you have applied to me for a written answer to your communication to me about your business with Mr. Macnin a jew of Mogador I have to state that I am no lawyer, & neither can or wish to make myself master of the contents of a voluminous set of papers which you have shown me, but if you have a demand against the said jew, have made that demand in a regular way and he refuses to pay it, state the matter to me in a concise way, adapted to the customs of the country & I will communicate the same to the Emperor of Morocco, & request that justice be done to your claims.[131]

Meir Macnin, no longer in England, was little affected by these proceedings. Having come into conflict with his nephew and substantially burned his bridges in commercial circles in London, it appears that he began dealing with Marseilles. Before long, Macnin was again embroiled in controversy, as we learn from a report of the French consulate in Essaouira to its counterpart in Tangier in 1820:

An order from His Majesty the Emperor of Morocco just arrived to the effect that if the rifles and bayonets that he ordered Messrs. Guedalla and Macnin to bring and which these two had commissioned to Mr. Joseph Taurel of Marseilles do not arrive within two months, they will have to pay a fine of $40,000 [*riyals*]. These Messrs. are consequently writing to Mr. Taurel to send these arms without any delay with the order to charter a ship for that purpose. It is therefore of the utmost importance that you would have the goodness to write directly to the authorities of Marseilles in order to remove any obstacle so that these arms can be shipped without any delay.[132]

Some of Macnin's London creditors also pursued him in Marseilles. Robert Burchall and William Smith were plaintiffs in a case against Macnin in the Tribunal of Commerce of Marseilles in 1822. Whether Meir Macnin abided by the court's judgment, and exactly what it decided, we do not know.[133] Burchall's claims against Macnin, however, continued for some years, as we will see later.

Whatever legal proceedings Meir Macnin's creditors may have undertaken against him in London or Marseilles, they did little harm to his career as the sultan's agent. He successfully cultivated his ties with the prince and future sultan, Mawlay ʿAbd al-Rahman, who served as governor of Essaouira for some time before Sultan Sulayman's death. The close ties forged became evident when ʿAbd al-Rahman became sultan of Morocco in 1822. Shortly thereafter, Meir Macnin became the new sultan's principal Jewish agent. Perhaps never before in Moroccan history would a Jew singularly amass so many diverse commissions and responsibilities.

CHAPTER SIX

The Sultan's Jew

On 21 November 1823 the authorities of Tangier convened the entire foreign consular corps in the casbah.[1] Meir Macnin presented two *dahirs* of Mawlay ʿAbd al-Rahman to the governor to be read in public. To the astonishment of most of those present, the *dahirs* revealed that Macnin had been delegated extraordinary powers, and was to be given as much assistance as possible by high officials. One of the decrees declared Meir Macnin the "Consul and Ambassador to all the Christian Nations"; that is, all such nations that had peaceful relations with Morocco. He was given the authority to appoint representatives in these countries. Apart from becoming a kind of secretary of state for foreign affairs, Macnin also became the chief financial representative for most of Morocco's foreign commerce. The *dahir* stated:

. . . we have granted to him permission to export from four of our ports (hitherto not ports of entry) namely Larache, Mazagan, Casablanca and Safi, the following articles: wheat, oxen, sheep, fowls, wax, hides, wool, and every article of *ritorno* (that is every article usually shipped from this Empire). We have ordered him to have at each of those ports, regular factors, and whoever wishes to ship articles from those ports, must ship it with the permission and understanding of him or his agents and give in a list to them of what is intended to be shipped, that they may send us a note of the same. When he shall make a grant of it, the duties will be settled between us and Mr. Macnin, as we intend to make a deduction from the customary duties in his favor, as shall be made convenient to him in consideration of his services and friendship to our high majesty.[2]

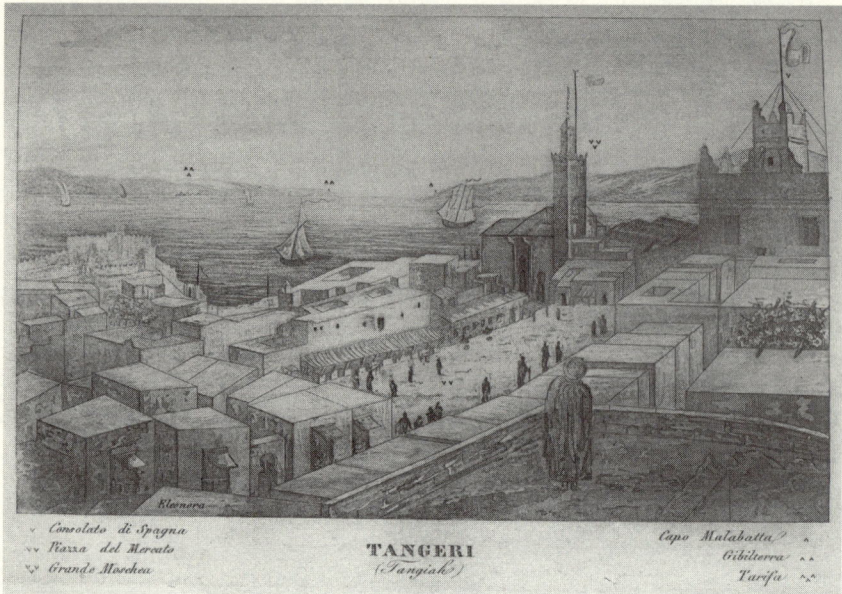

FIGURE 13. *Tangeri* (Tangier). From Jacopo Gråberg di Hemsö, *Specchio geografico e statistico dell'impero di Marocco* (Genoa: Dalla Tipografia Pellas, 1834).

The document further informed the consuls that the governors had been ordered not to demand duties from Macnin and his agents, and that he and his factors alone who were authorized to ship from the four ports would not be charged duties by the local authorities, but would settle later with the Makhzan.

At the same time that this *dahir* was issued, a decree was also sent to the governor of Tangier, Muhammad Umimun, and another to the chief financial administrator (who came from a notable Tetuani family), Muhammad ʿAshʿash,[3] informing them that Macnin had been granted the exclusive right to export oxen from the ports of Tangier and Tetuan. The only exception made was the customary eighty-three head of oxen granted to the British for export to their garrison in Gibraltar. The governor of Tangier was ordered to furnish Macnin with three to four thousand *riyals* if he required the money, and if ʿAshʿash had insufficient funds, then the governor of Tetuan was to supply him with this amount.[4] Macnin was also to be provided with a house for himself and his associates (which probably belonged to the Makhzan). The acting Dutch consular agent, Abraham Bendelac, noted in his diary that Macnin was to be given two horses (which in fact he received a few days later) together with eight dozen hens, five hundred eggs, a sack of semolina, a quantity of grain, olive oil, six large sugarloafs, and a basket of vegetables.[5] The gift of horses may have been particularly surprising to the Dutch consular agent, who was Jewish, since *dhimmi*s riding horses would have been prohibited by law.

The delegation of wide-ranging financial responsibilities to Jews had a long history in Morocco and in the Middle East. It was a common practice throughout the Ottoman Empire to appoint members of religious minorities to key financial posts.[6] In Morocco and elsewhere in the Maghrib, Jews were the only indigenous non-Muslim minority, and they therefore were frequently assigned roles as tax farmers and financial agents. The Makhzan appointed prominent and wealthy Jewish leaders who served as intermediaries between the palace and the Jewish community, linking the activities of the sultan's Jewish agents to the Jewish community as a whole. Because these individuals had no territorial base of power, except within their own Jewish community, they were entirely dependent on the ruler for support; the sultans' Jews would in turn use their royal connections to enhance their own status within the Jewish communities. Yet this close link to royal authority was risky and liable to backlash. Jews, as members of a religious minority, were vulnerable: the ruler could deflect discontent against unpopular financial policies by victimizing, at least in appearance, his Jewish agent and this could have reverberations for the Jewish community as a whole. Meir Macnin, however, was a real survivor of political intrigue, cleverly manipulating his role as indispensable financial operator. Superficially it seemed as if he was constantly falling in and out of favor. But this was often a charade, used by the sultan as a foil so that he could placate certain Makhzan officials who complained of Jewish haughtiness, and to affirm the Jew's ultimate dependency on the sharifian ruler.

Meir Macnin's promotion was also the result of changes in the Makhzan's tax and trade policies, and the advent of a new sultan. After Macnin returned to Morocco—exactly when and why is unknown—he established close ties with the chosen successor to the sharifian throne, the prince (*khalifa*) Mawlay ʿAbd al-Rahman. In 1821, ʿAbd al-Rahman was appointed governor of Essaouira.[7] The presence of the *khalifa* in Essaouira reflected a shift away from the sultan's dependence on the countryside for taxes, as well as on urban taxes on commerce—unreliable sources of revenue that often led to rural unrest or urban revolt. The new policy appears to have begun in 1817, with the easing of high tariffs and the promotion of grain exports. Revenue derived from foreign trade was used for controlling both rural and urban unrest.[8] Discontent over wheat exports at a time of food shortage and inflated prices of grain, however, caused Mawlay Sulayman to stop the exports. A plague epidemic from 1818 to 1820 considerably reduced trade. The British consul general was withdrawn, and Gibraltar also stopped its imports from Morocco. The French took advantage of the British absence to increase their foothold in the Moroccan market.[9] Rural unrest among the Berbers of the Middle Atlas in 1819 induced Mawlay Sulayman to resume the policy of encouraging exports as a source of revenue.[10] Urban rebellion in Fez and Tetuan between 1820 and 1822, and the proclamation of a rival sultan, Mawlay Ibrahim, who threatened to overthrow Sulayman,[11] may also have encouraged the sultan to shift away from a reliance on urban taxation. In 1820, seeking financial resources to reassert his control over the country, Mawlay Sulayman authorized the export of wool, and reduced tariffs on olive oil, goat skins, and almonds. Foreign commerce was again revived at Essaouira.[12]

Mawlay Sulayman's attempt to consolidate his position relied on Jewish traders, a policy that the ulama criticized. There were also Jews in the sultan's financial administration, such as Semtob Ben Attar in Essaouira, or Abraham Sicsu, who was appointed as the second customs administrator in Tangier in 1821.[13] In some ways reminiscent of the reaction against the Jews following the death of Sidi Muhammad b. ʿAbdallah, the Jews of Fez and Tetuan were subject to plundering and extortion during the urban rebellions of 1820–22. The *udaya* of Fez, on the rumor that the sultan had died, plundered the *mellah*, and Mawlay Sulayman's demand that the Jews' property be restored was ignored.[14] Mawlay Saʿid, who seized control of Fez and Tetuan in 1821 and who was known for his hostility toward Jews, looted Jewish stores in Fez.[15] Once again, following the news of the death of Mawlay Sulayman in late November 1822, the *udaya* pillaged the Jews of Fez.[16] Although these unfortunate events were much less devastating for the Jewish communities than the catastrophic bloodbath during Mawlay al-Yazid's reign, the urban rebellion of 1820–22 was a reminder that the alliance between royal power and the Jews came with considerable risks.

The end of the rebellion in Fez marked a new opening in the export trade.[17] Rural unrest, however, had cut Marrakesh's ties with Essaouira, and perhaps in an effort to avoid sole dependence on the royal port, El Jadida was opened for commerce; ʿAbd al-Malik ʿAshʿash was appointed as the new governor.[18] The projected revival of El Jadida as a commercial center anticipated a role later assigned to Meir Macnin.

Mawlay ʿAbd al-Rahman was a proponent of expanding trade with Europe, and his appointment as governor of Essaouira foreshadowed the changes in Moroccan policy after he became sultan. During his governorship in Essaouira, he fostered close ties with the Jewish and European merchant community of the port. After returning to Morocco, Meir Macnin was again one of the principal merchants in the port, trading with considerable amounts of credit from the Makhzan. He was able to deduct much of his accumulated debt by various dealings with the government, dispatching money or cloth to different locations, or giving iron and steel to a

Sufi lodge (*zawiya*).[19] He began to ship large quantities of ostrich feathers on ships chartered by Menachem Bensusan, a Moroccan Jew who had settled in London. He probably had obtained the government monopoly for this important export item.[20] Meir Macnin was again at the center of Essaouira's commercial life.

One of the other prominent commercial establishments that emerged in the 1820s, connected with the Macnin business, was the house of Bujnah (Busnach), associated with the most prominent Jewish commercial establishment in Algiers. The head of the house in Essaouira was referred to as "the most opulent man in Mogador."[21] His name was in fact, Aaron Amar, but he was known as "Bujnah" because of his connection with the Algerian merchant firm. Blida, Meir Macnin's only child, married Aaron Amar "Bujnah," "a man old enough to be her father, or even grandfather," remarked a British visitor in the early 1840s.[22] Thus was forged the alliance between the two most active commercial establishments in the port. In a *dahir* of ʿAbd al-Rahman on 1 September 1824, Aaron Amar "Bujnah" was formally awarded the honors due him as a merchant in the sharifian service, joining the other *dhimmi tujjar*.[23]

If there were still outstanding disputes between the Macnins and the Makhzan, they obviously in no way prevented Meir's rise to power in the early 1820s. The British consular representative in Essaouira had remarked on his close ties with ʿAbd al-Rahman: "It is well known to you, that HIM was for a few months Governor of this town, during which period Mr. Macnin showed him great attention, and was in the habit of continuously making very handsome presents. On HIM's departure, myself & Mr. Macnin accompanied him out the first day's journey, and I was not aware of the influence possessed by Mr. M. until we took our leave of HIM."[24]

Meir Macnin's influence in the town was well recognized by the Jewish leadership at this time. Although the *dayyanim* of the community were empowered to hear cases between Jews and impose fines, punishment was difficult to carry out and imprisonment required the cooperation of the Muslim authorities. Haim Pinto, the renowned rabbi and moral authority of the community, asked Meir to intercede with his Muslim connections to free a Jew who had been wrongly imprisoned.[25]

In the last months before Mawlay Sulayman's death, Meir Macnin (together with his brother Shlomo in Marrakesh)[26] was performing important tasks for the sultan. In the early 1820s, Sweden, Denmark, and Hamburg, which all had marginal interests in Morocco, still paid the annual "tribute" that a number of European countries had traditionally paid to the sultan to guarantee that their ships would be protected from piracy; and Sweden's tribute of twenty thousand *riyal*s for 1822 was delivered to Meir Macnin.[27] On 13 November 1822, Sultan Sulayman remitted a large sum of money

FIGURE 14. *The Interior of an Opulent Jew's House.* A European rendition of the house in the casbah of Essaouira where it is likely that Meir Macnin's daughter Blida lived, since she was married to Aaron Amar "Bujnah," the "opulent Jew," whose house is shown here. It is likely that Meir Macnin had also lived in this house. From G. Beauclerk, *Journey to Morocco* (London: Printed for Poole and Edwards, etc., 1828).

owed to the Makhzan by Shlomo, leaving no impediments to Meir's rise to prominence.[28] On 28 November, Sultan Sulayman died, and Mawlay ʿAbd al-Rahman, who had been relocated to Fez from Essaouira presumably following the successful suppression of the rebellion, was proclaimed sultan and received the customary declaration of loyalty (*bayʿa*) of the people of

Fez.²⁹ Soon thereafter, Mawlay ᶜAbd al-Rahman issued a proclamation announcing to the consular corps his succession as ruler of Morocco.³⁰

Mawlay ᶜAbd al-Rahman was to become more reliant on trade with Europe than his predecessor. Initially, the new sultan's chief agent for financial and foreign affairs was al-Talib b. Jallun, member of one of the wealthiest bourgeois families from Fez, who was sent to Tangier to replace Muhammad al-Salawi. Ibn Jailun was the principal organizer of the major trans-Saharan caravan which departed from Fez annually in April for Timbuktu. He himself had traveled there twice.³¹ Ibn Jallun was also a *hajj*, had traveled to Cairo, and was also regarded as the director of the caravan of pilgrims to Mecca (commerce and pilgrimage were often combined).³² While trade with Africa was mainly the responsibility of al-Talib b. Jallun, however, Meir Macnin seemed to be the natural choice of Mawlay ᶜAbd al-Rahman for implementing his new opening toward Europe. Nevertheless, Meir Macnin had needed to tread carefully to pave the way for his mandate, but the appointment that was read before the consular corps on 23 November 1823 probably concentrated more power in the hands of one Jew than ever before in the history of the ᶜAlawid dynasty. The extent of his delegation was impressive. How did it happen? Was it, as the British and French suggested, primarily because Macnin lavished gifts on the new sultan?

On 15 October 1823, shortly before Meir Macnin's appointment, a royal messenger reported to the acting Dutch consular agent, Bendelac, that he "had met near Fez the Jewish merchant Ben [son of] Macnin of Mogador who went, with a present, to meet the sultan."³³ Less restrained, the British vice consul in Essaouira wrote confidentially to the consul general in Tangier: "On being called to the throne, Mr. M. requested liberty to visit HIM, and I believe it was not until he had repeated the request several times that it was granted. Mr. M. did not set off on the journey to Fez, until he had prepared a very valuable present—and the result has been very favorable to him, so far."³⁴ On 28 October, in any event, the decree was issued. The following month, Meir Macnin was ordered to go to Tangier from Larache where he was engaged in some business.³⁵

Upon his arrival in Tangier, Meir Macnin immediately began engaging in diplomacy with the foreign consulates. Part of his responsibilities was to make arrangements to send all presents given by the consuls for the sultan. For example, Macnin and the governor summoned the consul of Denmark to deliver a royal letter asking that Denmark send an ambassador to pay tribute.³⁶ The following day, the *dahirs* on Macnin's appointment, as described above, were read to the consular corps. The foreign consulates grudgingly acknowledged the usefulness of Macnin to the sultan. The British consul general in Tangier remarked that "the Emperor's finances are in a very bad state and this man [Macnin] appears to be commissioned to raise money

FIGURE 15. Eugène Delacroix. *Muley-Abd-err-Rhahmann, sultan du Maroc, sortant de son palais de Méquinez, entouré de sa guarde et de ses principaux officiers,* 1845. Musée des Augustins, Toulouse.

how he can."[37] Similarly, the American consul, John Mullowny, commented on the motives for employing Macnin: Mr. Macnin is a Jew "who has traveled much in Europe, he has knowledge of commerce, intelligence of that kind, is much wanted by the ruling power of this country, all ways and means are used to increase funds, the mass of money left by Muley Soliman, in Meknes is still in the hands of the black troops, whom are consuming it. Neither the present king nor his opponents can reach it."[38]

While acknowledging that Macnin may have had some necessary experience useful to the sultan, many of the foreign representatives were reluctant to recognize the diplomatic credentials granted to Macnin. The British consul Douglas already had a history of dealing with disgruntled British creditors of Macnin. He wrote to the Foreign Office that

the Jew Meir Ben Macnin who His Majesty seems to place so much confidence in is a merchant of Mogadore, and has shown me papers constituting him a denizen of England of which he is proud, he does not do credit to our country in point of character, and I have reason to think that there are writs of arrest against him for debt at Gibraltar, ready to be put in execution unless the diplomatic character with which the emperor has invested him should be considered as a sufficient exemption from arrest.[39]

In response to Douglas's inquiry whether or not Macnin would be considered immune from arrest in Gibraltar, London replied "that the Emperor's Circular Communication cannot of itself invest the Jew Macnin with these privileges and immunities which are attached to the character of a Public Minister," and therefore, he would risk arrest if he went there. Douglas was urged to prevent Macnin from appearing in England: "Endeavour by all the means within your power to render abortive the measure of sending him here, and by stating if necessary to the Emperor that you have every reason to believe that the choice of a person of Mr. Macnin's station in life to represent him in this country would not be agreeable to His Majesty's Government."[40]

Still complaining about Macnin's appointment months later, the British consul offered a reason why Macnin was so interested in the appointment:

The Jew Macnin owes about £100,000 Louis d'or in different parts of Europe, but chiefly in England, his hopes were that a diplomatic character would screen him from arrest and I believe that he paid largely to the Emperor of Morocco for the circular letter by which he was named his ambassador & c. His first object was to go via Gibraltar to Madrid, Paris & London, the honor of a visit to Turin was reserved for some future occasion. The English government being occasionally in the habit of paying the expenses of asiatic & african missions, he hoped that the least they would do for him would be to give him a pension of £2,000 a year for the remainder of his life, he being a denizen subject of England . . . knowing that his presence in London would not be acceptable, or creditable to the Corps Diplomatique, I ventured to suggest to him that the Governor of Gibraltar not being a sovereign prince, could give no protection to his person, and that I knew there was a writ against him in the garrison ready to be enforced for £10,000 sterling on his arrival. He then proposed to go to London by sea. I had again to point out to him that his appointment from the Emperor would be no protection to him until he was received and accredited by the king of England and that great delays might occur before this could take place during which time he would be at the mercy of his creditors. This so alarmed him that he gave up the point. My business was already done when I received instructions from England to stop his voyage & if necessary to tell the Emperor that he would not be received.

Douglas's explanation seems plausible, and it also appears likely that the consul deterred him from traveling to Europe at this time.

The French consul, Sourdeau, also protested against the diplomatic powers granted to a Jew who, according to the consul, had a judgment against him for a debt of thirty thousand piastres. Macnin retorted that he owed nothing, but rather it was people in Marseilles who owed him eighty thousand piastres.[41] To the Foreign Ministry in Paris, Sourdeau complained about the bankrupt Jew, "who can neither set foot in Cadiz, nor in Livorno, nor in Marseilles."[42] The foreign representatives met to jointly protest the appointment of Macnin. But ʿAbd al-Rahman maintained his support for the appointment, insisting that if Macnin would be assisted in his tasks by the foreign representatives in Tangier, their efforts would be reciprocated. Another *dahir* surfaced at this time declaring that any presents offered to the sultan by the foreign representatives should be conveyed through Macnin.[43]

The vice consul, Willshire, who was one of the only European merchants at the port of Essaouira, described at some length the extraordinary powers conferred on Macnin. "It appears to me astonishing," Willshire wrote, "that a Mohametan Govʳ should invest with the dignity of ambassador, being an Israelite, instead of one of his Moorish [i.e., Muslim] subjects, and although HM may have overlooked this point, I shall be astonished if the consular corps at Tangier does, or the European powers, to whom he may be delegated."[44] The British consul could not really have been all that astonished. As a longtime resident and seasoned observer of Moroccan commerce and diplomacy, Willshire was well aware of the reasons that Jews were chosen as intermediaries, delegated with responsibilities in dealing with Europeans. Practically all travelers to Morocco, with far less experience in the country, made the observation that Jews were the indispensable middlemen.[45] Meir Macnin was obviously somewhat of a rival for Willshire, especially with his brother and partner Shlomo wielding considerable influence in Essaouira. By warning the British representative in Tangier about Macnin, Willshire was trying to cast doubt on Macnin's credentials and perhaps limit his utility to the Makhzan. But it was more complicated than that. Willshire was deeply ambivalent: "I do not hesitate to say," the vice consul continued, "that the great power conferred on Mr. Macnin, is better in his hands, than any other person I know belonging to his tribe, but such power in the hand of any one person is highly dangerous, and ought to be jealously watched by all Europeans residing in this country, whether in an official or mercantile capacity." Willshire's prediction of Macnin's importance to the Makzhan proved to be correct:

I have great doubts, whether it is possible for Mr. Macnin, to bring to maturity, and to set to work the different ports, which have exclusively been conferred upon him, evidently for the purpose of enriching the Royal Treasury, if he cannot, and that in a short period of time, it is very natural to suppose, his influence will gradually decline. Should he however be able to make the large contracts in the exportation of grain & cattle which he is reported to have agreed for, with the French Commissary and continue on the same scale of operations, his influence & power with HIM will be more firmly established, than ever.[46]

Willshire himself was one of a few merchants in Essaouira with close dealings with Macnin, other Jewish merchants, and the sultan. The vice consul was also, in effect, one of the royal *tujjar*, bound to the sultan in a contractual relationship of debt that was repaid to the Makhzan in monthly installments. By 1841, Willshire would have built up one of the largest debts of all the merchants in Essaouira.[47] In 1844 during the French naval attack against the port of Essaouira, he absconded, leaving behind considerable debts. His agent in Marrakesh, Shlomo Corcos, who had custody over the former vice consul's funds, was ordered by the sultan to move to Essaouira in 1846 to recover Willshire's debt.[48] But in 1823, Willshire was cautiously cultivating close ties with the sultan, as he reported to the Foreign Office: "I always met with the greatest attention and politeness from H.M., during his residence as governor of this town."[49] When the new sultan responded to a letter from the Essaouira merchants congratulating him on his succession to the throne, Willshire received special consideration:

In addition to the letter of H.M. addressed to the merchants generally, myself, Mr. Macnin & Mr. Guidalla, have been favored by a joint letter from H.M., received by express, wherein he assured us of his protection, and favor, couched in terms highly flattering, and to encourage us to carry on our trade, in the full assurance that no changes will be made to the advantage of the commerce of the port, but on the contrary, that he will encourage it all in his power. This special favor has excited a little envy to the other merchants.[50]

Willshire jealously guarded his privileged position, again receiving special attention in a letter favoring him together with Macnin and Guedalla.[51]

It is important to remember that this was all happening in the time before Morocco was compelled by foreign pressure to initiate a policy of free trade. The few European merchants in Morocco had to play by the sultan's rules, and were dependent on the sultan for special concessions and privileges.

Once Macnin's power was consolidated, the sultan began requesting that ambassadors be sent to him in his capital in Fez, bringing with them presents.[52] "Macnin has hinted to me that it would be respectful if an ambassador were sent from England and the same from Sardinia, to compliment the Emperor on his accession, the meaning of this is that the Emperor might get so much the more money by an ambassador, as the presents they bring are usually larger."[53] The British consul general Douglas was instructed in the name of King George IV to present himself to the sultan's court, and at the end of 1823 Douglas set out for Fez with his considerable supply of gifts.[54] Macnin was soon dealing with all the foreign consulates in Tangier. It was through Macnin that the Dutch negotiated the payment of tribute, or that the arrears on tribute still owed by Denmark and Sweden were remitted.[55] It was also through Macnin that the two thousand dollars of annual tribute and debts from the past years from Hamburg, the only German state with a treaty relationship with Morocco during this period, were to be delivered.[56]

Despite their misgivings, the consuls had little choice but to deal with Macnin, and therefore sometimes tried to win favor with him. The United States consul wrote in response to the letter which asked for special assistance to the sultan's agent, that Macnin, who spoke his language, would be assisted with pleasure.[57] The sultan also insisted that his governors should treat Macnin with special favor.[58]

The French, who were adamantly opposed to Macnin's appointment, also had to come to terms with him. While the British rights for exporting supplies to Gibraltar from Morocco were already guaranteed by treaty, the French had to negotiate an agreement through Macnin, who had the monopoly, if they wished to export provisions.[59] In 1823, provisions from Morocco were urgently needed to be sent to Cadiz to supply a French army that was engaged in a military intervention to support the consolidation of power by the Spanish monarch Ferdinand VII. The general munitioner of the French army in Spain, Victor Ouvrard,[60] negotiated a deal with Macnin to export quantities of barley and cattle for the French army through the Spanish ports of Cadiz, Tarifa, Algeciras, and Málaga. The contract was drawn up on November 25, and signed by Macnin and Ouvrard, in the presence of the *qaʾid* of Tangier, Muhammad Umimun, and the French consul general, providing for the export of four thousand oxen and three hundred thousand quintals of barley. Ouvrard agreed to pay a duty of five *riyal*s for the first two thousand head of cattle, twelve *riyal*s per head for the rest, and half a *riyal* for each quintal of barley, and to remit the sum of twenty thousand *riyal*s to the Moroccan government. The agreement was to be binding provided the French army remained in Spain, and all transactions were to be the responsibility of Meir Macnin. The contract referred to Macnin as responsible for the affairs of the consulates of all the Christian nations.[61] Soon after it was signed, the contract was dispatched for ratification by the sultan, the French, and Macnin.[62]

Macnin continued to be in charge of this operation, which proceeded very slowly. The agreed-upon duties went unpaid,[63] and much of the stipulated quantities of grain and oxen were not shipped. Ouvrard, pressed by creditors, ceded the contract in April 1824 to Jean Alexandre Ducroc and Jean

Dolfus. By August, the operation was suspended.[64] Disputes between the French and Moroccan governments over the fulfillment and terms of the contract dragged on for a few years.[65] In 1825, the agreement originally signed between Ouvrard and the Moroccans formally came to an end, to the former's disadvantage. The French consul in Tangier wrote to Macnin that the agreement should be regarded as a commercial affair between individuals.[66] Only 791 oxen and 895 quintals of barley had been exported.[67] The Moroccan government would claim a higher rate of duties and the French would make a claim for cattle that had not been exported.[68] For several years, Dolfus and Ducroc sought the intervention of the French Foreign Ministry on behalf of their claims against the Moroccan government. At this point the French consulate, wanting to wash its hands of the whole affair, responding that the contract was between the sultan and Ouvrard and could not be ceded to anyone else except the successor to the French munitioner in Spain.[69] It is doubtful that the rest of the cattle and barley was ever shipped.

Not only did the foreign consulates have to deal with Macnin, but so did the native population. Soon after his appointment, leading members of the Jewish community of Tangier also were required to give him their support. The governor of the town convened Jewish leaders ordering that they give Macnin one hundred ducats. He received a gift of a considerable quantity of eau-de-vie and wine from the Jewish community. Macnin convened all the Jewish and Muslim merchants in the port of Tangier, and in the presence of the governor, announced a reduction of duties, saying that commerce was suffering because of the high rates.[70]

The unusual concentration of power in Macnin's hands led him inevitably into a web of intricate rivalries with both the Moroccan administration and the consular corps, which often had opposing interests. One of the recurrent diplomatic problems between the British and the Moroccan authorities, as already seen previously, concerned jurisdiction over Jews from Gibraltar, many of whom were of Moroccan descent. The effort of Mawlay Sulayman to subject British Jews to *dhimmi* status again resurfaced. The Moroccan authorities began to require an exit tax from Gibraltarian Jews leaving Morocco, whether at the instigation of Mawlay ʿAbd al-Rahman or the governor of Tangier is unclear. In any case, the new policy led to the British consul coming into conflict with the governor. First there was a dispute over an exit tax demanded from the consul's servant when the two were on their way to Gibraltar.[71] Subsequently, as Douglas wrote, "my chief dispute with him [the governor] is on account of the two British subjects Jews, whom he imprisoned, contrary to the 7th article of the treaty, for not paying a tax never before paid or exacted from British subjects."[72]

The quarrel began to escalate when the governor refused to send a courier to the sultan with a message from the English consul; instead, Douglas had to write a letter and give it to his agent in Tetuan to be translated into Arabic and sent on to the sultan.[73] The other consulates joined in, and began to protest more generally against the arbitrariness of the governor,[74] and as the governor himself leveled his own accusations in the form of legal affidavits confirmed by the *qadi*s. In response to the counteraccusations of the governor, the sultan wrote a letter to the governor and the consuls in which, without specifying the nature of the accusations, he demanded that the consuls conduct themselves within the limits of their treaties.[75] The diplomatic corps in Tangier regarded the governor as a barbarian, ignorant of both diplomatic procedure and the treaties. "The governor of Tangier," wrote Douglas, "is a mountaineer of the Atlas, or Bereber [Berber], chief of the tribe of Garavan, totally unacquainted with Europeans or their customs, he having told me when he arrived here that I was the first European he had conversed with, he has little or no knowledge of what a treaty means, and a very high idea of his own commanding importance."[76] Macnin was the main intermediary in the disputes between the consulates and the Moroccan administration. Whether his pivotal role exacerbated the tensions between the foreign powers and the governor, even undermining the position of certain individuals, as Miège asserts, is not indicated by the sources.[77] What is clear, however, is that some of the consulates disapproved of Macnin's extraordinary mandate, but all the foreign representatives had to use his offices in this period.

When the French government began preparing an embassy to the sharifian court in 1824 to renew its treaty with the new sultan, Macnin once again served as the chief intermediary. The French had particular interests in maintaining good ties with the Makhzan because of the agreement, negotiated by Macnin, to ship provisions for their army in Spain. It was through Macnin that the embassy of the French consul to the sultan was arranged. An embassy, consisting of the French consular officers of Tangier, the two military purveyors who had replaced Ouvrard, Macnin, and the governor of Tangier, departed to meet the sultan. The party was met on the banks of the river Werga on the road to Fez. In addition to the customary gifts brought by the French, Macnin brought a present, and the governor brought twenty-five thousand *riyal*s from Essaouira, and twenty thousand owed from the original contract that Macnin had negotiated with the French.[78]

It can be surmised that the political intrigue in Tangier that preceded the embassy must have been aired before the sultan. The foreign consulates in particular saw the governor as a villain, disrespectful of the treaties and obstructing the normal conduct of diplomacy. The French had hoped to conclude a new treaty with an added stipulation that would give them most favored nation status. Although a treaty was concluded and the consul returned to Tangier with presents, including a lion to be sent to the king of France, the French failed to gain the commercial advantages of most favored nation and the consul was rebuked by the French foreign minister.[79] The British consul attributed the failure of the mission (though it is not clear if he knew exactly what the French hoped to gain) to the influence of the governor of Tangier. Macnin, according to the British consul, was also accused by the governor, and disgraced by the sultan for two days. Later, after the governor left, Macnin was able to meet with the sultan, "having been serviceable to the Emperor when governor of Mogadore, and in great favor," and he assured the British consul that he "completely opened the Emperor's eyes," and was able to exculpate himself.[80]

Whatever may have been Macnin's involvement in the practically unrelenting diplomatic intrigue in Tangier, his position and status, protected by the sultan, only grew. In April 1824, he moved, by royal order, to the lavish house of a Muslim notable who had had to liquidate his property because of a debt of some ten thousand *riyal*s claimed by the sultan.[81] The consuls were unable to dislodge him from his position of intermediary, and he continued to perform important tasks for the sultan. One such task was a renewed effort, initiated by Mawlay Sulayman through the Macnins and Guedallas, to expand the practically nonexistent Moroccan navy, which consisted of only fifteen frigates in 1824.[82] In February 1824, Meir Macnin approached the American consulate about the costs of acquiring an armed brig, and again in May requested three ships. In July, the sultan ordered Macnin's associate, Jacob Guedalla, to purchase four armed ships.[83] Macnin was also ordered to purchase two thousand muskets, and the sultan promised the French, probably at the time of their embassy, favor and generosity if the order were filled quickly.[84]

Apart from its negligible military power, in the first decades of the nineteenth century Morocco had relatively little value as a commercial market for the foreign powers, and ambitious foreign merchants there failed to gain the backing of their respective governments. The concentration of power in the hands of Macnin, as commissary, contractor, financial agent, and diplomat for the sultan reflected the extreme limitations of the Moroccan state and its few revenues. The American consul had serious doubts that the sultan's initiative to increase revenue through commerce would succeed, nor would the idea of grain exports to Europe pose any threat to American exports: "capitalists will not enter a trade so entangled with difficulties, as the commerce of this country ever will be, the design may yield some private or local advantage, but trifling to be injurious to any part of the United States, or I believe anywhere else."[85]

The intrigues against Macnin by foreign consuls failed to prevent him from serving as the chief intermediary between the Moroccan government and the diplomatic missions in Tangier. On 1 September 1824, he was ordered by the sultan, then in Marrakesh, to settle in Essaouira. It is doubtful that he went there, or at least if he did go, he did not remain long, since at the end of September he was called by the sultan to prepare for a trip from Tangier to Marrakesh. It is not exactly clear when he made his trip, but perhaps it was delayed because of the revolt of the Atlantic coastal provinces of Abda and Dukkala against the sultan. A month and a half after he was told to get ready to go to Marrakesh, he was still actively serving as an intermediary in Tangier; for example, he was asked to go with a Muslim to the house of the Spanish consul to remove books on Islam that a Franciscan father, who had been expelled from the country, had in his possession. On 27 January 1825, Meir Macnin accompanied the ambassador of the Spanish consul on a diplomatic mission that concerned the status of Spanish political refugees in Morocco, that brought fifteen crates of presents to the sultan. The mission reached Fez on February 7, and after being well received by the sultan, departed again for Tangier on the seventeenth with presents that included three horses and a lion for the king of Spain. Soon Macnin was back at the sultan's court, negotiating over the purchase of French muskets and cannons.[86]

The sultan's confidence in Macnin even seemed to grow. At the end of March 1825, Macnin was put in charge of customs at Tangier after his predecessor was sent to prison in Fez. The expansion of Macnin's authority must have incensed some of the foreign consulates. Both the French and the British continued to complain about employing Macnin, with his trail of unpaid debts in Marseilles, London, and elsewhere in Europe.[87]

Quite possibly, it was the cumulative effect of the protests against Macnin by the foreign consulates that led the sultan to remove him from his position in Tangier, though hardly to relinquish his services altogether. In June 1825, Macnin was appointed as chief administrator of customs at the port of El Jadida, charged with encouraging foreign trade from that port.[88] The foreign consuls were to settle their accounts with Macnin so that he could bring these funds to El Jadida, and he left on July 5.[89] His role as the principal intermediary between the Makhzan and the European powers in Tangier appears to have been again taken over by al-Talib b. Jallun, who was placed in charge as minister for all consular affairs. Ibn Jallun profited from his position in Tangier by engaging in foreign commerce.[90] The motives for the sultan to attempt to concentrate commerce in El Jadida instead of Essaouira are not divulged in the *dahir* to the governor. It was a period of drought in Morocco, as Bendelac noted in his diary on the last day of 1825: "God sent this year, in the Empire of Morocco, famine and drought." The French consul suggested that the purpose was to attract ships that could bring grain to these parts of Morocco where there were severe shortages, and the British consul corroborated this report. Ships loaded with grain soon began arriving at El Jadida. In 1826, Macnin wrote to Tangier about the sultan's orders to reduce port fees for ships loading at El Jadida.[91]

The fact that a Jew had achieved such position and influence, higher than would have even been conceivable in post-emancipation Europe of the early nineteenth century, must have been particularly irksome to the consular representatives, and they often expressed their contempt for Meir Macnin. But in Morocco, they were forced to resort to Jews in high places, both as intermediaries with the government and the population, and as consular agents in places where they had no reputable or influential nationals of their own. For most Europeans, practically the only social contact they had with native Moroccans was with the Jewish population. Jews were much more willing than Muslims to allow Christians into their homes and to permit them to participate in their festivals and celebrations.[92] While the world of the Muslim harem remained out of bounds and mainly the realm of erotic fantasy, Europeans were able to have greater access to the domestic space of Jewish women. This greater intimacy, however, did not usually serve to overturn their negative stereotypes of the Jews, who, in their minds, were untrustworthy, ugly, and dirty (with the partial exception of the young Jewish women who were the unwitting objects of the erotic fantasies of European male visitors). But negative stereotypes did not prevent Europeans from availing themselves of the indispensable services of the Jews. Everywhere in Morocco, Jews served European consulates as interpreters and agents; and it was Jews who hosted European diplomatic missions to the sultan.[93]

Furthermore, in the 1820s, only in Tangier and Essaouira were consular affairs represented by Europeans. In the rest of the ports, it was primarily Moroccan Jews who served as consular agents. Quite ironically, even Spain, where the Inquisition was still in force and where Jews were still not allowed to reside, employed Jews as its agents in Morocco. Meir Macnin's brother and commercial associate, Masud, served as consular agent of Spain and Portugal in Essaouira until his death in 1831.[94] With the effort to concentrate trade in El Jadida, the British consul Douglas wasted little time in appointing Meir Macnin consular representative to El Jadida, despite the consul's antipathy toward him. Meir, in turn, left his brother Shlomo in charge of the British consular agency in the port.[95] Prior to Meir Macnin's royal appointment to the customs at El Jadida, the French consul in Tangier took the initiative of appointing Macnin consular representative in Essaouira following the departure of the French agent there, "to please H.M. the Emperor whose favor he possesses." The former French consular agent, A. B. Casaccia of Genoa, had in fact "represented almost all the nations at Mogador,"[96] and thus Macnin may well have served as consular agent for other countries as well for short periods of time. When the customs were farmed out to Meir

FIGURE 16. *Court of a Jew's House, at Tetuan*. From J. Taylor, *A Picturesque Tour in Spain, Portugal, and along the Coast of Africa, from Tangiers to Tetuan* (Paris: Published by Robert Jennings, 1827). The text identifies the figure with his back to the viewer as "the old Jew Alboudarem, Vice-Consul of France." Abudarham was one of the leading families of notables and rabbis in Tetuan.

Macnin in El Jadida, the French joined the British in appointing him consular agent there. Macnin in the meantime delegated his brother in his place as agent for the French in Essaouira.[97] These appointments, it seems, were provisional and on an ad hoc basis, and were hardly mentioned in the ministerial correspondence. Despite the scathing assessment of Macnin only a few years previously by both the British and French consular authorities in Morocco and notwithstanding their efforts to undermine his privileged position, expediency prevailed over other considerations.

Macnin's appointment to El Jadida, and the consular offices conferred by the foreign diplomats, guaranteed that his services to the sharifian court were to be maintained. Though we lose track of his itinerary, it is clear that his appointment to El Jadida did not mean that he remained stationary in the port. In 1826, we find him in Marrakesh in the sultan's service. A British captain, Beauclerk, who was in Marrakesh in the late summer and early autumn of 1826 accompanying a British doctor whose assistance the sultan had requested, wrote of Macnin sardonically:

Mr. Macnean, whom our interpreter designated *the great* Mr. Macnean, came to see us, attended by a back-biting friend and servant: he told us with great freedom that he was delighted to have the pleasure of seeing us here, and that he had lived many years in London, whither he went with his brother, who was sent from the court of Morocco to that of St. James' as the Sultan's Minister, and he ended up assuring us of his goodwill towards us, and his desire to serve us by the Sultan, with whom he was, to use his own terms, "all the same Mr. Pitt, all the same Mr. Fox."[98]

The writer was already predisposed to considering Jews as duplicitous cheats. A Jew named Jacob, allegedly sent by the sultan to provide the British visitors with their needs "and to levy the payment on the Jewish community at large," convinced the Britons to cut their expenses because of the poverty of the Jewish community. Later, however, the visitors learned that they, as well as the sultan, had been duped, since the Jews were to be later repaid by the sultan, and Jacob had inflated the figures of the visitors' expenses.[99] "From the highest to the lowest; from the great Mr. Macnean who drove his four horses in London and became a willing bankrupt to the ruin of many, down to the paltry Jacob, our victualler, who had cheated the Sultan, ourselves, and his own brethren, such are the Jews."[100] Beauclerk did concede, however, that once the sultan had been cured of his ailment, Macnin prepared a feast in one of the royal gardens, at his own expense.[101]

But Meir Macnin's services were still needed in the effort to resuscitate El Jadida's trade. With that intention in mind, late in 1826 Mawlay ʿAbd al-Rahman dispatched him to England with the hope of attracting British merchants to the port. Already well advanced in years, Meir Macnin embarked for London on his last diplomatic mission for the sultan.

CHAPTER SEVEN

The Unwanted Emissary

The British responded with condescending indignation to the appointment of Meir Macnin as ambassador to the Court of St. James. But the fact that Sultan ʿAbd al-Rahman was intent on appointing Macnin, already the subject of considerable controversy on account of his trail of unsettled debts in several major European cities, attested not only to an entirely different conception of protocol, but also to the exceedingly weak presence of Morocco in Europe. While all the major and many of the minor Western nations were represented by consulates in Tangier, Essaouira, and sometimes other seaports, the Moroccans had practically no permanent establishments in any of the Western European countries with which they had diplomatic or commercial relations. On the rare occasions that Morocco appointed any kind of resident representative in a Christian country, a Jew generally held this post, but the nature of his duties and his precise relationship with the Makhzan was left nebulous and open to negotiation. Mawlay ʿAbd al-Rahman, in an effort to renew treaties with the European countries, negotiated the opening of a few Moroccan consulates in Europe. There was a short-lived attempt to establish a consulate in Marseilles that was to be represented by Jews.[1]

The only Moroccan mission established in this period with any permanence was in Gibraltar, where the sultan was represented by a consul general, the Moroccan Jew Judah Benoliel, "one of the most considerable and wealthy merchants in the place."[2] Benoliel was at the center of Morocco's political and financial relations with Europe in the 1820s. Not only was he a key intermediary between the British and the Moroccans, but he played an important role in negotiating treaties with Sardinia, Naples, and Austria. He was closely linked to Aaron Nunez Cardozo, the Jewish consul of both Tunis and Algiers in Gibraltar. In 1828, the Moroccan government considered the possibility of appointing Benoliel consul in Marseilles. In Gibraltar itself he played the role of middleman between the Jewish community and governing authorities and in Morocco he was involved in the problem of Spanish political refugees in Tangier. Benoliel was able to accumulate considerable wealth through extensive commercial ties with major Moroccan and Mediterranean ports. He supposedly left seventeen million francs at the time of his death.[3]

Benoliel's exceptional official and permanent role had to do with the fact that he was vitally needed, not so much to represent the interests of Moroccan subjects resident on the Rock of Gibraltar (since the many Moroccan Jews who lived there were anyway anxious to become British subjects), but to serve as a kind of banker for the state in charge of foreign exchange. Since the silver Spanish hard dollar was needed in increasing quantities for trade with Europe, Gibraltar was geographically well situated to serve as the center for Morocco's financial dealings. Because of Morocco's role as supplier of the British garrison, there was constant sea traffic with Tangier. Gold coins from Morocco were shipped to Benoliel in exchange for Spanish dollars. The proceeds of customs and taxes levied in northern Morocco could be transported to the southern capital of Marrakesh, by way of Benoliel in Gibraltar, who would ship the money to Essaouira.[4] The overland route from Essaouira to Marrakesh took only a few days, in contrast to a much more arduous and risky land journey from Tangier. Benoliel was also well positioned to ship other commodities to Morocco requested by the sultan—such as textiles, or grain in time of drought—or to negotiate the purchase of ships.[5]

Morocco's lack of representation abroad also reflected the unequal balance of power between the Islamic world and Western Europe. The European powers had for centuries established embassies and consulates in Muslim countries under the system known in the Ottoman Empire as "capitulations," treaty arrangements that enabled foreigners to reside and conduct trade in the empire while enjoying extraterritorial rights. Morocco concluded similar treaties with foreign countries that granted foreign residents extraterritorial rights under the protection of their consulates. Stipulations were made with both the Ottoman Empire and Morocco that the foreign consulates could issue patents of protection to native agents who would also enjoy the protection of the foreign powers. The Ottoman Empire and Morocco saw such treaties as necessary to facilitate trade, but during the nineteenth century the system of capitulations (and in Morocco, consular protection) became a major destabilizing force since it was used as a means of commercial penetration, often to the disadvantage of local merchants. The system of granting protection to native agents became widespread and much abused, as foreign states competed for new markets, and as natives increasingly vied for the protection of the consulates. This became a direct challenge to Muslim authority and sovereignty, especially since many of the natives who received patents of protection were *dhimmi*s, ironically the very people that the Islamic state was required to protect.[6]

While the various treaties between Morocco and the European states stipulated the extraterritorial rights that foreign nationals would enjoy on Moroccan soil, no such provisions were specified for Moroccans abroad. Within the Muslim world, where there were larger numbers of Moroccans, Islamic law was not considered territorial (i.e., it transcended political boundaries), and therefore Moroccans would not have had the need for extraterritorial rights. There were only a handful of permanent diplomatic representatives in foreign countries, but they were mostly limited to ports along the pilgrimage route to Mecca, in Tunis, Malta, Alexandria, and Cairo.[7] What exactly the Moroccan representatives in these ports did is not clear, but presumably they would have concerned themselves mainly with matters arising from pilgrim travel. There were no treaty arrangements for the establishment of permanent missions in European countries, and there was probably a kind of reluctance to make such arrangements by both sides. The small number of Muslim subjects in the Christian world would have, in any event, obviated the need for consular representation in foreign countries. A merchant marine was unknown in Morocco and hardly existed even in the Ottoman Empire; European countries, or occasionally the United States, conducted almost all commercial shipping. This gave the Europeans some obvious advantages, and it is therefore not surprising that Morocco attempted as much as possible to conduct diplomacy on its own territory where, often to the chagrin of the foreign representatives, the Europeans had to play by the sultan's rules.

Furthermore, very few Muslim merchants traveled to Europe. The exceptions were well known and often elicited comment in the newspapers or foreign consulates. In the 1820s, one such Muslim merchant was al-Hajj Ahmad Ahardan, a royal *tajir*, customs official, and Makhzan treasurer, who traveled to Marseilles, where he had business connections with Isaac Israel, as well as to England, Naples, Gibraltar, and Cadiz.[8] There were a few enterprising merchants from Fez who traveled to London, Manchester, and perhaps a few other locations in Europe in the nineteenth century, but for the most part the Christian continent to the north was a *terra incognita*, a forbidden and unknown land.

Since Morocco, like other Muslim states, rarely maintained permanent consulates abroad, diplomatic negotiations, when not occurring in Morocco, were conducted by special envoys selected by the ruler.[9] When these special missions were conducted by Muslims, the appointees were prominent and wealthy figures close to the Makhzan, who might be able to bear the expense of the mission themselves.[10] Other times, Jewish merchants were asked to help finance the missions. In 1789, when Tahir Fannish and Muhammad Bargash were sent on a mission to Holland, Mordecai de la Mar was asked to provide them with twenty-five thousand Spanish dollars via his brother in Amsterdam. The merchants of Essaouira were ordered to pay the emissaries' costs of passage to Europe.[11]

These observations are not meant to suggest that Muslims were averse to travel as such. Travel in Muslim culture served to link together the greater Islamic community, through pilgrimage or *hajj* to the holy shrines in the Hijaz, or through study in the centers of Islamic teaching.[12] Travel to the Christian world was much more problematic, since such a journey was "an inversion . . . a voyage to the unholy and the impure."[13] Thus, Muslim missions to the political realm of the infidel (*dar al-kufr*) needed also to be legitimized by the ulama by invoking the formula *masalih al-umma*, the "welfare of the Islamic people," which associated the Muslim traveler with the sacred pilgrimage.[14] Such embassies were unambiguously of an official nature, and the purpose of the mission was quite explicit.

When negotiations and diplomacy in Europe were conducted by Moroccan Jews, their official position was much more ambiguous, as was the case with Meir Macnin's mission to London in 1827. For one thing, such missions were often quite discreet since the very idea of a Jew representing the interests of the Islamic state could hardly be reconciled with the concept of the Muslim sacred pilgrimage. It is therefore not surprising that there is little trace in the Makhzan records of Jews on missions abroad. No mention of Macnin was discovered in the Moroccan archives nor in the chronicles of the period. Yet there is little doubt that Jews served as indispensable intermediaries for the Makhzan, since travel to Europe for Muslims was so much more problematic. The Jew, already an unbeliever, did not risk being corrupted by the impurity of the West.

Jews who served the Moroccan sultan abroad were men of wealth, who combined diplomacy with business for their own accounts. Yet the nature of the missions abroad were often left deliberately ambiguous by the sultan. Complicating matters further was the fact that often Moroccan Jews had ties abroad, either to members of their families residing in foreign countries or to governments to whom they were accredited. Even more problematic was when they were either denizens of Britain, like Macnin, or actual British subjects, as was the case with Jacob Benider, who was sent to London in 1772 to negotiate with the British on a variety of matters. Benider, it seems, who formerly resided in Gibraltar and had also served the British as their

first vice consul in the new port of Essaouira as well as their representative
in Agadir and Safi, failed to receive an audience at the Court of St. James
and was not recognized as Moroccan ambassador since he was a British subject. He succeeded only in receiving partial payment for services rendered
for the British.[15] Like Macnin, Benider was a man of wealth with property
in Essaouira, and likewise his reputation was questioned by the British authorities, who accused him of fraudulent activities.[16]

At the time of Meir Macnin's appointment to his last mission for the
Makhzan, the multiple claims against him must have been well known to the
sultan. His debts in London, Marseilles, and Livorno by this time allegedly
amounted to about one hundred thousand pounds sterling. In Gibraltar,
writs of arrest had been issued against him, and he had also been sentenced
to pay twenty-five thousand piastres by the commercial tribunal of Marseilles. Despite these substantial claims, Macnin continued to trade with
London and Marseilles through his nephew, Masud Pinto. The latter fled
England in 1825, pursued by his creditors, and the British consul in Tangier
unsuccessfully tried to have him arrested in Gibraltar. There was apparently
no legal means of doing so, in the absence of a power of attorney from his
creditors in London. In Morocco, the consul recognized that action would
be useless. The sultan consistently refused to take any action against Macnin,
despite the repeated diplomatic interventions of the Europeans.[17]

. . . Pinto, with his uncle Meir Macnin, who owes upwards of one hundred thousand
pounds, in England, France and Italy, chiefly for merchandize obtained in the same
swindling manner, having made a large present to the Emperor, or in other words
bribed his Imperial Majesty to become a party to their fraud, they have thus secured
themselves under his Majesty's protection from responsibility, and he has not condescended to answer either of my letters claiming his justice on the occasion.[18]

In any case, on 25 October 1826 ʿAbd al-Rahman issued a *dahir* addressed
to King George IV, appointing Macnin as ambassador to England. The
dahir read in translation:

The bearer, our tributary* subject, Mamarr ben Makneen, one of our merchants and
attached to our service, is proceeding thither, to your country, whom we recom-
mend to your Majesty's protection, and that he may be respected and protected by
all your chiefs and officers from any imposition or hindrance in his affairs, which of
course, are for us, in the same manner we regard and protect your servants and subjects, that come to our court.

*Note: This word is only used to distinguish either a Christian or a Jew from a
Mohammedan.[19]

The nuances of the Arabic text, in part, are somewhat different from the
Foreign Office's translation. For instance, a more literal translation of the
opening line would be: "This *dhimmi*, Meir b. Macnin, from the merchants

(*tujjar*) of our 'protected' people (*ahl dhimatina*) appointed to our service, is entrusted with affairs and duties in all lands." Protection is indeed demanded for Macnin, who in the Arabic text is appointed to the position of ambassador in all countries. The emphasis on the term *dhimmi* is more than just a cliché but it also specifically denotes a Jewish subject (since in Morocco, the word is applied only to Jews), attached to the sovereign of the Islamic state; indeed, subservient to the state. It evokes a sense of ownership, of potential vulnerability, and therefore, the official protection of the sultan renders the Jew theoretically inviolable. The same sort of protection could not be offered to a Muslim in the service of the sultan.

Soon after the Macnin's appointment, and prior to his departure for England, one of his major creditors, Robert Burchall, demanded the intervention of the British government for the restitution of his debt:

Meir Macnin was late a merchant in London, trading principally with the dominions of the Emperor of Morocco—he borrowed of me some years ago, certain sums of money amounting by authenticated account (with interest) to £17146.1.8. He is now residing in the aforesaid dominions, and I am told, that he is well able to pay my debt, altho' I can obtain no satisfaction from him in answer to my repeated requests to that effect.[20]

Burchall continued to press his claims via the Foreign Office, explaining the nature of the claim, and furnishing an affidavit with all the particulars of the debt contracted by Macnin. Burchall's claim on Macnin, it seems, dated from 1808 when Macnin had been commissioned by the Makhzan to purchase the brig *Arthur* from the British government. Macnin, however, was not supplied with adequate funds to purchase the ship, and Burchall had extended credit to Macnin by paying the Navy Office £5,128. "From the foregoing narrative, I hope your Lordship will be inclined to think this case is one, in which his Majesty's Government should interpose its authority, at least insofar as relates to the sum of £5128.5 paid to our Navy office and the interest there on, if not the whole sum of £17146.1.8."[21] The Foreign Office repeatedly informed Burchall that they would not be able to intervene with the Moroccan government on his behalf.[22] "I am desired to acquaint you that as your claim upon the Moorish Jew Macnin appears to have arisen out of private transactions and is not even supported by any other testimony than your own (however respectable that may be) it is impossible for his Majesty's Government to interfere in your favour, by applying for the extrajudicial interposition of the Moorish Government to compel Macnin to liquidate your claim."[23]

The French correspondence gives a more detailed account than the British of the purpose of Macnin's mission: "he is assigned the mission of presenting to the King of England from the Emperor a dozen horses, three hyenas, and a lion, and to urge His British Majesty to send to Mazagan [El

Jadida] English merchants to establish commercial houses where they would enjoy some privileges." The French consul reported further that "the general opinion of the consuls is that this is simply a trap to attract these merchants, to first receive them, to torment them in every manner, and then finally to strip them as usual."[24] The consul goes on to state that there are always ill-informed individuals who try to take advantage of seeming opportunities, but to their own detriment. Furthermore, El Jadida itself is "untenable for a large part of the year," and the inhabitants of the region are prone to revolt. "All the ports of Morocco," wrote the consul, "are without any commerce, and the Emperor does not know how to supply his Customs, his only and unique resource, in view of the fact that territorial importations are insignificant." The French consul's report of the El Jadida initiative is confirmed by a diary entry of the British vice consul in Essaouira, Chaillet, dating from 1828, that Masud Macnin had brought a letter from the sultan to his brother Meir in London, containing instructions to Meir to invite British merchants to settle in El Jadida.[25]

In early January 1827, Meir Macnin arrived in Essaouira, bringing with him four horses for his anticipated mission to England. He engaged Willshire for passage to England in the ship *Mitford*.[26] It was learned in late February that the sultan had chosen Macnin as his ambassador to convey letters to Lisbon and London.[27] The mission to London was confirmed in early April according to Bendelac, in a letter from the sultan to the governor of Essaouira.[28]

When the British learned of the impending mission, Douglas wrote to both the Foreign Office and to the British consular representative in Essaouira, Mr. Chaillet, not to issue Macnin a passport. Douglas was led to believe that as a consequence, Macnin had given up the idea of sailing on the *Mitford*, and had chartered a vessel bound for Lisbon, from where, Douglas surmised, he would probably proceed to England. The consul general mentioned a letter from the Foreign Office of 27 January 1824 that suggested that Macnin's appointment as ambassador "would not be agreeable to His Majesty's Government," but was not yet willing to communicate this to the sultan because of the uncertainty regarding Macnin's departure.[29] In early March, a Moroccan who served the British as interpreter visited the Foreign Office to report on the impending embassy of Macnin.[30]

The Foreign Office began to inquire about the rumors of Macnin's mission. Douglas was to formally represent to the Moroccan government that the British would refuse to receive him.[31] Likewise, the governor of Gibraltar was instructed not to admit Macnin in the capacity of ambassador for the sultan.[32] Officers at various British entry points were also instructed that if Macnin were to arrive in the country, he should not be allowed to proceed to London.[33] Since it was difficult to discover what the Makhzan's intention was, Douglas was to find out from Macnin himself, and to inform him of "the consequences which might happen from any injudicious attempt on his part to force himself on the notice of H. M.'s government, as the Emperor's ambassador."[34] Douglas subsequently wrote to the Foreign Office that he had formerly told Macnin he would not be received as ambassador in England, nor would he grant him a passport since he "never received the slightest intimation from the Emperor that such a mission was in contemplation." Douglas wrote to Chaillet instructing him not to grant Macnin a passport nor a bill of health. The consul had warned Macnin that his debts in England amounted to more than seventy thousand pounds, and that he would be arrested upon landing in the country. The consul learned that Macnin wished to be arrested "under the absurd idea, that the British government would pay his debts, to relieve the Emperor of Morocco's ambassador from so unpleasant a situation." To undermine Macnin's mission, Douglas stated: "I will have it conveyed to the Emperor by the Governor of this place, who dislikes Macnin, that he is not a proper person to be received in England as the Emperor's ambassador, that if the Emperor really has such an object in view, that he should select for the purpose one of his respectable Moorish subjects, and not a Jew who has a bad character in England and who cannot possibly be received."[35]

Douglas wrote before the news reached Tangier that Macnin had departed from Essaouira on April 12, reportedly with presents of six horses, four mules, a lion, and a tiger.[36] The British consul's dispatch was dated, in fact, a couple of days after Macnin had arrived at the quarantine station at Stangate Creek on board the *Mitford* (26 April 1827), where it was revealed by the officers at the quarantine station that he had brought with him five servants, six mules, and six Arabian horses (a slightly modified, but probably more accurate listing of the animals brought as gifts).[37] The authorities at the quarantine station had already been instructed to inform the government of the arrival of Macnin, "and to prevent unnecessary reports and accounts relating to that person from reaching the shore."[38] The British continued to be ambivalent about how he should be received. Downing Street sent an official by the name of Smith to Stangate Creek "for the purpose of ascertaining the real nature of the circumstances under which a person named Meir Macnin has arrived in this country reporting himself to be an ambassador from the Emperor of Morocco." Smith was asked to inspect Macnin's papers, and ascertain his claims as ambassador. These papers should be translated, but Smith should not give Macnin the impression that his diplomatic character would be recognized, and should decline to convey any documents to be presented to the king, "the acceptance of which might give Macnin a colourable pretext for asserting that he had been received as ambassador by the British government." Smith was instructed to inform Macnin, if he determined that his credentials as ambassador of the sultan were in order, that the British government would not receive him as a public minister and would assist him in returning to Morocco. If, however, he was not on an official mission, but his papers "are simply of a recommendatory nature," then the government would not prevent him from landing in the country but he would not be sheltered from any proceedings which might be effected by his creditors; further, Macnin would then be required to attest in writing that he would abide by the consequences of such legal proceedings.[39]

Smith's encounter with Macnin at Stangate Creek, as described in a letter to the Foreign Office, is revealing:

On going alongside of the vessel in which that person had come to this country, Sidi Boubarek, the Interpreter who accompanied me, immediately recognised him to be the Moorish Jew Meir Macnin. He also pointed out to me a Jew Broker of London, Macnin's nephew who, as I was informed by the Quarantine officers, had come from town on the preceding day and was admitted into quarantine with his uncle.

As I was not permitted to go on board Macnin's vessel, I intimated a wish that he should come off in a boat alongside of mine, to which he readily assented; but I did not assent that his nephew should accompany him.

Smith then offers the only known physical description of Macnin:

Macnin is an elderly man, whose countenance is strongly marked by that mingled impression of sagacity and submission which generally characterises Foreign Jews. He was dressed in the European fashion, but meanly.

Smith continues to describe his encounter with Macnin:

I desired the Interpreter to tell him that I was sent by His Majesty's Government to enquire what had brought him to this country.
He answered that he was the bearer of letters from the Emperor to the King.
Would he allow me to see those letters?
He said that his orders were to deliver them into the King's hands.
Did he know the contents of those letters?
He answered no.
I then notified to him that whatever might be the contents of those letters, he would not be received and treated in this country as the Emperor's Ambassador.
He showed it was [illegible].
I desired him further to understand with reference to what had passed between him and the British Consul General in Morocco, on a former occasion, that if he landed in England he would not be privileged from arrest.
He said he understood what I had said.
I intimated that there existed every probability that he would be arrested.
He folded his arms across his heart and said he was resigned to his fate.
I asked whether he would not therefore naturally prefer returning to Morocco or proceeding to Holland or France.
He said that he would land in England.

I desired the interpreter to ask him in the most distinct manner whether I was finally to understand that he came to this country mainly as the bearer of letters from the Emperor and not as the Emperor's ambassador.

He answered evasively that he brought letters from the Emperor and that the King would see from these letters what he really was.

Did he bring no papers from the British Consul General?

Yes and he would show them to me.

I then left him with the understanding that the papers should be sent to me on board the guardship—where I accordingly received them soon afterwards.

These papers consisted of a notarial copy of an Arabick letter dated in October 1823 from the Emperor of Morocco to the European Consuls at Tangier notifying to them the appointment of Macnin to be the Emperor's ambassador to all Christian Nations; of a translation of that letter and of a certificate from the British Consul General assenting for the authenticity of the signatures.

As the exhibition of these papers, although of a comparatively obsolete date and irregular in form, proved that there was a lasting desire in Macnin's mind not to renounce at last his pretensions to the ambassadorial character which his friends here had assigned to him. I determined to return the papers to him in conformity with my Instructions and to speak to him more pointedly than I had found it proper to do in the presence of the ship's crew and quarantine guards who had [illegible] him present at our first conversation.

Accordingly when I saw Macnin this morning, I returned his papers to him and told him most distinctly that this government would not receive him as the Emperor's ambassador, but that I should have to report to H.M. Government the fact of his having delivered these papers for my inspection. I was desirous of being enabled to state precisely in what character he proposed to land in this country.

Macnin never attempted to retract or qualify what he had said yesterday.

Smith and Macnin never came to any agreement. As instructed, Smith warned him of the consequences if he tried to land in England:

I showed to him Mr. Burchall's claim on him for £18,000. He had no doubt other creditors to satisfy. Was it not rashness to place himself in their power? Was it not worse than folly to deal disingenuously with His Majesty's Government?—He affected at first to treat these representations with indifference by saying that his creditors could do no more than enforce their demands, that he was under the Emperor's special protection and cared not for any thing that might happen; but finding apparently that it was useless or fatiguing to bring strains any longer, or as if determined to set himself right in the estimation of H.M. Government without further discussion, he drew two papers out of his pocket and throwing them at the guard exclaimed that there lay the Emperor's letters and that I might do with them what I pleased.

As soon as the old man had in some manner recovered from his emotions, I desired the interpreter to take cognizance of the contents of the letters which were open; and having ascertained that one of them, although addressed to the King, was in fact a mere letter of recommendation and the other paper in the nature of a general passport, I told Macnin that having now ascertained that he came here merely as a private individual, my mission was at an end; and I recommended that he should send the letters to the Secretary of State. But he intended me to deliver them in the proper quarter which I consented to do; and I left him with the assurance that he should obtain pratique as soon as the quarantine regulations could admit.

I have only further to add that I found it impossible to obtain any intelligible account of the horses and mules. Macnin stated generally that he brought them as presents from the Emperor to the King: but no mention is made of them in the letters and Sidi Ombark told me that he had heard from Mogador that Macnin himself had purchased them there before he embarked.[40]

There seems little reason to doubt that Macnin was dispatched in some sort of official capacity by the sultan of Morocco. The Moroccan understanding of diplomatic protocol was quite different from the British. It seems as if the sultan intentionally did not specify the nature of Macnin's mission, preferring instead to make use of him in London as circumstances arose. From the Moroccan point of view, a *dahir* issued in 1823 would still have been valid unless another decree had superseded it. And as we shall see, the Foreign Office did indeed receive the *dahir* of 1826, addressed to King George IV. As for the horses and mules, there is no way of knowing if the initiative for their purchase came from Macnin or the sultan, although even if Macnin had purchased them himself, he may have been asked to do so by the sultan. It was standard protocol for the sultan to give a lion as part of his diplomatic overtures to foreign powers (and sometimes a tiger and horses were also included).[41] Considering the great difficulties in transporting lions, it is likely that the diplomatic gesture was sponsored by the sharifian court. The British consulate reported in February that Macnin had arrived from Marrakesh, bringing with him ten horses, eight mules, and two lions (but that the lions had died en route).[42] For a Jew to accompany such a caravan of animals would have been improbable without official sanction.

Meir Macnin proceeded to London, taking up residence at 5 Sackville Street in Picadilly, and continued to approach the Foreign Office respecting his mission.[43] He complained that his credentials had been returned to him without any explanation:

As I *personally* left the said credentials for inspection, at your Lordship's Office in compliance with your Lordship's desire, and they have been returned me with the verbal observation *only*, that I should not be received in conformity to the tenor thereof, I require at your Lordship's hands, that a *written* document be sent me, containing your Lordship's decision, on the subject of my mission, in order that I may either forward or convey the same to my Imperial Master.

Macnin also asks for instructions as to what should be done with the mules and horses which the sultan wished to present to the king.[44] The reply to his request was rather evasive: "I am directed by Viscount Goderich," wrote

R. W. Hay, "to acknowledge the receipt of your letter of the 30th ulto and to acquaint you in reply that his Lordship will not fail to adopt such measures as he may consider most expedient for acquainting the Emperor of Morocco with the King's sentiments upon the subject to which your communication refers."[45]

Macnin's determined protests against the refusal of the British authorities to receive him in the capacity of ambassador ultimately led to a reply from King George IV to Sultan ʿAbd al-Rahman on May 31. His letter was consistent with the instructions concerning Macnin's status already circulated by the Foreign Office to various officials:

We desire to assure you that as long as Makneen shall reside here, and demean himself with propriety, he will enjoy the full protection of the Laws as well as receive from our ministers and the other officers of our government every favor and assistance which as a private individual he can reasonably require in furtherance of his lawful pursuits. But we think it right to inform your Imperial majesty that it has been represented to us that Makneen is largely indebted to various persons, our subjects and others in this country; and we feel assured that your Imperial Majesty will not desire that Makneen should be exempted from obedience to the Laws if he should be called upon by a regular decision of our courts of justice to satisfy his creditors.

As We have learnt, however, with surprize, that Makneen has brought with him a letter from your Imperial Majesty dated in October 1823, under the authority of which he has entertained the expectation of representing your Majesty at our Court in the character of your consul and ambassador. We think it necessary to apprize your Majesty that We cannot admit that individual to our court as your Majesty's Representative, because independently of the objection which would at all times exist to receive a person of his condition in the dignified character of your Majesty's Ambassador, We are persuaded that it never could have been your Majesty's intention to place him in a situation which would enable him to resist the payment of his debts, and even to contract new debts, with impunity.

We feel the less reluctance in declining to admit Macneen to Our Court, as your Majesty has it at all times in your power to communicate to us unreservedly by letter or through Our agent in your dominions whatever you may desire us to do for your Majesty's Service or gratification, it being one of the objects dearest to Our heart to cultivate your Majesty's friendship, and to convince you of our unalterable regard and affection. And so We pray to God to bless your Imperial Majesty with health and happiness.[46]

It is interesting to note that George IV's reply nowhere refers to the *dahir* of 25 October 1826 that ʿAbd al-Rahman addressed to him. In fact, copies of the *dahir*, in both the original Arabic and translation, together with Smith's written report, were received, as officially recorded by the Foreign Office on the documents themselves, the day after Macnin's interview at the quarantine station. But Smith only claimed to have received a copy of the earlier *dahir* that declared Meir Macnin "Consul and Ambassador to all the Christian Nations," read to the consular corps of Tangier in November 1823. Smith gives the impression that Macnin retained other letters so that he could deliver them directly to the king. Smith's account of his encounter is almost certainly inaccurate, perhaps even disingenuous. Once in London, Macnin complained to the secretary of state for the colonial department that the "two letters from His Imperial Majesty were delivered by me at Stangate Creek, to a gentleman who was deputed to communicate with me there, and I presume that they still remain with him."[47] It is unclear, therefore, at what level in the Foreign Office the subterfuge took place. Perhaps the Foreign Office intended by the king's reply to deliberately ignore the latter *dahir*, which was explicitly addressed to him, and, by referring to the earlier *dahir* of 1823, to impute false expectations to Macnin and thereby let the sultan off the hook.

Though he failed to receive an audience from the British government (at least as far as we know), Meir Macnin may have continued to represent himself as the ambassador from Morocco for a period of time.[48] The British must have accepted the gifts allegedly from Mawlay ʿAbd al-Rahman and brought by Macnin, since they reciprocated with a crate of jewels worth fifty thousand piastres.[49] Nothing prevented Macnin from settling in London again and resuming his commercial dealings. The principal victim in this diplomatic row between the Makhzan and the British government seems to have been Douglas rather than Macnin. Already in 1824, ʿAbd al-Rahman had asked King George IV to recall Douglas, perhaps due in part to the antipathy generated by the governor of Tangier. In addition, the conflict with the sultan orginated in allegations that Douglas had seduced three Jewish sisters, one of whom had had a child as a result.[50] But the final straw seems to have been the Macnin affair.[51]

Although claims were later to be lodged against Macnin, the legal proceedings threatened by Burchall and perhaps other creditors apparently never occurred while he was in England. Soon after his arrival in London, arrangements were worked out with his creditors through his correspondents already in London, who were well-established Moroccan Jewish merchants.

We the undersigned, Merchants of London, do hereby certify, that since the year 1821, we have acted as correspondents and agents of Mr. Meir Macnin, who was then at Mogadore and elsewhere in the Empire of Morocco, and that we received several cargoes of value from him, out of the proceeds of which we were desired by him, to apply sums of money, towards the liquidation of such few remaining debts to persons in London, whom his former agent had not paid before that period.

In conformity to such orders, we accordingly paid from time to time, several large sums of money, on his account for the purpose aforesaid, and amongst others two sums of money to Mr. Robert Burchall and we should have continued to pay more, had not a very great depreciation in the value of the goods sent here by Mr.

Meir Macnin, prevented us from carrying his orders into effect. And as produce is the *only* species of remittance (to any amount of consequence) that can be procured from the Empire of Morocco, owing to the exportation of specie being prohibited, had Mr. Macnin sent us more goods for the above stated purpose, it would have been at an enormous sacrifice. But we do honestly assert it, as our opinion, from Mr. Macnin's orders in his letters to us, that it was his *constant* intention, to discharge all such just claims as remained due from him as soon as he conveniently could.[52]

Despite the refusal of the British government to recognize Macnin's diplomatic credentials, the Foreign Office was hardly anxious to support his creditors. In light of a subsequent letter of Burchall, it seems likely that he was enjoined to reach an agreement with Macnin, as evidenced by his petition to the Foreign Office:

I the undersigned do hereby certify that I have visited Mr. Meir Macnin since his return to London, in a friendly manner, and that I am satisfied from the conversations which I have had with him, that it is his intention to arrange the matters between us amicably and as soon as he conveniently can.

I therefore declare that I do not mean to act in any hostile way towards the above named gentleman, but on the contrary, to render him all service, kindness and attention in my power.[53]

We know little about Macnin's commercial activities in London over the next five years, but we can infer that his debts continued to accrue. In 1829, for example, Macnin shipped a cargo on board the ship *Northumberland* to his brother Shlomo in El Jadida on behalf of Robert Burchall, probably still trying to settle his debts with the merchant. The ship was to procure products which represented the mainstay of Moroccan exports: gum, beeswax, almonds, calfskins, goatskins, etc.[54] Much of the commerce between London and Morocco was still being conducted by the House of Macnin.[55]

The British continued to employ Meir's brother Shlomo Macnin as consular representative in El Jadida, though not without misgivings. It is ironic that Shlomo Macnin was originally appointed by Douglas despite his bitter hostility to Meir Macnin, who eventually had been the cause of the British consul's loss of accreditation. Shlomo Macnin became embroiled in intrigue and disputes, which led the *qaʾid* of Azamur to seek his dismissal. The British consul of Tangier, commenting on Macnin, wrote:

although I have every desire, not only upon account of the evil fame of Shlomo Cohen Macnin, but on account of his extreme ignorance to appoint another agent, I have been hitherto deterred from this step by the singular difficulty of finding any man at Mazagan fit to undertake the duties of British agent, rarely as they are now called for in that place: and being moreover aware that scarcely any vessels, as I am informed, enter that Port from Great Britain, excepting those consigned to the House of the Macnins themselves.[56]

The immediate dispute involved the wreck of the *Northumberland*, one of only three British ships that had arrived in the port since Meir Macnin departed for England, leaving his brother in charge of the consulate.⁵⁷ Shlomo Macnin was accused by the *qaʾid* of Azamur of having been "actively instrumental in completing the wreck of the schooner."⁵⁸ While the *qaʾid* did not intimate any misconduct by the master of the vessel, the ship's crew accused their captain of doing nothing to save the ship once it had run aground because of a fraudulent deal with Macnin and the *qaʾid* of El Jadida concerning the sale of valuable parts from the wreckage.⁵⁹

Meir Macnin's questionable status in London seemed to have had no effect on his ability to reenter the oligarchic establishment of the Bevis Marks Synagogue, of which some of his relatives, such as Judah Guedalla, were among the leaders. He was again elected *parnas* of the congregation in September 1828, together with his nephew Solomon Sebag. In April 1829, he again became *presidente* of the Mahamad.⁶⁰

His nephew David Cohen Macnin, however, clashed with the leaders of the congregation shortly before Meir's return to England. In December 1826, he complained to the *parnasim* of the synagogue that he had been unfairly deprived of a *mitzvah* that he had enjoyed for nine consecutive years on Yom Kippur (presumably he meant an *aliyah* to the Torah). Unsatisfied with the response to his protests, he resigned from the congregation, declaring that he would no longer pay his *finta*. The congregation still sent him a bill, which he returned claiming that he no longer considered himself liable if his demands were not met.⁶¹ How his problems were resolved is not clear, but he seems to have returned to the congregation after they agreed to a reduced *finta*.⁶² In any event, they did not prevent Meir's return to prominence, which was probably the result of his marital ties with some of the most illustrious members of the congregation.

The problems that David encountered with the synagogue's leadership probably reflected his financial difficulties. Prior to Meir Macnin's departure from London, the House of Macnin was not doing very well. D. C. Macnin was declared bankrupt on 13 May 1831.⁶³ Some thirty-four creditors, including a number of Moroccan Jews in London, submitted claims that by 24 June amounted to £21,729, while £10,980 was assessed as debts owed to David Macnin's estate. The largest claim was that of Thomas Courtney, amounting to £7,363, while Meir Macnin claimed the next largest debt of £4,932, allegedly money he had lent to David. At the other end of the scale, Sarah Paines claimed £25 owed for rent and furnishings for his residence. Depositions were submitted, for example, by William Piggot, a clerk to Courtney and Sons, who attested to David Macnin's involvement in the Moroccan trade. Another witness testified to how David Macnin would hide from his creditors when they came to demand settlement: "Received orders and directions from the said David Cohen Macnin at His Counting house and usual place of business in Philpot Lane aforesaid that if any of the creditors of the said DCM should come to his said Counting House and enquire for him the said DCM this examinant should deny his the said DCM being at home."[64]

It is unclear exactly what Meir Macnin's role was in the proceedings against the estate of his nephew. It should be recalled that Meir was closely associated with his nephew in business for many years. Allusions are made in the proceedings—by the assignees to the estate, Jacob Benzaquen and Leonard Towne, who were appointed by the other creditors—to efforts to have Meir Macnin relinquish his claims to goods which were being assessed for the sale of the estate. Eventually, on 12 November, Macnin agreed to sign a letter abandoning his claim on the goods, which were to be sold. In any event, the debt to Meir was probably a smokescreen: by making the largest claim against his nephew's estate, he could then attempt to preempt the other creditors, and thereby protect his nephew with whom he was still associated.

What was not stated in the bankruptcy proceedings against his nephew was that Meir Macnin still had many unsettled debts himself, and had clearly incurred numerous new ones. As with David, one of his chief creditors in England was Thomas Courtney of Messrs. Courtney & Son at the Old Jewry in the City of London, a clothing contractor to the army and navy. Courtney claimed that Macnin owed him over twenty-two thousand pounds, declaring that "the said Meir Macnin declares and pretends that he is unable to pay the debt due from him to the said Thomas Courtney and George Courtney, but it is apprehended that the said Meir Macnin has a very large amount of property at Mogadore and elsewhere in the Kingdom of Morocco and that if such property can be made available for the payment of his debts he will be found solvent." The Courtneys appointed the British consul general in Tangier, E. W. A. Drummond Hay, as their attorney to assist them in enforcing payment of the debt.[65] According to Courtney, money had been advanced and goods sold and delivered to Macnin. In 1829, some sixteen bills of exchange "were drawn by the said Meir Macnin on and accepted by one Robert Burchall and were all dishonored and unpaid at the times they respectively became due." Further credit by five promissory notes had been drawn by Macnin and remained unpaid, and three additional bills of exchange are mentioned in Courtney's affidavit.[66] The case, it seems, came before the King's Bench, and it was anticipated that Macnin was to be declared bankrupt.[67] Courtney's solicitor wrote to the under secretary of state for foreign affairs, as well as to the consul general in Tangier, seeking the latter's assistance, and claiming that "Macnin has made very large consignments to Barbary with the view of putting his property beyond the control of his creditors."[68] The British consul general

in Tangier wrote to the vice consul in Essaouira on his intention to request
from the sultan that an attachment be placed on Macnin's property (which
was allegedly quite considerable in both Marrakesh and Essaouira). He asks
his consular agent to furnish him with information about Macnin's property, "and what steps you may have discovered to be taken by the agents of
Macnin with a view to sustain his swindling proceedings."[69] Hay wrote the
sultan, suggesting that the attachment on Macnin's property in Essaouira
and Marrakesh could be carried out in the presence of the British vice consul, or before an appointed agent of the vice consul.[70] To strengthen the impact of his request, the sultan's secretary, Sidi al-Mukhtar al-Jamaʿi, was also
enjoined to press the sultan on the issue.[71]

Consul Hay was well aware of the difficulties of reaching any settlement
on this issue, and he wrote to Courtney's solicitor on his efforts. His vice
consul in Essaouira, Willshire, was appointed as attorney, but he informed
Courtney's solicitor that the only way they would meet with success was if
presents were made, and asked that the expenses incurred be reimbursed.
"The first step which I have taken here," wrote Hay, "is of the greatest importance; whatever however may come of it I cannot divine, but it is in our
favour that the Court being on a journey, when my letters should reach it,
the Minister may be less open, as I trust, to the counteracting machinations
of intriguers for Meir Macnin."[72] Hay also wrote to Willshire, asking the
latter to attempt to gain the help of a former clerk, J. J. Riley, of the House
of Macnin in Essaouira regarding their property: "the service of this Riley
should I think be bought if needful, and from him you should draw all possible information with regard to the property of Macnin & C."[73] At the
same time he wrote the solicitor, he also wrote his relative R. W. Hay, the
under secretary of state, about the case, referring to his help to the "unfortunate victims, not the first, of the notorious Meir Macnin, the hero I believe of Cumberland's Comic Opera entitled '*The Jew of Mogador*.'" Hay
continues to assess the problem with the House of Macnin:

You may now call to mind what I wrote to you long ago about the character not dis-
similar of Meir Macnin's brother Solomon, whom the former left at Mazagan in
charge of our consular agency to which Meir had been appointed by Douglas.

Solomon died a few months ago at Mogador whither he had repaired a short
time before to superintend I believe his own and his brother's interests upon the recently previous decease of another of their *blessed* fraternity.

I will be curious to ascertain, as I hope we may to some extent, what has been
done with the great sums of property the Macnin brotherhood have been handling
of late years. I am informed that Meir Macnin took with him to London a few years
ago a considerable treasure in jewels. This is, I think, the 3d time he has been declared bankrupt. M. Renshaw writes me that a once wealthy man named Burchall
(of London I think) was totally ruined by this "Israelite indeed", and died of grief in
consequence, being unable to leave a shilling to his family.[74]

The sultan made it clear that he could not assist the British in their endeavor, being intent on protecting the Macnins' property:

Be it known to you, that Meer Benmacnin is so much in debt to our Treasury, that his property in this country will not suffice to liquidate more than a small portion of his other debts. He has no landed property at Sweerah, the houses in his occupation belong to the Treasury and he occupies them only for temporary purposes.

Regarding what he has in (the city of) Marocco [Marrakesh] the greatest debtor to him owes only twenty dollars; we inform you of this in order that you may be on the watch to inquire into it. The said Meer, is now in your Country, all his money and property is with him there, and the merchants his creditors may deal with him according to the known usage and in conformity with your Laws in like cases.[75]

Sidi al-Mukhtar al-Jamaᶜi wrote to Hay the same day, but merely stated that he had delivered the consul's letter and referred to the sultan's previous reply.[76]

There can be no doubt that the sultan was well aware of Macnin's landed assets, which would have been typical for a leading merchant. At any rate, the numerous transactions and deeds of Meir Macnin's property are preserved in the family collection, and although there is no extant document which includes the entire Macnin estate, there is a record of numerous transactions involving real estate throughout Macnin's career as a merchant, in both Essaouira and Marrakesh. So important was Macnin as a landowner in Marrakesh that throughout the nineteenth century and at least until the 1950s there was a street in the *mellah* known as "Darb Macnin."[77] A report on the *mellah* of Marrakesh in 1950 relates the tradition that the principal landowners were called Macnin.[78]

The correspondence between the Makhzan and the British representatives concerning the claims against Macnin continued. After receiving the sultan's letter, the consul wrote again to al-Mukhtar al-Jamaᶜi of the debt to Messrs. Courtney amounting to upwards of twenty thousand pounds. The creditors claimed that Macnin had sent property to Morocco which would cover the debt, and previously he had also had considerable goods already in store in Morocco. The consul, however, stated that he was unable to ascertain the truth of these claims without an inventory of Macnin's estate. Hay persisted by naming two Jewish brokers in Essaouira to assist in making an inventory of Macnin's property in the presence of the vice consul, and asking the sultan for his agreement.[79] The response of the secretary was somewhat ambiguous. In his reply, Macnin is considered an "eminent one among the Merchants, his vessels pass to and fro, when he sends [a cargo worth] ten thousand, fifteen thousand are sent [to him] in return, he is now in your Country and it is not just to search for his property, and consider within your own mind if such a thing can be done without proper documents."[80]

All proceedings were suspended when Hay received a letter from Courtney's solicitor, Van Sandan, that the parties had come to a compromise, and so all proceedings were suspended. "I have the honour to acknowledge the receipt of your esteemed favour and have to report that the bankruptcy of Messrs Courtney & Son reduced by the robberies practised on them by Meir Macnin has obliged them to yield to most unfair terms of compromise."[81]

Van Sandan was also no doubt frustrated by his dealings with Morocco. The problem of retrieving debts was explained by Willshire in a letter to the consul in Tangier. The various bills and documents of debtors upon which creditors can claim through an attorney are held by the *qadi* to enforce payment. Such documents submitted to the *qadi* cannot be assumed to be valid unless substantiated by evidence submitted by Muslims. During the reigns of Sidi Muhammad b. ʿAbdallah and Mawlay Sulayman, claims for debts against native merchants admitted the testimony of European courts. "In the latter end of the reign of Mulai Soleyman, or at the commencement of the present Sultan, Mulai Abdurahman which, I am not certain, the native hebrew merchants of this town, making use of the capacity of their Minister, obtained a letter from the Sultan, under the Imperial seal, that 'creditors must appear *personally* in this country to substantiate their claims.'"[82]

Courtney's claims were revived, as his solicitor intimated might happen, when Van Sandan, on behalf of his clients, "struck a docket," that is, initiated bankruptcy proceedings, on 18 January 1833.[83] Meir Macnin was declared bankrupt on 21 January 1833 at the Court of Bankruptcy on Basinghall Street.[84] The official assignee under the Bankruptcy Court to the estate of Meir Macnin, Alexander Brymer Belcher, conferred power of attorney upon E. W. A. Drummond Hay and William Willshire.[85] Belcher wrote to Consul Drummond Hay in Tangier, sounding a tone that was all too familiar among those dealing with Macnin's affairs:

I address to you with the accompanying power of Attorney requesting the weight of your official influence on behalf of the interests of the said Estate. I am perfectly sensible of the delicacy and difficulty of the task thus imposed but a very considerable amount of property being involved. I feel confident that whatever can be done will be accomplished for the benefit of those concerned so that justice as far as possible may be done to all parties. There is every reason to feel perfectly assured that property in goods or funds of some description to a large extent must be existing in your city either immediately possessed by him or in the hands of agents large shipments having been made and very inadequate returns received and it is of the utmost consequence that no time should be lost in securing it. The power herewith is I believe as ample and as formally drawn as it was possible to make it and I have only to add that duly appreciating the nature of the government under which you reside the fullest latitude is given to you and any arrangement will be acquiesced in which by a partial sacrifice to the government of a portion may save the remainder. You on the spot must necessarily be so much better acquainted with the best mode of effecting the object (in a country where the government is so despotic) than we can possibly be here that it is only needful to impress the propriety of promptness and decision and that not a moment be lost let your success be great or otherwise in realizing and transmitting to me such property as may be secured by you in the mode which may appear best adapted to serve the interests of the Estate without awaiting further instructions but acting as if for yourself.[86]

The British vice consul in Essaouira, William Willshire, reports in his diary that there was no hope of any part of Macnin's property being recovered for benefit of the creditors.[87] And indeed, after this date there is no further evidence of Macnin in either the archives of the Foreign Office or the Court of Bankruptcy. There is no indication that anything was ever resolved between Macnin and his creditors. In any case, he was soon far out of reach, retiring to Marrakesh, his city of birth, where he spent the last few years of his life.

CHAPTER EIGHT

Macnin's Legacy:
Sephardi and Oriental

Anglo-Jewry had entered a new era when Meir Macnin returned to England for his second lengthy stay in 1827. The formerly disdained Ashkenazi Jews had risen to much greater prominence in England, overshadowing the Sephardim. A mid-nineteenth-century history of the British Jews tells us:

It would appear that for upwards of thirty years after the appointment of Dr. Herschell to the chief Rabbiship of the German synagogues in England, the Ashcanazim, as the members of these communities are called, took the precedence of the Sephardim, or Spanish Jews, in almost everything appertaining to progress. The Ashcanazim were the authors of new works, the founders of new institutions, the advocates for the abolition of civil disabilities; in short, the prime movers of everything connected with national progress. The Sephardim remained in comparative quietude; though it must be acknowledged that the latter, were occasionally brought under particular notice. For instance, in 1805, Aaron Cardosa, Esq., was sent by the British Government to the Bey of Oran, to negotiate a treaty between the Court of St. James and the Mohammedan chief. Again in 1813, Masahod C. Machim, Esq., was appointed Envoy to the British Government from Muley Soliman, Emperor of Morocco. And again in 1827, Meir C. Machim, Esq. succeeded his father to his post in Morocco. With these few exceptions, and perhaps a couple more, up to the time of Sir Moses Montefiore's budding forth into a flourishing state . . . the Ashcanazim monopolized the attention of the British public.[1]

Only the prominent North African Jews engaged in diplomacy remain recorded in the memory of this period. (It was of course unknown to the writer that Meir Macnin's credentials were rejected by the British government, and he also mistakenly assumed that Masud was Meir's father.) Part of the reason for the declining prominence of Sephardim as a whole was their high degree of assimilation into Anglo-Jewish society. They probably felt less disadvantaged by the remaining civil disabilities than the Ashkenazim, which might explain why the latter were more determined to see all lingering legal discrimination removed.

For the Sephardi Jews, affiliation to the English nation became much more important than belonging to the "Portuguese Nation," with its sense of separateness. While retaining pride in being Sephardi, the leaders of Anglo-Jewry owed more to their prominence in Gentile society than to their connections to a supranational Sephardi world. While the division between Sephardi and Ashkenazi remained, the significance of this divide lessened as the real authority of communal institutions over their members declined. England was following in the wake of the emancipation of the Jews in France. It should be recalled that at the time of the Revolution, the French Sephardim were reluctant to grant emancipation to their poorer, less assimilated Ashkenazi coreligionists, lest they be identified with this undesirable element in society. Emancipation first came to the Sephardi Jews in 1790, but was then extended to all of French Jewry in the following year. Emancipation came at a price for the Sephardi Jews, who were required to give up their corporate privileges.[2] While civil rights came in a more piecemeal fashion in England, the separate status of Jews was never as well defined as in continental Europe. Consequently, there were fewer barriers to assimilation, and with the last legal hurdles removed in the first half of the nineteenth century, this assimilation was greatly accelerated.

Meir Macnin, unlike some of his relatives and other Moroccan immigrants to England, never established permanent roots in that country, preferring instead to remain until his dying day the sultan's Jew—privileged, but still a *dhimmi*. Many of the first generation of Morocco's international Jewish merchants left Morocco permanently. The most important merchant family of the eighteenth century, the Guedallas, who were as we have seen related to Meir Macnin through his marriage to Zohra Pinto, were already well established in England in the early nineteenth century. The connection of the Guedalla family to Morocco was through their property. Moses and Haim Guedalla of London still owned and rented extensive properties in Essaouira in the latter half of the nineteenth century, inherited from their father Judah and from the latter's father Jacob, and thus dating from the early existence of the town.[3]

But the Guedallas and other Moroccan families, such as the Macnins' close correspondent Menachem Bensusan, became an established part of Anglo-Jewry; their descendants were well integrated into British society. A few Macnins stayed in England. One branch of the family joined the Church of England, while a member of another branch, Abraham Cohen Macnin, joined the Stock Exchange. Although the latter was buried in the Novo Cemetery of the Bevis Marks Synagogue in 1840, he twice married outside his faith, as Albert Hyamson remarks disparagingly: " . . . he attained to undesirable prominence in the Synagogue records on account of his matrimonial relations and their connexion with his status as Cohen."[4] Meir's nephew David had a more ignominious end. After his dispute with the Mahamad and threatened resignation from the synagogue, he was again able to attain respectability in the Sephardi community, becoming first treasurer in 1830 and then president of the congregation's preparatory school for boys;[5] and despite bankruptcy in 1831 and his marriage to a non-Jew that same year, he was granted a prominent seat (*gaveta*) in the synagogue in 1835.[6] His good fortune, however, did not last. In 1851, he applied to the Mahamad for assistance, and was given five pounds on condition that he leave the country. He rebounded, however, repaying the congregation, including interest, for which he was praised by the Mahamad. But in 1866, he was admitted to the communal hospital, Beth Holim, as a pauper, died that year, and was buried in the Novo Cemetery.[7] Memory of the Macnins in England is perpetuated in a few families. One recent family history tells us:

According to family tradition Abraham Pinto [the son of Meir Pinto] was twenty years old when he came to London, and he had a considerable sum of money which somehow he managed to lose. But during this difficult period he was befriended by a relative, David Macnin, and by the time his son was married he seems to have been well established. In his will, dated about 1849, he lays upon his descendants the duty of always befriending the Macnins. But there are no Macnins left in the congregation, nor even in London as far as I know.[8]

Meir Pinto was Meir Macnin's father-in-law, and David Cohen Macnin was godfather (*sandak* in Hebrew: the man who holds the child in his lap at the circumcision ceremony) to Abraham Pinto's son, Moses, born in 1818.[9] Abraham also had another son, according to family tradition, named Meir after Meir Macnin.[10]

   In Morocco, the Macnins have disappeared from the collective memory. The family name there died with Meir, apart from the street in Marrakesh still known in the mid-twentieth century as "Darb Macnin."[11] Meir Macnin emblematized the growing dichotomy between the Jews of post-emancipation Europe and the Jews who remained outside the framework of the modern nation-state with its concepts of citizenship. Emancipation in Western Europe and the identification with the nation that accompanied the process of obtaining civil rights signaled fundamental changes in the relationship of Jews to the state. The period of the European court Jew came to a final end, and the Jews, not as mere instruments of the state but as independent entrepreneurs, were able to invest their capital in ways that were indistinguishable from those of non-Jews. Bourgeois society, while not ending prejudicial attitudes toward Jews, did, sometimes with reluctance, offer Jews the opportunity to enter society on equal terms.

Although Meir Macnin was by most accounts the largest property holder in Morocco's principal seaport, and for years, together with his brother, among the most important merchants of Morocco, his wealth hardly compared to that of the major capitalist families of Europe. In the absence of other forms of investment, all his capital was tied up in urban property in Essaouira and Marrakesh, and was always subject to sequestration by the sultan because of his debts to the state. As part of his contract as royal merchant, Macnin was required to obtain a loan from the Makhzan, which needed to be paid back on a monthly basis. Even if Meir Macnin and the other royal merchants wanted to acquit themselves of their debts, they were not allowed to do so. Indebtedness to the Makhzan was a *quid pro quo* of being a royal merchant.

This indebtedness was in fact a form of indenture, since even Macnin's wife could not travel outside of Morocco with him. In other words, she was kept as a kind of security that he would not permanently leave the country. There is no evidence that Zohra ever accompanied or resided with him during the many years he spent in London. It should be recalled that Meir Macnin left Morocco in 1799, shortly after his marriage. Since records of births were not kept in Morocco, the birth date of their daughter, Blida, is unknown, but it is likely that she was born shortly before Macnin's first departure for London, or perhaps a few years later during a visit to Essaouira.[12] His long absences from Morocco—he lived in London from 1800 to about 1817—perhaps offer an explanation why he and his wife were only able to have one child.

Meir Macnin wanted to guarantee that his vast property would remain within his family. It should be recalled as well that Zohra was descended from the Guedalla family through her maternal grandfather Jacob Guedalla, and that the Guedallas were the biggest property owners of Essaouira in the eighteenth century. Some of this property ended up in Macnin's hands. Frequently, Meir purchased property jointly with his brother Shlomo. There is no evidence that Shlomo ever married after having broken his engagement in 1815, and there would thus have been no one to dispute Blida's share of the property. Blida therefore became the principal heir of the Macnin property. To assure that his legacy would be transmitted, Meir Macnin bequeathed all his property in Essaouira and Marrakesh to Zohra and Blida on the eve of his departure for London in 1827.[13]

There is little record of the last two years of Meir Macnin's life. The absence of correspondence in the Foreign Office concerning his numerous British creditors points to the probability that he returned to Morocco in

1833. The eldest of the four Macnin brothers, Masud, who served as consular representative of Spain and Portugal in Essaouira, died in 1831,[14] and Shlomo, Meir's close commercial partner, died the following year, also in Essaouira. What became of the third brother, David, is unknown—most likely he died as a young man.

Meir returned to Marrakesh, the city of his birth, where he probably spent the last two years of his life. We know that Meir Macnin's son-in-law, Aaron Amar "Bujnah," was made the trustee of what must have been Meir's Makhzan houses in Essaouira in 1833, and the authorities ordered him to recuperate any losses that a current occupant, Eliyahu b. Avraham, might have incurred from his business transactions.[15]

We learn from an affidavit sworn some years later that Meir Macnin died in Marrakesh on 3 August 1835, 9 Av 5595 according to the Hebrew calendar[16]—on the evening of which day there began the annual Jewish fast, Tisha B'Av, that marks the destruction of the Temple. According to tradition, great tragedies in Jewish history often occurred on this date. Despite the symbolic importance of the date of his death, Meir Macnin and the family name were to be forgotten, and today are no longer a part of the collective memory of Moroccan Jews.

None of the four brothers left any known successors to the commercial enterprise. Only Masud had any male offspring, but they probably all settled in England, severing their ties with Morocco. There was also a woman named Mira, in all likelihood a Macnin sibling, whose name appears as representing the family interests in Essaouira when the brothers were in Marrakesh. What became of her is unknown. So among the elite merchants of Morocco, the name of Macnin was no longer heard after Meir's death, except as a fading memory.

Meir Macnin left behind considerable real estate in Essaouira and Marrakesh, and though there were undoubtedly many creditors in Europe who felt that they had never retrieved their money and were thus entitled to his property, Meir and his brothers also died with numerous debts still owed to them. In subsequent disputes regarding what must have amounted to the largest holdings of real estate in Essaouira, it is the name of "Bujnah" that is heard. Aaron Amar "Bujnah" was given by royal decree the right to recuperate from debtors, "Muslims and Jews," owing to the late Macnin brothers. To guarantee that he be empowered to do so, the *dahir* was sent to the governing authorities, who were ordered to take all steps to assist in the recovery of the debts. Presumably this also meant that Aaron would have been responsible for paying off the royal loan owed by the Macnins.[17] Aaron figured among Essaouira's prominent merchants for a number of years. The Makhzan continued to scrupulously protect the family against foreign creditors,[18] while assisting Aaron in his efforts to recover the family debts.[19]

The close bond that Mawlay ʿAbd al-Rahman maintained with Meir Macnin was inherited, in a sense, by the latter's daughter, Blida. The British antislavery campaigner James Richardson, who stayed in Essaouira in 1843, was greatly impressed by her:

Her father was a grandee at the Court in the days of former emperors, and the greatest merchant of his time, and she represented as an aristocrat among her people, a modern Esther, standing and pleading between the Sultan and her nation. This lady is the only native woman in the country, Mooress or Jewess, who has tact or courage enough to speak to the Emperor, and state her request with an unfaltering voice beneath the awful shadow of the Shereefian presence! Madame Bousac [*sic*] accompanied the merchants to Morocco [Marrakesh] to pay her respects to the Emperor. Among other modest or confidential demands which the lady made on the Imperial benevolence, was that of an advance to her husband of ten thousand dollars. His Imperial Highness was immediately obliged to give a formal assent before his court.[20]

In fact, as Madame Bujnah told Richardson, the sultan did not advance the loan as promised, but instead sent her a present of four fine white haiks, the outer garments commonly worn in North Africa.

Aaron Amar, who was already well on in years when he married Blida, died in 1845, a few months after the French attack on Essaouira, at a time when his children, Judah and Hanina, were still minors.[21] Blida lived until 1878,[22] but nevertheless, on the death of her husband and in the absence of any other male heir capable of assuming responsibility for the Macnin estate, the sultan effectively became the guardian of Blida and her two young children by taking charge of the property. A royal decree issued in 1847 by Sultan ʿAbd al-Rahman "conferred on the *dhimmiya* Blida daughter of Meir b. Macnin of Essaouira the right to reside in the house that she occupied from the various property of her father and to collect ten *mithqals* each month from the proceeds of the property to help her situation." The governor of the port of Essaouira, al-Hajj al-ʿArabi al-Tarris, was ordered to ensure that the authorities would implement the decree.[23] To further protect the family's inheritance against any spurious claims, two witnesses from Marrakesh swore to the date of Meir Macnin's death in Marrakesh, stating that "the notable Meir Hacohen b. Macnin, for all the days of his existence on the earth until the day of his death only had his one daughter Blida and left no other offspring who might be considered to inherit all that he left to his only daughter Blida."[24] The sultan continued to protect Blida's interests by maintaining the house she had inherited from her deceased father.[25]

The family preserved considerable official correspondence concerning these properties, since for some years the Makhzan was responsible for their maintenance and collecting their rent. Some of the inheritance held as security by the sultan was sold, such as a house in the *mellah* of Marrakesh that was purchased by Hadan b. al-Hazan Yaʿkub b. Muha in 1850.[26] The condition of Blida and her children as the sultan's wards was by no means easy, and clearly they had difficulty making ends meet. In 1860, in exchange for one hundred *mithqals*, Blida, Judah, and Hanina mortgaged a synagogue they owned to Makhluf Ohayon, formerly of Iligh. The synagogue was, in turn, leased to another tenant.[27]

As was common among other royal merchants, when Judah Amar "Bujnah" came of age, he was granted the status of his father by royal decree in 1863: "We include the merchant Judah b. Aaron Bujnah among our corps of official merchants and we renew the royal decrees he has from his father."[28] By conferring this status on Judah Amar, the sultan was in effect relinquishing his guardianship, and henceforth expected Judah Amar to pay back the monthly installments remitted by all the merchants for the debt they owed the sultan. Sultan Muhammad wrote to the *qaʾid* of Essaouira: "we granted to the *dhimmiya* Blida the daughter of the son of Macnin and her son, the son of Bujnah, profit from their properties that they have here in Marrakesh and there in the port of Essaouira, and we authorized their control of them, provided that they pay the monthly installment of the merchants."[29] Judah Amar thus inherited the debt of his father, which amounted to 21,954 *mithqals*.[30] The question of the Amar-Bujnah debt, and the properties they owned, continued to be the subject of dispute well into the French Protectorate period.

When Judah Amar joined the corps of royal merchants in the 1860s, the number of merchants in Essaouira was increasing. Foreign trade grew, especially with the inauguration of free trade established by the treaty with Great Britain in 1856, but this also brought fierce competition among the merchants. Some merchants made small fortunes, but others went bankrupt. The boom in trade also attracted Jewish migrants to the town, especially from the smaller communities of southern Morocco, but few were able to reap much benefit from the still rather modest foreign business. Poverty increased in the *mellah* as the number of inhabitants grew out of control. Rental property in the *mellah* also became a source of income for the Jewish merchant elite. By the late nineteenth century, when Essaouira's international trade seriously declined, the rents collected became for some of the Jewish elite of the casbah practically their only source of income. Complaints about the exploitation of the poor Jewish tenants of the *mellah* by the casbah landlords were well justified, but the elite itself was in decay. The formerly prosperous merchants had little left except their houses. They were a bourgeoisie in decline.[31]

In addition, the Makhzan also was hard pressed for cash. Spain's war against Morocco in 1859–60 and its occupation of Tetuan forced Morocco to pay a large indemnity, in exchange for Spanish withdrawal, that bankrupted the royal treasury. To repay its debt to Spain, Morocco had to accept the presence of Spanish officials at the ports, who were authorized to collect half of all the proceeds of customs duties. This significant loss of income at a time when the costs of government were mounting forced the Makhzan to adopt more drastic measures to collect revenue.[32] These financial pressures on the Makhzan probably explain why it tightened its requirement of merchants to repay their old loans.

Despite all his property, Judah Amar "Bujnah" was unable to compete with the most prominent Jewish merchants of Essaouira in the 1860s and 1870s. Judah began requesting an increase in the loan received from the sultan.[33] Of the twenty merchants who were granted the new royal loan of 1865, Judah Bujnah received ten thousand *riyals*, one of the largest sums distributed (only Joseph Elmaleh and his son received the larger amount of fifteen thousand *riyals*).[34] The minister Musa b. Ahmad assured Judah that he was "among the loved and faithful of the Sultan."[35] By 1867, Judah was requesting another loan from the Makhzan, claiming losses due to the decline in commerce, expenses in repairing properties, and a commercial loss due to the sale of the house in Marrakesh.[36] Judah persisted in this matter. Shortly thereafter, he gave another reason for requesting the loan: he was suffering considerable losses in rent from his properties because of the poverty of the tenants (who were unable to pay). He added that the amount he still owed to the sultan from the previous royal loan could be paid off by selling his property if he did not receive an additional loan. The selling of his property was authorized.[37] In a letter of Sultan Muhammad to the prince and future sultan, Mawlay al-Hasan, Judah was authorized to sell his property in Marrakesh to pay his debts to the treasury. If this still would not be sufficient, the remainder could be paid from his properties in Essaouira. The sultan wrote: "Help him sell it, on condition that he pays the amount that he sells it for to the financial officers in Marrakesh"; and added: "make clear to him that he should not sell his property to either Christians or those under their protection." Haim Corcos, a prominent Jewish merchant in Marrakesh, was delegated for him.[38] Since the opening of Morocco to free trade, foreign merchants and their agents had begun to settle in Marrakesh, and the government was concerned about the harm that this growing foreign penetration might cause. Under pressure from the financial agents in Essaouira to repay his ten-thousand-*riyal* loan, Judah requested a deferral until his properties could be sold in Marrakesh. An additional two months was granted.[39] It is noteworthy that, despite his difficulties, he still received the same gift of fine cloth that the sultan gave to all his Jewish merchants (*harqa zamuriyya*).[40] The properties were eventually put up for auction, but this was still not the end of the story. In the following year, Judah wrote that no one had offered to purchase the properties and he asked that a sharifian order be issued so that the treasury could take the amount for which the properties were assessed.[41] Owing to the auctioning of Judah's Marrakesh property in 1869, the sultan would have presumably released his mortgaged property in Essaouira. But the story continued, since money was still claimed by the treasury from the old debt of his father. Two years later, Judah requested that his properties be taken and assessed in Essaouira to pay off the rest of his debt to the Makhzan.[42] His properties were sequestered and about a year and half later assessed at 37,862 *mithqal*s and 5 *uqiya*s, but the financial officials added that they were overvalued in light of their dilapidated condition.[43]

Judah's sister, Hanina, also had an interest in these proceedings, especially since she had married Judah b. Samuel Levy "Ben Hamu," from another prominent family, in 1862. In the marriage agreement concerning the dowry (*nedunya*, "that which is given" in Hebrew/Aramaic), Hanina was to receive from her mother and brother property and sundry other precious items such as gold and silver belonging to Blida and Judah which were not specified. In exchange for this pledge, Hanina would renounce any other claims on their property. The property in Hanina's dowry included half of a synagogue in the *mellah* known as "Ben Saʿdya," and one-third of the house in the casbah where they lived (which was known as "Dar Ben Macnin"). Significantly, it was specified that the sultan held property as mortgage, and if he were to return it, she and her husband would receive one-third.[44] As we have seen, the property was released to Judah from mortgage in 1863.

The husband's marriage gift, which he was obligated to give by religious law so as to provide for the wife in case of death or divorce, would have been preserved in the marriage contract, the *ketubah*, which unfortunately was not preserved. In any event, it is highly probable that, as was customary, the bride's dowry was considerably higher than the groom's gift since the latter would still be only beginning to gain economic independence.[45]

The property offered as Hanina's dowry was far from certain, since a part of it was contingent on the family's ability to retrieve its mortgaged property from the sultan. Although the property was probably released in 1863, as we have seen, it was again seized in 1873. Hanina consequently delegated her brother-in-law, Meir Ben Hamu (Levy), who complained to the sultan that the various properties of her late father Aaron Amar "Bujnah," of which she was entitled to a third, had been seized for her father's debts. They were then released on condition that the debt that Aaron Amar owed the Makhzan be repaid. She claimed, however, that she had settled a third of the debt that her father had owed.[46] The arrangements established in the dowry of Hanina with her brother, Judah Amar, and her mother, Blida, were later reiterated. It was further declared that the ten thousand *riyal*s had been loaned entirely for the use of Judah Amar and Blida, and in return for

Hanina and her husband's not participating in the payment of the debt, they gave up their rights to a synagogue and house in Marrakesh.[47]

The financial difficulties of the family, and its continued difficulties in meeting the demands of the Makhzan, did not prevent the new sultan, Mawlay al-Hasan (1873–94), from renewing the decrees of his predecessors for Judah b. Aaron Bujnah,[48] and issuing another loan of one thousand *riyals*.[49] As with Judah's notorious ancestor, Meir Macnin, it was in the interest of the Makhzan to continue the relationship from generation to generation, not only because of the outstanding debt it claimed, but also because of its desire to closely control the activities of the merchant community. This was becoming increasingly difficult, especially with the expansion of foreign consular protection. In the latter half of the nineteenth century, nearly all the merchants with any significant business with Europe came under the protection of one foreign power or another. The protection offered by the foreign powers began to challenge the protection (*dhimma*) offered by the Islamic state, represented by the sultan.

Of those enjoying foreign protection, a disproportionate number were Moroccan Jews. In 1863–64, the most venerable leader of London's Jewish community, Sir Moses Montefiore (by now an elderly man), visited Morocco on a mission to obtain equal rights for Moroccan Jews. Montefiore, who made the arduous journey from Essaouira to Marrakesh in a sedan, was received by Sultan Muhammad and succeeded in obtaining a decree that promised the Jews justice and an end to corporal punishment.[50] However, whereas the Tanzimat reforms in the Ottoman Empire effectively did away with *dhimmi* status (at least in theory), and established new civil courts, the Moroccan sultan was from his point of view simply ratifying the existing system of justice within the framework of Islamic law: in other words, no civil status with equality for all was established, and Jews continued to pay *jizya*.

Thus, the means by which Jews could escape *dhimmi* status were not the legal changes implemented by the Moroccan state, but rather, becoming subjects or citizens of foreign powers, or protégés of foreign nations represented in Morocco. Jews who had formerly been employed by the sharifian state as a way to limit foreign influence now became agents of foreign penetration when Morocco was forced to liberalize trade under European pressure. Yet the reasons that many Jews invested their political futures in Europe affected the very nature of the relationship between Jews and the ʿAlawid state. As imperialism undermined the legitimacy of the Islamic polity, Jews in growing numbers repudiated the *dhimma* pact offered by the state and sought the protection of a foreign power. Foreign governments were increasingly encroaching on the sovereign rights of the Moroccan sultan.[51] A virtual marketplace developed whereby patents of protections were sold to the natives.

Competition between the foreign powers contributed to the rapid expansion of the system of protection. Efforts to end the abuses of protection, such as the convening of the international Madrid conference, failed to stem the tide.[52]

Thus, for Moroccan Jews, especially those in contact with foreign consulates, Europe and European Jewry had now become important arbiters of their welfare. No longer was their sole recourse the sultan of Morocco; they were now prepared to call on the assistance of the foreign powers whenever an injustice was committed. The British, who were the most important trading partners of Morocco, were seen as the most influential foreign power, and had numerous protégés. But the French were also important competitors. French influence in Morocco was helped by their invasion of neighboring Algeria in 1830, which became a French colony. Algerian Jews were considered subjects of France, and after 1870 with the issuance of the so-called Crémieux Decree, Algerian Jews were made French citizens en bloc. A growing number of Moroccan Jews went to Algeria, became subjects of France after a short stay, and then returned to Morocco with newfound rights.[53]

Although Aaron Amar "Bujnah" came to Morocco prior to France's occupation of Algeria, and though his wife was a native Moroccan subject, he and his family were subsequently to be regarded as beneficiaries of French protection. The Levy "Ben Hamu" family were more frequently protégés of the British, and members of the family settled in London where they continued to trade with Morocco. One of Hanina and Judah Levy's children, Haim, settled in London, and used for his telegraphic address "BEN-MACKNIN, LONDON," thus perpetuating the identity of his redoubtable ancestor.[54] Thus the question of the Macnin-Amar "Bujnah"-Levy "Ben Hamu" property was no longer simply a matter between the heirs and the sultans, but the foreign consulates as well became ensnared in the dispute. All the parties involved in the inheritance were prepared to vigorously assert their rights to the many properties.

In 1881 Judah Amar Bujnah introduced a new demand in his effort to acquit himself of his debt. He requested from the sultan that half his old debt be deducted, as had been done for all the merchants in 1270 (1853/54), and that it should be calculated in *mithqal*s. Because of inflation and losses in revenue, the Makhzan began translating debts that had been assessed in the money of account (*mithqal*s) into the silver currency (*riyal*s) at the current market rate of exchange. This was, of course, disadvantageous to the merchants paying off their old debt, and therefore he was cleverly requesting that the old system be applied retroactively to the old debt.[55] He also asked that his debt be reduced by the amount of the rent collected from his properties that was paid to the treasury from 1262 (1845/46) to 1280 (1863/64), and for his five houses sold in Marrakesh, whose price was also paid to the treasury. One of the five houses he bought back from the Makhzan by order of the sultan, and he claimed this should be deducted from his debt. Money, he claimed, should also be deducted from monthly installments that he paid to the financial officers of Essaouira.[56]

Unable to obtain any redress from the sultan for his grievances, Judah now turned to the French consulate, which sympathized with his plight and began entering into a correspondence with the financial officers of Essaouira. The French pointed out that the reduction of the merchants' debt by half was a concession made by Sultan ʿAbd al-Rahman due to the pillaging of the city during the French bombardment in 1844. "In his capacity as protégé of the most favored nation," argued the consular agent, "Judah Boudjenah should have naturally benefited from this advantage, but he was a minor and was unable to act by himself for his interests." The Makhzan submitted a claim of 21,977, while Judah claimed that the sultan owed him 19,222 *riyals*. The authorities would not agree to deduct from the debt for rent paid on the mortgaged properties, and they disputed the fact that all the debtors had had their obligations reduced by half after 1844. They did agree to look for the old account books concerning the property in Marrakesh and rental dues, but failed to locate the records.[57] Apparently, nothing was resolved at this time, with the Makhzan, the French, and the Amar family contesting both the debt and the property. What is certain is that much of the real estate remained in the hands of the two branches of Meir Macnin's descendants: Amar "Bujnah" and Levy "Ben Hamu," and the various family documents preserve a record of the inheritance of the properties and various rental agreements with individuals in Essaouira and Marrakesh.

The claims of Meir Macnin's descendants to the property did not go unchallenged. The French consulate in Mogador had been unwavering in its support of Amar, but the French legation in Tangier began making efforts to control the abusive expansion of protection. Consequently, in 1890, Judah Amar was one of three Jews removed from the list of those receiving patents of protection from the French consulate in Mogador. The justification for his removal was that the Crémieux Decree, which offered Algerian Jews French nationality, was issued after Judah had left Algeria.[58] Several years later, he protested this decision, supplying the consulate with declarations from persons in Algiers attesting to his having stayed in Algiers in 1883 and 1887, but his appeal was denied.[59] However, two of his sons, Aaron and David Amar, moved to Algiers, where they were able to obtain French nationality, probably serving in the French army in World War I.[60]

Morocco increasingly came into France's sphere of influence, and in 1912, French domination over most of Morocco was secured with the beginning of the occupation of the country, which was to last until 1956. Spain occupied the northern coastal regions and some of the adjoining hinterlands, while the city of Tangier was given international status. Unlike their colony in Algiers, the French classified Morocco with Tunisia which had been occupied in 1882, as a "protectorate." What this signified in theory was that Moroccan institutions were to remain intact, but were simply to be reformed under French tutelage. In fact, only the skeleton of the former Moroccan administration remained, while true power rested in the hands of the French authorities, headed by a resident-general.

Two separate systems of administration were formed, one led by the sultan and the other by the resident-general. French courts were established, independent of the indigenous courts, to judge any cases involving Europeans. Jews who had been French protégés before the protectorate lost their privileged status (though protégés of other foreign countries generally retained their status). The Westernized Jews hoped to be made subject to the European courts, but they were to be disappointed. Moroccan Jews were still considered subjects of the sultan and under sharifian jurisdiction. Cases between Moroccans, regardless of their religion, were to come under the jurisdiction of the Makhzan. Although the Jews were no longer subject to the stipulations governing the *dhimmi*s, nor subject to the inequities and disabilities of the *shariᶜa* courts based on the Maliki school of jurisprudence, they were formally recognized as "indigenous," a status resented by the Westernized elite. What constituted Moroccan nationality remained deliberately ambiguous. The protectorate authorities thus effectively eliminated *dhimmi* status, without establishing a coherent new legal framework for the Jews.[61]

The various aspects of the Moroccan administration, including the institutions of Jewish self-government, were taken over, reorganized, and supervised by the French authorities within a few years after the establishment of the protectorate. The administration of property, whether private or belonging to religious endowments (*hubus*) or the Makhzan, was registered and controlled by the French administration (the "Contrôle des Domaines"). The instrument of control on a local level was the French *contrôleur civil*. In this new framework of administration, the question of the various Macnin/Bujnah/Levy properties again reemerged.

Essaouira's role as an international port rapidly declined in the twentieth century, as the center of commerce shifted northward to the rapidly developing seaport of Casablanca, soon to become Morocco's biggest city. Few opportunities existed in the colonial economy for the merchants of Essaouira, and the number who were able to make a living from trade, as well as the size and geographical scope of their business, grew considerably smaller. For those of the Jewish elite who stayed in Essaouira, often little remained of their former wealth other than the rent derived from property whose value was undoubtedly diminishing. The Amar and Levy families reflected this situation of diminishing returns, living off the income of their jointly held rental property in Essaouira and Marrakesh.[62]

Already in 1918, authorities began demanding evidence that the many properties held by the family were truly inherited or that they had obtained the right of tenancy for the many properties. In the 1920s, of the two branches of the family, Aaron Levy was a British protégé, and Haim Levy was a naturalized British subject, while Aaron and David Amar were French citizens; both sides of the family claimed to jointly hold considerable property.[63] In 1925, the French administration challenged their right to the properties, and evoking the story of the old debt owed the sultan, demanded evidence that they were freehold rather than Makhzan-owned.[64] The case was sent to the Service des Domaines in Rabat, the capital of the French protectorate. The family vigorously protested this attack on their inheritance, and were ultimately victorious. In a letter to the attorney representing the family in Casablanca, the head of the Service des Domaines in Rabat wrote: "I have just authorized the inspector of my department in Mogador to bring to an end the opposition of the Service des Domaines to establishing title to the requested property by the heirs of Amar Bou Jenah [*sic*] for the properties they own in Mogador."[65] The properties of the heirs of the late Judah Amar Bujnah and Judah Ben Hamu Levy in Essaouira were finally assessed and registered by the government authorities as well as by the notaries of the rabbinical court. This included various houses and parts of houses, shops, half of a caravanserai (*funduq*), a mill, an oven, and a synagogue. Other properties were also inherited in Marrakesh.[66]

It was thanks to Samuel Lévy-Corcos, the grandson of Hanina and Judah Levy "Ben Hamu," and the great-great-grandson of Meir Macnin, living modestly in Paris in the 1980s, that this story is told through the family papers. It is now clear why so many of the documents pertaining to real estate holdings were kept for generations, for it was through these properties that the descendants of Meir Macnin were able to live a life of relative affluence until their departure from Morocco. As Essaouira's economic position declined, the value of these properties and the rents that the family derived from them diminished significantly. Some of the old elite of Morocco, unable to adapt to the new conditions imposed by the colonial economy, became a decadent bourgeoisie, with their houses little more than large empty shells, and with hardly enough money to subsist on.

The growth of trade with Europe following the era of the Macnins gave considerable opportunities to Moroccan Jewish merchants, and this has been seen as marking the beginning of "Jewish capitalism" in Morocco.[67] This "Jewish capitalism," however, remained confined to a marginal sector. The Jewish merchants hardly constituted a social class. Investment opportunities

were lacking in Morocco, and as a result, few Moroccan merchants were independent agents. Jewish merchants, including Macnin, Amar-Bujnah, and
Levy, were *dhimmi*s, tied to the sultan in a relationship of debt. Since the
Makhzan itself was plunging deeper and deeper into debt, the situation
hardly provided these merchants with any kind of assurance of economic
protection. Consequently, by the end of the century, many Moroccan Jewish
merchants were in serious financial trouble or went bankrupt. Both the
Makhzan, hard pressed for money to repay its own debts, and foreign creditors quarreled over claims on the assets of these Moroccan Jewish merchants. Those who were able to protect their fortunes did so because they
sent their investments abroad.[68] The Moroccan Jewish merchants, therefore,
did not represent an independent social class, emerging from changes in the
local economy. Traditionally a marginal group without any significant political roots, many of the wealthiest Jews became even more marginal in the
nineteenth century, as protégés of foreign powers.

The story of Meir Macnin and his legacy reveals the extent to which en-
trepreneurial opportunities were limited in Morocco. Indebted either to
the Makhzan or to the foreign powers, the Jewish elite in Morocco was vulnerable and relatively powerless in the expanding market with Europe, unless they chose to plant their roots deeply in foreign soil. They were rarely
agents of transition, but tended instead to be conservative, even reluctant,
partners in the modernization of the Jewish community.

Despite the many years that Meir Macnin lived in England, he did not
return to Morocco with ideas about how to transform his own society. He
belonged instead to the Moroccan community, a symbol of the time when
two contrasting worlds were growing further and further apart.

The final rupture between Western European Jewry and Moroccan and
other Jewish communities of Asia and Africa took place during the span of
Meir Macnin's life. At the beginning of his story, there was still some sense
of an interconnected Sephardi world; but by the 1830s, the Sephardi Diaspora that had formerly bridged both the Mediterranean and the Atlantic
had lost much of its meaning. The perception of a sharp division between
the Muslim world and Europe, between East and West, now profoundly affected the Jewish world. The Sephardi origins of Jews of North Africa and
the Middle East were no longer of great relevance to European Jews, who
now viewed their coreligionists in Muslim countries as "Oriental" Jews, belonging to a decayed civilization that awaited emancipation. This sense of a
great cultural divide in the Jewish world between East and West still exists
today, especially in Israel, where the majority of "Oriental" Jews now live.

Reference Matter

Notes

The following abbreviations of archival sources are used in the notes:

AEP   Ministère des Affaires Etrangères, Paris
AEN   Ministère des Affaires Etrangères, Nantes
ANP   Archives Nationales, Paris
ARH   Algemeen Rijksarchief, The Hague
  CO   Colonial Office records, Public Record Office, London
  FO   Foreign Office records, Public Record Office, London. Unless otherwise indicated, these references cite reports to the Foreign Office in London.
  KH   al-Khizanat al-Hasaniyya, Rabat
  LP   Private Papers of S. Lévy, Paris. Unless otherwise indicated, the names following the dates of documents are those of rabbis or notaries who were signatories.
  NA   National Archives, Diplomatic Branch, Washington, D.C.
PRO   Public Record Office, London
  SP   State Papers, Public Record Office, London
SPJC   Spanish and Portuguese Jews' Congregation (Bevis Marks), London

Chapter 1. Introduction: Court Jews and Muslim-Jewish Relations in Morocco

    1. A recent study of the phenomenon of the court Jew in Morocco treats the period only up until Meir Macnin's career begins. See Nicole S. Serfaty, *Les courtisans juifs des sultans marocains: Hommes politiques et hauts dignitaires, XIIIe–XVIIIe siècles* (Paris: Editions Bouchène, 1999).
    2. Most influential in establishing this view of medieval Spanish Jewry was the

German-Jewish historian Heinrich H. Graetz. See his *History of the Jews*, 6 vols. (Philadelphia: Jewish Publication Society of America, 1891–98), vol. 3. Both Eliyahu Ashtor, *The Jews of Moslem Spain*, 3 vols. (Philadelphia: Jewish Publication Society of America, 1973–84), and Yitzhak Baer, *A History of the Jews in Christian Spain*, 2 vols. (Philadelphia: Jewish Publication Society of America, 1961), devote much attention to the court Jews who come to emblematize a particular age in Hispano-Jewish history. See Eleazar Gutwirth, "Abraham Seneor: Social Tensions and the Court-Jew," in *Michael*, vol. 11, ed. Eleazar Gutwirth and Shlomo Simonsohn (Tel-Aviv: The Diaspora Research Institute, 1989), 169–70.

3. *The Jews of Spain: A History of the Sephardi Experience* (New York: The Free Press, 1992), 44.

4. Cf. Norman A. Stillman and Yedida K. Stillman, "The Jewish Courtier Class in Late Eighteenth-Century Morocco as Seen through the Eyes of Samuel Romanelli," in *Essays in Honor of Bernard Lewis: The Islamic World from Classical to Modern Times*, ed. C. E. Bosworth et al. (Princeton, N.J.: Darwin Press, 1988), 845.

5. Studies of the court Jew have been inspired by the famous *Hofjuden* of western and central Europe, the subject of the influential book by Selma Stern, *The Court Jew: A Contribution to the History of Absolutism in Central Europe* (Philadelphia: Jewish Publication Society of America, 1950). Following her lead, and using primarily Arabic sources, Walter J. Fischel studied the "court Jews" of the medieval Islamic world in *Jews in the Economic and Political Life of Mediaeval Islam* (New York: Ktav Publishing House, 1969). One of Fischel's main portraits, that of Yaʿqub Ibn Killis, is taken out of context since this famous vizier in the tenth-century Fatimid court was a convert to Islam and totally devoted to the Ismaʿili creed of the Egyptian state. See Yaacov Lev, "The Fatimid Vizier Yaʿqub Ibn Killis and the Beginning of the Fatimid Administration in Egypt," *Der Islam* 58 (1981): 238.

6. Michel Abitbol, *Le passé d'une discorde: Juifs et Arabes depuis le VIIᵉ siècle à nos jours* (Paris: Perrin, 1999), 96–104. On two prominent courtiers, see Cecil Roth, *The House of Nasi: The Duke of Naxos* (Philadelphia: Jewish Publication Society of America, 1948); idem, *Doña Gracia of the House of Nasi* (Philadelphia: Jewish Publication Society of America, 1948).

7. For a discussion of Jewish courtiers in the Marinid period from the thirteenth to the fifteenth centuries, see Maya Shatzmiller, "An Ethnic Factor in a Medieval Social Revolution: The Role of Jewish Courtiers under the Marinids," in *Islamic Society and Culture: Essays in Honour of Professor Aziz Ahmad*, ed. Milton Israel and N. K. Wagle (New Delhi: Manohar, 1983), 149–163; idem, *The Berbers and the Islamic State: The Marinid Experience in Pre-Protectorate Morocco* (Princeton, N.J.: Markus Wiener, 2000), 57–68.

8. Yosef Kaplan, "Court Jews before the *Hofjuden*," in *From Court Jews to the Rothschilds: Art, Patronage, and Power, 1600–1800*, ed. Vivian B. Mann and Richard I. Cohen (Munich: Prestel, 1996), 13–16.

9. Stern, *The Court Jew*, 3–11; Michael Graetz, "Court Jews in Economics and Politics," in Mann and Cohen, *From Court Jews to the Rothschilds*, 27.

10. Serfaty, *Les courtisans juifs*, 203.

11. See, especially, H. Z. Hirschberg, *A History of the Jews in North Africa*, 2 vols. (Leiden: Brill, 1974–81), 2:88ff.

12. Norman A. Stillman, *The Jews of Arab Lands* (Philadelphia: Jewish Publication Society of America, 1979), 78–85; idem, "The Moroccan Jewish Experience: A Revisionist View," *Jerusalem Quarterly* 9 (1978); Jane Gerber, "The Pact of ʿUmar in Morocco: A Reappraisal of Muslim-Jewish Relations," in *Proceedings of the Seminar on Muslim-Jewish Relations in North Africa* (New York: World Jewish Congress 1975). Bernard Lewis argues that the two main communities that were outside the Ottoman Empire, the Jews of Morocco and Iran, fared worse. *The Jews of Islam* (Princeton, N.J.: Princeton University Press, 1984), 148–50. For a critique of this book, see my review in *International Journal of Middle East Studies* 21 (1989): 601–5.

13. See especially Germain Ayache, "La minorité juive dans la Maroc précolonial," *Hespéris-Tamuda* 25 (1987): 147–68. The protective role of the government in the construction of Jewish quarters is emphasized by ʿAbd al-ʿAziz al-Khamlishi, "Hawla masʾala binaʾ al-mahattat bi-al-mudun al-maghribiya," *Dar al-Niyaba* 4 (spring 1987): 21–28, 5 (summer/fall 1988): 30–41.

14. Mohammed Kenbib, "Les relations entre Musulmans et Juifs au Maroc, 1859–1944: Essai bibliographique," *Hespéris-Tamuda* 23 (1985): 92–98; and more generally, idem, *Juifs et Musulmans au Maroc, 1859–1948* (Rabat: Université Mohammed V, Publications de la Faculté des Lettres et des Sciences Humaines, 1996), and idem, *Les protégés: contribution à l'histoire contemporaine du Maroc* (Rabat: Université Mohammed V, Publications de la Faculté des Lettres et des Sciences Humaines, 1994), 225–32; Ayache, "La minorité juive," 162–63; Simon Lévy, "La communauté juive dans le contexte de l'histoire du Maroc du 17ᵉ siècle à nos jours," in *Juifs du Maroc: identité et dialogue* (Grenoble: Editions La Pensée Sauvage, 1980), 105–52. See also Leland Bowie, "An Aspect of Muslim-Jewish Relations in Late Nineteenth-Century Morocco: A European Diplomatic View," *International Journal of Middle Eastern Studies* 7 (1976): 3–19. On the impact of foreign interference on Muslim-Jewish relations in Demnat, see Ahmad Tawfiq, *al-Mujtamaʿ al-maghribi fi al-qarn al-tasiʿ ʿashr: Inultan (1850–1912)*, 2 vols. (Rabat: Manshurat Kulliyat al-Adab wa-al-ʿUlum al-Insaniyya bi-al-Rabat, 1978–1980), 1:304–10.

15. For the title of the book by Bernard Lewis, see note 12. For an effort at broad generalizations about the condition of Jews in Islam, see G. E. von Grunebaum, "Eastern Jewry under Islam," *Viator* 2 (1971): 365–72.

16. Cf. Bernard Lewis, "The Pro-Islamic Jews," *Judaism* 17 (1968): 401–4; I. G. Marcus, "Beyond the Sephardic Mystique," *Orim* 1 (1985): 35–38.

17. Most influential was S. D. Goitein's *Jews and Arabs: Their Contacts through the Ages* (New York: Schocken, 1955); his ideas on symbiosis are further elaborated in *A Mediterranean Society*, 6 vols. (Berkeley: University of California Press, 1967–1993), vol. 2: *The Community*. For a nuanced reconsideraton of the use of the concept of symbiosis in early Islam, see Steven M. Wasserstrom, *Between Muslim and Jew: The Problem of Symbiosis under Early Islam* (Princeton, N.J.: Princeton University Press, 1995).

18. S. D. Goitein, *A Mediterranean Society*, vol. 1: *Economic Foundations* (Berkeley: University of California Press, 1967), 1–2.

19. Goitein, *Jews and Arabs*, 10–11.

20. Lewis, *The Jews of Islam*, 57–58, 140ff.

21. Goitein, *A Mediterranean Society*, 1:ix. Curiously, neither Goitein nor Lewis

draws comparisons to the Jews in the Hellenistic world, despite the fact that Islamic civilization was at least in part heir to this earlier cultural matrix.

22. Lewis, *The Jews of Islam.*

23. *Études et recherches sur la vie intellectuelle juive au Maroc de la fin du 15ᵉ au début du 20ᵉ siècle,* 3 vols. (Paris: Geuthner, 1972–80).

24. Haïm Zafrani, *Mille ans de vie juive au Maroc* (Paris: G.-P. Maisonneuve et Larose, 1983), 290.

25. Bat Ye'or, *The Dhimmi: Jews and Christians under Islam* (Rutherford, N.J.: Fairleigh Dickinson University Press, 1985); David Littman, "Jews under Muslim Rule in the Late Nineteenth Century," *Wiener Library Bulletin* 28 (1975): 65–76. The terms "antisemitism" and "pogroms" are sometimes applied to the Moroccan scene. See, for instance, Shalom Bar-Asher, "Antisemitism and Economic Influence: The Jews of Morocco (1672–1822)," in *Antisemitism through the Ages,* ed. Shmuel Almog (Oxford: Pergamon Press, 1988), 195–215.

26. See the debate between Mark R. Cohen, "The Neo-Lachrymose Conception of Jewish-Arab History," *Tikkun* 6, no. 3 (1991): 55–60, and Norman Stillman, "Myth, Counter-Myth and Distortion," ibid., 60–64. See also Mark R. Cohen, *Under Crescent and Cross* (Princeton, N.J.: Princeton University Press, 1994), 3ff.

27. Daniel Boyarin and Jonathan Boyarin, "Diaspora: Generation and the Ground of Jewish Identity," *Critical Inquiry* 19 (1993): 720–23.

28. *After Jews and Arabs: Remaking Levantine Culture* (Minneapolis: University of Minnesota Press, 1993), 128–43.

29. James Clifford, *Routes: Travel and Translation in the Late Twentieth Century* (Cambridge, Mass.: Harvard University Press, 1997), 274.

30. A classic study of *dhimmi* status is Antoine Fattal, *Le statut légal des non-musulmans en pays d'Islam* (Beirut: Impr. Catholique, 1958). For other useful discussions, see Stillman, *Jews of Arab Lands,* 24–26; Lewis, *Jews of Islam,* 3ff; Cohen, *Under Crescent and Cross,* 52–74; C. E. Bosworth, "The 'Protected Peoples' (Christians and Jews) in Medieval Egypt and Syria," *Bulletin of the John Rylands University Library of Manchester* 62 (1979), 11–36; idem, "The Concept of *Dhimma* in Early Islam," in *Christians and Jews in the Ottoman Empire,* ed. Benjamin Braude and Bernard Lewis, 2 vols. (New York: Holmes & Meier, 1982), 1:37–51.

31. S. D. Goitein, *A Mediterranean Society,* 1:66–70.

32. Abdallah Laroui, *Les origines sociales et culturelles du nationalisme marocain, 1830–1912* (Paris: Maspero, 1977), 310–14.

33. The reasons for the disappearance of indigenous Christians in the Maghrib are far from clear, but a number of factors should be mentioned: the weak Christianization of many regions before the rise of Islam, the rapid Islamization of the Berber tribes after the Muslim conquests, the expansion of the Hillalian Bedouin into the Maghrib in the eleventh century, and the persecution of non-Muslims by the Almohads in the twelfth century. See Xavier de Planhol, *Minorités en Islam: Géographie politique et sociale* (Paris: Flammarion, 1997), 194–201.

34. For discussions of the variety of Muslim-Jewish relations in Morocco, see Moshe Shokeid, "Jewish Existence in a Berber Environment," in *Les relations entre Juifs et Musulmans en Afrique du Nord, XIXᵉ–XXᵉ siècles* (Paris: Centre National de la Recherche Scientifique, 1980), 62–71; Norman A. Stillman, "Muslims and Jews in

Morocco: Perceptions, Images, Stereotypes," in *Proceedings of the Seminar on Muslim-Jewish Relations in Morocco*, 13–26; Lawrence Rosen, "Muslim-Jewish Relations in a Moroccan City," *International Journal of Middle Eastern Studies* 3 (1972): 435–49; Allan R. Meyers, "Patronage and Protection: The Status of Jews in Precolonial Morocco," in *Jews among Muslims: Communities in the Precolonial Middle East*, ed. Shlomo Deshen and Walter Zenner (London: Macmillan, 1996), 83–97.

35. Lawrence Rosen, *Bargaining for Reality: The Construction of Social Relations in a Muslim Community* (Chicago: University of Chicago Press, 1984), 162.

36. Henry Munson, Jr., "Muslim and Jew in Morocco: Reflections on the Distinction between Belief and Behavior," *Poznań Studies in the Philosophy of the Sciences and Humanities* 48 (1996): 376.

37. Cf. Rosen, *Bargaining for Reality*, 152–53; Daniel J. Schroeter, "Trade as a Mediator in Muslim-Jewish Relations: Southwestern Morocco in the Nineteenth Century," in *Jews among Arabs: Contacts and Boundaries*, ed. Mark R. Cohen and Abraham L. Udovitch (Princeton, N.J.: Darwin Press, 1989), 113–14; Kenneth L. Brown, "Mellah and Madina: A Moroccan City and Its Jewish Quarter (Salé, ca. 1880–1930)," in *Studies in Judaism and Islam*, ed. S. Morag et al. (Jerusalem: Magnes Press, The Hebrew University, 1981), 253–81.

38. See my "Royal Power and the Economy in Precolonial Morocco: Jews and the Legitimation of Foreign Trade," in *In the Shadow of the Sultan: Culture, Power, and Politics in Morocco*, ed. Rahmah Bourqia and Susan G. Miller (Cambridge, Mass.: Harvard University Press, 1999), 74–102.

39. Cf. Andrew C. Hess, *The Forgotten Frontier* (Chicago: University of Chicago Press, 1978); Jacques Berque, *L'intérieur du Maghreb, XVᵉ–XIXᵉ siècle* (Paris: Gallimard, 1978), 171–76; Johan de Bakker, "Slaves, Arms, and Holy War: Moroccan Policy *vis-à-vis* the Dutch Republic during the Establishment of the ʿAlawi Dynasty," (Ph.D. diss., University of Amsterdam, 1991), 4–9.

40. Patricia Mercer, "Palace and *Jihad* in the Early ʿAlawi State in Morocco," *Journal of African History* 18 (1977): 535, 546–53.

41. Hayyim Bentov, "le-Demuto shel ha-sar Shmuel ibn Sunbal," in *Zekhor le-Avraham: kovets maʾamarim le-zekher R. Avraham Elmalih*, ed. H. Z. Hirschberg (Jerusalem: Vaʿad ʿAdat ha-Maʿaravim bi-Yerushalayim, 1972); Cecil Roth, "The Amazing Clan of Buzaglo," *Transactions of the Jewish Historical Society of England* 23 (1971): 11–22; idem, "Jacob Benider: Moroccan Envoy at the Court of St. James (1772)," *Miscellanies of the Jewish Historical Society of England* 2 (1935): 84–90. On the Palaches, see Herbert I. Bloom, *The Economic Activities of the Jews of Amsterdam in the Seventeenth and Eighteenth Centuries* (Williamsport, Pa.: The Bayard Press, 1937), 79–82; David Corcos, "Shmuel Palache ve-mishpato be-London," in *Studies in the History of the Jews of Morocco* (Jerusalem: Rubin Mass, 1976).

42. Cf. John Waterbury, *The Commander of the Faithful* (London: Weidenfeld and Nicolson, 1970), 16–18.

43. This sense of separation of both monarchs and court Jews has been examined for seventeenth-century central Europe. See Stern, *The Court Jew*, 9–12.

44. Muhammad Daʾud, *Tarikh Titwan* (Tetuan: Imprimerie Royale, 1979), 8:81–82, cited and analyzed by Ayache, "La minorité juive," 155.

45. An example of this is in a letter found in the Corcos papers from the prince

and future sultan, Muhammad b. ʿAbd al-Rahman, concerning the prominent merchant Shlomo Corcos in 1843. Michel Abitbol, *Tugʾar al-sultan: ʿIlit kalkalit yehudit be-Maroko* (Jerusalem: Mekhon Ben Tsevi, 1994), 1, 2 n. 5. The term, however, implies more a sense of proprietorship than simple friendship and familiarity suggested in this analysis of the text.

46. LP, 13 Rabiʿ II 1209 = 7 November 1794, Mawlay ʿAbd al-Salam to Mawlay ʿAbd al-Malik. It is Meir Macnin who is referred to as "our chattel."

47. Slaves were also not merely objects but also persons, according to Islamic law. In Morocco, there was a wide variety of slave statuses, depending on functions and whether they were slaves of the Makhzan or individuals. See Mohammed Ennaji, *Serving the Master: Slavery and Society in Nineteenth-Century Morocco* (New York: St. Martin's Press, 1999), 88–96; John Hunwick, "Black Africans in the Mediterranean World: Introduction to a Neglected Aspect of the African Diaspora," *Slavery and Abolition* 13, no. 1 (1992): 6–14.

48. John Hunwick, "Islamic Law and Polemics over Race and Slavery in North and West Africa (16th–19th Century)," in *Slavery in the Islamic Middle East*, ed. Shaun E. Marmon (Princeton, N.J.: Markus Wiener, 1999), 44.

49. *Power and Powerlessness in Jewish History* (New York: Schocken Books, 1986), 6.

50. Salo W. Baron, *A Social and Religious History of the Jews*, 2d ed., 18 vols. (New York: Columbia University Press, 1952–83), 4:41, 70ff.

51. Kenneth R. Stow, "Papal and Royal Attitudes toward Jewish Lending in the Thirteenth Century," *Association for Jewish Studies Review* 6 (1981): 161–74.

52. Léon Poliakov, *Les Banchieri juifs et le Saint-Siège du XIIIᵉ au XVIIIᵉ siècle* (Paris: Ecole Pratique des Hautes Etudes, 1965), 50–66.

53. Schroeter, "Royal Power," 84–86.

54. E.g., the community of Tetuan in 1184 = 1770–1771. ʿAbd al-Rahman Ibn Zaydan, *Ithaf aʿlam al-nas bi-jamal akhbar hadirat Miknas*, 5 vols. (Rabat: al-Matbaʿat al-Wataniya "li-Sahibiha ʿAbbas al-Thanani wa-Muhammad al-Qabbaj," 1929–33), 3:255.

55. For the history of this period, I have relied on the authoritative study of Mohamed El Mansour, *Morocco in the Reign of Mawlay Sulayman* (Wisbech, Cambridgeshire: MENAS Press, 1990).

56. Ibid., 22.

57. Ibid., 137–43; see also Rachid Abdallah El-Nasser, "Morocco from Kharijism to Wahhabism: The Quest for Religious Purism" (Ph.D. diss., University of Michigan, 1983), 478ff.

Chapter 2. The Rise of the Macnins

1. Birthdays were generally unknown, and there is no record of Meir Macnin's birth. The earliest document with Meir Macnin's name dates from 1787, a legal document in which the "young man" (*bahur*) Meir purchases a piece of property in Essaouira. LP, 2 Heshvan 5548 = 14 October 1787, signed Yehuda b. Masʿud Alʿankri (second signature unclear).

2. Jacopo Gråberg di Hemsö, *Specchio geografico e statistico dell'impero di Marocco* (Genoa: Dalla Tipografia Pellas, 1834), 58; Gaston Deverdun, *Marrakech, des origines à 1912*, 2 vols. (Rabat: Editions Techniques Nord-Africaines, 1959–66), 1:597–98. An

earlier European traveler who visited Marrakesh in 1804 cites two thousand Jews. Domingo Badia y Leyblich, *Travels of Ali Bey* (London: Longman, Hurst, Rees, Orme and Brown, 1816), 155. The small number of Jewish inhabitants in 1804 might reflect the high death rate during the bubonic plague of 1799–1800.

3. John Davidson, *Notes Taken during Travels in Africa* (London: Printed by J. L. Cox and Sons, 1839), 39.

4. Scholars differ in interpreting sources on the Jews of Marrakesh in this period. David Corcos quite emphatically states that there were Jews, and even Jewish mercenaries, in Marrakesh at the time of the Almohad conquest. "Le-ofi yahasim shel shalite ha-Almawahhidun le-Yehudim," in *Studies in the History of the Jews of Morocco* (Jerusalem: Rubin Mass, 1976), 326–27. H. Z. Hirschberg, however, does not believe that Jews lived there at the time of conquest. *A History of the Jews in North Africa*, 2 vols. (Leiden: Brill, 1974–81), 1:124–25. Deverdun, citing Yusuf b. Taghibirdi, *al-Nujum al-Zahira*, writes that the Jews probably took refuge within the ramparts of Marrakesh during the Almohad siege, and only those who embraced Islam saved their lives. *Marrakech*, 1:277.

5. Corcos, "Le-ofi yahasim," 320–21.

6. Ibid., 54.

7. Deverdun, *Marrakech*, 1:338–39; Hirschberg, *History of the Jews*, 1:428–29.

8. Roger Le Tourneau, *Fez in the Age of the Marinides* (Norman: University of Oklahoma Press, 1961), 11–13; Ahmed Khaneboubi, *Les premiers sultans Mérinids (1269–1331)* (Paris: Editions L'Harmattan, 1987), 56–58.

9. A number of studies have focused on the creation of the *mellah* in Marrakesh, frequently citing a local Jewish tradition that 1557 marked the date. Corcos, "Les Juifs au Maroc et leurs *mellahs*," in *Studies*, 81–85; Deverdun, *Marrakech*, 1:363–66; Hirschberg, *History of the Jews*, 2:190. The tradition of this date is probably associated with the rise of the Saʿdian sultan, Mawlay ʿAbdallah al-Ghalib, to power in Marrakesh that year. For a recent and persuasive explanation of the formation of the *mellah* of Marrakesh, see Emily R. Gottreich, "Jewish Space in the Moroccan City: A History of the Mellah of Marrakesh, 1550–1930" (Ph.D. diss., Harvard University, 1999), 19–65. On the etymology of the word *mellah*, see Simon Lévy, "Hara et Mellāḥ: les mots, l'histoire et l'institution," in *Histoire et linguistique*, Colloques et Seminaires nº 20, ed. Abdelahad Sebti (Rabat: Université Mohammad V, Publications de la Faculté des Lettres et des Sciences Humaines, 1992), 41–50.

10. Gottreich, "Jewish Space," 65–72.

11. This tradition is found in a late nineteenth-century manuscript, but apparently based on older family papers. The list of these families is found in Corcos, "Juifs au Maroc," 109. I was not able to locate this manuscript in the family collection, but have no reason to doubt its authenticity and Corcos's critical judgment. The Spanish archives report that at the end of August 1778, an agreement was reached between Sumbal and the Sultan. Sumbal was to pay eleven thousand ducats and to present four guarantors of that amount; in exchange he was put in charge of the port of Mogador. Mariano Arribas Palau, "Datos sobre Samuel Sumbel y sus relaciones con España," *Sefarad* 40 (1980): 134; Ramón Lourido Díaz, "Los Judios en Marruecos durante el sultanato de Sidi Muhammad b. Abd Allah (1757–1790)," *Miscelánea de Estudios Arabes y Hebraicos*, 26–28, (1977–79): 341–45.

12. Louis Chénier, *Un Chargé d'Affaires au Maroc: Le correspondance du consul Louis Chénier: 1767–1782*, ed. Pierre Grillon (Paris: S.E.V.P.E.N., 1970), 101.

13. Ibid., 111–12; Georg Høst, *Histoire de l'Empereur du Maroc Mohamed Ben Abdallah*, trans. F. Damgaard and P. Gailhanou, with a preface by Jean-Louis Miège (Rabat: Editions La Porte, 1998; first published in Danish in 1791), 29, 31.

14. From a Makhzan register book. ʿAbd al-Rahman Ibn Zaydan, *Ithaf aʿlam al-nas bi-jamal akhbar hadirat Miknas*, 5 vols. (Rabat: al-Matbaʿat al-Wataniya "li-Sahibiha ʿAbbas al-Thanani wa-Muhammad al-Qabbaj," 1929–33), 3:254.

15. Ahmad ibn al-Mahdi al-Ghazzal, *Natijat al-ijtihad fi al-muhadanah wa-al-jihad*: "rihlat al-Ghazzal wa-safaratuh ila al-Andalus" (Algier: Diwan al-Matbuʿat al-Jamiʿiya, 1984), 38; Ahmad b. Khalid al-Nasiri, *al-Istiqsaʾ li-akhbar duwal al-Maghrib al-Aqsa*, 9 vols., 2d ed. (Casablanca: Dar al-Kitab, 1954–56), 8:20–21; Louis Chénier, *Recherches historiques sur les Maures et histoire de l'Empire de Maroc*, 3 vols. (Paris: l'Imprimerie Polytype, 1787), 3:39–40, 468–69; idem, *Un chargé d'Affaires*, 69, 130–31, 197, 297, 715; ANP, AE/B¹/843, "Mémoire sur le commerce de Mogador," 7 February 1789; AEP, Mémoires et Documents, 2 (1775), fol. 447; Høst, *Histoire de l'Empereur*, 33–34, 36; Raymond Thomassy, *Le Maroc et ses caravanes ou relations de la France avec cet Empire* (Paris: F. Didot Frères, 1845), 324–27.

16. Based on the same manuscript, Corcos refers to the arrival of the Macnin family, but without giving a precise date. He mentions Abraham's two sons, Masud and Meir, but does not mention Shlomo and David. Corcos, "Juifs au Maroc," 114. Shlomo is referred to in the European documents as Solomon and Salomon, as Shlomo in the Hebrew documents, and as Shlomo and Shalom in the Arabic sources. Since his career was spent in Morocco, I write "Shlomo," as the Hebrew name is commonly spelled. Several errors in chronology and some confusion in the roles of the different brothers is found in David Corcos's article "Macnin," in *Encyclopaedia Judaica*, 11:675. Abraham had at least two daughters, since reference is made to his two sons-in-law.

17. Colonel Keatinge, *Travels in Europe and Africa*, 2 vols. (London: Printed for Henry Colburn, 1816), 1:193. Mohamed El Mansour pointed out to me that this still happens today whenever there is a shortage of hotel suites, especially during international meetings when the palace accommodates its guests in the private homes of rich Moroccans; it is considered an honor to host royal guests.

18. Maxime Rodinson, *Islam and Capitalism* (Austin: University of Texas Press, 1978), 14–19; for a comparison of Christian and Muslim attitudes toward profit and interest, see Mark R. Cohen, *Under Crescent and Cross: The Jews in the Middle Ages* (Princeton, N.J.: Princeton University Press, 1994), 77–103.

19. Tahir Fannish was one of the principal diplomatic agents of the sultan. He negotiated with the foreign diplomatic representatives in Morocco; he was, for example, involved in concluding a treaty with the United States in 1786. He was an ambassador on numerous foreign missions, engaged in negotiations to obtain arms, release Muslim captives, among other matters, in London (1773–74), Paris (1778), Gibraltar (1778), and Istanbul (1783–84, 1787–88, 1790); he may also have been governor of Essaouira around 1777–78. On his various activities, see Ramón Lourido Díaz, *Marruecos y el mundo exterior en la segunda mitad del siglo XVIII* (Madrid: Agencia Española de Cooperación Internacional, 1989), passim; see also Høst, *His-*

toire de l'Empereur, 76, 96–97, 117. On his negotiations with the United States, see Mariano Arribas Palau, "Documentación española sobre las primeras relaciones entre Marruecos y los Estados Unidos de America del Norte," *Hespéris-Tamuda* 17 (1976–77): 116–17. Correspondence on his embassy to London is found in SP 71/21, 20 December 1773; and FO 52/3, 3 August 1773, Charles Logie (British consul general in Tangier). Al-Nasiri (*al-Istiqsaʾ*, 8:60) also refers to a mission to Istanbul in 1200 = 1785/86; it is possible that his date is incorrect.

20. AEN, Tanger 87, Mogador, 9 July 1789, Anᵈ Layton & Compᵉ to Du Rocher. He was still reported to be in prison by the Dutch consular agent: ARH, Consulaat Tanger 1, 17 July 1789, Subremont to Blount. Fannish had served the sultan as emissary to England in 1773; FO 52/3, Gibraltar, 3 August 1773, Logie. He continued to work as a diplomatic agent in Morocco; FO 52/4, Mogador, 11 February 1782.

21. A very static view of the functions of the *nagid*, who is seen as often presiding over the *maʿamad* or council of the community, is given by Haïm Zafrani, *Etudes et recherches sur la vie intellectuelle juive au Maroc de la fin du 15ᵉ siècle au début du 20ᵉ siècle*, vol. 1: *Pensée juridique et environnement social, économique et religieux* (Paris: Geuthner, 1972), 106–9. The role and influence of the *nagid* was in fact malleable, shaped more by his relationship with Muslim potentates and his own personality than his formal position. See Shlomo Deshen, *The Mellah Society: Jewish Community Life in Sherifian Morocco* (Chicago: University of Chicago Press, 1989), 53–61.

22. Cf. Deshen, *Mellah Society*, 57–58.

23. Samuel Romanelli, *Travail in an Arab Land*, trans. Yedida K. Stillman and Norman A. Stillman (Tuscaloosa: The University of Alabama Press, 1989).

24. Ibid., 124.

25. Pierre Flamand, *Diaspora en terre d'Islam: les communautés israélites du sud marocain* (Casablanca: Presses des Imprimeries Réunies, n.d.), 51. James Grey Jackson, *An Account of Timbuctoo and Housa* (London: Longman, Hurst, Rees, Orme, and Brown, 1820), 87. Local Jewish traditions on the early period of the town also see Jacob Guedalla, resident in the casbah, as the richest merchant in the town.

26. Romanelli, *Travail*, 124; Meir Pinto is referred to as the former vice consul for France. This tradition is found in a hagiographic book about the life and miracles of Rabbi Haim Pinto of Essaouira. Avraham Ben ʿAttar, *Shanot Hayyim* (Casablanca: Imprimerie Simplex A. Soussan, 1958), 3. The book was translated from Hebrew into Judeo-Arabic, with additions, by Haim Zafrani (Casablanca: David A. Amar, 1961). Census records from Livorno suggest that Akrish resettled in the Italian port in 1793 (listed as Isache di David Acris from Mogador). See Jean Pierre Filippini, "La ballottazione a Livorno nel Settecento," *La Rassegna Mensile di Israel* 40 (1983): 256; he may have originally been born in Morocco, reaching Livorno by way of Gibraltar in 1769. See idem, "Livorno e gli ebrei dell'Africa del Nord nel Settecento," in *Gli Ebrei in Toscana dal medioevo al Risorgimento* (Florence: L. S. Olschki, 1980), 22. Abudarham was a family, originally from Tetuan, that settled in Livorno in 1794 (see Filippini, "La ballotazione," 256).

27. LP, testimony regarding presents sent from London by Judah Guedalla, 10 Iyar 5665 = 15 May 1905. This document clarifies the family connections between the Guedalla family and Meir Macnin.

28. Chambre de Commerce, Marseilles, J. 1553, Mogador, 4 September 1786.

Signed by Mordejay Delamar, Gwyn & Hutchinson, Aº Dᶜ Leonardi e Compa, Meir Pinto, Haim Guedalla y Ca, Salomon Sebag, Wilson & Mackarness, Guiseppe e don Chiappe, Gieo Battista [Ricio?]. The affairs of the corps of foreign merchants were subject to the regulations and decisions of the Tribunale de Commercio, because of the preponderant influence of the Genoese in the town. Several later accounts mention that only the Jew Guedalla was admitted to the company of foreign merchants (which the aforementioned petition contradicts). Jackson, *An Account of Timbuctoo and Housa*, 87; FO 52/29, Gibraltar, 3 June 1828, R. Chaillet (vice consul in Essaouira) to Smith; Chaillet, "Observations on the Western Coast of the Morocco State during My Journey from Mogador to Tangier in July and August 1830: Memorandum Respecting the Foundation of Mogador, its Trade, etc.," Royal Geographical Society, MS 1828, fols. 48–49, 67–68.

29. Keatinge, *Travels*, 1:179.

30. Ibid., 1:191.

31. Information on their activities is found scattered through the correspondence of the Dutch consular agent David Jean Subremont with the Dutch consul general in Tangier, Webster Blount. ARH, Consulaat Tanger 1, 8 July 1788. The merchants of the town are listed in a letter dated 7 October 1786. Their involvement in the trade with Marseille is found in correspondence between Essaouira and the French consulate in Tangier. AEN, Tanger 87.

32. FO 52/4, 26 October 1782, Mordecai De La Mar to Masahod; ARH, Consulaat Tanger, 1. It is inaccurate to state that only "Europeans" directly shipped goods to European ports. See Ahmed Farouk, "Aperçu de trafic du port de Mogador avec les principales places européenes (1786–1787)," *Hespéris-Tamuda* 26–27 (1988–1989): 97.

33. Mordecai De La Mar was an important intermediary in ransoming European captives. AEN, Tanger 87, 9 September 1786, 19 August 1787, Cabanes & Depras to Du Rocher. See also Manon Hosotte-Reynaud, "Un négociant français à Mogador à la fin du XVIIIᶜ siècle et sa correspondance avec le consul de France à Salé," *Hespéris* 44 (1957): 341. The consular archives refer constantly to Jews involved in ransoming European captives, and from the very beginnings of Essaouira, the port was a transit point for releasing Europeans held in the south. Saugnier and Brisson, *Voyages to the Coast of Africa* (London: G. G. J. Robinson, 1792), 48, 57, 398–99, 412–14; ANP, AE/Bᴵᴵᴵ/319, August 1765; FO 52/1, 1 January 1766, Hosier and Adams (British merchants at Essaouira). For a description of the hazards for ships on this coast, see James Gray Jackson, *An Account of the Empire of Marocco and the Districts of Sus and Tafilelt*, 3d ed. (London: Printed by William Bulmer and Co., 1814), 269–72.

34. Jackson, *Account of the Empire of Marocco*, 272–73.

35. Ibid., 279–80.

36. Saugnier and Brisson, *Voyages*, 279–80.

37. AEN, Tanger 87, 9 September 1786, 19 August 1787, Cabanes and Depras to Du Rocher.

38. Hosotte-Reynaud, "Un négociant français," 341–42.

39. John Paddock, *Narrative of the Shipwreck of the Oswego on the Coast of South Barbary* (New York: Published by Captain James Riley, 1818), 185–86. A similar ex-

perience is described by a French sailor, held captive in Wad Nun in 1819. Charles Cochelet, *Naufrage du brick français La Sophie*, 2 vols. (Paris: Librairie Universelle de P. Mongie Aîné, 1821), 1:288ff.

40. René Basset, *Relation de Sidi Brahim de Massat* (Paris, 1883), 26–27; al-Nasiri, *al-Istiqsaʾ*, 8:20.

41. Daniel J. Schroeter, *Merchants of Essaouira: Urban Society and Imperialism in Southwestern Morocco, 1844–1886* (Cambridge: Cambridge University Press, 1988), 12–13.

42. FO 52/4, 1 June 1782, 26 October 1782, 29 October 1782, translated excerpts of letters from Mordecai De La Mar to his brother Masahod in Amsterdam; see Eliezer Bashan, *mi-Mizrah shemesh ʿad mevoʾo* (Lod: Orot Yahadut Hamaghreb, 1996), 228–29; and G. Rogers, *A History of Anglo-Moroccan Relations to 1900* (London: Foreign and Commonwealth Office, n.d.), 114.

43. FO 52/6, 3 January 1786, Masahod De La Mar; FO 52/7, Tangier, 16 July 1787, Matra.

44. Chénier, *Un Chargé d'affaires*, 664 (letter dated 18 June 1778); ARH, Consulaat Tanger 1, 19 June 1789, Subremont to Blount; AEN, 19 June 1789, Sicard to Du Rocher.

45. Jackson, *Account of Timbuctoo*, 88–89.

46. ARH, Consulaat Tanger 1, 31 January 1789, Subremont. On the grain trade during this period, see Mohamed El Mansour, *Morocco in the Reign of Mawlay Sulayman* (Wisbech, Cambridgeshire: MENAS Press, 1990), 55–56; El-Nasser, "Morocco from Kharijism to Wahhabism," 373–374; Ramón Lourido Díaz, "El comercio del trigo entre Marruecos y la Peninsula Iberica en el siglo xviii," *Almenara* 9 (1976): 29–61.

47. ARH, Consulaat Tanger 1, 9 August 1790, Subremont.

48. Lourido Díaz, *Marruecos y el mundo*, 251; idem, "Los judios en Marruecos," 29–30.

49. ARH, Consulaat Tanger 1, 19 June 1789, Subremont; AEN, 10 July 1789, Sicard to Du Rocher.

50. Cf. Hayyim Bentov, "Le-demuto shel ha-sar Shmuel Ibn Sunbal," in *Zekhor le-Avraham: Kovets maʾamarim le-zekher R. Avraham Elmalih*, ed. H. Z. Hirschberg (Jerusalem: Vaʿad ʿAdat ha-Maʿaravim bi-Yerushalayim, 1972), 47–49.

51. Francesco Chiappe was appointed in 1784 as the sultan's interpreter and secretary, responsible for European affairs. MʾBarek Zaki, "Le Maroc et Gênes: Quelques aspects des relations entre 1700 et 1800," *Revue Maroc-Europe* no. 2 (1992): 49. He was represented as having the title of "secretary for foreign affairs." FO 52/6, Tangier, 11 August 1786, Duff. Francesco's brothers were also prominent in trade and diplomacy: Giacomo Girolamo served as the Venetian consul in Tangier, Giovanni Battista as consular representative in Casablanca, and Giuseppe (Joseph) represented the commercial interests of the Marquis Viale in Essaouira, serving also as Genoese consul general, and Spanish chargé d'affaires. The brothers became intricately linked to Moroccan foreign relations, and received various commercial privileges in the country. See Vincenzo Marchesi, "Le relazioni tra la Repubblica veneta ed il Marocco dal 1757 al 1797," *Rivista Storica Italiana* 3 (1886): 72ff.; Mariano Arribas Palau, "Los hermanos Chiappe en Marruecos," in *La Conoscenza dell'Asia e dell'Africa in Italia nei secoli XVIII e XIX*, vol. 1, pt. 2 (Naples: Istituto Universitario Orientale, 1984), 813–69; idem, "La

actividad comercial del marqués Viale en Marruecos," *Revista de Archivos, Bibliotecas y Museos* 79 (1976): 3, 16; idem, "Reclamaciones de marqués Viale contra la casa comercial española de Casablanca y el consul Salmon," *Cuadernos de la Biblioteca Española de Tetuán*, 17–18 (1978): 40ff.; Enrico de Leone, "Veneziani e Genovesi nel Marocco nella seconda metà del secolo XVIII," *Levante* 10 (1963): 5–11; Maria Nallino, "Documenti arabi sulle relazioni tra Genova e il Marocco nella seconda metà del secolo XVIII," *Rivista degle Studi Orientali* 21 (1946): 56–57; ARH, Consulaat Tanger 1, 2 October 1794, Subremont to Blount. On these and other Jewish courtiers, see Lourido Díaz, *Marruecos y el mundo*, 250.

52. Høst, *Histoire de l'Empereur*, 17, 45, 51, 69, 108–10, 118, 124. For other sources on Sumbal, see: Lourido Díaz, *Marruecos y el mundo*, 250–51; Bentov, "Le-demuto," 51–52; Alexander Jardine, *Letters from Barbary, France, Spain, Portugal, &C. by an English Officer* (London: Printed for T. Cadell, 1788), 44–45; Hirschberg, *A History of the Jews*, 2:284. On the cases before the rabbinical courts, see Bentov, "Le-demuto," 51–56; an epitaph on Sumbal's gravestone marks his death on 17 Heshvan 5543 = 25 October 1782. On his role in relations with Spain, see Mariano Arribas Palau, "Datos sobre Samuel Sumbel," 121–39. His brother or nephew, Meir, served as interpreter for the French consulate; when he died in 1796, his son returned from London to take over the position. Hosotte-Reynaud, "Un négociant," 336.

53. Analyzed by Norman A. Stillman and Yedida K. Stillman, "The Jewish Courtier Class in Late Eighteeenth-Century Morocco As Seen Through the Eyes of Samuel Romanelli," in *Essays in Honor of Bernard Lewis: The Islamic World from Classical to Modern Times*, ed. C. E. Bosworth et al. (Princeton, N.J.: Darwin Press, 1988), 848–51. It is worth noting here that descendants of Meir Macnin and Eliahu Levi were linked in marriage. He came from a family of prominent merchants, *nagids*, rabbis, and courtiers (who were also known by their *kinui*, Ibn Yuli). See Bentov, "Mishphat ha-Levi Ibn Yuli," in *mi-Mizrah u-mi-ma'arav*, ed. E. Bashan, A. Rubinstein, and S. Schwarzfuchs (Ramat Gan: Universitat Bar-Ilan, 1980): 131–58.

54. Lourido Díaz, *Marruecos y el mundo*, 250–51; Levi was arrested and imprisoned in 1788, but is soon found actively engaging in commerce for the sultan. ARH, Consulaat Tanger 1, 31 October 1788, 19 June 1789, Subremont to Blount.

55. Bashan, *mi-Mizrah shemesh*, 217–18. He was involved in negotiating the peace treaty with the United States in 1786. Arribas Palau, "Documentación española sobre las primeras relaciones entre Marruecos y los Estados Unidos de America del Norte," 125. He is mentioned as reading a royal letter to the consuls of Tangier. FO 52/6, 25 September 1785, Duff.

56. Manuel Conrotte, *España y los países musulmanes durante el ministerio de Floridablanca* (Madrid: Impr. del Patronato de Huérfanos de Administración, 1909), 277.

57. *Travail*, 142.

58. The source is a lawsuit involving his other wife. Bentov, "Mishpahat ha-Levi," 141–42.

59. FO 52/4, Mogador, 1 June 1782, Gwyn & Hutchinson; ARH, Consulaat Tanger 1, 12 May 1793, Subremont to Blount.

60. FO 52/3, 9 Sha'ban 1186 = 5 November 1772, sultan to King George III (explaining reasons for the expulsion of the Christians from Tetuan).

61. FO 52/2, Gibraltar, 17 August 1770, Sampson.

62. Jackson, *Account of the Empire of Marocco*, 258.

63. Keatinge, *Travels*, 1:272.

64. In this period, Jews began appearing in Spain on diplomatic missions for the Moroccan government. Special provisions of safe conduct were needed from the General Inquisitor to allow the Jews to travel in Spain. Such was the case with Abraham Masahod, who arrived in Algeciras, but whose mission to Madrid was aborted when his credentials as diplomatic representative were questioned by the Moroccan authorities. See Mariano Arribas Palau, "La misión frustrada de Abraham Masahod a España en 1766," *Sefarad* 43 (1983): 109–33. Another courtier, Isaias b. ʿAmmur, on a mission to negotiate a peace treaty with Genoa in 1768, traveled by way of Barcelona, which raised some eyebrows in the inquisitorial tribunal. He later offered his services to the Spanish. Mariano Arribas Palau, "Notas sobre el Judío Isaías B. ʿAmmur en Marruecos," *Sefarad* 48 (1988): 235–44; he was apparently born in Gibraltar and was considered a British subject. SP 71/21, 31 March 1772.

65. David Cardozo in Agadir, and Malca in Safi, the brother-in-law of Mordecai De La Mar. ARH, Consulaat Tanger 1, 2 October 1794, Subremont to Blount.

66. ARH, Consulaat Tanger 1, 2 November 1794, Subremont to Blount; FO 52/11, 23 January 1801.

67. For a study of this question that deals with Muslim merchants in Fez, see Norman Cigar, "Socio-Economic Structures and the Development of an Urban Bourgeoisie in Pre-Colonial Morocco," *Maghreb Review* 6, nos. 3–4 (1981): 55–76.

68. Mariano Arribas Palau, *Cartas árabes de Marruecos del tiempo de Mawlay al-Yazid (1790–1792)* (Tetuan: Cremades, 1961), 42.

69. From a chronicle of events in Fez and elsewhere in Morocco recorded by the Ibn Danan family, called *Divre ha-yamim shel Fez*; the part of the chronicle that describes atrocities of Mawlay al-Yazid was written by Judah b. Obed Attar (1725–1812), in a work called *Zikharon li-bene Yisraʾel*, which was translated into French by Georges Vajda, *Un recueil de textes historiques judéo-marocains* (Paris: Larose, 1951), 79–96.

70. Cf. Jane S. Gerber, "The Pact of ʿUmar in Morocco: A Reappraisal of Muslim-Jewish Relations," in *Proceedings of the Seminar on Muslim-Jewish Relations in North Africa* (New York: World Jewish Congress, 1975): 40–50.

71. William Lempriere, *A Tour from Gibraltar to Tangier, Sallee, Mogodore, Santa Cruz, and Tarudant; and Thence over Mount Atlas to Morocco* (Philadelphia: Printed by T. Dobson, 1794), 137. The British consul correctly predicted that Attal would probably be killed if the sultan died. FO 52/8, 19 December 1789, Matra. On Attal's diplomatic activities, see Bashan, *Mi-mizrah shemesh*, 213–19. On Attal, and others executed by Mawlay al-Yazid, see Hirschberg, *History of the Jews*, 2:291; Romanelli, *Travail*, 143; Olof Agrel, *Neue Reise nach Marokos* (Nuremberg: Adam Gottlieb Schneider und Weigel, 1798), 123–24, 133–38.

72. FO 52/8, 6 May 1790, Matra.

73. Muhammad al-Duʿayyif, *Tarikh al-Duʿayyif*, ed. Ahmad al-ʿAmari (Rabat: Dar al-Maʾthurat, 1986), 202.

74. [Robert Heron], *Account of the Life of Muley Liezit, Late Emperor of Morocco* (London, 1797), 39, 42–44, 55, 132; Agrel, *Neue Reise*, 132ff. Norman A. Stillman, "Two Accounts of the Persecution of the Jews of Tetouan in 1790," *Michael*, vol. 5,

ed. Daniel Carpi, Yehuda Nini, and Shlomo Simonsohn (Tel-Aviv: Diaspora Research Institute, 1978), 130–142 [the first account is from Franz von Dombay, the Hapsburg consular agent, and the second is from al-Duᶜayyif's manuscript, which has since been edited and published]; FO 52/8, 6 May 1790, Matra. Foreign accounts are corroborated by the detailed description in al-Duᶜayyif, *Tarikh*, 202.

75. Vajda, *Recueil de textes*, 79–96 (based on a manuscript of Jacob Ibn Danan of Fez, entitled "Divre ha-yamim shel Fez," and containing an account by Judah b. ᶜObed Ibn ᶜAttar; a translation is also found in Hirschberg, *A History of the Jews*, 2:293–300); Louis Brunot and Elie Malka, *Textes judéo-arabes de Fès* (Rabat: Ecole du Livre, 1939), 198–99; al-Duᶜayyif, *Tarikh*, 207; Agrel, *Neue Reise*, 177, 237.

76. Agrel, *Neue Reise*, 261, 283–84, 308. In normal times, Jews were often required to take their shoes off while walking past a mosque or Muslim shrine.

77. al-Nasiri, *al-Istiqsaʾ*, 8:82–83.

78. al-Duᶜayyif, *Tarikh*, 233–34. A detailed description of the bloodbath in Marrakesh is found in Agrel, *Neue Reise*, 409–411; see also a letter dated 30 April 1792, written by the Danish consul in Tangier, in Jean-Louis Miège, "Un bicentenaire: Schousboue, botaniste et consul," *Maroc-Europe*, 5 (1993): 211–12.

79. Romanelli, *Travail*, 136ff.

80. *Account of the Life of Muley Liezit*, 148. This source refers to 150 persons. Agrel mentions sixty of the elite, including nine Christians and one consul; *Neue Reise*, 411. The Danish consul also reports on this: Miège, "Schousboue," 212.

81. ARH, Consulaat Tanger 1, 29 February 1792, Subremont. I have changed the spelling of the Jewish names. The details of the procedure are not that clear. It seems that the sultan had ordered the consuls, merchants, and governors to go to Marrakesh. ARH, Consulaat Tanger 1, 16 February 1792, Subremont. Probably, the sultan's plans to execute them were discovered after his death.

82. On the support of Ibn Nasir for Mawlay Hisham, see al-Duᶜayyif, *Tarikh*, 218, 229–30; Agrel, *Neue Reise*, 407–9. Jackson reports an accusation that the merchants had supplied the rebel with ammunition. *Account of Timbuctoo*, 285.

83. ARH, Consulaat Tanger 1, 29 November 1790, Subremont to Blount.

84. Tahir Fannish was appointed by Mawlay al-Yazid to replace the former governor of Tangier, Muluk b. ᶜAbd al-Malik, who was executed in September 1790. Agrel, *Neue Reise*, 236–39, 312. It should be noted that Tahir Fannish's father, ᶜAbd al-Haqq Fannish, had been governor of Salé and had been executed by Sidi Muhammad during the early part of his reign. al-Nasiri, *al-Istiqsaʾ*, 8:29–30.

85. *Account of the Life of Muley Liezit*, 146–47; Romanelli, *Travail*, 142–47; ARH, Consulaat Tanger 1, 10 December 1790, 29 February 1792, Subremont. Eliahu Levi was also a courtier under Sidi Muhammad, but was arrested in 1788. He seems to have been released, for it was reported in the following year that he had arrived in Essaouira from Marrakesh for the purpose of shipping wheat (presumably from Essaouira to another port). ARH, Consulaat Tangier 1, 31 October 1783, 19 June 1789, Subremont to Blount.

86. ARH, Consulaat Tanger 1, 19 September 1790, and 31 July 1791, Subremont to Blount.

87. Cf. El Mansour, *Morocco in the Reign of Mawlay Sulayman*, 15, 88.

88. Algemeen Rijksarchief Aanwinstein, Consulaat Tanger (Amsterdam), 1906,

I, 91, quoted in Mohammed Kenbib, *Juifs et musulmans au Maroc, 1859–1948* (Rabat: Université Mohammed V, Publications de la Faculté des Lettres et des Sciences Humaines, 1994), 49 n. 109. The letter is dated 24 Muharram 1205, which corresponds to 3 October 1790, rather than 20 October 1791 as indicated in the footnote.

89. ARH, Consulaat Tanger 1, 31 July 1791, Subremont to Blount. He refers to the "governor's Jew," Meir.

90. ARH, Consulaat Tanger 1, El Jadida, 15 March 1791, Subremont to Blount; FO 52/10, 27 April 1799, Matra.

91. John Rylands Library, Manchester, Dombay Papers, Mss. 286, fol. 2, 1 Safar 1199 = 14 December 1784, *dahir* of the sultan ("we have charged him [Chiappe] with writing foreign [language] letters exchanged between us and Christian countries, and for ambassadors, consuls, merchants, and other Christians coming to us he will be the intermediary between us and them"). See also Arribas Palau, "Los hermanos," 825.

92. FO 52/10, 19 October 1791, Matra; Arribas Palau, "Reclamaciones," 61.

93. FO 52/10, 30 October 1790, Matra; ARH, Consulaat Tanger 1, 20 November 1790, Subremont to Blount.

94. 28 February 1792, Jackson to James Willis (former British consul for Senegambia) in Jackson, *Account of Timbuctoo*, 56.

95. 7 March 1792, Jackson to Willis, ibid., 58–61.

96. ARH, Consulaat Tanger 1, 4 April 1792, Subremont to Blount; FO 52/10, Gibraltar, 15 April 1792, Matra.

97. FO 52/10, Gibraltar, 27 May 1792, Matra; Tangier, 10 April 1793, Matra.

98. ARH, Consulaat Tanger 1, 18 October 1792, Subremont to Blount.

99. FO 52/10, 12 December 1792, Matra.

100. ARH, Consulaat Tanger 1, 2 October 1794, 13 May 1795, Subremont to Blount; al-Nasiri, *al-Istiqsa*, 8: 102–3.

101. al-Duᶜayyif, *Tarikh*, 295; al-Nasiri, *al-Istiqsa*, 8:101–2.

102. El Mansour, *Morocco in the Reign of Mawlay Sulayman*, 89–98; ARH, Consulaat Tanger 1, Subremont to Blount, 16 March 1796; FO 52/11, 21 March 1795, 30 December 1795, 16 June 1797, 5 September 1797, Matra, 30 January 1801.

103. For example, there is a reference to a wreck in the harbor of Essaouira of a ship consigned to Meir Macnin from Lisbon. ARH, Consulaat Tanger 1, 20 January 1796, Subremont to Blount.

104. 28 February 1792, and 7 March 1792, Jackson to Willis, in Jackson, *Account of Timbuctoo*, 56–61; ARH, Consulaat Tanger 1, 24 February 1791, 25 April 1792, 15 May 1792, 22 May 1792, 31 May 1792, 29 June 1792, 12 September 1792, Subremont to Blount; Jackson, *Account of the Empire of Marocco*, 278.

105. Mawlay ᶜAbd al-Malik al-Zayzun, nephew of the sultan, was governor of Agadir and Tarudant, but later became virtually independent. See El Mansour, *Morocco in the Reign of Mawlay Sulayman*, 95; see also al-Duᶜayyif, *Tarikh*, 221, 260.

106. LP, 13 Rabiᶜ II 1209 = 7 November 1794, Mawlay ᶜAbd al-Salam to Mawlay ᶜAbd al-Malik. ᶜAbd al-Salam, a brother of the sultan, was the father of ᶜAbd al-Malik.

107. LP, 24 Rabiᶜ II 1211 = 27 October 1796 (signatures unclear).

108. ᶜAbd al-Malik was called to Marrakesh in early 1797, and Agadir was declared closed; no European merchant was to remain there. See Jackson, *Account of*

Timbuctoo, 79–80. ʿAbd al-Malik's property was seized in Agadir and he was sent to Fez to live with his father at the end of Ramadan 1212 = March 1798. al-Duʿayyif, *Tarikh*, 302, 304.

109. El Mansour, *Morocco in the Reign of Mawlay Sulayman*, 56; Agadir was finally closed in 1798, FO 52/11, 3 February 1798, Matra; ARH, Consulaat Tanger 1, 21 February 1798, 10 March 1798, 22 March 1798, Subremont to Blount. Meir Macnin, together with Guedalla and Pinto, was required to assist in the liquidation of the business of a Christian merchant, Pacifico, from Agadir. In 1799, Mawlay Sulayman ordered all the Christian merchants to leave Safi for Essaouira. According to one source, Ibn Nasir died the same year from the plague, and Chiappe, who had been closely tied to the old regime and to Ibn Nasir, was expelled from the country several months later. FO 52/11, 28 November 1799, 13 December 1799, 19 May 1800, Matra. However, in a letter dated 1802, the British merchant Jackson reported that "The Bashaw of Abda *Abdrahaman ben Nassar*, received me with his accustomed urbanity and hospitality . . . "; Jackson, *Account of Timbuctoo*, 136. The letter gives only a year, in contrast to most other letters included in the book, and therefore the date may have been in error.

110. This was also the case elsewhere in the Jewish world. For early modern Central Europe, see *The Memoirs of Glückel of Hameln*, trans. Marvin Lowenthal (New York: Schocken Books, 1977); for a new interpretation of this work, see Natalie Zemon Davis, *Women on the Margins: Three Seventeenth-Century Lives* (Cambridge, Mass.: Harvard University Press, 1995), 5–62.

111. ARH, Consulaat Tanger 1, 24 December 1796, Subremont to Blount. The daughter in question was Zohra.

112. ARH, Consulaat Tanger 1, 31 January 1789, 9 August 1790, 20 September 1790, 24 February 1791, Subremont to Blount.

113. ARH, Consulaat Tanger 1, 31 January 1799, Subremont to Blount.

114. For a description and analysis of Jewish weddings in Morocco, see Issachar Ben-Ami, *Le judaïsme marocain* (Jerusalem: Rubin Mass, 1975), 9ff.

115. The splendor of an elite Jewish wedding captivated Eugène Delacroix, who spent some months in Morocco in 1832. Notes on the Jewish wedding he attended in Tangier are found in Eugène Delacroix, *The Journal of Eugène Delacroix* (New York: Viking Press, 1972), 106–8. It inspired a famous painting. See also *Delacroix in Morocco*, exhibition organized by the Institut du Monde Arabe (Paris: Flammarion, 1994–95). There are other descriptions of Moroccan Jewish weddings from the early nineteenth century. See, e.g., William Robertson, *A Residence at Gibraltar and a Visit to the Peninsula in the Summer of 1841* (Edinburgh: A. Fullarton & Co., 1844), 232–36. See also Alexandre Dumas, *Le Véloce ou de Cadix à Tunis* (Paris: Editions François Bourin, 1990), 61–71.

116. LP, 29 Elul 5540 = 29 September 1780. Translation of a document drawn up in Essaouira; declaration of Solomon [Shlomo], son of Abraham Cohen, known as Ben Macnin. He received a piece of property in Marrakesh to pay off all debts of a family to which he was creditor. Deeds for Marrakesh, however, were not found in the family collection, although legal documents refer to the various properties left there by Meir Macnin to his wife, Zohra. Other legal documents pertaining to inheritance refer to his property in Marrakesh. Evidence also of his extensive property

comes from a census taken of the *mellah* of Marrakesh, dated 6 Rabiᶜ II 1308 = 19 November 1890. In this document, reference is made to "*Darb* Maqnin ("Street of Macnin") as the fourth quarter of the *mellah*. KH, *al-tartib al-ᶜam*. Published and analyzed by Khalid Ibn al-Saghir, "Wathiqa ghayr manshura ᶜan millah Marrakish fi nihayat al-qarn al-tasiᶜ ᶜashar," *Hespéris-Tamuda* 35 (1997): 60. I am grateful to the author for sending me a copy of his article, and to Emily Gottreich for alerting me to this information. FO 52/11, 18 September 1801, Matra.

117. LP, 2 Heshvan 5548 = 14 October 1787, signed Yehuda b. Masᶜud Alᶜankri and [second signature unclear].

118. LP, 5 Jumadi II 1209 = 28 December 1794. A later testimony about this property is found in a notarized rabbinic document dated 6 Tevet 5558 = 25 December 1797 [partially torn]. It is unclear why a transaction between Jews would have required an Arabic deed. The Spanish Franciscan mission had been established in 1769, but had been forced to close down in 1790. Fr. A. Luengo, "Mogador—fondación de la misión católica," *Mauritania*, 1 August 1940, 249.

119. The house was eventually sold, after some negotiation, to Guedalla & Cⁱᵉ, for two thousand "ducats," but apparently the deal was never closed. ARH, Consulaat Tanger 1, 16 March 1796, 10 September 1796, 14 October 1796, 3 December 1797, Subremont to Blount.

120. ARH, Consulaat Tanger 1, 1 February 1797, Subremont to Blount.

121. LP, 1 Shaᶜban 1211 = 30 January 1797 (signatures unclear), and 30 Jumadi I 1212 = 20 November 1797, signed Muhammad b. Ahmad, Mansur b. Muhammad.

122. LP, 22 Adar 5558 = 10 March 1798 (signatures unclear); 15 Kislev 5559 = 23 November 1798, signed Yehuda b. Masᶜud Alᶜankri, Yishuᶜa [   ] Ben Mor Yosef.

123. LP, mid-Dhu al-Hijja 1214 = May 1800, signed ᶜAbd al-Rahman, Muhammad b. Ahmad.

124. LP, 21 Hijja 1211 = 17 June 1797, declaration of a loan from Meir Macnin to Muhammad b. Dahman.

125. LP, 26 Adar 5559 = 3 March 1799, contract notarized by Yehuda Levi Yuli and [   ] Saᶜdon.

126. Paul Pascon, "Le commerce de la Maison d'Iligh d'après le registre comptable de Husayn b. Hachem (Tazerwalt, 1850–1875)," *Annales ESC* 35 (1980): 702–3; another version of this article appears in Paul Pascon, et al., *La Maison d'Iligh et l'histoire sociale du Tazerwalt* (Rabat: Société Marocaine des Editeurs Réunis, 1984).

127. Robert Adams, *The Narrative of Robert Adams* (London: Printed for John Murray, 1816), 76.

128. According to al-Duᶜayyif, Sidi Hashim declared himself ruler ("declared the caliphate") during his rebellion, but was routed by the sultan's governor in Tarudant, Wild Aghnaj. *Tarikh*, 353.

129. Adams, *Narrative*, 150–51. Besides the editor of Robert Adams's account, Joseph Dupuis, the British consular agent, wrote many of the notes in the book.

130. On the Jews of Iligh, see Paul Pascon and Daniel J. Schroeter, "Le cimetière juif d'Iligh (1750–1956): Etude des épitaphes comme documents d'histoire sociale (Tazerwalt, sud-ouest marocain)," *Revue de l'Occident Musulman et de la Méditerranée* 34, no. 2 (1982): 39–62; another version appears in Pascon et al., *La Maison d'Illigh*.

Chapter 3. The Plague and the World of Mediterranean Jewry

1. The distinction between "great plague" and "small plague" is made in Hebrew in the *geniza*. See S. D. Goitein, *A Mediterranean Society*, 6 vols. (Berkeley:
University of California Press, 1967–1993), vol. 5: *The Individual*, 113.

2. On the plague in the medieval Middle East, see Michael W. Dols, *The Black
Death in the Middle East* (Princeton, N.J.: Princeton University Press, 1977).

3. Mohamed El Mansour, *Morocco in the Reign of Mawlay Sulayman* (Wisbech,
Cambridgeshire: MENAS Press, 1990), 99.

4. ARH, Consulaat Tanger 1, 27 February 1799, Subremont to Blount; an Arabic
chronicle gives 10 Ramadan 1213 = 15 February 1799 as the beginning of the outbreak.
See Muhammad al-Duʿayyif, *Tarikh al-Duʿayyif*, ed. Ahmad al-ʿAmari (Rabat: Dar al-
Maʾthurat, 1986), 314. Some sources refer to April; James Grey Jackson, *An Account
of Timbuctoo and Housa* (London: Longman, Hurst, Rees, Orme, and Brown, 1820),
167. Jackson's book contains the most detailed contemporary description of the
plague (pp. 156–90). The British consul general, Matra, reports in April that by that
month the plague had already been in Fez for more than eight months, though this
is not corroborated by other sources. FO 52/11, 26 April 1799. For a study of plagues,
epidemics, and famines in Morocco in the eighteenth and nineteenth centuries, see
Muhammad al-Amin al-Bazzaz, *Tarikh al-awbiʾa wa-al-majaʿat bi-al-Maghrib fi al-
qarnayn al-thamin ʿashar wa-al-tasiʿ ʿashar* (Rabat: Jamiʿat Muhammad al-Khamis,
Manshurat Kulliyat al-Adab wa-al-ʿUlum al-Insaniya bi-al-Rabat, 1992); for the plague
of 1799–1800, see ibid., 89–99. See also H.-J. Renaud, "La peste de 1799 d'après des
documents inédits," *Hespéris* 1 (1923): 160–82; idem, "Un nouveau document marocain sur la peste de 1799," *Hespéris* 5 (1923): 83–90. The best analysis of the social, economic, and political consequences of the plague is found in El Mansour, *Morocco in
the Reign of Mawlay Sulayman*, 98–100.

5. See Daniel Panzac, *La peste dans l'Empire Ottoman, 1700–1850* (Louvain: Edi-
tions Peeters, 1985), 134ff; on the spread of the plague in the Maghrib, see Lucette
Valensi, *On the Eve of Colonialism: North Africa before the French Conquest* (New
York: Africana Publishing Company, 1977), 1–4.

6. Ibid., 146.

7. al-Duʿayyif, *Tarikh*, 314.

8. al-Bazzaz, *Tarikh al-awbiʾa*, 91–92.

9. Contemporary historians attributed the spread of the plague to the movement
of the Sultan's army. Al-Duʿayyif, *Tarikh*, 315; al-Bazzaz, *Tarikh al-awbiʾa*, 92–94; El
Mansour, *Morocco in the Reign of Mawlay Sulayman*, 98–99.

10. ARH, Consulaat Tanger 1, 13 June 1799, 29 June 1799, Subremont to Blount.

11. Jackson, *An Account of Timbuctoo*, 158–62; FO 52/11, Gibraltar, 5 February
1800 and 19 May 1800, Matra. Early in August, thirty to forty deaths per day were
reported by the Dutch consular agent. ARH, Consulaat Tanger 1, 5 August 1799,
Subremont to Blount.

12. Jackson, *An Account of Timbuctoo*, 156ff.; other reports on the death toll of
the plague are found in ARH, Consulaat Tanger 1, 5 August 1799, 8 September 1799,
7 October 1799, 15 November 1799, Subremont to Blount. The report to the House
of Commons gave the figure of seventy-five hundred, which seems even more im-

plausible. *Parliamentary Papers*, House of Commons, Reports, vol. 28, 1799–1800, no. 169, p. 11.

13. Ahmad b. Khalid al-Nasiri, *Kitab al-istiqsaʾ li-akhbar duwal al-Maghrib al-Aqsa*, 2d ed., 9 vols. (Casablanca: Dar al-Kitab, 1954–56), 8:106; al-Duʿayyif, *Tarikh*, 315–18; El Mansour, *Morocco in the Reign of Mawlay Sulayman*, 200.

14. al-Duʿayyif, *Tarikh*, 315.

15. FO 52/11, Gibraltar, 13 September 1799, Matra.

16. Renaud, "La peste de 1799," 181.

17. Cf. Fernand Braudel, *Civilization and Capitalism: Fifteenth–Eighteenth Century*, vol. 1: *The Structures of Everyday Life: The Limits of the Possible* (New York: Harper & Row, 1981), 83–88. On responses to the plague in Tunisia, see Nancy E. Gallagher, *Medicine and Power in Tunisia, 1780–1900* (Cambridge: Cambridge University Press, 1983), 24–32.

18. Renaud, "La peste de 1799," 171.

19. David G. LoRomer, *Merchants and Reform in Livorno, 1814–1868* (Berkeley: University of California Press, 1987), 19–22.

20. For details on this charter, see Attilo Milano, "La constituzione 'livornina' del 1593," *Rassegna Mensile di Israel* 34 (1958): 15–27; Guido Sonnino, *Storia della tipografia ebraica in Livorno* (Turin: Casale Monf.–Tip. Giuseppe Lavagno, 1912), 7–8; Renzo Toaff, *La Nazione ebrea a Livorno e a Pisa: 1591–1700* (Florence: L. S. Olschki, 1990), 41ff.; Alfredo S. Toaff, "Cenni storici sulla comunità ebraica e sulla sinagoga di Livorno," *Rassegna Mensile di Israel* 21 (1955): 356.

21. Attilo Milano, "Uno sguardo sulle relazioni tra la Livorno ebraica e i paesi della Berberia," in *Miscellanea di studi in memoria de Dario Disegni*, ed. E. M. Artom, L. Caro, and S. J. Sierra (Turin: Instituto di Studi Ebraica Scuola Rabbinica, "S. H. Margulies–D. Disegni," 1969), 139–40.

22. Jonathan I. Israel, *European Jewry in the Age of Mercantilism, 1550–1750* (Oxford: Clarendon Press, 1985), 49, 113, 164, 175, 238; Aron di Leone Leoni, *La Nazione ebraica spagnola e portoghese negli Stati Estensi* (Rimini: Luisè Editore, 1992), 27–28. Growth in the eighteenth century was less spectacular, but even so, by 1784 there were 4,327 Jews in Livorno.

23. Jean-Pierre Filippini, "Les Juifs d'Afrique du Nord et la communauté de Livourne au XVIIIᵉ siècle," in *Les relations intercommunautaires juives en méditerranée occidentale, XIIIᵉ–XXᵉ siècles* (Paris: Centre National de la Recherche Scientifique, 1984), 60; Haïm Zafrani, *Etudes et recherches sur la vie intellectuelle juive au Maroc de la fin du 15ᵉ siècle au début du 20ᵉ siècle*, vol. 1: *Pensée juridique et environnement social, économique et religieux* (Paris: Geuthner 1972), 209–10. On North African Jews publishing their works in Livorno, see M. Mitchell Serels, "Sephardic Printing as a Source of Historical Material," in *The Sephardi and Oriental Jewish Heritage*, ed. Issachar Ben-Ami (Jerusalem: Magnes Press, The Hebrew University, 1982), 123–31.

24. Renzo Toaff, "Livorno, comunità sefardita," *Rassegna Mensile di Israel* 38 (1972): 203–9.

25. Jean-Pierre Filippini, "Les négociants juifs de Livourne au XVIIIᵉ siècle," *Revue des Etudes Juives* 132 (1973): 672–73.

26. Jean-Pierre Filippini, "La ballottazione a Livorno nel Settecento," *Rassegna Mensile di Israel* 40 (1983); idem, "Livorno e gli ebrei dell'Africa del Nord nel Sette-

cento," in *Gli Ebrei in Toscana dal medioevo al Risorgimento* (Florence: L. S. Olschki, 1980): 21–22; idem, "Juifs emigrés et immigrés dans le port de Livourne pendant la période Napoléonienne," in *East and Maghreb*, ed. S. Schwarzfuchs, vol. 4 (Ramat-Gan: Bar-Ilan University Press, 1983), 51–53; idem, "Juifs d'Afrique," 60.

27. Toaff, *La Nazione ebrea*, 467–71; Simon Schwarzfuchs, "La 'Nazione Ebrea' livournaise au Levant," *Rassegna Mensile di Israel* 50 (1984): 707–24; Maurice Eisenbeth, "Les Juifs en Algérie et en Tunisie à l'époque turque (1516–1830)," *Revue Africaine* 96 (1952): 155–61; Richard Ayoun, "Les Juifs livournais en Afrique du Nord," *Rassegna Mensile di Israel* 50 (1984): 650–705; Michele Cassandro, *Aspetti della storia economica e sociale degli ebrei di Livorno nel seicento* (Milan: Dott. A. Giuffrè Editore, 1983), 70–83, 103; Minna Rozen, *bi-Netive ha-Yam ha-Tikhon: ha-pezurah ha-yehudit-Sefaradit be-meʾot ha-16–18* (Tel Aviv: ha-Katedrah le-Heker ha-Tarbut ve-ha-Historiyah shel Yehude Saloniki ve-Yavan, Universitat Tel Aviv, 1993), 11–12; idem, "The Leghorn Merchants in Tunis and Their Trade with Marseilles at the End of the 17th Century," in *Les relations intercommunautaires*, 51–59; Eliezer Bashan, "Teʾudot ʿal kesharim bayn Livorno le-Yehude Algier, Bône, Tunis ve-Tripoli be-meah ha-yud-het," in *Michael*, vol. 5, ed. Daniel Carpi, Yehuda Nini, and Shlomo Simonsohn (Tel Aviv: Diaspora Research Institute, 1978), 134ff.; Miège, "Juifs de Gibraltar," 100.

28. Minna Rozen, "Contest and Rivalry in Mediterranean Maritime Commerce in the First Half of the Eighteenth Century: The Jews of Salonika and the European Presence," *Revue des Etudes Juives* 147 (1988): 322–24; cf. Schwarzfuchs, "La 'Nazione Ebrea.'"

29. Rozen, "Leghorn Merchants," 51–53.

30. Isaac Abrami, "ʿEdat ha-Grana be-Tunis le-or pinkaseha: ha-maʾavak ʿal ha-otonomiyah," in *Judaïsme d'Afrique du Nord aux XIXᵉ–XXᵉ siècles*, ed. Michel Abitbol (Jerusalem: Institut Ben-Zvi , 1980), 68–72; idem, "La contribution des sources internes, hébraiques, judéo-arabes et arabes à l'histoire des Juifs livournais à Tunis," *Rassegna Mensile di Israel* 50 (1984): 725–39; D. Cazès, *Essai sur l'histoire des Israélites de Tunisie* (Paris: Librairie Armand Durlacher, 1888), 124–29; Eisenbeth, "Les Juifs en Algérie," 161–63; Ayoun, "Juifs livournais," 677–88; Milano, "Uno sguardo," 144.

31. Filippini, "La ballottazione," 215.

32. Filippini, "Juifs d'Afrique," 60–63. In the census of 1834, 108 Jews are listed from Tunis, 90 from Algiers, 52 from Tripoli, and 33 from Morocco. Milano, "Uno sguardo," 149. The number of descendants of Jews from the Maghrib was undoubtedly higher.

33. Filippini, "La ballotazione," 248–64.

34. Filippini, "Juifs d'Afrique," 62–63; idem, "Juifs emigrés," 50–52.

35. Idem, "Livourne et l'Afrique du Nord au 18ᵉ siècle," *Revue d'Histoire Maghrébine* 7–8 (1977): 142–49.

36. Filippini, "Livorno e gli ebrei," 27; see also idem, "Le rôle des négociants et des banquiers juifs de Livourne dans le grand commerce international en Méditerranée au XVIIIᵉ siècle," in *The Mediterranean and the Jews: Banking, Finance and International Trade (XVI–XVIII Centuries)*, ed. Ariel Toaff and Simon Schwarzfuchs (Ramat Gan: Bar-Ilan University Press, 1989), 129ff.

37. Eliezer Bashan, *Shivya u-fedut ba-hevrah ha-yehudit be-artsot ha-Yam ha-Tikhon (1391–1830)* (Ramat Gan: Hotsaʾat Universitat Bar Ilan, 1980), 251–60; Rozen,

"Leghorn Merchants," 51–52; Eisenbeth, "Les Juifs en Algérie," 356–63; Ayoun, "Juifs livournais."

38. ANP, F² I 441; text in Filippini, "Juifs emigrés," 75.

39. Filippini, "Juifs émigrés," 59–62.

40. Ayoun, "Juifs livournais," 661–62.

41. Filippini, "Juifs d'Afrique," 60–61.

42. David Corcos, "Les Juifs au Maroc et leurs mellahs," in *Studies in the History of the Jews of Morocco* (Jerusalem: Rubin Mass, 1976), 114; Samuel Romanelli, *Travail in an Arab Land*, trans. Yedida K. Stillman and Norman A. Stillman (Tuscaloosa: The University of Alabama Press, 1989), 124; Filippini, "La ballotazione," 248–64.

43. Filippini, "Juifs émigrés," 31ff.

44. Ibid., 32ff.

45. Published in Pisa in 1812.

46. The sources dealing with Abraham Coriat are conflicting. According to the *Encyclopedia Judaica*, he left Gibraltar during the siege, and finished his career as a *dayyan* in Livorno, where he died in 1806. David Corcos writes that Coriat became *dayyan* in Livorno at the request of Livornese in Essaouira; "Juifs au Maroc," 112. Another author writes that Abraham Raphael Coriat came to Essaouira and was chief rabbi about 1788, was in Gibraltar in 1790 and 1794 and again in Essaouira in 1828, and died in 1836. Abraham I. Laredo, *Les noms des Juifs du Maroc* (Madrid: Consejo Superior de Investigaciones Científicas, Instituto "B. Arias Montano," 1978), 1080. Another source says that he came to Essaouira about 1787 for three years, leaving before "the outrages" (presumably of Mawlay al-Yazid), and then in 1791–92 he was in Gibraltar, and later in Livorno. Yosef Ben Naʾim, *Malke rabanan* (Jerusalem: Defus ha-Maʿarav, 1930–31), fol. 10. Most likely he died about 1808 since from police archives in Livorno we learn that his son Judah came to Livorno to see "sa mère veuve depuis 5 ans d'Avraham Curiat, son père aussi rabbin, et décédé à Livourne." Filippini, "Juifs emigrés," 49. There was another Abraham Coriat, the author of numerous works, who was also a chief rabbi in Essaouira in the eighteenth and nineteenth centuries. Laredo, *Les noms*, 1080.

47. See Serels, "Sephardic Printing," 123–31. Among Meir Macnin's contemporaries (though sometimes their books were published posthumously), see Avraham Koriyat, *Berit avot* (Livorno: Printed by Eliyahu Ben Amozeg, 1861/62); Yosef Elmalih, *Tokfo shel Yosef*, vol. 1 (Livorno: Printed by Eliyahu Ben Amozeg, 1854/55), vol. 2 (Livorno: Printed by Yaʿakov Tobiyana, 1801/1802); Abraham Belaʿish, *Pri ets hayyim* (Livorno: Printed by Moshe and Yisraʾel Palache, 1845/56). Harvey Goldberg indicated to me in a personal communication that he has learned from Libyan Jews that rabbis often stayed in Livorno and even became naturalized as Livornese when they went to publish their books there.

48. LP, Promise of marriage, Livorno, 23 May 1820.

49. On the Bujnah in Livorno, see Filippini, "Juifs d'Afrique," 61, 63.

50. On connections with Marseilles, see Paul Masson, *Marseille depuis 1789*, 2 vols. (Paris, E. de Boccard, 1916–18), 2:185–91.

51. Morton Rosenstock, "The House of Bacri and Busnach: A Chapter from Algeria's Commercial History," *Jewish Social Studies* 14 (1952): 343–64; Françoise Hildesheimer, "Grandeur et décadence de la maison Bacri de Marseille," *Revue des*

Etudes Juives 136 (1977): 389–413; Magali Morsy, *North Africa 1800–1900* (London: Longman, 1984), 84–86; Eisenbeth, "Les Juifs en Algérie," 372–83.

52. In 1808 David Busnach (Bujnah) wrote in a petition to the French consul general that he "abandonned 22 years ago the country of Algiers in order to escape the inconveniences of which his family had been the victim." Filippini, "Juifs d'Afrique," 61, 63; see also idem, "Juifs émigrés," 52–56, 63, 78–79.

53. LP, 22 March 1822.

54. AEN, Tanger 87, 7 February 1838, Extrait des minutes de la Chancellerie du consulat de France à Mogador.

55. G. Beauclerk, *Journey to Morocco* (London: Printed for Poole and Edwards, etc., 1828), 251.

56. Mesod Benady, "The Settlement of Jews in Gibraltar, 1704–1783," *Transactions of the Jewish Historical Society of England* 26 (1979): 88–97; Jean-Louis Miège, "Les Juifs de Gibraltar au XIXᵉ siècle," in *Les relations intercommunitaires*, 99–101; Magali Morsy, "Les Juifs marocains à Gibraltar au 18ᵉ siècle: Histoire d'une minorité manipulée," *Pluriel* (1976): 51, 59–60.

57. Morsy, "Les Juifs marocains à Gibraltar," 48–50.

58. Benady, "Settlement of Jews in Gibraltar," 100; for 1754, see Thomas James, *The History of the Herculean Straits, Now Called the Straits of Gibraltar*, 2 vols. (London: Printed by Charles Rivington, 1771), 2:320.

59. CO 91/90, Gibraltar, 11 November 1826. For various estimates of the Jewish population of Gibraltar in the nineteenth century, see Miège, "Les Juifs de Gibraltar," 104–5.

60. Julio Caro Baroja, *Los Judíos en la España moderna y contemporánea*, 2d ed., 3 vols. (Madrid: Ediciones ISTMO, 1978), 3:157–60, 202–12.

61. James Picciotto, *Sketches of Anglo-Jewish History* (London: Trubner & Co., 1875), 320.

62. "Tableau de l'état actuel du Judaïsme dans les différentes parties du globe," *Revue Orientale* 1 (1841): 247–50.

63. Descendants of these families are still part of the Jewish community of Lisbon today. See José Maria Abecassis, *Genealogia hebraica Portugal e Gibraltar sécs. XVII a XX*, 5 vols. (Lisbon: J. M. Abecassis, Distribuição, Livraria Ferin, 1990–91), 2:677–82 (Coriat family), 3:588 (Pinto family).

64. George Borrow, *The Bible in Spain* (London: J. Murray, 1843), 31.

65. Jean-Louis Miège, *Le Maroc et l'Europe, 1830–1894*, 4 vols. (Paris: Presses Universitaires de France, 1961–63), 2:96 n. 3.

66. Albert M. Hyamson, *The Sephardim of England* (London: Methuen, 1951), 97. H. Z. Hirschberg, "Jews and Jewish Affairs in the Relations between Great Britain and Morocco in the 18th Century," in *Essays Presented to Chief Rabbi Israel Brodie on the Occasion of His Seventieth Birthday*, ed. H. H. Zimmels et al. (London: Soncino Press, 1967), 158–59. The influx of Jews from Morocco was pointed out by the noted Anglo-Jewish historian Cecil Roth, "Why Anglo-Jewish History?" *Transactions of the Jewish Historical Society of England* 22 (1970): 24.

67. On this network of Jewish traders, see H. Z. Hirschberg, *A History of the Jews in North Africa*, vol. 2: *From the Ottoman Conquests to the Present Time*, 2d ed. (Leiden: Brill, 1981), 212–35; Herbert I. Bloom, *The Economic Activities of the Jews of*

Amsterdam in the Seventeenth and Eighteenth Centuries (Williamsport, Pa.: The Bayard Press, 1937), 75–82; Jonathan I. Israel, "The Economic Contribution of Dutch Sephardi Jewry to Holland's Golden Age, 1593–1713," *Tijdschrift voor Geschiedenis* 96 (1983): 512, 517–18. Primary sources on Dutch-Moroccan relations are found in *Les sources inédites de l'histoire du Maroc de 1530 à 1845: Dynastie saadienne, archives et bibliothèques des Pays Bas*, ed. H. De Castries et al., 1st ser., 6 vols. (Paris: E. Leroux, 1906–23). See also Johan de Bakker, "Slaves, Arms, and Holy War: Moroccan Policy *vis-à-vis* the Dutch Republic during the Establishment of the ʿAlawi Dynasty (1660–1727)" (Ph.D. diss., University of Amsterdam, 1991).

68. George Rudé, *Hanoverian London, 1714–1808* (Berkeley: University of California Press, 1971), 33–36.

69. Alfred C. Wood, *A History of the Levant Company* (New York: Barnes & Noble, 1964), 180–87.

70. Jean-Louis Miège, "Entre désert et ocean: L'espace économique d'Essaouira au XIXᵉ siècle," *Revue Maroc-Europe*, no. 4 (1993): 50–51.

71. *Parliamentary Papers*, House of Commons, Reports, vol. 28, 1799–1800, no. 169.

72. FO 52/11, Tangier, 1 August 1801, Matra.

73. Sources dispute the number of ships that reached the port of Essaouira annually. One study, without specifying the sources for each year, refers to 30–40 ships per year in the 1780s, and lists 30 ships for 1798, 32 for 1799, 28 for 1800, 40 for 1801, and 25 for 1803. Miège, "Entre désert et ocean," 49, 60. Another source mentions 60 ships for 1798. AEP, Correspondance Consulaire et Commerciale, 21, cited in El Mansour, *Morocco in the Reign of Mawlay Sulayman*, 62.

74. See *Gentleman's Magazine* 78 (1808): 983. On trade in Morocco generally during this period, see El Mansour, *Morocco in the Reign of Mawlay Sulayman*, 42–46.

75. Michel Labarraque certifies that Citizens Antoinette Spahi (?) and Joseph Maru (?) "part de ce Port pour se rendre à Lisbonne fuyant la maladie contagieuse qui malheureusement aff[lige] cette ville & contreer [?] sur le brigantin Anglais le Lark." And two days later, he " . . . certifie que le nomme Baruk Ben Jacob Baruk sujet de l'Empereur du Maroc, part de ce Port pour se soustraire de la Maladie contagieuse qui reigne, sur le Brigantin Anglais le Lark Ca Gray." AEN, Tanger, Mogador 92, 5 Fructidor year 7, and 7 Fructidor year 7, Michel Labarraque.

76. ARH, Consulaat Tanger 1, 31 May 1799, David Jean Subremont (Dutch consular agent in Mogador) to Webster Blount (Dutch consul general in Tangier).

77. *Parliamentary Papers*, House of Commons, Reports, vol. 28, 1799–1800, no. 169, pp. 21, 25.

78. ARH, Consulaat Tanger 1, 8 September 1799, Subremont to Blount.

79. Miège, *Le Maroc et l'Europe*, 2:23.

80. ARH, Consulaat Tanger 1, 5 August 1799, Subremont to Blount.

81. ARH, Consulaat Tanger 1, 7 October 1799, Subremont to Blount.

82. FO 52/11, Gibraltar, 26 September 1799, James Matra.

83. *Parliamentary Papers*, House of Commons, Reports, vol. 28, 1799–1800, no. 169.

84. Ibid.

85. The burning of the ships from Essaouira, which resulted in public expense,

underlined the inadequate quarantine facilities; later that year, Parliament passed a bill to build a lazaret. Charles F. Mullet, "A Century of English Quarantine (1709–1825)," *Bulletin of the History of Medicine* 23 (1949): 534–35.

86. Mullet, "A Century of English Quarantine," 512.

87. P. Froggatt, "The Lazaret on Chetney Hill," *Medical History* 8 (1964): 46–47.

88. Mullet, "A Century of English Quarantine," 534.

89. Review of Thomas Hancock, *Researches into the Laws and Phenomena of Pestilence* (London: W. Phillips, 1821), *Quarterly Review* 27 (1822): 545–46. The author does not reject the notion that the plague is a communicable disease, but also believes that it can originate spontaneously and sporadically.

90. *Quarterly Review* 33 (1826): 218–57.

91. Cf. Gallagher, *Medicine and Power*, 11–12; Froggatt, "The Lazaret," 44–45.

92. Hancock, *Researches*, 247–51.

93. Review of *Results of an Investigation Respecting Epidemic and Pestilential Disease; Including Researches in the Levant Concerning the Plague*, by Charles Maclean, M.D., &c. &c. (1818), *Quarterly Review* 27 (1822): 534–35.

94. Gallagher, *Medicine and Power*, 13. On Islamic medical theories of the plague, see Dols, *The Black Death*, 84–109.

95. Ann Thomson, *Barbary and Enlightenment: European Attitudes towards the Maghreb in the Eighteenth Century* (Leiden: Brill, 1987), 20. This stereotypical view of the passive response of Muslims to the plague is reproduced in William H. McNeill, *Plagues and Peoples* (New York: Anchor Books, 1976), 166–67.

96. Xavier Durrieu, *The Present State of Morocco: A Chapter of Mussulman Civilisation* (London: Longman, Brown, Green, and Longmans, 1854), 4–5.

97. James Grey Jackson, *An Account of the Empire of Marocco and the Districts of Suse and Tafilelt*, 3d ed. (London: Printed by William Bulmer and Co., 1814), 175–77. Matra reported that the sultan regarded quarantine by land as a great sin. FO 52/11, 26 April 1799. The gates of Marrakesh were shut when it was learned of the plague in Fez and Meknes. ARH, Consulaat Tanger 1, 4 May 1799, Subremont to Blount. Tunisians, however, employed a variety of practices (such as quarantine), similar to those of Europeans, to prevent the spread of contagion and to treat the plague. In the case of Tunisia, it has been shown how the bey adopted public health policies to prevent the spread of the epidemic, and medical treatments were also employed. Gallagher, *Medicine and Power*, 24–26.

98. El Mansour, *Morocco in the Reign of Mawlay Sulayman*, 100.

99. al-Duᶜayyif, *Tarikh*, 313.

100. FO 174/2, 3 Rabiᶜ I 1213 = 15 August 1798. Translation of a dispatch from the Ottoman sultan to the Moroccan sultan.

101. El Mansour, *Morocco in the Reign of Mawlay Sulayman*, 104.

102. FO 52/11, 23 January 1801, Matra.

103. The governor's arrest is reported on 2 Shawwal 1215 = 16 February 1801, by a contemporary historian of this period. See al-Duᶜayyif, *Tarikh*, 321. Macnin is not mentioned in this account. The author, who lived in Rabat, reports that the sultan went to Essaouira and had the governor arrested. This seems unlikely since the sultan's arrival would have been mentioned by the consulates. The sultan did arrive in November of that year (ibid., 32). See also Rachid Abdallah El-Nasser, "Morocco,

from Kharijism to Wahhabism: the Quest for Religious Purism" (Ph.D. diss., University of Michigan, 1983), 440–41.

104. FO 52/11, Tangier, 1 August 1801, James Matra; 18 September 1801, Matra; AEN, Tanger 87, 14 March 1801, Michel Labaraque (Essaouira) to A. Guillet, consul general of France in Tangier. See also El-Nasser, "Morocco from Kharijism to Wahhabism," 440–41.

105. FO 52/14, London, 10 June 1801, petition of the creditors to the Foreign Office.

106. FO 52/14, London, 10 June 1801, petition to "His Imperial Majesty the Emperor of Morocco, High and Mighty Sovereign of all the Barbary States."

107. FO 52/11, 18 September 1801, Matra.

108. Ibid.

109. Ibid.

110. FO 52/11, Tangier, 2 October 1801, Matra.

111. FO 52/11, Tangier, 21 November 1801, Matra.

112. FO, 52/14, 26 Muharram 1217 = 29 May 1802 (the translation is that of the British Foreign Office).

113. FO, 52/11, Tangier, 2 October 1801, Matra.

114. FO 52/11, 23 December 1801, Matra.

115. FO 174/284, 18 November 1802, Pelham to Matra.

116. AEN, Tanger 87, 16 October 1801, Du Mellet and Sabatier (Essaouira) to Guillet.

117. AEN, Tanger 87, 20 Vendémiaire year 11, [   ] to Guillet (1803).

Chapter 4. The 'Berberiscos' of London

1. PRO, Index to Denizations, Meir Cohen Macknin, of Morocco, To be a free Denizen and to have all rights, etc., to free Denizens belonging, 11 May 1802. For a list of Jews who became denizens or were naturalized before 1800, see W. S. Samuel, "A List of Jewish Persons Endenizened and Naturalised 1609–1799," *Transactions of the Jewish Historical Society of England* 22 (1970): 111–44.

2. H. S. Q. Henriques, *The Jews and the English Law* (Oxford: Oxford University Press, 1908), 234; on denization, see also Gerald Berkeley Hertz, *British Imperialism in the Eighteenth Century* (London: Archibald Constable and Co., 1908), 61.

3. Frank Felsenstein, *Anti-Semitic Stereotypes: A Paradigm of Otherness in English Popular Culture, 1660–1830* (Baltimore: The Johns Hopkins University Press, 1995), 187ff.; Henriques, *The Jews and the English Law*, 241–45; Hertz, *British Imperialism*, 64ff.; David S. Katz, *The Jews in the History of England, 1485–1850* (Oxford: Clarendon Press, 1994), 240–53, 384; Todd M. Endelman, *The Jews of Georgian England, 1714–1830* (Philadelphia: Jewish Publication Society of America, 1979), 24–26.

4. See Mark R. Cohen, *Under Crescent and Cross: The Jews in the Middle Ages* (Princeton, N.J.: Princeton University Press, 1994), 99.

5. Cf. Lionel Kochan, *Jews, Idols and Messiahs: the Challenge from History* (Oxford: Basil Blackwell, 1990), 81.

6. James Picciotto, *Sketches of Anglo-Jewish History* (London: Trubner & Co., 1875), 190.

7. Todd M. Endelman, *Radical Assimilation in English Jewish History, 1656–1945* (Bloomington: Indiana University Press, 1990), 33.

8. This information comes from the only remaining descendant in England who still bears the Macnin name. Letter from Audrey Macnin, 20 April 1998. David Cohen Macnin married Priscilla Mitchell on 17 February 1831. Parish records of St. James, Westminster, London.

9. Philo-Semitism was also an important movement prior to the readmission of the Jews in the seventeenth century. However, the growing idea of toleration at that time reflected millenarian tendencies rather than any actual encounters with Jews (since only crypto-Jews would have then resided in England). See David S. Katz, *Philo-Semitism and the Readmission of the Jews to England, 1603–1655* (Oxford: Clarendon Press, 1982).

10. Picciotto, *Sketches*, 237–40.

11. See Katz, *Jews in the History of England*, 343–45. Richard J. Dircks, *Richard Cumberland* (Boston: Twayne, 1976), 86; Louis Zangwill, "Richard Cumberland Centenary Memorial Paper," *Transactions of the Jewish Historical Society of England* 7 (1915): 170–73; Gerald Reitlinger, "The Changed Face of English Jewry at the End of the Eighteenth Century," *Transactions of the Jewish Historical Society of England* 23 (1971): 38–39; M. J. Landa, *The Jew in Drama* (New York: KTAV Publishing House, 1969), 141.

12. *The Examiner* (1808): 299. Other reviews were hardly more generous. See, e.g., *Edinburgh Annual Register* 1, no. 2 (1808): 275–76; *European Magazine* 53 (1808): 381. For a discussion of the play, see Lewis I. Newman, *Richard Cumberland: Critic and Friend of the Jews* (New York: Bloch Publishing Company, 1919), 22–28.

13. FO 52/54, 29 November 1823. He reiterates his assertion in FO 174/154, 12 April 1824.

14. He wrote and published his memoirs before *The Jew of Mogadore*, and his published letters are also not revealing. See Richard Cumberland, *Memoirs of Richard Cumberland* (London: Printed for Lackington, Allen, & Co., 1806); Richard Cumberland, *The Letters of Richard Cumberland*, ed. Richard J. Dircks (New York: AMS Press, 1988).

15. He apparently also had another son, Judah, who also lived in London. See Manon Hosotte-Reynaud, "Un négociant français à Mogador à la fin du XVIIIᵉ siècle et sa correspondance avec le consul de France à Salé," *Hespéris* 44 (1957): 336.

16. Leah Wells Sumbel, *Memoirs of the Life of Mrs. Sumbel, Late Wells*, 3 vols. (London: C. Chapple, 1811). She changed her name to Leah upon converting to Judaism.

17. Ibid., 1:190–91; Kalmin A. Burnim, "The Jewish Presence in the London Theatre, 1660–1800," *Transactions of the Jewish Historical Society of England* 33 (1992–94): 89.

18. Ibid., 1:194–95.   19. Ibid., 3:182–83.

20. Ibid., 3:184–85.   21. Ibid., 1:200–201.

22. Ibid., 1:207.   23. Ibid., 2:78.

24. Ibid., 2:93.   25. Ibid., 2:102–3.

26. Ibid., 2:101.

27. Hayyim Bentov, "Le-demuto shel ha-sar Shmuel Ibn Sunbal," in *Zekhor le-Avraham: Kovets maᵓamarim le-zekher R. Avraham Elmalih*, ed. H. Z. Hirschberg (Jerusalem: Vaᶜad ᶜAdat ha-Maᶜaravim bi-Yerushalayim, 1972), 51. The author refers

to documents belonging to his friend David Corcos. These documents may be the same ones that David Corcos mentions in connection with Samuel Sumbal's selection of ten families to settle in Essaouira. I was unable to locate these in the family collection (see above, Chapter 2, note 11).

28. On the stereotype, from the late 1750s, of Jews as peddlers and old clothes men, see Endelman, *Jews of Georgian England*, 105–7; and Felsenstein, *Anti-Semitic Stereotypes*, 78–79. For a general portrait of Jewish peddlers and old clothes men, see Betty Naggar, *Jewish Pedlars and Hawkers, 1740–1940* (Camberley, Surrey: Porphyrogenitus, 1992).

29. Felsenstein, *Anti-Semitic Stereotypes*, 88.

30. Edward Napier, *Excursions along the Shores of the Mediterranean*, 2 vols. (London: H. Colburn, 1842), 1:271–72.

31. Katz, *Jews in the History of England*, 344–45.

32. Ursula Henriques, *Religious Toleration in England, 1787–1833* (Toronto: University of Toronto Press, 1961), 175; Michael Ragussis, *Figures of Conversion: "The Jewish Question" and English National Identity* (Durham, N.C.: Duke University Press, 1995), 15–26; Endelman, *Jews of Georgian England*, 71ff.; Picciotto, *Sketches*, 241–43, 282.

33. There is disagreement on the reasons for the readmission of the Jews under Cromwell. For a mercantilist and political view, see Jonathan I. Israel, *European Jewry in the Age of Mercantilism, 1550–1750* (Oxford: Clarendon Press, 1985), 158–60; a more religious explanation is given by Katz, *Philo-Semitism*, passim; idem, *Jews in the History of England*, 108ff.; see the discussion in Endelman, *Jews of Georgian England*, 16–17. The most complete description of the Whitehall Conference is in found, *Philo-Semitism*, 205–31.

34. Miriam Bodian, *Hebrews of the Portuguese Nation* (Bloomington: Indiana University Press, 1997), 12–13.

35. Picciotto, *Sketches*, 152. For an assessment of the wealth of the London Jewish community based on dues paid to the Sephardi synagogue, see Edgar R. Samuel, "The Jews in English Foreign Trade—A Consideration of the 'Philo Patriae' Pamphlets of 1753," in *Remember the Days*, ed. John M. Shaftesley (London: Jewish Historical Society of England, 1966), 131–33.

36. Albert M. Hyamson, *The Sephardim of England* (London: Methuen, 1951), 222.

37. Endelman, *Radical Assimilation*, 10–11; Elkan Nathan Adler, *London* (Philadelphia: The Jewish Publication Society of America, 1930), 150.

38. Harold Pollins, *Economic History of the Jews in England* (Rutherford, N.J.: Fairleigh Dickinson University Press, 1982), 48–58; George Rudé, *Hanoverian London, 1714–1808* (Berkeley: University of California Press, 1971), 53–54.

39. *Catalogue of an Exhibition of Anglo-Jewish Art and History* (London: Victoria & Albert Museum, 1956), 58.

40. Katz, *Jews in the History of England*, 185–88; Endelman, *Jews of Georgian England*, 22; Pollins, *Economic History of the Jews*, 56–57.

41. Robert Southey, *Letters from England*, ed. Jack Simmons (London: Cresset Press, 1951), 397.

42. F. A. Wendeborn, *A View of England towards the Close of the Eighteenth Century*, vol. 2 (London: Printed for G. G. J. and G. Robinson, 1791), 471. The distinc-

tion between Ashkenazim and Sephardim is made by the author's contemporary, Johan Wilhelm von Archenholz, *A Picture of England* (Dublin: Printed by P. Byrne, 1790), 113–14. On these stereotypes of Sephardim and Ashkenazim held by non-Jews, see Felsenstein, *Anti-Semitic Stereotypes*, 51–53.

43. Patrick Colquhoun, *A Treatise on the Police of the Metropolis*, 7th ed. (London: Printed for J. Mawman et al., 1806), 119–21; on German Jews assisting in the traffic of counterfeit coins, see 182–83, 190. See the discussion in Felsenstein, *Anti-Semitic Stereotypes*, 71–72. These observations about and attitudes toward the Jews are echoed in numerous other accounts of the period. See, e.g., John Corry, *A Satirical View of London at the Commencement of the Nineteenth Century* (London: Kearsley, 1801), 47–49; Richard King, *The Frauds of London Detected* (London: A. Hogg, 1770), 110–12.

44. Charles H. L. Emanuel, *A Century and a Half of Jewish History Extracted from the Minute Books of the London Committee of Deputies of the British Jews* (London: George Routledge & Sons, 1910).

45. Bodian, *Hebrews*, 125–31.

46. Yosef Kaplan, "The Portuguese Community in 17th-Century Amsterdam and the Ashkenazi World," in *Dutch Jewish History*, vol. 2, ed. Jozeph Michman (Jerusalem: Institute for Research on Dutch Jewry, Hebrew University of Jerusalem; Assen/Maastricht: Van Gorcum, 1989), 23–45.

47. *Bevis Marks Records*, pt. 1: *The Early History of the Congregation from the Beginnings until 1800*, ed. Lionel D. Barnett (Oxford: Oxford University Press, 1940), 29–32; Katz, *Jews in the History of England*, 180–83; Endelman, *Jews of Georgian England*, 167; Bodian, "Amsterdam, Venice, and the Marrano Diaspora in the Seventeenth Century," in Michman, *Dutch Jewish History*, 2:63–64. On the prejudice of Sephardim toward Ashkenazim, see Picciotto, *Sketches*, 117, 133.

48. Emanuel, *A Century and a Half of Jewish History*, 11.

49. Katz, *Jews in the History of England*, 272–73.

50. Emanuel, *A Century and a Half of Jewish History*, 11.

51. *El Libro de los Acuerdos, Being the Records and Accompts of the Spanish and Portuguese Synagogue of London*, ed. Lionel Barnett (Oxford: Printed at the University Press by John Johnson, 1931).

52. Bodian, "Amsterdam," 62–63; Gerard Nahon, *Métropoles et périphéries sefarades d'Occident: Kairouan, Amsterdam, Bayonne, Bordeaux, Jérusalem* (Paris: Editions du Cerf, 1993), 71–87; Evelyne Oliel-Grausz, "La circulation du personnel rabbinique dans les communautés de la diaspora sépharade au XVIIIᵉ siècle," in *Transmission et passages en monde juif*, ed. Esther Benbassa (Paris: Publisud, 1997), 313–34.

53. Eliezer Bashan, *Shivya u-fedut ba-hevrah ha-yehudit be-artsot ha-Yam ha-Tikhon (1391–1830)* (Ramat Gan: Hotsaʾat Universitat Bar Ilan, 1980), 269–70; R. D. Barnett, "The Correspondence of the Mahamad of the Spanish and Portuguese Congregation of London during the Seventeenth and Eighteenth Centuries," *Transactions of the Jewish Historical Society of England* 20 (1964): 23–25.

54. Moses Gaster, *History of the Ancient Synagogue of the Spanish and Portuguese Jews* (London: Printed by Harrison & Sons, 1901), 40–41, 145–46, 149.

55. Endelman, *Jews of Georgian England*, 168–169.

56. Robert Cohen, "Passage to a New World: The Sephardi Poor of Eighteenth

Century Amsterdam," in *Neveh Yaʿakov: Jubilee Volume Presented to Dr. Jaap Meijer on the Occasion of His Seventieth Birthday*, ed. Lea Dasberg and Jonathan N. Cohen (Assen: Van Gorcum, 1982), 34–35; Katz, *Jews in the History of England*, 181.

57. Gaster, *History of the Ancient Synagogue*, 149.

58. Endelman, *Jews of Georgian England*, 170.

59. R. D. Barnett, "Correspondence of the Mahamad of the Spanish and Portuguese Congregation," 15; Mesod Benady, "The Settlement of Jews in Gibraltar, 1704–1783," *Transactions of the Jewish Historical Society of England* 26 (1979): 106–7; Picciotto, *Sketches*, 190–91; Cecil Roth, *A History of the Jews in England* (Oxford: Oxford University Press, 1941), 231–32.

60. Henry Mayhew, *London Labour and the London Poor*, 4 vols. (London: Frank Cass, 1967), 1:452–54; Endelman, *Jews of Georgian England*, 170–71.

61. Alfred Rubens, "Portrait of Anglo-Jewry, 1656–1836," *Transactions of the Jewish Historical Society of England* 19 (1960): 18; and idem, *A Jewish Iconography* (London: The Jewish Museum, 1954), 29, 42; Richard Phillips, *Modern London; Being the History and Present State of the British Metropolis* (London: R. Phillips, 1804), plate and text (no page number); Naggar, *Jewish Pedlars*, 45–46.

62. *Monthly Repository*, no. 119 (October 1815): 719, cited in Katz, *Jews in the History of England*, 370 n. 133.

63. Paul Goodman, *Moses Montefiore* (Philadelphia: Jewish Publication Society of America, 1925), 24–30; Lucien Wolf, *Sir Moses Montefiore: A Centennial Biography* (New York: Harper & Brothers, 1885).

64. Picciotto, *Sketches*, 169, 310; Katz, *Jews in the History of England*, 196–201, 278–79; Gaster, *History of the Ancient Synagogue*, 160–64; Moses Margoliouth, *The History of the Jews in Great Britain*, 3 vols. (London: R. Bentley, 1851), 2:2, 52, 74–75; R. D. Barnett, "Haham Meldola and Hazan de Sola," *Transactions of the Jewish Historical Society of England* 21 (1968): 1–10; Guido Sonnino, *Storia della tipografia ebraica in Livorno* (Turin: Casale Monf.–Tip. Giuseppe Lavagno, 1912), 10, 28, 45; Alfredo Toaff, "Il Collegio rabbinico di Livorno," *Rassegna Mensile di Israel* 12 (1938): 190. On the network of recruitment for Sephardi rabbis, see Oliel-Grausz, "La circulation du personnel rabbinique," 313–34.

65. Southey, *Letters*, 367–68.

66. R. D. Barnett, "Anglo-Jewry in the Eighteenth Century," in *Three Centuries of Anglo-Jewish History*, ed. V. D. Lipman (Cambridge: Published for the Jewish Historical Society of England by W. Heffer and Sons Limited, 1961), 61.

67. Meir Macnin, merchant, first appears in the *London Directory*, at 3 Haydon Square in 1802. See Edward Murray Tomlinson, *A History of the Minories* (London: J. Murray, 1922), 333–34, 337.

68. On the Buhillals, see Daniel J. Schroeter, *Merchants of Essaouira: Urban Society and Imperialism in Southwestern Morocco, 1844–1886* (Cambridge: Cambridge University Press, 1988), 53.

69. FO 52/14, 17 June 1799, and 6 March 1800, Petitions to Duke of Portland.

70. Evidence of this is found in the *ketubot* (marriage contracts) preserved in the congregation. See *Bevis Marks Records*, pt. 2: *Abstracts of the Ketubot or Marriage-Contracts of the Congregation from Earliest Times until 1837*, ed. Lionel D. Barnett (Oxford: Printed at the University Press by J. Johnson, 1949).

71. SPJC, Minutes, MS 108, fols. 257, 288, 296. Macnin is listed as either Meir Cohen Macnin or Meir Cohen.

72. SPJC, Minutes, MS 108, fols. 257, 312. On these procedures of the congregation, see Hyamson, *Sephardim*, 189. The *finta* was assessed every two years following the annual meeting of the Mahamad. Neville Laski, *The Laws and Charities of the Spanish and Portuguese Jews Congregation of London* (London: Cresset Press, 1952), 35–37. On the oligarchal structure of synagogues in England, see V. D. Lipman, "Synagogal Organization in Anglo-Jewry," *Jewish Journal of Sociology* 1 (1959): 80–93.

73. In 1809, the congregation decided to increase the maximum *finta* of a single member to fifty-six pounds (4 percent of fourteen hundred pounds). Hyamson, *Sephardim*, 241.

74. SPJC, Minutes, MS 109, fol. 286.

75. SPJC, Minutes, MS 110, fols. 128, 156.

76. Laski, *Laws and Charities*, 40.

77. Picciotto, *Sketches*, 165.

78. *Anglo-Jewish Letters*, ed. Cecil Roth (London: The Soncino Press, 1938), 157, 237–39; A. L. Shane, "Isaac D'Israeli and his Quarrel with the Synagogue—a Reassessment," *Transactions of the Jewish Historical Society of England* 29 (1988): 165–75.

79. SPJC, Mahamad Papers, MS 295, no. 58, 30 September 1829. See *El Libro de los Acuerdos*, 6.

80. *Diaries of Sir Moses and Lady Montefiore*, 2 vols., ed. L. Loewe (London: Griffith Farran Okeden & Welsh, 1890), 1:9.

81. David Corcos, "Les Juifs au Maroc et leurs mellahs," in *Studies in the History of the Jews of Morocco* (Jerusalem: Rubin Mass, 1976), 114; Lucien Wolf, *Essays in Jewish History*, ed. Cecil Roth (London: The Jewish Historical Society of England, 1934), 400–401.

82. The marriage took place on 5 Shebet 5573. *Bevis Marks Records*, 2:119.

83. Esther de Samuel Haim de Moses Montefiore, on 12 Heshvan 5572. *Bevis Marks Records*, 2:118.

84. Paul Goodman, *Think and Thank* (London: Oxford University Press, 1933), 119.

85. Examples are scattered in the records of *ketuvot*, in *Bevis Marks Records*, pts. 2 and 3. See also Wolf, *Essays*, 221; Hyamson, *Sephardim*, 206.

86. Hyamsom, *Sephardim*, 190.

87. Picciotto, *Sketches*, 164.

88. Benady, "Settlement of Jews in Gibraltar," 102.

89. Autobiographical information is found in Moshe b. Yitshak Edraᶜi, *Yad Moshe* (Amsterdam, 1808/9). See also Yosef Ben Naʾim, *Malke rabanan* (Jerusalem: Defus Ha-Maᶜarav, 1930–31), fols. 92–92a; Abraham I. Laredo, *Les noms des Juifs du Maroc* (Madrid: Consejo Superior de Investigaciones Científicas, Instituto "B. Arias Montano," 1978), 233; see also Hyamson, *Sephardim*, 263.

90. SPJC, MS 755, vol. 2. On the Meldolas, see R. D. Barnett, "Haham Meldola and Hazan de Sola"; Gaster, *History of the Ancient Synagogue*, 160–64.

91. On this publishing market, see M. Mitchell Serels, "Sephardic Printing as a Source of Historical Material," in *The Sephardi and Oriental Jewish Heritage*, ed. Issachar Ben-Ami (Jerusalem: Magnes Press, The Hebrew University, 1982), 123–31.

92. David Hasin, *Tehilah le-David* (Amsterdam: Proops, 1807); see Corcos, "Juifs

au Maroc," 114 n. 115. On Hasin, see André E. Elbaz, "Quelques précisions inédites sur la vie et l'oeuvre de David Ben Hassine," in *Misgav Yerushalayim Studies in Jewish Literature*, ed. Ephraim Hazan (Jerusalem: Misgav Yerushalayim, 1987), 41–51.

93. Laredo, *Les noms*, 596.

94. Gaster, *History of the Ancient Synagogue*, 154.

95. Ibid., 169–71.

96. Miriam Bodian, "The Escamot of the Spanish-Portuguese Jewish Community of London, 1664," in *Michael*, vol. 9, ed. Daniel Carpi and Shlomo Simonsohn (Tel Aviv: Diaspora Research Institute, 1985), 9–15 (contains the original *escamot* in Spanish); for an English translation, see *El Libro de los Acuerdos*.

97. Meir Benyahu, "Vikuhim ba-kehilah ha-Sefaradit ve-ha-Portugezit be-London u-teshuvot ha-hakham Rabi Rafaʾel Meldola," in *Michael*, vol. 10, ed. Robert A. Rockaway and Shlomo Simonsohn (Tel Aviv: Diaspora Research Institute, 1986), 10, 15–20; Gaster, *History of the Ancient Synagogue*, 171; Hyamson, *Sephardim*, 235–38.

Chapter 5. The Macnins in Morocco

1. FO 174/13, 17 May 1802.

2. FO 174/13, 14 October 1803.

3. *Gentleman's Magazine* 78 (1808): 983.

4. Mohamed El Mansour, *Morocco in the Reign of Mawlay Sulayman* (Wisbech, Cambridgeshire: MENAS Press, 1990), 61–65. In 1815, four Christian merchants are mentioned. James Riley, *An Authentic Narrative of the Loss of the American Brig Commerce. . . .* (Hartford, Conn.: S. Andrus and Son, 1846), 198.

5. Riley, *Authentic Narrative*, 199–200.

6. Reference to merchant firms in Essaouira during these years is found in FO 174/13, December 1808, 1 June 1809, Gwyn to Green; FO 174/20, 4 May 1814, Dupuis to Green; 1 February 1810, 5 April 1810, 1 March 1811, 2 July 1811, 3 April 1812; 29 April 1812, Gwyn to Green.

7. Jean-Louis Miège, "Le Maroc et les premières lignes de navigation à vapeur," *Bulletin de l'Enseignement Public au Maroc*, no. 236 (1956): 37–47.

8. Riley, *Authentic Narrative*, 203.

9. Jean-Louis Miège, "L'activité maritime d'Essaouira, 1765–1840," in *Essaouira: Mémoire et empreintes du présent* (Agadir: Université Ibnou Zohr, Publications de la Faculté des Lettres et des Sciences Humaines, 1994), 20.

10. Muhammad al-Duᶜayyif, *Tarikh al-Duᶜayyif*, ed. Ahmad al-ᶜAmari (Rabat: Dar al-Maʾthurat, 1986), 274, 276.

11. Abu al-Qasim al-Zayyani, "Jamharat al-tijan wa-fahrisat al-yaqut wa-al-luʾllu wa-al-murjan fi dhikr al-muluk al-ᶜAlawiyyin wa-ashyakh Mawlana Sulayman" (KH, Ms. sig. MM 6778), cited in Rachid Abdallah El-Nasser, "Morocco from Kharijism to Wahhabism: The Quest for Religious Purism" (Ph.D. diss., University of Michigan, 1983), 446.

12. al-Zayyani, "*Alfiyat al-suluk*," Bibliothèque Générale (al-Khizanat al-ᶜAmma), Rabat, Ms. K.224, fol. 210, in Mohamed El Mansour, "Political and Social Developments in Morocco during the Reign of Mawlay Sulayman, 1792–1822" (Ph.D. thesis, University of London, 1981), appendices, 143.

13. Roger Le Tourneau, *Fès avant le protectorat* (Casablanca: SMLE, 1949), 380–81; see also Norman Cigar, "Socio-Economic Structures and the Development of an Urban Bourgeoisie in Pre-Colonial Morocco," *Maghreb Review* 6, nos. 3–4 (1981): 55–76.

14. FO 8/5, Instructions to Consuls, Mogador, 14 June 1814, Dupuis (?) to Green; regarding a debt owed to the late Mr. Gwyn.

15. FO 631/1 Mogador, 29 July 1813, and 21 August 1813, Dupuis (?) to Green.

16. FO 631/1 Mogador, 22 June 1814, [Dupuis] to Green.

17. For a description of this system, see James Richardson, *Travels in Morocco*, 2 vols. (London: Charles J. Skeet, 1860), 1:10–11.

18. Based on the two Judeo-Arabic account books in the Lévy papers. The first account book, concerning the affairs of Shlomo Macnin, runs from 17 Sivan 5574 = 5 June 1814 to 3 Heshvan 5576 = 6 November 1815 (hereafter LP, JA I). The other account book, belonging to Meir Macnin, which is less complete, covers the years 1820 to 1822 (hereafter LP, JA II).

19. LP, JA I, 24 Sivan 5574 = 12 June 1814. During the reign of Mawlay Sulayman, the minting of silver coins was very irregular. In 1221 (= 1806–7), a *dirham* of 1.954 grams was minted, of less weight than earlier *dirham*s, the coinage of which had been suspended. In subsequent years, the "new" *dirham* was struck only sporadically. Daniel Eustache, *Corpus des Monnaies ʿAlawites*, 3 vols. (Rabat: Banque du Maroc, 1984), 1:248–249.

20. LP, JA I, 21 Sivan 5574 = 9 June 1814. The *mithqal* had been sometimes a gold and sometimes a silver coin, but during this period, it was an accounting currency. See Eustache, Corpus, 1:245–52 passim.

21. LP, 21 Dhu al-Qaʿda 1220 = 10 February 1806.

22. See, e.g., Amnon Cohen, *Jewish Life under Islam: Jerusalem in the Sixteenth Century* (Cambridge, Mass.: Harvard University Press, 1984), 115–19.

23. For a discussion of the Judeo-Arabic of Morocco, see Joseph Chetrit, "Niveaux, registres de langue et sociolectes dans les langues judéo-arabes du Maroc," in *Les Relations entre juifs et musulmans en Afrique du Nord, XIXᵉ–XXᵉ siècles* (Paris: Editions du Centre National de la Recherche Scientifique, 1980), 129–43; idem, "Tradition du discours et discours de la tradition dans les communautés juives du Maroc: Etude socio-pragmatique," in *Communication in the Jewish Diaspora*, ed. Sophia Menache (Leiden: Brill, 1996), 339–407. For further discussion and a detailed case study, see Norman A. Stillman, *The Language and Culture of the Jews of Sefrou, Morocco: An Ethnolinguistic Study* (Manchester: University of Manchester Press, 1988); for one of the first extensive studies, see Louis Brunot and Elie Malka, *Glossaire judéo-arabe de Fès* (Rabat: Ecole du Livre, 1940), and idem, *Textes judéo-arabes de Fès* (Rabat: Ecole du Livre, 1939).

24. On the history and culture of tea in Morocco, see ʿAbd al-Ahad al-Sibti and ʿAbd al-Rahman Lakhsassi, *Min al-shaʾ ila al-tayʾ: al-ʿadah wa-al-tarikh* (Rabat: Manshurat Kulliyat al-Adab wa-al-ʿUlum al-Insaniya bi-al-Rabat, 1999).

25. LP, 1 Elul 5580 = 11 August 1820, signed Haim Pinto, David Elhazan.

26. LP, 4 Iyar 5575 = 14 May 1815, signed Musa b. Yehuda b. David Ohayon, Yisraʾel [   ] Harrush. I was unable to determine if David Cohen Macnin, Meir's nephew in London, was Shlomo's or Masud's son, or related to Meir in some other way.

27. André Chouraqui, *La Condition juridique de l'Israélite marocain* (Paris: Presses du Livre Français, 1950), 156; Haïm Zafrani, *Etudes et recherches sur la vie intellectuelle juive au Maroc de la fin du 15ᵉ siècle au début du 20ᵉ siècle*, vol. 1: *Pensée juridique et environnement social, économique et religieux* (Paris: Geuthner, 1972), 88.

28. LP, 24 Jumadi I 1224 = 7 July 1809.

29. LP, 8 Ramadan 1224 = 17 October 1809, seal unclear. Addressed "*dhimmi* our sharifian servant, the merchant Shlomo b. Macnin." Another letter only dated 1224 = 1809/10 also acknowledges receipt of the present that was given to the sultan as asked.

30. LP, JA I.

31. Rahma Bourqia, "Don et théatralité: Réflexion sur le rituel du don (*hadiyya*) offert au sultan au XIXᵉ siècle," *Hespéris-Tamuda* 31 (1993): 61–75.

32. Ibid., 70.

33. As related to James Richardson; Richardson, *Travels in Morocco*, 1:153–54.

34. From evidence later in the century, it seems that the Jewish merchants would typically receive pieces of linen, while Muslim merchants received completed garments. KH, 28 Muharram 1285 = 21 May 1868.

35. Richardson, *Travels in Morocco*, 1:146–48.

36. Cf. Abdellah Hammoudi, *Master and Disciple: The Cultural Foundations of Moroccan Authoritarianism* (Chicago: University of Chicago Press, 1997), 49–51.

37. See Mohammed Ennaji, *Expansion européene et changement social au Maroc (XVIᵉ–XIXᵉ siècles)* (Casablanca: Editions Eddif, 1996), 28–30.

38. FO 52/13, 9 May 1807; on Sulayman's restrictive policies, see the introduction to Antoine Burel, *La mission du Capitaine Burel au Maroc en 1808*, ed. Jacques Caillé (Paris: Arts et Métiers Graphiques, 1953), 9.

39. From a *fatwa* on a request by Jews to build a *hammam* in Fez in 1252/1836–37. Paul Paquignon, "Quelques documents sur la condition des Juifs au Maroc," *Revue du Monde Musulman* 9 (1909): 117.

40. Ramón Lourido Díaz, "Los Judíos en Marruecos durante el Sultanato de Sidi Muhammad b. Abd Allah (1757–1790)," *Majallat Dar al-Niyaba/Revue Dar al-Niaba* 3, no. 12 (1986): 26.

41. "A Reminder for the Children of Israel," Ben Zvi Institute, ms. 1742, cited in Shalom Bar-Asher, "Antisemitism and Economic Influence: The Jews of Morocco (1672–1822)," in *Antisemitism through the Ages*, ed. Shmuel Almog (Oxford: Pergamon Press, 1988), 203.

42. John Buffa, *Travels through the Empire of Morocco* (London: J. J. Stockdale, 1810), 113–14.

43. These observations were made by most European writers on Morocco. See, e.g., William Lempriere, *A Tour from Gibraltar to Tangier, Sallee, Mogodore, Santa Cruz, and Tarudant; and Thence over Mount Atlas to Morocco* (Philadelphia: Printed by T. Dobson, 1794), 5, 110, 135; Arthur de Capell Brooke, *Sketches in Spain and Morocco* (London: Henry Colburn and Richard Bentley, 1831), 249–50, 338–39.

44. Buffa, *Travels*, 69.

45. See Susan G. Miller, "*Dhimma* Reconsidered: Jews, Taxes and Royal Authority in Nineteenth-Century Tangier," in *In the Shadow of the Sultan: Culture, Power, and Politics in Morocco*, ed. Rahma Bourqia and Susan G. Miller (Cambridge, Mass.: Harvard University Press, 1999), 103–26.

46.   Domingo Badia y Leyblich, *Travels of Ali Bey* (London: Longman, Hurst, Rees, Orme and Brown, 1816), 147.

47.   James Grey Jackson, *An Account of Timbuctoo and Housa* (London: Printed for Longman, Hurst, Rees, Orme and Brown, 1820), 296–97.

48.   Norman A. Stillman, *The Jews of Arab Lands* (Philadelphia: Jewish Publication Society, 1979), 367, citing FO 174/10. For an analysis of this incident, see Bernard Lewis, *The Jews of Islam* (Princeton, N.J.: Princeton University Press, 1984), 154–55. This was not the first time that Jews having a claim to the protection of a European state sought the intervention of their government with a Muslim power, as Lewis asserts.

49.   Riley, *Authentic Narrative*, 257.

50.   Jean-Louis Miège, *Chronique de Tanger, 1820–1830: Journal de Bendelac* (Rabat: Editions La Porte, 1995), 277–78.

51.   FO 52/53, 22 Jumada I 1247 = 29 October 1831 (original English translation); FO 174/126, 29 October 1831.

52.   Riley, *Authentic Narrative*, 200, 205–6.

53.   G. Beauclerk, *Journey to Morocco* (London: Printed for Poole and Edwards, etc., 1828), 231.

54.   Jackson, *Account of Timbuctoo*, 297.

55.   Mark R. Cohen, *Under Crescent and Cross* (Princeton, N.J.: Princeton University Press, 1994), 69–71; Lewis, *Jews of Islam*, 14–15.

56.   Riley, *An Authentic Narrative*, 199; also found in Stillman, *The Jews of Arab Lands*, 368–69.

57.   AEN, Tanger 88, Mogador, 17 May 1844, Hélouis-Jorelle to Doré de Nion.

58.   Cf. Miller, "*Dhimma* Reconsidered," 108–9.

59.   LP, mid-Hijja 1214 = May 1800.

60.   For the different cities, see David ʿOvadiyah, *Kehilat Sefru*, 3 vols. (Jerusalem: Makhon la-Heker Toldot Kehilot Yehude Maroko, 1975–76), 1:103–4. On Tetuan, see Muhammad Daʾud, *Tarikh Titwan*, 6 vols. (Tetuan: Maktabat al-Talib, 1959–66), 3:238–39. A French translation of the *dahir* sent to the governor of Tetuan is found in Jean-Louis Miège, Mʾhammad Benaboud, and Nadia Erzini, *Tétouan: Ville andalouse marocaine* (Paris: CNRS Editions, 1996; Rabat: Kalila wa dimna, 1996), 82–84. On Essaouira, see FO 174/13, Mogador, 1 July 1807, Gwyn. On Rabat and Salé, see al-Duʿayyif, *Tarikh*, 334; Jacques Caillé, *La Ville de Rabat jusqu'au protectorat français* (Paris: Nanoest, 1949), 323–24; Kenneth L. Brown, "Mellah and Madina: A Moroccan City and its Jewish Quarter (Salé ca 1880–1930)," in *Studies in Judaism and Islam*, ed. S. Morag et al. (Jerusalem: Magnes Press, The Hebrew University, 1981), 254–55.

61.   Thomas James, *The History of the Herculean Straits, Now Called the Straits of Gibraltar*, 2 vols. (London: Printed by Charles Rivington, 1771), 2:22.

62.   Antoine Fattal, *Le Statut légal des non-musulmans en pays d'Islam* (Beirut: Impr. Catholique, 1958), 93; Georges Vajda, "Un traité maghrébin 'adversus judaeos': 'Aḥkam ahl al-dimma' du šayḫ Muḥammad b. ʿAbd al-Karīm al-Maġīlī," in *Etudes d'orientalisme dediées à la mémoire de Lévi-Provençal*, vol. 2 (Paris: G.-P. Maisonneuve et Larose, 1962), 808; al-Wansharisi, *al-Miyar al-Maghrib*, trans. Emile Amar, "La pierre de touche des fétwas," *Archives Marocaines* 12 (1908): 231–32.

63. See El-Nasser, "From Kharijism to Wahhabism," 395.

64. Brown, "A Moroccan City," 254.

65. Ibid., 254–55.

66. Stillman, *The Jews of Arab Lands*, 79–81.

67. David Corcos, "Les Juifs au Maroc et leurs *mellahs*," in his *Studies in the History of the Jews of Morocco* (Jerusalem: Rubin Mass, 1976), 104.

68. Daʾud, *Tarikh*, 3:238–39; Corcos, "Juifs au Maroc," 92–93.

69. Corcos, "Juifs au Maroc," 121–22.

70. Al-Duʿayyif, *Tarikh*, 346.

71. Brown, "A Moroccan City"; Corcos, "Juifs au Maroc," 103.

72. FO 174/13, 1 July 1807, Gwyn.

73. Archibald Robbins, *A Journal Comprising an Account of the Loss of the Brig Commerce. . . .* (Hartford, Conn.: Silas Andrus & Son, 1851), 252–53.

74. *Gentleman's Magazine* 78 (1808): 982–84.

75. This is discussed in a responsum of Yosef Elmalih, *Tokfo shel Yosef*, vol. 1 (Livorno: Printed by Eliyahu Ben Amozeg, 1854/55), analyzed in Corcos, "Juifs au Maroc," 122. In July 1807, the British consular agent reported that a government official came to pay the Jews for their houses, and that an augmentation on the value of them was ordered. It is likely that the augmentation, however, was after the Jews were paid, as evidenced from the responsum.

76. KH, Kᵍ³. See Daniel J. Schroeter, *Merchants of Essaouira: Urban Society and Imperialism in Southwestern Morocco, 1844–1886* (Cambridge: Cambridge University Press, 1988), 32.

77. Riley, *Authentic Narrative*, 200, 225.

78. Ibid., 200.

79. LP, 24 Jumadi II 1222 = 29 August 1807, Muhammad b. Ahmad [   ], Ibrahim [   ].

80. LP, 28 Jumadi II 1222 = 2 September 1807, Muhammad b. [   ]; al-ʿAyashi b. al-Hasan al-Shabbani.

81. LP, 25 Rabiʿ II 1222 = 2 July 1807, Muhammad b. Ahmad [   ], Ibrahim [   ]; the property was previously sold in 1803. LP, 5 Rabiʿ II 1218 = 25 July 1803, signatures unclear.

82. LP, end of Jumadi I 1224 = July 1809.

83. LP, mid-Safar 1226 = March 1811, signatures unclear.

84. LP, 4 Iyar 5563 = 26 April 1803, David Elhazan and (Haim) Pinto; 25 Tishri 5562 = 2 October 1801, Haim Pinto and David Elhazan.

85. LP, 21 Tevet 5571 = 17 January 1811, Haim Pinto and Moshe b. Avraham Sabbah.

86. LP, 29 Sivan 5578 = 3 July 1818, Haim Pinto and David Benʿattar.

87. LP, JA II, 5583 = 1822/23.

88. LP, 10 Elul 5582 = 27 August 1822, signed Yaʿkov b. Elazar Hacohen.

89. LP, 10 Tevet 5565 = 12 December 1804, Haim Pinto and David Elhazan. Initially three hundred *riyal*s were paid, and twenty were added on 24 Sivan 5565 = 21 June 1805.

90. LP, mid-Rabiʿ I 1239 = November 1823.

91. LP, 5 Adar 5587 = 5 March 1827, signed David Elhazan (?).

92. LP, Shevat 5587 = January/February 1827. On the institutions of the synagogue, see Zafrani, *Etudes*, 126–27.

93. LP, 16 Shevat 5587 = 13 February 1827, signed Ya°kov b. Elazar Hacohen and Mordekhai b. Mas°ud Malka; LP, 5 Adar 5587 = 5 March 1827, signed Haim Pinto and David Elhazan.

94. Recorded in LP, JA I, 144 Adar B 5575 = 26 March 1815.

95. There are several published hagiographies of Rabbi Haim Pinto. See, e.g., Avraham Ben°attar, *Shanot Hayyim* (Casablanca: Imprimerie Simplex A. Soussan, 1958); Ehud Mikhelson, *ha-Shoshelet le-vet Pinto: toldot rabane ha-mishpahah u-ma°ase mofet* (Tel Aviv: Gale-Alfa Tikshoret, 1992).

96. The issue of community versus privately owned synagogues is analyzed in detail by Shlomo Deshen, *The Mellah Society: Jewish Community Life in Sherifian Morocco* (Chicago: University of Chicago Press, 1989), 90–103.

97. FO 52/14, 10 October 1808, Macnin to Castlereagh.

98. FO 52/12, Tangier, 16 September 1804, 12 October 1804, 20 October 1804, Matra; cf. El Mansour, *Morocco in the Reign of Mawlay Sulayman*, 431. On °Ash°ash, see Schroeter, *Merchants*, 118.

99. FO 174/13, Mogador, 1 August 1807, Gwyn to Matra.

100. FO 8/5, instructions to Consul, Downing Street, 2 June 1807, Castlereagh to Green.

101. FO 52/14, 22 April 1807.

102. FO 52/14, 29 December 1807, affidavit of Moses Stanton.

103. FO 52/14, 28 Dhu al-Hijja 1222 = 26 February 1808, sultan to Ahmad b. °Abd al-Sadiq; 16 Rabi° I 1223 = 12 May 1808, °Abd al-Sadiq to principal secretary of state; 26 April 1808, Meir Macnin to Castlereagh.

104. FO 174/13, 24 May 1808, Downing Street, E. Cooke to Meir Macnin.

105. FO 52/14, 6 July 1808.

106. FO 52/14, 26 July 1808, Macnin to Cooke.

107. FO 52/14, 24 October 1909.

108. FO 52/14, 16 November 1808, Macnin to Cooke.

109. FO 174/20, 2 July 1811, Gwyn.

110. FO 52/16, 18 June 1812, Moses Abitbol to Bathurst.

111. See my "Royal Power and the Economy in Precolonial Morocco: Jews and the Legitimation of Foreign Trade," in *In the Shadow of the Sultan*, 75.

112. FO 52/16, 6 Safar 1228 = 8 February 1813.

113. FO 52/16, 22 March 1813.

114. FO 52/16, 26 April 1813, Macnin to Chapman.

115. FO 52/16, 5 May 1813, Macnin to Bunbury.

116. FO 52/16, 12 May 1813, Macnin to Bunbury.

117. *Maqam* is literally "position" or "rank," but is a standard title used for the sultan.

118. FO 52/17, 8 Rabi° I 1231 = 7 February 1816, Sultan Sulayman to Castlereagh; FO 52/18, 7 Jumada I 1232 = 25 March 1817, °Abd al-Khalid b. °Abd al-Qadir °Ash°ash to Castlereagh.

119. FO 52/24, 23 February 1823, Douglas to Talib Benjalun.

120. FO 52/17, 18 September 1816, D. C. Macnin to Earl Bathurst.

121. FO 174/286, Ahmad b. Mubarak to the English vice consul, n.d. (in Arabic); this is attested to by a letter sent by Meir Macnin, 8 Sivan 5576 = 4 June 1816 (in

Judeo-Arabic). Ahmad b. Mubarak was a minister in the court of Sulayman, the "Keeper of the Seal" (*sahib al-khatim*). See Ahmad b. Khalid al-Nasiri, *Kitab al-Istiqsaʾ li-akhbar duwal al-Maghrib al-Aqsa*, 2d ed., 9 vols. (Casablanca: Dar al-Kitab, 1954–56), 9:130–31.

122. FO 174/286, 9 Muharram 1232 = 29 November 1816, Ahmad b. Mubarak.

123. FO 52/17, 28 December 1816. Navy Office.

124. FO 174/286, 9 Muharram 1816 = 29 November 1816 (English translation; there is also a Spanish translation, but the Arabic original is missing).

125. FO 52/18, 11 February 1817. J. Guedalla and D. C. Macnin to Bathurst.

126. LP, 28 Safar 1233 = 7 January 1818.

127. FO 52/21, 15 March 1820, D. C. Macnin to Bathurst.

128. FO 52/19, 8 June 1818, Ben Ribuh to Bathurst.

129. FO 52/19, 2 November 1818, J. Guedalla and D. C. Macnin (now of 110 Fenchurch Street) to Earl Bathurst.

130. FO 174/286, 16 January 1822.

131. FO 174/286, 17 January 1822.

132. AEN, Tanger 87, Mogador, 14 July 1820, Casaccia to Sourdeau.

133. Evidence was found only in register books where judgments are listed for 15 July 1822. Archives Départementales des Bouches-du-Rhône, Marseilles, 545 U 156, and 545 U 1.

Chapter 6. The Sultan's Jew

1. The event is described in the diary of a Moroccan Jew who was the acting consular agent in Tangier for the Netherlands. This diary, found in the Dutch archives (ARH), was edited with extensive cross-referencing of other consular archives by Jean-Louis Miège, *Chronique de Tanger, 1820–1830: Journal de Bendelac* (Rabat: Editions La Porte, 1995). On the event of 21 November 1823, see p. 215.

2. FO 52/24, translation of the *dahir* of 22 Safar 1239 = 28 October 1823. The date of the document is incorrectly translated as 19 November 1823, two days before the *dahir* was read. Translations are also found in AEP, CCC Maroc 28; NA, RG 84 Tangier. The Arabic document probably reads "Tit" instead of "Mazagan" (as appears in the French and American translation, and a copy of the American translation is also found in FO 52/28). Tit was an Atlantic port next to El Jadida (the latter known to Europeans as Mazagan), established by Sidi Muhammad b. ʿAbdallah, that failed to develop.

3. On Muhammad ʿAshʿash and his governmental service, see Muhammad Daʾud, *Tarikh Titwan*, 6 vols. (Tetuan: al-Maktabat al-Mahdiyya, 1959–66), 3:276–83.

4. Translations of these letters are found in FO 52/24, 22 Safar 1239 = 28 October 1823; AEP, CCC Maroc 28; NA, RG 84 Tangier. Both the British and the French incorrectly translated the Muslim date.

5. Miège, *Journal de Bendelac*, 215, 217.

6. See Charles Issawi, *An Economic History of the Middle East and North Africa* (New York: Columbia University Press, 1982), 89–91; for a general discussion on the Jews of the Ottoman Empire, see Avigdor Levy, *The Sephardim in the Ottoman Empire* (Princeton, N.J.: Darwin Press, 1992), 28–34.

7. FO 52/24, 24 November 1823, Douglas; Ahmad b. Khalid al-Nasiri, *Kitab al-istiqsa³ li-akhbar duwal al-Maghrib al-Aqsa*, 2d ed., 9 vols. (Casablanca: Dar al-Kitab, 1954–56), 8:155.

8. Cf. Mohamed El Mansour, *Morocco in the Reign of Mawlay Sulayman* (Wisbech, Cambridgeshire: MENAS Press, 1990), 68–71.

9. Ibid., 187.

10. Ibid., 69.

11. On this rebellion, see ibid., 119–208. See also Miège, *Journal de Bendelac*, 45ff.

12. El Mansour, *Morocco in the Reign of Mawlay Sulayman*, 69–70.

13. Miège, *Journal de Bendelac*, 78.

14. Georges Vajda, *Un recueil de textes historiques judéo-marocains* (Paris: Larose, 1951), 100; El Mansour, *Morocco in the Reign of Mawlay Sulayman*, 192.

15. Miège, *Journal de Bendelac*, 81.

16. Ibid., 136.

17. El Mansour, *Morocco in the Reign of Mawlay Sulayman*, 219.

18. FO 174/28, Mogador, 2 November 1822, Willshire to Douglas. Possibly the governor was ʿAbd al-Rahman rather than ʿAbd al-Malik ʿAshʿash. See Miège, *Journal de Bendelac*, 126–27 nn. 86, 87.

19. His debts over two years (1236–37 = 1820–22) amounted to 102,035 *riyals*. LP, JA II.

20. Report of the amount paid for the *sakat al-rish*. LP, JA II.

21. G. Beauclerk, *Journey to Marocco* (London: Printed for Poole and Edwards, etc., 1828), 251.

22. James Richardson, *Travels in Morocco*, 2 vols. (London: Charles J. Skeet, 1860), 1:298.

23. LP, 7 Muharram 1240 = 1 September 1824. Evidence of the close ties between Macnin and Amar comes from Meir's 1822 account book. LP, JA II.

24. FO 174/28, 31 December 1823, Willshire.

25. LP, 17 Shevat 5582 = 8 February 1822, signed Haim Pinto and David Elhazan.

26. During this period, Meir was sending goods to his brother in Marrakesh. LP, JA II.

27. Miège, *Journal de Bendelac*, 120. The previous year, Denmark agreed to remit one hundred thousand *riyals* of arrears in tribute. El Mansour, *Morocco in the Reign of Mawlay Sulayman*, 202. On the history of the annual tribute paid by Sweden and Denmark, see Jacques Caillé, "L'abolition des tributs versés au Maroc par la Suède et le Danemark," *Hespéris* 45 (1958): 203–38.

28. LP, 27 Safar 1238 = 13 November 1822, *dahir* of Sultan Sulayman.

29. al-Nasiri, *al-Istiqsa³*, 8:155, 166; FO 52/24, 24 November 1823, Douglas; Miège, *Journal de Bendelac*, 131.

30. Miège, *Journal de Bendelac*, 134–35.

31. Ibid., 150–51 n. 24, 183; FO 52/23, 28 June 1822; FO 52/24, 10 April 1823, Douglas. See also Mustafa Bushuʿara³, *al-Istitan wa-al-himaya bi-al-Maghrib, 1280–1311/ 1865–1894*, 4 vols. (Rabat: al-Matbaʿat al-Malikiya, 1984–89), 1:80–81.

32. AEP, CCC Maroc 29, 19 July 1825, Sordeau.

33. Miège, *Journal de Bendelac*, 201.

34. FO 174/28, 31 December 1823, Willshire.

35. Miège, *Journal de Bendelac*, 213–14.

36. Ibid., 214; AEP, CCC Maroc 28, 24 Safar 1239 = 30 October 1823.

37. FO 52/24, 29 November 1823, Douglas.

38. NA, RG 84 Tangier, 22 November 1823.

39. FO 52/24, 29 November 1823, Douglas.

40. FO 8/8, Downing Street, London, 27 January 1824, R. W. Horton to Douglas.

41. Miège, *Journal de Bendelac*, 215. Perhaps this refers to the judgment of 15 July 1822 (see above, Chapter 5, note 133).

42. AEP, CCC Maroc 28, 28 November 1823, Tangier, Sourdeau.

43. NA, RG 84 Tangier, 8 Rabiᶜ I 1239 = 12 November 1823, Sultan to Umimun. The date is incorrectly translated as 6 November 1823.

44. FO 174/28, 31 December 1823.

45. See, e.g., Arthur de Capell Brooke, *Sketches in Spain and Morocco* (London: Henry Colburn and Richard Bentley, 1831), 249.

46. FO 174/28, 31 December 1823, Willshire.

47. AEP, CCC Mogador 1, 2 January 1841, Delaporte; see also Daniel J. Schroeter, *Merchants of Essaouira: Urban Society and Imperialism in Southwestern Morocco, 1844–1886* (Cambridge: Cambridge University Press, 1988), 24–25.

48. Private papers of the Corcos family (Jerusalem), 28 Jumada II 1263 = 23 June 1846. The amount of debt is listed in a letter dated 14 Safar 1263 = 1 February 1847, ᶜAbd al-Rahman in an order to al-Hajj al-ᶜArabi al-Tarris, the governor of Essaouira. This letter is reproduced with a translation in Hebrew in Michel Abitbol, *Tugᵊar al-sultan: ᶜIlit kalkalit yehudit be-Maroko* (Jerusalem: Makhon Ben Tsevi, 1994), 2–3.

49. FO 174/28, 21 April 1923.

50. FO 174/28, 21 April 1823, Willshire.

51. FO 174/28, 3 June 1823, Willshire.

52. Miège, *Journal de Bendelac*, 223, 225, 227–28.

53. FO 52/24, 29 November 1823, Douglas. The sultan wished to have Sardinia pay an annual tribute as did Denmark and Sweden, but after negotiations with the Sardinian consul, he agreed to sign a treaty without requiring tribute. François Mugnier, "Relation d'un voyage à Fez en 1825," *Mémoires et Documents de la Société Savoisienne d'Histoire et d'Archéologie* 26 (1887): 363–64, 419–20.

54. Miège, *Journal de Bendelac*, 230. On Douglas's embassy to Fez, see P. G. Rogers, *A History of Anglo-Moroccan Relations to 1900* (London: Foreign and Commonwealth Office, n.d.), 135–36. The sultan also wished that the United States would send an embassy, with substantial presents, to the royal court. The American consul Mullowny was able to evade this request. Luella J. Hall, *The United States and Morocco, 1776–1956* (Metuchen, N.J.: Scarecrow Press, 1971), 103–4.

55. Miège, *Journal de Bendelac*, 225–30, 249.

56. FO 174/125, 21 Shaᶜban 1239 = 21 April 1824, translation of a letter from the sultan to the Hamburg Nation. On relations between Hamburg and Morocco, see Pierre Guillen, *L'Allemagne et le Maroc de 1870 à 1905* (Paris: Presses Universitaires de France, 1967), 4–6.

57. NA, RG 84 Tangier, 15 December 1823 (letter sent 24 November).

58. LP, letter to the sultan, with date and signature effaced. From the context it

can be deduced that it is from the governor of Tangier. "Année 1824" was added on the bottom.

59. Macnin's control of cattle exports in Tangier and Tetuan was reaffirmed by the sultan on 5 March 1824. Miège, *Journal de Bendelac*, 251.

60. Maurice Payard, *Le financier G.-J. Ouvrard, 1770–1846* (Reims: Académie Nationale de Reims, 1958), 113; Jacques Wolff, *Le financier Ouvrard* (Paris: Librairie Jules Tallandier, 1992), 198–99.

61. FO 52/24, 29 November 1823, Douglas; AEN, Tanger 57, 22 Rabiᶜ I 1239 = 25 November 1823. The contract was translated by the French vice consul, Delaporte, who had an excellent command of Arabic, and he signed it on 24 May 1824. Bendelac reports this transaction in his diary for November 26, and he refers to six thousand oxen, and a half-*riyal* duty per *fanega* of barley (another measurement). Other correspondence refers to these latter amounts, according to Miège, *Journal de Bendelac*, 217–18 n. 178. However, in contrast to Miège's interpretation, the contract in Arabic refers only to the four thousand oxen, and to quintals rather than *fanegas*. The contract is published in ᶜAbd al-Rahman Ibn Zaydan, *Ithaf aᶜlam al-nas bi-jamal akhbar hadirat Miknas*, 5 vols (Rabat: al-Matbaᶜat al-Wataniya "li-Sahibiha ᶜAbbas al-Thanani wa-Muhammad al-Qabbaj," 1929–33), 5:156–59.

62. Miège, *Journal de Bendelac*, 220.

63. Ibid., 237, 242. Delaporte was sent to Cadiz to obtain the twenty thousand *riyal*s to cover the contract.

64. AEN, Tanger 57, 4 August 1824, Sourdeau to Dolfus.

65. Miège, *Journal de Bendelac*, 299 n. 7, 309 n. 32.

66. AEN, Tanger 57, 22 April 1825 = 3 Ramadan 1240, Sourdeau to Meir Macnin.

67. Miège, *Journal de Bendelac*, 219 n. 178. Miège found no evidence in the archives that the rest of the shipments were ever made.

68. Ibid., 418 n. 3; FO 52/27, 10 December 1826, Douglas.

69. AEP, Affaires Diverses Politiques, Maroc 1, 28 September 1829, 31 August 1831, Dolfus and Ducroc.

70. Miège, *Journal de Bendelac*, 219, 221.

71. Ibid., 247. On the general antipathy between the governor and Douglas, see Mugnier, "Relation d'un voyage," 360–63.

72. FO 52/25, 4 June 1824, Douglas. See also Miège, *Journal de Bendelac*, 259.

73. Miège, *Journal de Bendelac*, 260.

74. Ibid., 261–62 n. 64.

75. Ibid., 262–63 n. 65.

76. FO 52/25, 4 June 1824, Douglas.

77. *Journal de Bendelac*, 262 n. 64.

78. Ibid., 255, 264, 266 n. 74; FO 52/25, 4 June 1824, Douglas.

79. Jacques Caillé, Le Consulat de Tanger (des origines à 1830) (Paris: Editions A. Pedone, 1967), 107–9; Journal de Bendelac, 271 n. 85.

80. FO 52/25, 4 June 1824, Douglas.

81. Miège, *Journal de Bendelac*, 258. There are few letters in the Lévy-Corcos collection from this period. A *dahir*, dated 22 Ramadan 1239 = 21 May 1824, orders "our servant the merchant Meir b. Macnin to pay our secretary Sidi Mukhtar al-Jamaᶜi twenty *riyal*s from money that he has that is owed to us."

82. AEP, Mémoires et Documents, Afrique 5, cited in Miège, *Journal de Bendelac*, 279 n. 102.

83. NA, RG 84 Tangier, 20 February 1824, Mullowny; Miège, *Journal de Bendelac*, 278–79 n. 102.

84. AEP, CCC Maroc 28, 18 Ramadan 1239 = 17 May 1824 (translated incorrectly as 18 May), ʿAbd al-Rahman to Sordeau.

85. NA, RG 84 Tangier, 22 November 1823, Mullowny.

86. Miège, *Journal de Bendelac*, 297 n. 1, 302, 305, 317, 334, 337, 339 n. 28, 345 n. 47.

87. Ibid., 349 n. 59.

88. NA, RG 84 Tangier, 4 Dhu al-Qaʿda 1240 = 20 June 1825 (incorrectly translated as 19 June), translated *dahir* to the governor.

89. Miège, *Journal de Bendelac*, 372, 380. Miège's suggestion that this move represented a precipitous fall of influence, and a "demi-exil" (371 n. 109) seems a little exaggerated.

90. AEN, Tanger 57, 25 Rabiʿ I 1241 = 7 November 1825, French consul to Ibn Jallun. He was sent to Tangier in December 1825. Miège, *Journal de Bendelac*, 409. Merchandise belonging to Ibn Jallun shipped on a Sardinian ship to Tunis is reported in the entry for 24 December 1826 (ibid., 461). Ibn Jallun is mentioned as being at the royal court in Fez in June of 1825, prior to his arrival in Tangier, in Mugnier, "Relation d'un voyage," 404, 413–14, 420–24. On Ibn Jallun's diplomatic negotiations with the Two Sicilies, see Giovanni Iannettone, *Il Marocco negli atti consolari del regno delle Due Sicilie* (Naples: Editrice Cymba, 1967), 111ff. Foreign sources frequently refer to him as Ibn Jallul (Benjelul, Benjeloul, etc.).

91. Miège, *Journal de Bendelac*, 373 n. 110, 406–8, n. 50, 415, 441. Supposedly eighteen hundred Jews died of hunger in Fez. Vajda, *Recueil de textes*, 100.

92. See, e.g., Mugnier, "Relation d'un voyage," 368–69.

93. Ibid., 407–8.

94. AEN, Tanger 87, 12 May 1831, Addy Delevante to Dellaporte (in Italian).

95. Douglas himself does not refer to the appointment in his correspondence with the Foreign Office, but his successor, R. W. Hay, does: FO 52/36, 2 June 1832.

96. National Archives, Stockholm, Svenska Konsulers skrivelser 51 Tanger, 20 June 1825, cited in Miège, *Journal de Bendelac*, 110 n. 44.

97. AEP, CCC Maroc 29, 6 May 1826, Sordeau. The archives and seal of the French consulate remained in Masud's house until the appointment of Addy Delevante as consular agent in 1828. Miège, *Journal de Bendelac*, 529.

98. Beauclerk, *Journey*, 151. Reference here is to the British political rivals, William Pitt and Charles Fox, who constantly attempted to outflank each other in positions of power. Both died in 1806, and are buried next to each other in Westminster Abbey.

99. Ibid., 153–54.

100. Ibid., 247.

101. Ibid., 173.

Chapter 7. The Unwanted Emissary

1. In 1828, Harun b. Itshak Israʾil [Aaron ben Isaac Israel], and in 1835, Nessim Cohen Solal were appointed, but objections were raised since Muslims would be

under the jurisdiction of a Jew. AEN, Tanger 82, "Correspondances et notes relatives aux projects conçus par le Sultan de créer un consulat marocain à Marseille," 1827–1835, *dahir*s of 23 Dhu al-Qaʿda 1243 = 6 June 1828, and 27 Safar 1251 = 24 June 1835. See Jean-Louis Miège, *Le Maroc et l'Europe, 1830–1894*, 4 vols. (Paris: Presses Universitaires de France, 1961–63), 2:89. Miège also refers to a chargé d'affaires accredited to the court of Turin who resided in Genoa, but is unclear on his source and does not give the period or duration of the appointment. He writes that it was "so discreet that he disappeared without anyone noticing" (29). Elsewhere he refers to "the Jew Modena at Genoa, the only other Moroccan consul [besides Benoliel in Gibraltar] officially accredited in Europe." His name appears in some of the consular records, but rarely in the state archives of Turin. Idem, *Chronique de Tanger, 1820–1830: Journal de Bendelac* (Rabat: Editions La Porte, 1995), 36 n. 23, 319–20 n. 58.

2. Arthur de Capell Brooke, *Sketches in Spain and Morocco*, 2 vols. (London: Henry Colburn and Richard Bentley, 1831), 1:132. See also G. Beauclerk, *Journey to Morocco* (London: Printed for Poole and Edwards, etc., 1828), 1.

3. Miège, *Journal de Bendelac*, 17, 115 n. 60, 203–4 n. 145, 470 n. 12; idem, *Le Maroc et l'Europe*, 2:89 n. 3.

4. Miège, *Journal de Bendelac*, 125, 156, 158, 159, 338.

5. Ibid., 157, 330 n. 5, 337–38 n. 23.

6. Cf. Mohammed Kenbib, *Les protégés: contribution à l'histoire contemporaine du Maroc* (Rabat: Université Mohammed V, Publications de la Faculté des Lettres et des Sciences Humaines, 1996), 29–40.

7. Mustafa Bushuʿaraʾ, *al-Istitan wa-al-himaya bi-al-Maghrib, 1280–1311/1865– 1894*, 4 vols. (Rabat: al-Matbaʿat al-Malikiya, 1984–89), 1:58.

8. Miège, *Journal de Bendelac*, 75–76 n. 103, 330. He was customs agent in Tangier in the 1820s (94, 153), and "head of the treasury" (159).

9. See the introduction to Muhammad al-Saffar, *Disorienting Encounters: Travels of a Moroccan Scholar in France in 1845–1846: The Voyage of Muhammad as-Saffar*, trans. and ed. Susan Gilson Miller (Berkeley: University of California Press, 1992), 12.

10. Ibid., 13–14.

11. FO 52/8, Tangier, 21 August 1789, Matra.

12. Abderrahmane El Moudden, "The Ambivalence of *Rihla*: Community Integration and Self-Definition in Moroccan Travel Accounts, 1300–1800," in *Muslim Travelers: Pilgrimage, Migration, and the Religious Imagination*, ed. Dale F. Eickelman and James Piscatori (Berkeley: University of California Press, 1990), 69.

13. al-Saffar, *Disorienting Encounters*, 53.

14. Ibid., 53–54.

15. SP 71/21, 7 August 1772, 28 December 1772, and 23 February 1773, Benider to Earl of Rochford. The British decided to appoint Benider to Essaouira when it became clear that it was becoming the principal port. FO 52/2, Gibraltar, 19 May 1770, 17 August 1770, J. Sampson. Benider remained in London, and in 1784 he petitioned the British government for passage to return to Gibraltar. His petition came before the commissioner appointed by Parliament for the indemnification of the American loyalists (AO 13/79), and is published by Cecil Roth, "Jacob Benider: Moroccan Envoy at the Court of St. James (1772)," *Miscellanies of the Jewish Historical Society of En-*

gland 2 (1935): 84–90. A Muslim ambassador, Sidi Tahir Fannish, was appointed to England in 1773. FO 52/3, Gibraltar, 3 August 1773, Logie.

16. FO 52/3, Gibraltar, 12 April 1773, 13 May 1773, Logie; Georg Høst, *Histoire de l'Empereur du Maroc Mohamed Ben Abdallah*, trans. F. Damgaard and P. Gailhanou (Rabat: Editions La Porte, 1998; first published in Danish in 1791), 66–67.

17. See Miège, *Le Maroc et l'Europe*, 2:40–41, 142, 184, 3:187; FO 52/24, 29 November 1823, Tangier, Douglas; FO 52/25, 1824; FO 52/26, 17 June 1825, Tangier, Douglas; FO 52/28, 22 Safar 1239 = 28 October 1823, Sultan ʿAbd al-Rahman to King George IV.

18. FO 52/26, 17 June 1825, Douglas; FO 95/166, Downing Street, 23 September 1825, R. W. Hay to A. Glennie, Smith, Griffith, and Richardson.

19. FO 52/28, 25 October 1826, Sultan ʿAbd al-Rahman to King George IV (Arabic original and English translation).

20. FO 52/27, Nº 9 Mincing Lane, 28 November 1826, Robᵗ Burchall to Earl Bathurst. Subsequently, Burchall sent his account with Macnin to the Foreign Office. FO 52/28, 10 February 1827.

21. FO 52/28, 2 March 1827, Burchall.

22. FO 95/166, Downing Street, 8 January 1827, 22 February 1827, R. W. Hay to R. Burchall; 15 February 1827, R. W. Hay to His M's Advocate General.

23. FO 95/166, Downing Street, 14 March 1827, R. W. Hay to Burchall.

24. AEP, CP Maroc 2, 6 November 1826, Sourdeau.

25. FO 52/31, 2 October 1828.

26. FO 174/28, 27 January 1827, Chaillet to Douglas; Miège, *Journal de Bendelac*, 469.

27. Miège, *Journal de Bendelac*, 471.

28. Ibid., 475.

29. FO 52/28, 26 February 1827.

30. FO 52/28, Downing Street, 12 March 1827.

31. FO 95/164, 26 March 1827, Bathurst to Douglas.

32. CO 91/91, 21 May 1827, Sir George Don to Viscount Goderich (responding to a despatch of 28 March).

33. FO 95/166, Downing Street, 13 March 1827, R. W. Hay to H. Hobhouse.

34. FO 95/164, 27 March 1827, Bathurst to Douglas.

35. FO 52/28, 28 April 1827, Douglas.

36. The news reached Tangier on 6 May: Miège, *Journal de Bendelac*, 477.

37. FO 52/28, 26 April 1827, Stangate Creek, Dixon.

38. FO 95/166, Downing Street, 27 March 1827, R. W. Hay to Captain Marshall Ru.

39. FO 52/28, 27 April 1827, R. W. Hay.

40. FO 52/28, 29 April 1827.

41. Miège, *Journal de Bendelac*, 430 n. 34; Høst, *Histoire de l'Empereur*, 76.

42. FO 52/28, 11 February 1827.

43. FO 52/28, 14 May 1827, Macnin. Copy of reply in FO 95/166, 16 May 1827, R. W. Hay.

44. FO 52/28, 30 May 1827.

45. FO 95/166, 4 June 1827.

46. FO 95/164.

47. FO 52/28, 14 May 1827, Meir Macnin to Lord Goderich.

48. FO 95/166, Downing Street, 11 July 1827, R. W. Hay to Mr. Ackroyd.

49. Miège, *Journal de Bendelac*, 482.

50. FO 52/31, 20 January 1829, diary of vice consul Chaillet.

51. See P. G. Rogers, *A History of Anglo-Moroccan Relations to 1900* (London: Foreign and Commonwealth Office, n.d.), 137–38.

52. FO 52/28, London, 17 May 1827, M. S. Bensusan & Co.

53. FO 52/58, London, 17 May 1827, Burchall.

54. FO 52/32, Tangier, 12 March 1830, copy of an original agreement to charter the vessel *Northumberland*.

55. FO 52/30, 19 March 1830.

56. FO 52/32, 12 March 1830, E. W. A. Drummond Hay.

57. FO 52/32, 9 September 1829, Shlomo Macnin. The letter is written in Judeo-Arabic, with an English translation.

58. FO 52/32, Tangier, 12 March 1830, E. W. A. Drummond Hay to R. W. Hay.

59. FO 52/32, Mogador, 29 December 1829, Vice Consul Chaillet to E. W. A. Drummond Hay.

60. SPJC, Minutes, MS 112, fol. 211, 242.

61. SPJC, Mahamad Papers, MS 295, no. 14, 13 December 1826, David Macnin to wardens (*parnasim*); MS 296, no. 10, 30 March 1827, David Macnin to Solomon Almosnino.

62. Albert M. Hyamson refers to a dispute involving Abraham Cohen, but this is probably an error. It was David who was having financial difficulties at the time. See *The Sephardim of England* (London: Methuen, 1951), 207.

63. PRO, Court of Bankruptcy, B 3/3615, Office of the Commissioners of Bankrupts and Court of Bankruptcy. Bankruptcy Commission Files. It was only in 1831, the year of D. C. Macnin's bankruptcy, that the Court of Bankruptcy was established by an act that made the Bankruptcy Commissioners officers of the court. See Sheila Marriner, "English Bankruptcy Records and Statistics before 1850," *Economic History Review* 33 (1980): 352.

64. PRO, Court of Bankruptcy, B 3/3615.

65. FO 174/287, 8 May 1832, Thomas and George Courtney, appointing E. W. A. Drummond Hay as attorney.

66. FO 174/287, 8 May 1832, Thomas Courtney.

67. This is mentioned in a note from Andrew Van Sandan to E. W. A. Drummond Hay attached to Courtney's affidavit.

68. FO 52/36, 30 April 1832, And^w Van Sandan to R. W. Hay. E. W. A. Drummond Hay in Tangier speculates that Macnin may either have been imprisoned or placed under some constraint by Courtney, but there is no further evidence on this matter. FO 52/36, Tangier, 25 May 1832, Hay to Willshire.

69. FO 52/36, 25 May 1832, Hay to Willshire.

70. FO 174/126, 26 May 1832, Hay to sultan (with an Arabic translation).

71. FO 174/126, 26 May 1832, Hay to Sidi al-Mukhtar al-Jamaᶜi (with an Arabic translation).

72. FO 52/36, 2 June 1832, Hay to Van Sandan.

73. FO 52/36, 1 June 1832, Hay to Willshire.

74. FO 52/36, 2 June 1832, private letter of Hay.

75. FO 174/126, 8 Muharram 1248 = 7 June 1832; only the English translation was found in the archives. The Muslim date is incorrectly converted to 8 June in the document as translated.

76. FO 174/126, same date as above.

77. See Chapter 2, note 116.

78. Report on the population of the *mellah*, 1950. Archives of the Ittihad-Maroc (Casablanca), Moroccan branch of the Alliance Israélite Universelle (AIU). These archives have since been sent to the central AIU archives in Paris.

79. FO 174/126, 29 Muharram 1248 = 28 June 1832, Arabic, with English translation. The Muslim date is incorrectly converted to 29 June in the document as translated.

80. FO 174/126, 13 Safar 1248 = 12 July 1832, Sidi al-Mukhtar to Hay.

81. FO 174/287, received 21 July (letter undated); this is reported by Hay to Willshire, in FO 52/36.

82. FO 174/40, 26 September 1832, Willshire to Hay.

83. PRO, B4/45. Docket Book. "Striking a docket" initiated bankruptcy proceedings, "declaring the intention of rendering a debtor bankrupt." Marriner, "English Bankruptcy Records," 354–55. In the case of Macnin, this is recorded in B5/109, 21 January 1833, signed by Van Sandan.

84. PRO, B5/95, 22 January 1833, Register of Fiats of Bankruptcy, entered 22 March 1833. A copy is found in FO 174/287. Unfortunately, bankruptcy records were only sporadically preserved. While the file for the case of D. C. Macnin remains, Meir's has disappeared.

85. FO 174/287, 20 March 1833; witnessed by William Henry Nevill, clerk to Andrew van Sandan; a notary public also certified the signature of P. Laurie, the Lord Mayor and Chief Magistrate of the City of London; FO 635/1, 27 March 1833, diary of Willshire, reports receiving the letter with enclosed power of attorney.

86. FO 174/287, London, 22 March 1833, Alexander Brymer Belcher to Drummond Hay. A document is annexed, signed by Meir Macnin, "late of Finsbury Circus in the City of London, merchant against whom a fiat of Bankruptcy has been duly awarded and issued under which I have been duly found and declared Bankrupt and under which, Alexander Brymer Belcher of King's Arms Yard in the City of London Esquire has been duly appointed assignee." Signed 17 March 1833. This is the last document with Macnin's signature.

87. FO 635/1, 22 May 1833, diary of Willshire.

Chapter 8. Macnin's Legacy: Sephardi and Oriental

1. Moses Margoliouth, *The History of the Jews in Great Britain*, 3 vols. (London: R. Bentley, 1851), 2:196–97.

2. Frances Malino, *The Sephardic Jews of Bordeaux: Assimilation and Emancipation in Revolutionary and Napoleonic France* (Tuscaloosa: University of Alabama Press, 1978), 40ff.

3. LP, 8 Tamuz 5619 = 10 July 1859, Declaration of Haim and Moses Guedalla.

4. Albert M. Hyamson, *The Sephardim of England* (London: Methuen & Co.,

1951), 207. He died on 25 November 1840. *Bevis Marks Records*, pt. 6: *The Burial Register (1733–1918) of the Novo (New) Cemetery of the Spanish and Portuguese Jews' Congregation, London*, ed. Miriam Rodrigues-Pereira and Chloe Loewe (London: The Spanish & Portuguese Jews' Congregation, 1997). There is an obituary in *Gentleman's Magazine* 15 (January 1841): 105.

5. Hyamson, *Sephardim*, 208.

6. SPJC, Minutes, MS 113, 22 September 1835.

7. Hyamson, *Sephardim*, 208. He died on 11 July 1866; *Burial Register*, 133.

8. Sarah F. Orkin, *Roots and Recollections* (London: Published by the author, 1995), 167.

9. Miriam Rodrigues-Pereira and Chloe Loewe, eds., *The Birth Register (1767–1881) of the Spanish & Portuguese Jews' Congregation, London* (London: The Spanish & Portuguese Jews' Congregation, 1993), 68.

10. Reported by Esther Pinto, "The Pinto Family" (unpublished paper, 1922). Thanks to Barbara Barnett for giving me a copy.

11. Khalid b. al-Saghir, "Wathiqa ghayr manshura ʿan millah Marrakish fi nihayat al-qarn al-tasiʿ ʿashar," *Hespéris-Tamuda* 35 (1997): 60. See Chapter 2, note 116.

12. A description, based on observations made in 1843, of a "Madam Bousac" must refer to Blida "Bujnah." The author guessed that she was about thirty years old. James Richardson, *Travels in Morocco*, 2 vols. (London: Charles J. Skeet, 1860), 1:294–98.

13. LP, 2 Nisan 5587 = 30 March 1827, Haim Pinto and David Elhazan of Essaouira.

14. AEN, Tanger 87, 12 May 1831, Addy Delevante to Della Porte (in Italian). He died on 28 April.

15. LP, 11 Shawwal 1248 = 3 March 1833, Sultan to Aaron Amar (al-Tajir Harun Bujnah).

16. LP, 15 Av 5608 = 14 August 1848, affidavit of Meir Hadida of Marrakesh and Moshe Sabbah of the death of Meir Macnin and his burial in Marrakesh; also testifying that he had only one daughter, Blida, and no other heirs.

17. LP, 4 Ramadan 1255 = 11 November 1839, *dahir* of Sultan ʿAbd al-Rahman.

18. AEN, Tanger 87, 15 April 1838, Delaporte. Concerning the dispute between Stellato and Bujenah.

19. LP, 19 Dhu al-Qaʿda 1256 = 12 January 1841, a long declaration of numerous Muslim debtors to Shalom Macnin, specifying the date of debt, its amount, and other particulars.

20. Richardson, *Travels in Morocco*, 1:294–95.

21. AEN, Tanger, Mogador 92, 18 May 1881, "Lettre adréssée par le Consul de France aux Administrateurs de la Douane de Mogador."

22. LP, Notes from an old prayer book of Judah Amar, 20 Heshvan 5639 = 16 November 1879.

23. LP, 19 Rajab 1263 = 3 July 1847, ʿAbd al-Rahman. This was later raised to twenty *mithqal*s. AEN, Tanger, Mogador 92, 12 September 1881, Mahon ("Réclamations de Boudjenah").

24. LP, 15 Av 5608 = 14 August 1848, copy of affidavit of Meir Hadida and Moshe Sabbah. Meir Macnin's death also came to the attention of the British consulate. The British consular representative Grace writes to the merchant Samuel L.

Bensusan of London, representing a merchant firm that had considerable dealings with the Macnins, that Meir Hadida, the person whom Bensusan had designated to make a declaration before Grace regarding the death of Macnin, has refused to do so. FO 830/1, 15 August 1848. The reasons for his refusal are not disclosed, but as we saw above, he gave his affidavit to the Jewish authorities in Hebrew and Judeo-Arabic.

25. LP, 10 Rajab 1263 = 24 June 1847, *dahir* of Sultan ʿAbd al-Rahman.

26. LP, 11 Ramadan 1266 = 21 July 1850. Authorization of sultan for sale of proceeds of house, 22 Safar 1267 = 27 December 1850; the sale was later validated by the declaration of Hadan b. Muha that he had purchased the house from the property that Judah Bujnah had inherited (presumably after the latter was an adult), 4 Jumadi II 1280 = 16 November 1863.

27. LP, 3 Nisan 5620 = 26 March 1860; the same document states that additional money was received in French currency, 21 Tevet 5621 = 3 January 1861. The money was returned in Tishri 5621 = September/October 1860.

28. LP, 24 Safar 1280 = 10 August 1863, Sultan Muhammad b. ʿAbd al-Rahman.

29. LP, 8 Rabiʿ I 1280 = 23 August 1863, Sultan Muhammad b. ʿAbd al-Rahman. Some of these properties were government (Makhzan) houses that had been leased to the Macnins and other merchants in Essaouira. Many merchants sublet their properties. In a register book from Essaouira listing the town's revenue and expenditure, rent from the Macnin/Bujnah properties is listed separately from "houses of the merchants." KH, K⁴⁶, Rabiʿ II–Shawwal 1279 = September 1862–April 1863.

30. AEN, Tanger, Mogador 92, 22 September 1881, Mahon. Aaron Amar had considerable difficulty, together with the other merchants, in repaying the monthly installments in the period before the 1844 war. AEN, Tanger 88, 18 February 1842, Beuscher (Amar is referred to as Boudjnah).

31. See Daniel J. Schroeter, *Merchants of Essaouira: Urban Society and Imperialism in Southwestern Morocco, 1844–1886* (Cambridge: Cambridge University Press, 1988), 203, 209–14.

32. On the Spanish-Moroccan war and its impact, see Edward Szymański, "La guerre hispano-marocain 1859–1860: début de l'histoire du Maroc contemporain (essai de périodisation)," *Rocnik Orientalistyczny* 29, no. 2 (1965): 53–65; Abdallah Laroui, *Les origines sociales et culturelles du nationalisme marocain (1830–1912)* (Paris: Maspero, 1977), 278–82; Germain Ayache, *Etudes d'histoire marocain* (Rabat: Société Marocaine des Editeurs Réunis, 1979), 97–109.

33. LP, 5 Jumadi II 1280 = 17 November 1863, Musa b. Ahmad; and 29 Rajab 1280 = 9 January 1864, Musa b. Ahmad.

34. KH, K²⁹⁵ (a register of customs, town revenue, and expenditure 1865–66), 1 Dhu al-Hijja 1281 = 27 April 1865.

35. LP, 28 Muharram 1283 = 12 June 1866.

36. LP, 13 Rajab 1284 = 10 November 1867, Musa b. Ahmad.

37. LP, 2 Shaʿban 1284 = 29 November 1867, Musa b. Ahmad. The new loan of 1865 is not mentioned, but later it becomes apparent that he still owed money from the old debt of his father.

38. LP, 26 Muharram 1285 = 19 May 1868.

39. LP, 24 Jumadi II 1285 = 12 October 1868, al-Tayyib b. al-Yamani (Bu ʿAshrin) to Judah Bujnah.

40. KH, 28 Muharram 1285 = 21 May 1868, Musa b. Ahmad.

41. LP, 26 Safar 1286 = 7 June 1869, al-Tayyib b. al-Yamani (Bu ʿAshrin) to Judah Bujnah.

42. LP, 4 Jumadi I 1288 = 22 July 1871, Musa b. Ahmad to Judah Bujnah Amar.

43. Direction des Archives Royales (Mudiriya al-Wathaʾiq al-Malikiya), Rabat, 12 Dhu al-Qaʿda 1288 = 23 January 1872, al-ʿArabi Faraj and ʿAbd al-Rahman Aqasbi to al-Hajj Muhammd b. al-Madani Bannis.

44. There are two documents, both signed on the same day. The first is the agreement on what Blida and Judah would give for the dowry, while the second is the dowry itself. 10 Adar B 5622 = 12 March 1862, signed Yosef Elmaleh and Yosef b. Aharon Elmaleh. The dowry agreement was later signed in Marrakesh (because of the property there) in the month of Sivan 5622 = May/June 1862, by Shmuel Yaʿkov, Rafael Yosef Harush, Yaʿkov Siboni, Aharon Sabbah, and Masʿud Pinto. Another signature on the bottom is dated Tevet 5629 = December 1868/January 1869, Avraham b. Yaʿkov Benʿattar, probably an indication that the property was freed from mortgage.

45. Cf. S. D. Goitein, *A Mediterranean Society*, 6 vols. (Berkeley: University of California Press, 1967–93), vol. 3: *The Family*, 130–31.

46. LP, 16 Safar 1290 = 15 April 1873, Muhammad b. ʿAbd al-Rahman to *umanaʾ* of Essaouira.

47. LP, 20 Shebet 5634 = 24 January 1874, signed Avraham b. Yaʿkov Benʿattar, Moshe Hacohen.

48. LP, 28 Rabiʿ I 1293 = 23 April 1876, Sultan al-Hasan.

49. AEN, Tanger, Mogador 92, 12 September 1881, Mahon.

50. The visit is recounted in *Diaries of Sir Moses and Lady Montefiore*, ed. L. Loewe, 2 vols. (London: Griffith, Farran, Okedan & Welsh, 1890), 2:145–61. See also the account of a doctor who accompanied Montefiore on his mission: Thomas Hodgkin, *Narrative of a Journey to Morocco in 1863 and 1864* (London: T. C. Newby, 1866); official Moroccan documents on the missions are published in *al-Wathaʾiq* 4 (1978): 266–95. For an interpretation of the impact of the Montefiore mission to Morocco, see Michel Abitbol, *Le passé d'une discorde: Juifs et arabes depuis le VIIe siècle* (Paris: Perrin, 1999), 168–72; Mohammed Kenbib, *Juifs et Musulmans au Maroc, 1859–1948* (Rabat: Université Mohammed V, Publications de la Faculté des Lettres et des Sciences Humaines, 1994), 142–73.

51. The rejection of the *dhimma* and Muslim reactions to this is discussed by Laroui, *Les origines sociales*, 310–14. This was occurring all over the Muslim world in this period. Bernard Lewis, *The Jews of Islam* (Princeton, N.J.: Princeton University Press, 1984), 169–70.

52. The problem of consular protection has been the subject of numerous studies. See especially Mohammed Kenbib, *Les protégés: contribution à l'histoire contemporaine du Maroc* (Rabat: Université Mohammed V, Publications de la Faculté des Lettres et des Science Humaines, 1996); Leland Bowie, *The Impact of the Protégé System on Morocco, 1880–1912* (Athens: Ohio University Center for International Studies, 1970); F. V. Parsons, *The Origins of the Moroccan Question, 1880–1900* (London: Duckworth, 1976).

53. On Moroccan Jews becoming naturalized French citizens in Algeria and then

returning to Morocco, see Jean-Louis Miège, *Le Maroc et l'Europe: 1830–1894*, 4 vols. (Paris: Presses Universitaires de France, 1961–63), 2:674–77.

54. LP, 28 July 1911, H. J. S. Levy to Samuel Lévy (his nephew and the late owner of the documents on which this study is based).

55. For a discussion of how the monetary system worked, see Thomas K. Park, "Inflation and Economic Policy in 19th Century Morocco: The Compromise Solution," *Maghreb Review* 10, nos. 2–3 (1985): 51–56. See also Schroeter, *Merchants*, 142–52.

56. LP, 27 Jumadi I 1298 = 27 April 1881 (declaration).

57. AEN, Tanger, Mogador 92, 12 September 1881, Mahon. Includes numerous letters exchanged between the consulate and the financial officers of Essaouira translated from Arabic.

58. AEN, Tanger, Mogador, 95, 15 April 1890, Patenôtre to Lacoste.

59. LP, 11 October 1895, Tangier, [   ] to Leriche, Gérant du Consulat de France, Mogador; 20 January 1896, Algiers, Müller to Judah Amar.

60. LP, 12 December 1901, minutes of court case in Algiers, regarding testimony on Aaron Amar's birth (in the absence of a birth certificate). That the two brothers obtained French nationality is evident from later legal documents, e.g., LP, 14 March 1918, copy of a notarized document signed by the justice of the peace in Mogador and registered by the clerk of the court.

61. Doris Bensimon-Donath, *Evolution du judaïsme marocain sous le protectorat français, 1912–1956* (Paris: Mouton, 1968), 102–3; Michael M. Laskier, *The Alliance Israélite Universelle and the Jewish Communities of Morocco, 1862–1962* (Albany: State University of New York Press, 1983), 163–65; André Chouraqui, *La condition juridique de l'Israélite marocain* (Paris: Presses du Livre Français, 1950), 63.

62. LP, 22 August 1923, letter from Aaron Levy in Essaouira to David Amar in Algiers, giving an account of money sent from rents on their joint property in Essaouira and Marrakesh.

63. LP, Statement of freehold property held in Mogador, 8 April 1918, Aaron J. Levy; LP, November 1, 1918, Makhzen and Habous Property to Aaron Judah Levy and H. J. S. Levy, asking that the brothers produce a rabbinical document for a particular shop.

64. LP, 16 December 1925, 10 March 1926, notes of a conversation with the *contrôleur des domaines*.

65. LP, 12 April 1926, Chef du Service des Domaines to Felix Guedj.

66. LP, 11 August 1926 (government), and 12 August 1926 (notaries of rabbinical court). Further details of the property are found in the original rabbinical document, based on various deeds, signed 2 Elul 5686 = 12 August 1926, Yehuda Benabu and Mordekhai Ohayon. Agreement was reached between the various heirs of the property on 2 Av 5686 = 13 July 1926; earlier proceedings in the rabbinical court, dated 7 Kislev 5686 = 24 November 1925, signed by the above notaries and the following *dayyanim*: Avraham Bensusan (president of the rabbinical court), David Knafo, and Moshe Bensimhon. Details of the properties in Marrakesh are not given (since this would have been under the jurisdiction of the rabbinical court in Marrakesh).

67. Miège, *Le Maroc et l'Europe, 1830–1894*, 2: 91–92; and idem, "La bourgeoisie juive du Maroc au XIXe siècle: Rupture ou continuité?" in *Judaïsme d'Afrique du*

Nord aux XIXe– XXe siècles, ed. Michel Abitbol (Jerusalem: Institut Ben-Zvi, 1980), 25–36. For a general discussion of capitalism and its meaning in Morocco, see Mohammed Ennaji, *Expansion européene et changement social au Maroc (XVIe–XIXe siècles)* (Casablanca: Editions Eddif, 1996), 7ff.

68. For further details, see my *Merchants*, 21ff.

Bibliography

I. Archives and Manuscripts

France

Alliance Israélite Universelle, Paris
   Archives of Ittihad-Maroc (the Moroccan branch of the AIU), formerly in Casablanca
      Miscellaneous reports on Moroccan communities, 1940s–1950s
Archives Départementales des Bouches-du-Rhône, Marseilles
   545 U Répertoire des Jugements, Tribunal de Commerce
Archives Nationales, Paris
   Affaires Etrangères
      AE/B^{III} Consulats: Mémoires et Documents
Ministère des Affaires Etrangères, Paris
   Affaires Diverses Politiques, Maroc
      Correspondance Consulaire et Commercial, Maroc
      Correspondance Consulaire et Commercial, Mogador
      Correspondance Politique, Maroc
Ministère des Affaires Etrangères, Nantes
   Série A. Archives de la Légation de France au Maroc
   Tanger. Correspondance avec le Ministère de la Guerre
   Tanger. Correspondance avec le Consulat de France à Mogador
   Tanger, Mogador. Consulat de France à Mogador

Private Papers of Samuel Lévy-Corcos, Paris
Correspondence
Legal documents
Account books
Miscellaneous records

Chambre de Commerce, Marseilles
J. 1553 Consulat de Salé. Lettres de J.-B. du Rocher, consul (1786–93)

Great Britain

Public Record Office, London

Colonial Office
91 Gibraltar: Original Correspondence
714 Indexed Précis of Incoming Correspondence
    (Governors' correspondence, Gibraltar)

Office of the Commissioners of Bankrupts and Court of Bankruptcy
B 3 Bankruptcy Commission Files
B 4 Bankruptcy Commission Docket Book
B 5 Bankruptcy Enrolment Books

Foreign Office
8 War and Colonial Department: General Correspondence, Barbary States
    (Instructions to Consuls)
52 General Correspondence, Morocco, Series I
95 Political and other Departments: Miscellanea (Morocco: Consuls, Do-
    mestic)
99 General Correspondence, Morocco, Series II
174 Consulate and Legation, Tangier, and Embassy, Rabat, Morocco: Gen-
    eral Correspondence
631 Consulate, Mogador, Morocco: General Correspondence
635 Consulate, Mogador, Morocco: Miscellanea

Index to Denizations

State Papers, Foreign
71 Barbary States

The John Rylands Library, Manchester
Dombay Papers

Spanish and Portuguese Jews' Congregation (Bevis Marks), London
Mahamad Minutes
Mahamad Papers
MS 755 Hebrew letters addressed to H. H. R. Meldola and Dayan D. Meldola,
    vol. 2: Letters from North Africa

Israel

Private Papers of the Corcos Family, Jerusalem
Correspondence
Miscellaneous papers

Morocco

Bibliothèque Royale (al-Khizanat al-Hasaniyya), Rabat
General Correspondence, Period of Mawlay ʿAbd al-Rahman
General Correspondence, Period of Muhammad IV
Registers (Kananish)
    K46 Customs, town revenue, and expenditure of Essaouira, 1279 = 1862–63
    K93 Lists of Makhzan property in various cities, 1296–97 = 1878–80
    K295 Customs, town revenue, and expenditures of Essaouira, 1282 = 1865–66

Direction des Archives Royales (Mudiriya al-Wathaʾiq al-Malikiya), Rabat
Correspondence with officials in Essaouira

Netherlands

Algemeen Rijksarchief (Dutch State Archives), The Hague
Consulaat Tanger 1 (Correspondence with Mogador consulate)

United States

National Archives, Diplomatic Branch, Washington, D.C.
Record Group 84. Consulate General, Tangier, Morocco

II. Printed Works

Abecassis, José Maria. *Genealogia Hebraica Portugal e Gibraltar Sécs. XVII a XX.* 5 vols. Lisbon: J. M. Abecassis, Distribuição, Livraria Ferin, 1990–1991.

Abitbol, Michel. *Le passé d'une discorde: Juifs et Arabes depuis le VIIe siècle*. Paris: Perrin, 1999.

——. *Tugʾar al-sultan: ʿIlit kalkalit yehudit be-Maroko.* Jerusalem: Makhon Ben Tsevi, 1994.

Abrami, Isaac. "La contribution des sources internes, hébraiques, judéo-arabes et arabes à l'histoire des Juifs livournais à Tunis." *Rassegna Mensile di Israel* 50 (1984): 725–39.

——. "ʿEdat ha-Grana be-Tunis le-or pinkaseha: ha-maʾavak al ha-otonomiyah." In *Judaïsme d'Afrique du Nord aux XIXe–XXe siècles*, edited by Michel Abitbol, 64–95. Jerusalem: Institute Ben-Zvi, 1980.

Adams, Robert. *The Narrative of Robert Adams.* London: Printed for John Murray, 1816.

Adler, Elkan Nathan. *London*. Philadelphia: Jewish Publication Society of America, 1930.

Afa, ʿUmar. *Masʾalat al-nuqud fi tarikh al-Maghrib fi al-qarn al-tasiʿ ʿashar (Sus 1822–1906).* Agadir: Jamiʾat al-Qadi ʿIyad, Manshurat Kulliyat al-Adab wa-al-ʿUlum al-Insaniya bi-Agadir, 1988.

——. al-Nuqud al-Maghribiya fi al-qarn al-thamin ʿashar: inzamitiha wa-anzimatiha fi mintaqat Sus. Rabat: Manshurat Kulliyat al-Adab wa-al-ʿUlum al-Insaniya bi-al-Rabat, 1993)

Agrel, Olof. *Neue Reise nach Marokos.* Nürnberg: Adam Gottlieb Schneider und Weigel, 1798.

Alcalay, Ammiel. *After Jews and Arabs: Remaking Levantine Culture*. Minneapolis: University of Minnesota Press, 1993.

Archenholz, Johan Wilhelm von. *A Picture of England*. Dublin: Printed by P. Byrne, 1790.

Arribas Palau, Mariano. "La actividad comercial del marqués de Viale en Marruecos." *Revista de Archivos, Bibliotecas y Museos* 79 (1976): 3–25.

———. *Cartas árabes de Marruecos del Tiempo de Mawlay al-Yazid (1790–1792)*. Tetuan: Cremades, 1961.

———. "Datos sobre Samuel Sumbel y sus relaciones con España." *Sefarad* 40 (1980): 121–39.

———. "Documentación española sobre las primeras relaciones entre Marruecos y los Estados Unidos de America del Norte." *Hespéris-Tamuda* 17 (1976–77): 97–136.

———. "Los hermanos Chiappe en Marruecos." In *La Conoscenza dell'Asia e dell'Africa in Italia nei secoli XVIII e XIX*, vol. 1, pt. 2, pp. 813–69. Naples: Istituto Universitario Orientale, 1984.

———. "La misión frustrada de Abraham Masahod a España en 1766." *Sefarad* 43 (1983): 109–33.

———. "Notas sobre el Judío Isaías B. ᶜAmmur en Marruecos." *Sefarad* 48 (1988): 235–44.

———. "Reclamaciones de marqués Viale contra la casa comercial española de Casablanca y el consul Salmón." *Cuadernos de la Biblioteca Española de Tetuán* 17–18 (1978): 39–82.

Ashtor, Eliyahu. *The Jews of Moslem Spain*. 3 vols. Philadelphia: Jewish Publication Society of America, 1973–84.

Ayache, Germain. *Etudes d'histoire marocain*. Rabat: Société Marocaine des Editeurs Réunis, 1979.

———. "La minorité juive dans le Maroc précolonial." *Hespéris-Tamuda* 25 (1987): 147–68.

Ayoun, Richard. "Les Juifs livournais en Afrique du Nord." *Rassegna Mensile di Israel* 50 (1984): 650–705.

Badia y Leyblich, Domingo. *Travels of Ali Bey*. London: Longman, Hurst, Rees, Orme and Brown, 1816.

Baer, Yitzhak. *A History of the Jews in Christian Spain*. 2 vols. Philadelphia: Jewish Publication Society of America, 1961.

Bakker, Johan de. "Slaves, Arms, and Holy War: Moroccan policy vis-à-vis the Dutch Republic during the Establishment of the ᶜAlawi Dynasty." Ph.D. diss., University of Amsterdam, 1991.

Bar-Asher, Shalom. "Antisemitism and Economic Influence: The Jews of Morocco (1672–1822)." In *Antisemitism Through the Ages*, edited by Shmuel Almog, 195–215. Oxford: Pergamon Press, 1988.

Barnett, R. D. "Anglo-Jewry in the Eighteenth Century." In *Three Centuries of Anglo-Jewish History*, edited by V. D. Lipman, 45–68. Cambridge: Published for the Jewish Historical Society of England by W. Heffer and Sons Limited, 1961.

———. "The Correspondence of the Mahamad of the Spanish and Portuguese Congregation of London during the Seventeenth and Eighteenth Centuries." *Transactions of the Jewish Historical Society of England* 20 (1964): 1–50.

———. "Haham Meldola and Hazan de Sola." *Transactions of the Jewish Historical Society of England* 21 (1968): 1–38.

Baron, Salo W. *A Social and Religious History of the Jews*. 2d ed. 18 vols. New York: Columbia University Press, 1952–83.

Bashan, Eliezer. *mi-Mizrah shemesh ʿad mevoʾo*. Lod: Orot Yahadut Hamaghreb, 1996.

———. *Shivya u-fedut ba-hevrah ha-yehudit be-artsot ha-Yam ha-Tikhon (1391–1830)*. Ramat Gan: Hotsaʾat Universitat Bar Ilan, 1980.

———. "Teʾudot ʿal kesharim bayn Livorno le-Yehude Algier, Bône, Tunis ve-Tripoli be-meah ha-yud-het." In *Michael*, vol. 5, edited by Daniel Carpi, Yehuda Nini, and Shlomo Simonsohn, 134–67. Tel Aviv: Diaspora Research Institute, 1978.

Basset, René. *Relation de Sidi Brahim de Massat*. Paris: Nancy, 1883.

Bat Yeʾor. *The Dhimmi: Jews and Christians under Islam*. Rutherford, N.J.: Fairleigh Dickinson University Press, 1985.

al-Bazzaz, Muhammad al-Amin. *Tarikh al-awbiʾa wa-al-majaʿat bi-al-Maghrib fi-al-qarnayn al-thamin ʿashar wa-al-tasiʿ ʿashar*. Rabat: Jamiʿat Muhammad al-Khamis, Manshurat Kulliyat al-Adab wa-al-ʿUlum al-Insaniya bi-al-Rabat, 1992.

Beauclerk, G. *Journey to Morocco*. London: Printed for Poole and Edwards, etc., 1828.

Belaʿish, Avraham. *Pri ets hayyim*. Livorno: Printed by Moshe and Yisraʾel Palache, 1845/56.

Benady, Mesod. "The Settlement of Jews in Gibraltar, 1704–1783." *Transactions of the Jewish Historical Society of England* 26 (1979): 87–110.

Ben-Ami, Issachar. *Le judaïsme marocain*. Jerusalem: Rubin Mass, 1975.

Ben ʿAttar, Avraham. *Shanot Hayyim*. Casablanca: Imprimerie Simplex A. Soussan, 1958.

Ben Naʾim, Yosef. *Malke rabanan*. Jerusalem: Defus ha-Maʿarav, 1930/31.

Bensimon-Donath, Doris. *Evolution du judaïsme marocain sous le protectorat français, 1912–1956*. Paris: Mouton, 1968.

Bentov, Hayyim. "Le-demuto shel ha-sar Shmuel ibn Sunbal." In *Zekhor le-Avraham: kovets maʾamarim le-zekher R. Avraham Elmalih*, edited by H. Z. Hirschberg, 47–68. Jerusalem: Vaʿad ʿAdat ha-Maʿaravim bi-Yerushalayim, 1972.

———. "Mishpahat ha-Levi Ibn Yuli." In *mi-Mizrah u-mi-maʿarav*, edited by E. Bashan, A. Rubinstein, and S. Schwarzfuchs, 131–58. Ramat Gan: Universitat Bar-Ilan, 1980.

Benyahu, Meir. "Vikuhim ba-kehilah ha-Sefaradit ve-ha-Portugezit be-London u-teshuvot ha-haham Rabi Rafaʾel Meldola." In *Michael*, vol. 10, edited by Robert A. Rockaway and Shlomo Simonsohn, 9–77. Tel Aviv: Diaspora Research Institute, 1986.

Berque, Jacques. *L'intérieur du Maghreb, XVe–XIXe siècle*. Paris: Gallimard, 1978.

Bevis Marks Records, pt. 1. *The Early History of the Congregation from the Beginnings until 1800*. Edited by Lionel D. Barnett. Oxford: Oxford University Press, 1940.

———, pt. 2. *Abstracts of the Ketubot or Marriage-Contracts of the Congregation from Earliest Times until 1837*. Edited by Lionel D. Barnett. Oxford: Printed at the University Press by J. Johnson, 1949.

———, pt. 6. *The Burial Register (1733–1918) of the Novo (New) Cemetery of the Spanish & Portuguese Jews' Congregation, London*. Edited by Miriam Rodrigues-Pereira and Chloe Loewe. London: The Spanish and Portuguese Jews' Congregation, 1997.

Biale, David. *Power and Powerlessness in Jewish History*. New York: Schocken Books, 1986.

Bloom, Herbert I. *The Economic Activities of the Jews of Amsterdam in the Seventeenth and Eighteenth Centuries*. Williamsport, Pa.: Bayard Press, 1937.

Bodian, Miriam. "Amsterdam, Venice, and the Marrano Diaspora in the Seventeenth Century." In *Dutch Jewish History*, vol. 2, edited by Jozeph Michman, 47–65. Jerusalem: Institute for Research on Dutch Jewry, Hebrew University of Jerusalem; Assen/Maastricht: Van Gorcum, 1989.

——. "The Escamot of the Spanish-Portuguese Jewish Community of London, 1664." In *Michael*, vol. 9, edited by Daniel Carpi and Shlomo Simonsohn, 9–26. Tel Aviv: Diaspora Research Institute, 1985.

——. *Hebrews of the Portuguese Nation*. Bloomington: Indiana University Press, 1997.

Borrow, George. *The Bible in Spain*. London: J. Murray, 1843.

Bosworth, C. E. "The Concept of *Dhimma* in Early Islam." In *Christians and Jews in the Ottoman Empire*, vol. 1, edited by Benjamin Braude and Bernard Lewis, 37–51. New York: Holmes & Meier, 1982.

——. "The 'Protected Peoples' (Christians and Jews) in Medieval Egypt and Syria." *Bulletin of the John Rylands University Library of Manchester* 62 (1979): 11–36.

Bourqia, Rahma. "Don et théatralité: Réflexion sur le rituel du don (*hadiyya*) offert au sultan au XIXᵉ siècle." *Hespéris-Tamuda* 31 (1993): 61–75.

Bowie, Leland. "An Aspect of Muslim-Jewish Relations in Late Nineteenth-Century Morocco: A European Diplomatic View." *International Journal of Middle Eastern Studies* 7 (1976): 3–19.

——. *The Impact of the Protégé System on Morocco, 1880–1912*. Athens: Ohio University Center for International Studies, 1970.

Boyarin, Daniel, and Jonathan Boyarin. "Diaspora: Generation and the Ground of Jewish Identity." *Critical Inquiry* 19 (1993): 693–725.

Braudel, Fernand. *Civilization and Capitalism: 15th–18th Century*. vol. 1: *The Structures of Everyday Life: The Limits of the Possible*. New York: Harper & Row, 1981.

Brooke, Arthur de Capell. *Sketches in Spain and Morocco*. London: Henry Colburn and Richard Bentley, 1831.

Brown, Kenneth L. "Mellah and Madina: A Moroccan City and Its Jewish Quarter (Salé ca 1880–1930)." In *Studies in Judaism and Islam*, edited by S. Moraget et al., 253–81. Jerusalem: Magnes Press, The Hebrew University, 1981.

Brunot, Louis, and Elie Malka. *Glossaire judéo-arabe de Fès*. Rabat: Ecole du Livre, 1940.

——. *Textes judéo-arabes de Fès*. Rabat: Ecole du Livre, 1939.

Buffa, John. *Travels Through the Empire of Morocco*. London: J. J. Stockdale, 1810.

Burel, Antoine. *La mission du Capitaine Burel au Maroc en 1808*. Edited by Jacques Caillé. Paris: Arts et Metiers Graphiques, 1953.

Burnim, Kalmin A. "The Jewish Presence in the London Theatre, 1660–1800." *Transactions of the Jewish Historical Society of England* 33 (1992–94): 65–96.

Bushuʿaraʾ, Mustafa. *al-Istitan wa-al-himaya bi-al-Maghrib, 1280–1311/1865–1894*. 4 vols. Rabat: al-Matbaʿat al-Malikiya, 1984–89.

Caillé, Jacques. "L'abolition des tributs versés au Maroc par la Suède et le Danemark." *Hespéris* 45 (1958): 203–38.

——. *Le Consulat de Tanger (des origines à 1830)*. Paris: Editions A. Pedone, 1967.

——. *La Ville de Rabat jusqu'au protectorat français*. Paris: Nanoest, 1949.

Caro Baroja, Julio. *Los Judíos en la España moderna y contemporánea*. 2d ed. 3 vols. Madrid: Ediciones ISTMO, 1978.

Cassandro, Michele. *Aspetti della storia economica e sociale degli ebrei di Livorno nel seicento*. Milan: Dott. A. Giuffrè Editore, 1983.

Castries, Henry de, ed. *Les sources inédites de l'histoire du Maroc de 1530 à 1845*. 1st ser: *Dynastie saadienne, archives et bibliothèques des Pays Bas*. 6 vols. Paris: E. Leroux, 1906–23.

Catalogue of an Exhibition of Anglo-Jewish Art and History. London: Victoria & Albert Museum, 1956.

Cazès, D. *Essai sur l'histoire des Israélites de Tunisie*. Paris: Librairie Armand Durlacher, 1888.

Chénier, Louis. *Un Chargé d'Affaires au Maroc: La correspondance du consul Louis Chénier, 1767–1782*. Edited by Pierre Grillon. Paris: S.E.V.P.E.N., 1970.

——. *Recherches historiques sur les Maures et histoire de l'Empire de Maroc*. 3 vols. Paris: l'Imprimerie Polytype, 1787.

Chetrit, Joseph. "Niveaux, registres de langue et sociolectes dans les langues judéo-arabes du Maroc." In *Les Relations entre juifs et musulmans en Afrique du Nord, XIXᵉ–XXᵉ siècles*, 129–43. Paris: Editions du Centre National de la Recherche Scientifique, 1980.

——. "Tradition du discours et discours de la tradition dans les communautés juives du Maroc: étude socio-pragmatique." In *Communication in the Jewish Diaspora*, edited by Sophia Menache, 339–407. Leiden: Brill, 1996.

Chouraqui, André. *La Condition juridique de l'Israélite marocain*. Paris: Presses du Livre Français, 1950.

Cigar, Norman. "Socio-Economic Structures and the Development of an Urban Bourgeoisie in Pre-Colonial Morocco." *Maghreb Review* 6, nos. 3–4 (1981): 55–76.

Clifford, James. *Routes: Travel and Translation in the Late Twentieth Century*. Cambridge, Mass.: Harvard University Press, 1997.

Cochelet, Charles. *Naufrage du brick français la Sophie*. 2 vols. Paris: Librairie Universelle de P. Mongier Ainé, 1821.

Cohen, Amnon. *Jewish Life under Islam: Jerusalem in the Sixteenth Century*. Cambridge, Mass.: Harvard University Press, 1984.

Cohen, Mark R. *Under Crescent and Cross: The Jews in the Middle Ages*. Princeton, N.J.: Princeton University Press, 1994.

——. "The Neo-Lachrymose Conception of Jewish-Arab History." *Tikkun* 6, no. 3 (1991): 55–60.

Cohen, Mark, and Yedida Stillman. "Genizat Kahir ve-minhage geniza shel Yehude ha-mizrah." *Peʿamim* 24 (1985): 3–35.

Cohen, Robert. "Passage to a New World: The Sephardi Poor of Eighteenth Century Amsterdam." In *Neveh Yaʾakov: Jubilee Volume Presented to Dr. Jaap Meijer on the Occasion of his Seventieth Birthday*, edited by Lea Dasberg and Jonathan N. Cohen, 31–41. Assen: Van Gorcum, 1982.

Colquhoun, Patrick. *A Treatise on the Police of the Metropolis*. 7th ed. London: Printed for J. Mawman et al., 1806.

Conrotte, Manuel. *España y los países musulmanes durante el ministerior de Floridablanca*. Madrid: Impr. del Patronato de Huérfanos de Administración, 1909.

Corcos, David. "Les Juifs au Maroc et leurs mellahs." In *Studies in the History of the Jews of Morocco*, 64–130.

——. "Le-ofi yahasam shel shalite ha-Almawahhidun le-Yehudim." In *Studies in the History of the Jews of Morocco*, 319–342.

——. "Macnin." *Encyclopaedia Judaica*, 11:675.

——. *Studies in the History of the Jews of Morocco*. Jerusalem: Rubin Mass, 1976.

Corry, John. *A Satirical View of London at the Commencement of the Nineteenth Century*. London: Kearsley, 1801.

Cumberland, Richard. *The Letters of Richard Cumberland*. Edited by Richard J. Dircks. New York: AMS Press, 1988.

——. *Memoirs of Richard Cumberland*. London: Printed for Lackington, Allen, & Co., 1806.

Daʾud, Muhammad. *Tarikh Titwan*. 6 vols. Tetuan: Maktabat al-Talib, 1959–66.

Davidson, John. *Notes Taken during Travels in Africa*. London: Printed by J. L. Cox and Sons, 1839.

Davis, Natalie Zemon. *Women on the Margins: Three Seventeenth-Century Lives*. Cambridge, Mass.: Harvard University Press, 1995.

Delacroix, Eugène. *The Journal of Eugène Delacroix*. New York: Viking Press, 1972.

Delacroix in Morocco. Exhibition organized by the Institut du Monde Arabe. Paris: Flammarion, 1994–95.

Deshen, Shlomo. *The Mellah Society: Jewish Community Life in Sherifian Morocco*. Chicago: University of Chicago Press, 1989.

Deverdun, Gaston. *Marrakech, des origines à 1912*. 2 vols. Rabat: Editions techniques nord-africaines, 1959–66.

Diaries of Sir Moses and Lady Montefiore. Edited by L. Loewe. London: Griffith, Farran, Okedan & Welsh, 1890.

Dircks, Richard J. *Richard Cumberland*. Boston: Twayne Publishers, 1976.

Dols, Michael W. *The Black Death in the Middle East*. Princeton, N.J.: Princeton University Press, 1977.

al-Duʿayyif, Muhammad. *Tarikh al-Duʿayyif*. Edited by Ahmad al-ʿAmari. Rabat: Dar al-Maʾthurat, 1986.

Dumas, Alexandre. *Le Véloce ou de Cadix à Tunis*. Paris: Editions François Bourin, 1990.

Durrieu, Xavier. *The Present State of Morocco: A Chapter of Mussulman Civilisation*. London: Longman, Brown, Green, and Longmans, 1854.

Edraʿi, Moshe b. Yitshak. *Yad Moshe*. Amsterdam: 1808/9.

Eisenbeth, Maurice. "Les Juifs en Algérie et en Tunisie à l'époque turque (1516–1830)." *Revue Africaine* 96 (1952): 114–87, 343–84.

Elbaz, André E. "Quelques précisions inédites sur la vie et l'oeuvre de David Ben Hassine." In *Misgav Yerushalayim Studies in Jewish Literature*, edited by Ephraim Hazan, 41–51. Jerusalem: Misgav Yerushalayim, 1987.

Elmalih, Yosef. *Tokfo shel Yosef*. Vol. 1. Livorno: Printed by Eliyahu Ben Amozeg, 1854/55. Vol. 2. Livorno: Printed by Yaᶜakov Tobiyana, 1801/2.

El Mansour, Mohamed. *Morocco in the Reign of Mawlay Sulayman*. Wisbech, Cambridgeshire: MENAS Press, 1990.

———. "Political and Social Developments in Morocco during the Reign of Mawlay Sulayman, 1792–1822." Ph.D. thesis, University of London, 1981.

El Moudden, Abderrahmane. "The Ambivalence of *Rihla*: Community Integration and Self-Definition in Moroccan Travel Accounts, 1300–1800." In *Muslim Travellers: Pilgrimage, Migration, and the Religious Imagination*, edited by Dale F. Eickelman and James Piscatori, 69–84. Berkeley: University of California Press, 1990.

El-Nasser, Rachid Abdallah. "Morocco, from Kharijism to Wahhabism: The Quest for Religious Purism." Ph.D. diss., University of Michigan, 1983.

Emanuel, Charles H. L. *A Century and a Half of Jewish History Extracted from the Minute Books of the London Committee of Deputies of the British Jews*. London: George Routledge & Sons, 1910.

Endelman, Todd M. *The Jews of Georgian England, 1714–1830*. Philadelphia: Jewish Publication Society of America, 1979.

———. *Radical Assimilation in English Jewish History, 1656–1945*. Bloomington: Indiana University Press, 1990.

Ennaji, Mohammed. *Expansion européene et changement social au Maroc (XVIᵉ–XIXᵉ siècles)*. Casablanca: Editions Eddif, 1996.

———. *Serving the Master: Slavery and Society in Nineteenth-Century Morocco*. New York: St. Martin's Press, 1999.

Eustache, Daniel. *Corpus des Monnaies ᶜAlawites*. 3 vols. Rabat: Banque du Maroc, 1984.

Farouk, Ahmed. "Aperçu de trafic du port de Mogador avec les principales places européennes (1786–1787)." Hespéris-Tamuda 26–27 (1988–89): 93–105.

Fattal, Antoine. *Le statut légal des non-musulmans en pays d'Islam*. Beirut: Impr. Catholique, 1958.

Felsenstein, Frank. *Anti-Semitic Stereotypes: A Paradigm of Otherness in English Popular Culture, 1660–1830*. Baltimore: The Johns Hopkins University Press, 1995.

Filippini, Jean-Pierre. "La ballottazione a Livorno nel Settecento." *Rassegna Mensil di Israel* 40 (1983): 199–268.

———. "Les Juifs d'Afrique du Nord et la communauté de Livourne au XVIIIᵉ siècle." In *Les relations intercommunautaires juives en méditerranée occidentale, XIIIᵉ–XXᵉ siècles*, 60–69. Paris: Centre National de la Recherche Scientifique, 1984.

———. "Juifs emigrés et immigrés dans le port de Livourne pendant la période Napoléonienne." In *East and Maghreb*, vol. 4, edited by S. Schwarzfuchs, 31–91. Ramat-Gan: Bar-Ilan University Press, 1983.

———. "Livorno e gli ebrei dell'Africa del Nord nel Settecento." In *Gli Ebrei in Toscana dal medioevo al Risorgimento*, 21–32. Florence: L. S. Olschki, 1980.

———. "Livourne et l'Afrique du Nord au 18ᵉ siècle." *Revue d'Histoire Maghrébine* 7–8 (1977): 125–49.

———. "Les négociants juifs de Livourne au XVIIIᵉ siècle." *Revue des Etudes Juives* 132 (1973): 672–73.

———. "Le rôle des négociants et des banquiers juifs de Livourne dans le grand commerce international en Méditerranée au XVIIIᵉ siècle." In *The Mediterranean and the Jews: Banking, Finance and International Trade (XVI–XVIII Centuries)*, edited by Ariel Toaff and Simon Schwarzfuchs, 123–49. Ramat Gan: Bar-Ilan University Press, 1989.

Fischel, Walter J. *Jews in the Economic and Political Life of Mediaeval Islam*. New York: Ktav Publishing House, 1969.

Flamand, Pierre. *Diaspora en terre d'Islam: les communautés israélites du sud marocain*. Casablanca: Presses des Imprimeries Réunies, n.d.

Gallagher, Nancy E. *Medicine and Power in Tunisia, 1780–1900*. Cambridge: Cambridge University Press, 1983.

Gaster, Moses. *History of the Ancient Synagogue of the Spanish and Portuguese Jews*. London: Printed by Harrison & Sons, 1901.

Gerber, Jane S. *The Jews of Spain: A History of the Sephardic Experience*. New York: Free Press, 1992.

———. "The Pact of ᶜUmar in Morocco: A Reappraisal of Muslim-Jewish Relations." In *Proceedings of the Seminar on Muslim-Jewish Relations in North Africa*, 40–50. New York: World Jewish Congress, 1975.

al-Ghazzal, Ahmad ibn al-Mahdi. *Natijat al-ijtihad fi al-muhadana wa-al-jihad: "rihlat al-Ghazzal wa-safaratuh ila al-Andalus."* Algiers: Diwan al-Matbaᶜat al-Jamiᶜiya, 1984.

Glückel of Hameln. *The Memoirs of Glückel of Hameln*, translated by Marvin Lowenthal. New York: Schocken Books, 1977.

Goitein, S. D. *Jews and Arabs: Their Contacts through the Ages*. New York: Schocken, 1955.

———. *A Mediterranean Society*. 6 vols. Berkeley: University of California Press, 1967–93.

Goodman, Paul. *Moses Montefiore*. Philadelphia: Jewish Publication Society of America, 1925.

———. *Think and Thank*. London: Oxford University Press, 1933.

Gottreich, Emily R. "Jewish Space in the Moroccan City: A History of the Mellah of Marrakesh, 1550–1930." Ph.D. diss., Harvard University, 1999.

Gråberg di Hemsö, Jacopo. *Specchio geografico e statistico dell'impero di Marocco*. Genoa: Dalla Tipografia Pellas, 1834.

Graetz, Heinrich H. *History of the Jews*. 6 vols. Philadelphia: Jewish Publication Society of America, 1891–98.

Grunebaum, G. E. von. "Eastern Jewry under Islam." *Viator* 2 (1971): 365–72.

Guillen, Pierre. *L'Allemagne et le Maroc de 1870 à 1905*. Paris: Presses Universitaires de France, 1967.

Gutwirth, Eleazar. "Abraham Seneor: Social Tensions and the Court-Jew." In *Michael*, vol. 11, edited by Eleazar Gutwirth and Shlomo Simonsohn, 169–229. Tel-Aviv: Diaspora Research Institute, 1989.

Hammoudi, Abdellah. *Master and Disciple: The Cultural Foundations of Moroccan Authoritarianism*. Chicago: University of Chicago Press, 1997.

Hancock, Thomas. *Researches into the Laws and Phenomena of Pestilence*. London: W. Phillips, 1821.

Hasin, David. *Tehilah le-David*. Amsterdam: Proops, 1807.

Henriques, H. S. Q. *The Jews and the English Law*. Oxford: Oxford University Press, 1908.

Henriques, Ursula. *Religious Toleration in England, 1787–1833*. Toronto: University of Toronto Press, 1961.

[Heron, Robert]. *Account of the Life of Muley Liezit, Late Emperor of Morocco*. London, 1797.

Hertz, Gerald Berkeley. *British Imperialism in the Eighteenth Century*. London: Archibald Constable and Co., 1908.

Hess, Andrew C. *The Forgotten Frontier*. Chicago: University of Chicago Press, 1978.

Hildesheimer, Françoise. "Grandeur et décadence de la maison Bacri de Marseille." *Revue des Etudes Juives* 136 (1977): 389–413.

Hirschberg, H. Z. *A History of the Jews in North Africa*. 2d ed., translated from Hebrew. 2 vols. Leiden: Brill, 1974–81.

——. "Jews and Jewish Affairs in the Relations between Great Britain and Morocco in the 18th Century." In *Essays Presented to Chief Rabbi Israel Brodie on the Occasion of His Seventieth Birthday*, edited by H. H. Zimmels et al., 153–81. London: Soncino Press, 1967.

Hodgkin, Thomas. *Narrative of a Journey to Morocco in 1863 and 1864*. London: T. C. Newby, 1866.

Hosotte-Reynaud, Manon. "Un négociant français à Mogador à la fin du XVIIIᵉ siècle et sa correspondance avec le consul de France à Salé." *Hespéris* 44 (1957): 335–45.

Høst, Georg. *Histoire de l'Empereur du Maroc Mohamed Ben Abdallah*. Translated by F. Damgaard and P. Gailhanou, with a preface by Jean-Louis Miège. Rabat: Editions La Porte, 1998; first published in Danish in 1791.

Huhner, Leon. "Moses Elias Levy: An Early Florida Pioneer and the Father of Florida's First Senator." *Florida Historical Quarterly* 19 (1941): 319–45.

Hunwick, John. "Black Africans in the Mediterranean World: Introduction to a Neglected Aspect of the African Diaspora." *Slavery and Abolition* 13, no. 1 (1992): 6–14.

——. "Islamic Law and Polemics over Race and Slavery in North and West Africa (16th–19th Century)." In *Slavery in the Islamic Middle East*, edited by Shaun E. Marmon, 43–68. Princeton, N.J.: Markus Wiener, 1999.

Hyamson, Albert M. *The Sephardim of England*. London: Methuen, 1951.

Iannettone, Giovanni. *Il Marocco negli atti consolari del regno delle Due Sicilie*. Naples: Editrice Cymba, 1967.

Ibn al-Saghir, Khalid. "Wathiqa ghayr manshura ᶜan millah Marrakish fi nihayat al-qarn al-tasiᶜ ᶜashar." *Hespéris-Tamuda* 35 (1997): 25–71.

Ibn Zaydan, ᶜAbd al-Rahman. *Ithaf aᶜlam al-nas bi-jamal akhbar hadirat Miknas*. 5 vols. Rabat: al-Matbaᶜat al-Wataniya "li-Sahibiha ᶜAbbas al-Thanani wa-Muhammad al-Qabbaj," 1929–33.

Israel, Jonathan I. "The Economic Contribution of Dutch Sephardi Jewry to Holland's Golden Age, 1593–1713." *Tijdschrift voor Geschiedenis* 96 (1983): 505–36.

——. *European Jewry in the Age of Mercantilism, 1550–1750*. Oxford: Clarendon Press, 1985.

Issawi, Charles. *An Economic History of the Middle East and North Africa*. New York: Columbia University Press, 1982.

Jackson, James Grey. *An Account of the Empire of Marocco and the Districts of Suse and Tafilelt.* 3d ed. London: Printed by William Bulmer and Co., 1814.

——. *An Account of Timbuctoo and Housa.* London: Longman, Hurst, Rees, Orme and Brown, 1820.

James, Thomas. *The History of the Herculean Straits, Now Called the Straits of Gibraltar.* 2 vols. London: Printed by Charles Rivington, 1771.

Jardine, Alexander. *Letters from Barbary, France, Spain, Portugal, & C. by an English Officer.* London: Printed for T. Cadell, 1788.

Kaplan, Yosef. "Court Jews before the *Hofjuden.*" In *From Court Jews to the Rothschilds: Art, Patronage, and Power, 1600–1800,* edited by Vivian B. Mann and Richard I. Cohen, 11–25. Munich: Prestel, 1996.

——. "The Portuguese Community in 17th-Century Amsterdam and the Ashkenazi World." In *Dutch Jewish History,* vol. 2, edited by Jozeph Michman, 23–45. Jerusalem: Institute for Research on Dutch Jewry, Hebrew University of Jerusalem; Assen/Maastricht: Van Gorcum, 1989.

Katz, David S. *The Jews in the History of England, 1485–1850.* Oxford: Clarendon Press, 1994.

——. *Philo-Semitism and the Readmission of the Jews to England, 1603–1655.* Oxford: Clarendon Press, 1982.

Keatinge, Colonel. *Travels in Europe and Africa.* 2 vols. London: Printed for Henry Colburn, 1816.

Kenbib, Mohammed. *Juifs et Musulmans au Maroc, 1859–1948.* Rabat: Université Mohammed V, Publications de la Faculté des Lettres et des Sciences Humaines, 1994.

——. *Les protégés: contribution à l'histoire contemporaine du Maroc.* Rabat: Université Mohammed V, Publications de la Faculté des Lettres et des Sciences Humaines, 1996.

——. "Les relations entre Musulmans et Juifs au Maroc, 1859–1944: Essai bibliographique." *Hespéris-Tamuda* 23 (1985): 83–104.

al-Khamlishi, ʿAbd al-ʿAziz. "Hawla masʾala binaʾ al-millahat bi-al-mudun al-maghribiya." *Dar al-Niyaba* 4 (spring 1987): 21–28; 5 (summer/fall 1988): 30–41.

Khaneboubi, Ahmed. *Les premiers sultans Mérinids (1269–1331).* Paris: Editions L'Harmattan, 1987.

King, Richard. *The Frauds of London Detected.* London: A. Hogg, 1770.

Kochan, Lionel. *Jews, Idols, and Messiahs: The Challenge from History.* Oxford: Basil Blackwell, 1990.

Koriyat, Avraham. *Berit avot.* Livorno: Printed by Eliyahu Ben Amozeg 1861/62.

Landa, M. J. *The Jew in Drama.* New York: KTAV Publishing House, 1969.

Laredo, Abraham. *Les noms des Juifs du Maroc.* Madrid: Consejo Superior de Investigaciones Científicas, Instituto "B. Arias Montano," 1978.

Laroui, Abdallah. *Les origines sociales et culturelles du nationalisme marocain, 1830–1912.* Paris: Maspero, 1977.

Laski, Neville. *The Laws and Charities of the Spanish and Portuguese Jews Congregation of London.* London: Cresset Press, 1952.

Laskier, Michael M. *The Alliance Israélite Universelle and the Jewish Communities of Morocco, 1862–1962.* Albany: State University of New York Press, 1983.

Lempriere, William. *A Tour from Gibraltar to Tangier, Sallee, Mogodore, Santa Cruz, and Tarudant; and thence over Mount Atlas to Morocco*. Philadelphia: Printed by T. Dobson, 1794.

Leone, Enrico de. "Veneziani e Genovesi nel Marocco nella seconda metà del secolo XVIII." *Levante* 10 (1963): 3–13.

Leoni, Aron di Leone. *La Nazione ebraica spagnola e portoghese negli Stati Estensi*. Rimini: Luisè Editore, 1992.

Le Tourneau, Roger. *Fès avant le protectorat*. Casablanca: SMLE, 1949.

———. *Fez in the Age of the Marinides*. Norman: University of Oklahoma Press, 1961.

Lev, Yaacov. "The Fatimid Vizier Yaʿqub Ibn Killis and the Beginning of the Fatimid Administration in Egypt." *Der Islam* 58 (1981): 237–49.

Levy, Avigdor. *The Sephardim in the Ottoman Empire*. Princeton, N.J.: Darwin Press, 1992.

Lévy, Simon. "La communauté juive dans le context de l'histoire du Maroc du 17ᵉ siècle à nos jours." In *Juifs du Maroc: identité et dialogue*, 105–52. Grenoble: Editions La Pensée Sauvage, 1980.

———. "Hara et Mellāḥ: les mots, l'histoire et l'institution." In *Histoire et linguistique*, Colloque et Seminaires nᵒ 20, edited by Abdelahad Sebti, 41–50. Rabat: Université Mohammed V, Publications de la Faculté des Lettres et des Sciences Humaines, 1992.

Lewis, Bernard. *The Jews of Islam*. Princeton, N.J.: Princeton University Press, 1984.

———. "The Pro-Islamic Jews." *Judaism* 17 (1968): 391–404.

El Libro de los Acuerdos, Being the Records and Accompts of the Spanish and Portuguese Synagogue of London. Edited by Lionel Barnett. Oxford: Printed at the University Press by John Johnson, 1931.

Lindo, E. H. *A Jewish Calendar*. London: Printed by L. Thompson, 1838.

Lipman, V. D. "Sephardi and Other Jewish Immigrants in 18th Century England." In *Migration and Settlement: Proceedings of the Anglo-American Jewish Historical Conference*, 37–62. London: Jewish Historical Society of England, 1971.

———. "Synagogal Organization in Anglo-Jewry." *Jewish Journal of Sociology* 1 (1959): 80–93.

Littman, David. "Jews under Muslim Rule in the Late Nineteenth Century." *Wiener Library Bulletin* 28 (1975): 65–76.

LoRomer, David G. *Merchants and Reform in Livorno, 1814–1868*, 19–22. Berkeley: University of California Press, 1987.

Lourido Díaz, Ramón. "El comercio del trigo entre Marruecos y la Peninsula Iberica en el siglo xviii." *Almenara* 9 (1976): 29–61.

———. "Los Judíos en Marruecos durante el Sultanato de Sidi Muhammad b. Abd Allah (1757–1790)." *Miscelánea de Estudios Arabes y Hebraicos* 26–28 (1977–79): 327–55.

———. *Marruecos y el mundo exterior en la segunda mitad del siglo XVIII*. Madrid: Agencia Española de Cooperación Internacional, 1989.

Luengo, Fr. A. "Mogador: Fundación de la mission católica." *Mauritania* (1 August 1940): 249–51.

Malino, Frances. *The Sephardic Jews of Bordeaux: Assimilation and Emancipation in Revolutionary and Napoleonic France*. Tuscaloosa: University of Alabama Press, 1978.

Marchesi, Vincenzo. "Le relazioni tra la Repubblica veneta ed il Marocco dal 1757 al 1797." *Rivista Storica Italiana* 3 (1886): 34–87.

Marcus, I. G. "Beyond the Sephardic Mystique." *Orim* 1 (1985): 35–53.

Margoliouth, Moses. *The History of the Jews in Great Britain.* 3 vols. London: R. Bentley, 1851.

Marriner, Sheila. "English Bankruptcy Records and Statistics before 1850." *Economic History Review* 33 (1980): 351–66.

Masson, Paul. *Marseille depuis 1789.* 2 vols. Paris, E. de Boccard, 1916–18.

Mayhew, Henry. *London Labour and the London Poor.* 4 vols. London: Frank Cass, 1967.

McNeill, William H. *Plagues and Peoples.* New York: Anchor Books, 1976.

Mercer, Patricia. "Palace and *Jihad* in the Early ʿAlawi State in Morocco." *Journal of African History* 18 (1977): 531–53.

Meyers, Allan R. "Patronage and Protection: The Status of Jews in Precolonial Morocco." In *Jews Among Muslims: Communities in the Precolonial Middle East,* edited by Shlomo Deshen and Walter Zenner, 83–97. London: Macmillan, 1996.

Miège, Jean-Louis. "L'activité maritime d'Essaouira, 1765–1840." In *Essaouira: Mémoire et empreintes du présent, 15–31.* Agadir: Université Ibnou Zohr, Publications de la Faculté des Lettres et des Sciences Humaines, 1994.

——. "Un bicentenaire: Schousboue, botaniste et consul." *Maroc-Europe* 5 (1993): 211–12.

——. "La bourgeoisie juive du Maroc au XIXᵉ siècle: Rupture ou continuité." In *Judaïsme d'Afrique du Nord aux XIXᵉ–XXᵉ siècles,* edited by Michel Abitbol, 25–36. Jerusalem: Institut Ben-Zvi, 1980.

——. "Entre désert et ocean: l'espace economique d'Essaouira au XIXᵉ siècle." *Revue Maroc-Europe* no. 4 (1993): 45–60.

——. "Les Juifs de Gibraltar au XIXᵉ siècle." In *Les relations intercommunautaires juives en méditerranée occidentale, XIIIᵉ–XXᵉ siècles,* 99–118. Paris: Centre National de la Recherche Scientifique, 1984.

——. "Le Maroc et les premières lignes de navigation à vapeur." *Bulletin de l'Enseignement Public au Maroc,* no. 236 (1956): 37–47.

——. *Le Maroc et l'Europe: 1830–1894.* 4 vols. Paris: Presses Universitaires de France, 1961–63.

——, ed. *Chronique de Tanger, 1820–1830: Journal de Bendelac.* Rabat: Editions La Porte, 1995.

Miège, Jean Louis, Mʾhammad Benaboud, and Nadia Erzini. *Tétouan: Ville andalouse marocaine.* Paris: CNRS Editions, 1996; Rabat: Kalila wa dimna, 1996.

Mikhelson, Ehud. *ha-Shoshelet le-vet Pinto: Toldot ha-mishpahah u-maʾase mofet.* Tel Aviv: Gale-Alfa Tikshoret, 1992.

Milano, Attilo. "La constituzione 'livornina' del 1593." *Rassegna Mensile di Israel* 34 (1958): 15–27.

——. "Uno Sguardo sulle relazioni tra la Livorno ebraica e i paesi della Berberia." In *Miscellanea di studi in memoria de Dario Disegni,* edited by E. M. Artom, L. Caro, and S. J. Sierra, 139–51. Turin: Instituto di Studi Ebraica Scuola Rabbinica "S. H. Margulies–D. Disegni," 1969.

Miller, Susan G. "*Dhimma* Reconsidered: Jews, Taxes, and Royal Authority in Nineteenth-Century Tangier." In *In the Shadow of the Sultan*, 103–26.

Morsy, Magali. "Les Juifs marocains à Gibraltar au 18ᵉ siècle: Histoire d'une minorité manipulée." *Pluriel* (1976): 47–60.

———. *North Africa 1800–1900*. London: Longman, 1984.

Mugnier, François. "Relation d'un voyage à Fez en 1825." *Mémoires et Documents de la Société Savoisienne d'Histoire et d'Archéologie* 26 (1887): 351–433.

Mullet, Charles F. "A Century of English Quarantine (1709–1825)." *Bulletin of the History of Medicine* 23 (1949): 527–45.

Munson, Henry, Jr. "Muslim and Jew in Morocco: Reflections on the Distinction between Belief and Behavior." *Poznań Studies in the Philosophy of the Sciences and Humanities* 48 (1996): 357–79.

Naggar, Betty. *Jewish Pedlars and Hawkers, 1740–1940*. Camberley, Surrey: Porphyrogenitus, 1992.

Nahon, Gerard. *Métropoles et périphéries sefarades d'Occident: Kairouan, Amsterdam, Bayonne, Bordeaux, Jérusalem*. Paris: Editions du Cerf, 1993.

Nallino, Maria. "Documenti arabi sulle relazioni tra Genova e il Marocco nella seconda metà del secolo XVIII." *Rivista degle Studi Orientali* 21 (1946): 51–76.

Napier, Edward. *Excursions along the Shores of the Mediterranean*. 2 vols. London: H. Colburn, 1842.

al-Nasiri, Ahmad b. Khalid. *Kitab al-istiqsaʾ li-akhbar duwal al-Maghrib al-Aqsa*. 2d ed. 9 vols. Casablanca: Dar al-Kitab, 1954–56.

Newman, Lewis I. *Richard Cumberland: Critic and Friend of the Jews*. New York: Bloch Publishing Company, 1919.

Oliel-Grausz, Evelyne. "La circulation du personnel rabbinique dans les communautés de la diaspora sépharade au XVIIIᵉ siècle." In *Transmission et passages en monde juif*, edited by Esther Benbassa, 313–34. Paris: Publisud, 1997.

Orkin, Sarah F. *Roots and Recollections*. London: Published by the author, 1995.

ʿOvadiyah, David. *Kehilat Sefru*. 3 vols. Jerusalem: Makhon la-Heker Toldot Kehilot Yehude Maroko, 1975–76.

Paddock, John. *Narrative of the Shipwreck of the Oswego on the Coast of South Barbary*. New York: Published by Captain James Riley, 1818.

Panzac, Daniel. *La peste dans l'Empire Ottoman, 1700–1850*. Louvain: Editions Peeters, 1985.

Paquignon, Paul. "Quelques documents sur la condition des Juifs au Maroc." *Revue du Monde Musulman* 9 (1909): 112–23.

Park, Thomas K. "Inflation and Economic Policy in 19th Century Morocco: The Compromise Solution." *Maghreb Review* 10, nos. 2–3 (1985): 51–56.

Parsons, F. V. *The Origins of the Moroccan Question, 1880–1900*. London: Duckworth, 1976.

Pascon, Paul. "Le commerce de la Maison d'Iligh d'après le registre comptable de Husayn b. Hachem (Tazerwalt, 1850–1875)." *Annales: ESC* 35 (1980): 700–729. (Another version of this article appears in Pascon et al., *La maison d'Iligh*, 43–90.)

Pascon, Paul, with A. Arrif, D. Schroeter, M. Tozy, and H. Van Der Wusten. *La Maison d'Iligh et l'histoire sociale du Tazerwalt*. Rabat: Société Marocaine des Editeurs Réunis, 1984.

Pascon, Paul, and Daniel J. Schroeter. "Le cimetière juif d'Iligh, 1751–1955: Etude des épitaphes comme documents d'histoire sociale." *Revue de l'Occident Musulman et de la Méditerranée* 34, no. 2 (1982): 39–62. Another version of this article appears in Pascon et al., *La Maison d'Iligh*, 113–40.

Phillips, Richard. *Modern London; Being the History and Present State of the British Metropolis*. London: R. Phillips, 1804.

Picciotto, James. *Sketches of Anglo-Jewish History*. London: Trubner & Co., 1875.

Planhol, Xavier de. *Minorités en Islam: Géographie politique et sociale*. Paris: Flammarion, 1997.

Poliakov, Léon. *Les Banchieri juifs et le Saint-Siège du XIIIᵉ au XVIIIᵉ siècle*. Paris: Ecole Pratique des Hautes Etudes, 1965.

Pollins, Harold. *Economic History of the Jews in England*. Rutherford, N.J.: Fairleigh Dickinson University Press, 1982.

Ragussis, Michael. *Figures of Conversion: "The Jewish Question" and English National Identity*. Durham, N.C.: Duke University Press, 1995.

Reitlinger, Gerald. "The Changed Face of English Jewry at the End of the Eighteenth Century." *Transactions of the Jewish Historical Society of England* 23 (1971): 31–41.

Renaud, H.-P.-J. "La peste de 1799 d'après des documents inédits." *Hespéris* 1 (1923): 160–82.

———. "Un nouveau document marocain sur la peste de 1799." *Hespéris* 5 (1923): 83–90.

Richardson, James. *Travels in Morocco*. 2 vols. London: Charles J. Skeet, 1860.

Riley, James. *An Authentic Narrative of the Loss of the American Brig Commerce*. Hartford, Conn.: S. Andrus & Son, 1846.

Robbins, Archibald. *A Journal Comprising an Account of the Loss of the Brig Commerce*. Hartford, Conn.: Silas Andrus & Son, 1851.

Robertson, William. *A Residence at Gibraltar and a Visit to the Peninsula in the Summer of 1841*. Edinburgh: A. Fullarton & Co, 1844.

Rodinson, Maxime. *Islam and Capitalism*. Austin: University of Texas Press, 1978.

Rodrigues-Pereira, Miriam, and Chloe Loewe, eds. *The Birth Register (1767–1881) of the Spanish & Portuguese Jews' Congregation, London*. London: The Spanish & Portuguese Jews' Congregation, 1993.

Rogers, P. G. *A History of Anglo-Moroccan Relations to 1900*. London: Foreign and Commonwealth Office, n.d.

Romanelli, Samuel. *Travail in an Arab Land*. Translated by Yedida K. Stillman and Norman A. Stillman. Tuscaloosa: University of Alabama Press, 1989.

Rosen, Lawrence. *Bargaining for Reality: The Construction of Social Relations in a Muslim Community*. Chicago: University of Chicago Press, 1984.

———. "Muslim-Jewish Relations in a Moroccan City." *International Journal of Middle Eastern Studies* 3 (1972): 435–49.

Rosenstock, Morton. "The House of Bacri and Busnach: A Chapter from Algeria's Commercial History." *Jewish Social Studies* 14 (1952): 343–64.

Roth, Cecil. "The Amazing Clan of Buzaglo." *Transactions of the Jewish Historical Society of England* 23 (1971): 11–22.

———. *Doña Gracia of the House of Nasi*. Philadelphia: Jewish Publication Society of America, 1948.

——. *A History of the Jews in England*. Oxford: Oxford University Press, 1941.

——. *The House of Nasi: The Duke of Naxos*. Philadelphia: Jewish Publication Society of America, 1948.

——. "Jacob Benider: Moroccan Envoy at the Court of St. James (1772)." *Miscellanies of the Jewish Historical Society of England* 2 (1935): 84–90.

——. "Why Anglo-Jewish History?" *Transactions of the Jewish Historical Society of England* 22 (1970).

——, ed. *Anglo-Jewish Letters*. London: Soncino Press, 1938.

Rozen, Minna. *bi-Netive ha-Yam ha-Tikhon: ha-pezurah ha-Yehudit-Sefaradit be-me³ot ha-16–18*. Tel Aviv: Ha-Katedrah le-Heker ha-Tarbut ve-ha-Historiyah shel Yehude Saloniki ve-Yavan, Universitat Tel Aviv, 1993.

——. "Contest and Rivalry in Mediterranean Maritime Commerce in the First Half of the Eighteenth Century: The Jews of Salonika and the European Presence." *Revue des Etudes Juives* 147 (1988): 309–52.

——. "The Leghorn Merchants in Tunis and their Trade with Marseilles at the End of the 17th Century." In *Les relations intercommunautaires juives en méditerranée occidentale, XIIIᵉ–XXᵉ siècles*, 51–59. Paris: Centre National de la Recherche Scientifique, 1984.

Rubens, Alfred. *A Jewish Iconography*. London: The Jewish Museum, 1954.

——. "Portrait of Anglo-Jewry, 1656–1836." *Transactions of the Jewish Historical Society of England* 19 (1960): 13–52.

Rudé, George. *Hanoverian London, 1714–1808*. Berkeley: University of California Press, 1971.

al-Saffar, Muhammad. *Disorienting Encounters: Travels of a Moroccan Scholar in France in 1845–1846: The voyage of Muhammad as-Saffar*. Translated and edited by Susan Gilson Miller. Berkeley: University of California Press, 1992.

Said, Edward W. *Orientalism*. New York: Vintage Books, 1979.

Samuel, Edgar R. "The Jews in English Foreign Trade—A Consideration of the 'Philo Patriae' Pamphlets of 1753." In *Remember the Days*, edited by John M. Shaftesley, 123–43. London: Jewish Historical Society of England, 1966.

Samuel, W. S. "A List of Jewish Persons Endenizened and Naturalised 1609–1799." *Transactions of the Jewish Historical Society of England* 22 (1970): 111–44.

Saugnier and Brisson. *Voyages to the Coast of Africa*. London: G. G. J. Robinson, 1792.

Schroeter, Daniel J. "La découverte des Juifs berbères." In *Relations Judéo-Muslmanes au Maroc: perceptions et realités*, edited by Michel Abitbol, 169–87. Paris: Editions Stavit, 1997.

——. "The Jewish Quarter and the Moroccan City." In *New Horizons in Sephardic Studies*, edited by Yedida K. Stillman and George K. Zucker, 67–81. Albany: State University of New York Press, 1993.

——. *Merchants of Essaouira: Urban Society and Imperialism in Southwestern Morocco, 1844–1886*. Cambridge: Cambridge University Press, 1988.

——. "Orientalism and the Jews of the Mediterranean." *Journal of Mediterranean Studies* 4, no. 2 (1994): 183–96.

——. Review of Bernard Lewis, *The Jews of Islam*. *International Journal of Middle East Studies* 21 (1989): 601–5.

——. "The Royal Palace Archives of Rabat and the Makhzan in the 19th Century." *Maghreb Review* 7, nos. 1–2 (1982): 41–45.

———. "Royal Power and the Economy in Precolonial Morocco: Jews and the Legitimation of Foreign Trade." In *In the Shadow of the Sultan: Culture, Power, and Politics in Morocco*, edited by Rahmah Bourqia and Susan G. Miller, 74–102. Cambridge, Mass.: Harvard University Press, 1999.

———. "Trade as a Mediator in Muslim-Jewish Relations: Southwestern Morocco in the Nineteenth Century." In *Jews among Arabs: Contacts and Boundaries*, edited by Mark R. Cohen and Abraham L. Udovitch, 113–40. Princeton, N.J.: Darwin Press, 1989.

Schwarzfuchs, Simon. "La 'Nazione Ebrea' livournaise au Levant." *Rassegna Mensile di Israel* 50 (1984): 707–24.

Serels, M. Mitchell. "Sephardic Printing as a Source of Historical Material." In *The Sephardi and Oriental Jewish Heritage*, edited by Issachar Ben-Ami, 123–31. Jerusalem: Magnes Press, The Hebrew University, 1982.

Serfaty, Nicole S. *Les courtisans juifs des sultans marocains: hommes politiques et hauts dignitaires XIIᵉ–XVIIIᵉ siècles*. Paris: Editions Bouchène, 1999.

Shane, A. L. "Isaac D'Israeli and His Quarrel with the Synagogue—A Reassessment." *Transactions of the Jewish Historical Society of England* 29 (1988): 165–75.

Shatzmiller, Maya. *The Berbers and the Islamic State: The Marinid Experience in Pre-Protectorate Morocco*. Princeton, N.J.: Markus Wiener, 2000.

———. "An Ethnic Factor in a Medieval Social Revolution: The Role of Jewish Courtiers under the Marinids." In *Islamic Society and Culture: Essays in Honour of Professor Aziz Ahmad*, edited by Milton Israel and N. K. Wagle, 149–63. New Delhi: Manohar, 1983.

Shokeid, Moshe. "Jewish Existence in a Berber Environment." In *Les relations entre Juifs et Musulmans en Afrique du Nord, XIXᵉ–XXᵉ siècles*, 62–71. Paris: Centre National de la Recherche Scientifique, 1980.

al-Sibti, ʿAbd al-Ahad and ʿAbd al-Rahman Lakhsassi. *Min al-shaʾ ila al-tayʾ: al-ʿadath wa-al-tarikh*. Rabat: Manshurat Kulliyat al-Adab wa-al-ʿUlum al-Insaniya bi-al-Rabat, 1999.

Sonnino, Guido. *Storia della tipografia ebraica in Livorno*. Turin: Casale Monf.–Tip. Giuseppe Lavagno, 1912.

Southey, Robert. *Letters from England*. Edited by Jack Simmons. London: Cresset Press, 1951.

Stern, Selma. *The Court Jew: A Contribution to the History of Absolutism in Central Europe*. Philadelphia: Jewish Publication Society of America, 1950.

Stillman, Norman A. *The Jews of Arab Lands*. Philadelphia: Jewish Publication Society of America, 1979.

———. *The Language and Culture of the Jews of Sefrou, Morocco: An Ethnolinguistic Study*. Manchester: University of Manchester Press, 1988.

———. "The Moroccan Jewish Experience: A Revisionist View." *Jerusalem Quarterly* 9 (1978): 111–23.

———. "Muslims and Jews in Morocco: Perceptions, Images, Stereotypes." In *Proceedings of the Seminar on Muslim-Jewish Relations in North Africa*, 13–26. New York: World Jewish Congress, 1975.

———. "Myth, Counter-Myth and Distortion." *Tikkun* 6, no. 3 (1991): 60–64.

———. "Two Accounts of the Persecution of the Jews of Tetouan in 1790." In

Michael, vol. 5, edited by Daniel Carpi, Yehuda Nini, and Shlomo Simonsohn, 130–42. Tel-Aviv: Diaspora Research Institute, 1978.

Stillman, Norman A., and Yedida K. Stillman. "The Jewish Courtier Class in Late Eighteenth-Century Morocco as Seen through the Eyes of Samuel Romanelli." In *Essays in Honor of Bernard Lewis: The Islamic World from Classical to Modern Times*, edited by C. E. Bosworth et al., 845–54. Princeton, N.J.: Darwin Press, 1988.

Stow, Kenneth R. "Papal and Royal Attitudes toward Jewish Lending in the Thirteenth Century." *Association for Jewish Studies Review* 6 (1981): 161–74.

Sumbel, Leah Wells. *Memoirs of the Life of Mrs. Sumbel, Late Wells*. 3 vols. London: C. Chapple, 1811.

Szymański, Edward. "La guerre hispano-marocain 1859–1860: début de l'histoire du Maroc contemporain (essai de périodisation)." *Rocnik Orientalistyczny* 29, no. 2 (1965): 53–65.

Tawfiq, Ahmad. *al-Mujtamaᶜ al-maghribi fi al-qarn al-tasiᶜ ᶜashr: Inultan (1850–1912)*. 2 vols. Rabat: Manshurat Kulliyat al-Adab wa-al-ᶜUlum al-Insaniya bi-al-Rabat, 1978–80.

Taylor, J. *A Picturesque Tour in Spain, Portugal, and along the Coast of Africa, from Tangiers to Tetuan*. Paris: Published by Robert Jennings, 1827.

Thomassy, Raymond. *Le Maroc et ses caravanes ou relations de la France avec cet Empire*. Paris: F. Didot Frères, 1845.

Thomson, Ann. *Barbary and Enlightenment: European Attitudes towards the Maghreb in the 18th Century*. Leiden: Brill, 1987.

Toaff, Alfredo S. "Cenni storici sulla comunità ebraica e sulla sinagoga di Livorno." *Rassegna Mensile di Israel* 21 (1955): 355–430.

———. "Il Collegio rabbinico di Livorno." *Rassegna Mensile di Israel* 12 (1938): 184–95.

Toaff, Renzo. "Livorno, comunità sefardita." *Rassegna Mensile di Israel* 38 (1972): 203–9.

———. *La Nazione ebrea a Livorno e a Pisa: 1591–1700*. Florence: L. S. Olschki, 1990.

Tolédano, Joseph. *La Saga des familles: les Juifs du Maroc et leurs noms*. Tel Aviv: Editions Stavit, 1983.

Tomlinson, Edward Murray. *A History of the Minories*. London: J. Murray, 1922.

Vajda, Georges. *Un recueil de textes historiques judéo-marocains*. Paris: Larose, 1951.

———. "Un traité maghrébin 'adversus judaeos': 'Aḥkam ahl al-dimma' du šayḥ Muḥammad b. ᶜAbd al-Karīm al-Maǧīlī," In *Etudes d'orientalisme dediées à la mémoire de Lévi-Provençal*, 2:805–13. Paris: G.-P. Maisonneuve et Larose, 1962.

Valensi, Lucette. *On the Eve of Colonialism: North Africa before the French Conquest*. New York: Africana Publishing Company, 1977.

al-Wansharisi. *al-Miyar al-Maghrib*. Translated by Emile Amar, "La pierre de touche des fétwas." *Archives Marocaines* 12 (1908):12–13.

Wasserstrom, Steven M. *Between Muslim and Jew: The Problem of Symbiosis under Early Islam*. Princeton, N.J.: Princeton University Press, 1995.

Waterbury, John. *The Commander of the Faithful*. London: Weidenfeld and Nicolson, 1970.

Wendeborn, F. A. *A View of England towards the Close of the Eighteenth Century*. London: Printed for G. G. J. and J. Robinson, 1791.

Williams, Stanley Thomas. *Richard Cumberland: His Life and Dramatic Works*. New Haven, Conn.: Yale University Press, 1917.

Wolf, Lucien. *Essays in Jewish History*. Edited by Cecil Roth. London: Jewish Historical Society of England, 1934.

———. *Sir Moses Montefiore: A Centennial Biography*. New York: Harper & Brothers, 1885.

Wood, Alfred C. *A History of the Levant Company*. New York: Barnes & Noble, 1964.

Zafrani, Haïm. *Etudes et recherches sur la vie intellectuelle juive au Maroc de la fin du 15ᵉ siècle au début du 20ᵉ siècle*, vol. 1: *Pensée juridique et environnement social, économique et religieux*. Paris: Geuthner, 1972.

———. *Mille ans de vie juive au Maroc*. Paris: G.-P. Maisonneuve et Larose, 1983.

Zaki, MᵉBarek. "Le Maroc et Gênes: Quelques aspects des relations entre 1700 et 1800." *Revue Maroc-Europe*, no. 2 (1992): 81–110.

Zangwill, Louis. "Richard Cumberland Centenary Memorial Paper." *Transactions of the Jewish Historical Society of England* 7 (1915): 147–79.

Jewish acculturation in, 62, 65, 68–69, 75–76; Jewish civil status in 55–56, 60–61; Jewish immigration to, 45–50, 60–61, 67–68; 145–56; Public Record Office, xii, xiv, 52, 143, 147–48; and readmission of the Jews, 60–61; Sephardim in, 55–56, 59, 60–76, 144–46; and trade with Morocco 19, 20, 23, 46–47, 52–53, 60, 62, 67, 69, 70, 77–79, 82, 98, 126, 127, 138, 154. *See also* Gibraltar; London

Guedalla, David, 47, 78, 101

Guedalla, Haim, 19, 23, 30, 31, 32, 52, 71, 78, 79, 89, 93, 97, 102, 170*n*28, 176*n*109

Guedalla, Haim (son of Judah), 73, 145

Guedalla, Jacob, 28, 145, 147

Guedalla, Judah, 47, 71, 73, 75, 78, 97, 101–2, 103, 138, 145

Guedalla, Moses, 145

Guedalla family, 19, 28, 29, 30, 31, 32, 46, 47, 48, 71, 73, 75, 77, 78, 93, 115, 119, 145, 147

Hadida family, 71

Hadith, 8

Hadiyya. *See* Gifts and the sharifian court

Haha region, 30

Hajj, 111, 127

Halakhah (*halakhic*), 8, 33, 66, 74

Hamburg, 66, 67, 116

Hamet a Moussa. *See* Sidi Ahmed U Musa

Hancock, Thomas, 50

al-Hasan, Mawlay (sultan), 151

Hashim b. ʿAli (Abu Damiʿa), 34

Hawz region, 27

Hay, E. W. A. Drummond, 139–42

Hay, R. W., 134–35

Hebrew language, xix, 152

Hekdesh (Jewish religious endowments), 59

Hijaz, 127

Hisham, (Mawlay), 25, 27, 28, 29–30, 31

Hofjude. *See under* Court Jews

Holland, 40, 46, 65, 66, 67, 116, 127, 132; consuls of, in Morocco, 28, 29, 31, 32, 33, 47, 116, 106–7, 111, 120; Moroccan trade with, 20, 29, 30, 45–46, 53. *See also* Amsterdam

Høst, Georg, 24

Iberian peninsula, 39, 98–100, 116

Ibn al-Talib, ʿAbd al-Karim, 96

Ibn Jallun, al-Talib, 111, 120, 201*n*90

Ibn Nasir, ʿAbd al-Rahman, 24, 25, 26, 28, 30, 176*n*109

Ibrahim (Mawlay), 80, 108

Ida U Tanan, 82

Iligh, 22, 34, 150

Imin Tanaʾute, 82

Islam: and commerce, 18; and *hajj*, 111, 127; idea of Muslim-Jewish symbiosis in, 5–7; and interest and usury, 12, 18, 34, 94; and legality of grain exports, 99–100; and position of Jews compared to Christian world, 8–9, 56, 121, 158; and taxation, 99; and travel to Christian world, 127. *See also Dhimmi*; *Jihad*; *Shariʿa*

Ismaʿil, Mawlay (sultan), 27, 38

Israel, Isaac, 100, 126

Istanbul, 19, 66

Italian language, 40, 63, 82

Italy, 67, 70, 128

Izmir, 40

Jackson, James Gray, 20–21, 23, 25, 29, 31, 38, 78, 80, 89

al-Jamaʿi, Sidi al-Mukhtar, 140–41

Jew Bill, 55

The Jew (Cumberland), 57

The Jew of Mogadore: A Comic Opera in Three Acts (Cumberland), 57, 140

Jewish quarter. See *Mellah*

Jihad, 10–11, 87, 101

Jizya, 8, 13, 88, 90, 153

Journal of the Plague Year (Defoe), 50

Judeo-Arabic language, xvii, 41, 82. *See also* Arabic language

Judeo-Spanish language, 73. *See also*, Spanish language

Keatinge, Colonel, 18

Ketubah (pl. *ketubot*), 84, 152

Larache, 105

Law. See *Halakhah*; Maliki school of jurisprudence; Rabbinical courts; *Shariʿa*

Layton, Andrew, 28, 30

Levi, Eliahu, 23, 24, 28, 172*n*53; 174*n*85

Levi, Shlomo, 94

Levy (Ben Hamu), Haim, 154

Levy (Ben Hamu), Judah, 152, 154, 157

Levy (Ben Hamu), Meir, 152

Levy (Ben Hamu) family, 152, 154, 155, 156, 157. *See also* Amar (Bujnah) family

115*n*16; and Darb Macnin ("Street of Macnin"), 141, 146, 177*n*116; descendants and heirs of, xi, xiv, 148–58; in England, 57, 72–73, 145–46, 148; in Marrakesh, 17, 84, 147–48; and name, xiii, 15, 146, 148

Madina. See under Essaouira

Madrid Conference, 154. *See also* Protection and protégés

Mahamad (*ma*ʿ*amad*). *See under* Spanish and Portuguese Jews' Congregation

Makhzan (central administration of Moroccan government). *See* ʿAlawid dynasty; Merchants; Property; *and individual sultans.*

Málaga, 116

Malik Ibn Anas, 79

Maliki school of jurisprudence, 79, 156

Malta, 126

al-Maʾmun (sultan), 16

Manchester, 126

Marinid dynasty, 2, 16

Marital practices and strategies, 32, 41, 43, 73, 84–86, 109, 145, 147, 152, 176*n*115

Marrakesh, xi, xiii, 15–17, 18, 24, 82, 96, 97, 108, 116, 125, 134, 140, 143, 147–53, 155, 157; court of sultans in, 23, 25, 29, 30, 31, 52, 80, 92, 119–20, 123, 149, 153; foundation of, 15–16; Jewish community of, 15–17, 74, 95, 96; Jewish merchants in, 18, 23, 81–85, 109, 115, 152, 156; Jews settle in, 15–17, 167*n*4; and Mawlay Hisham, 25, 30, 31; *mellah* of, 16–17, 90, 95, 141, 146, 150, 177*n*116; pillaged during al-Yazid's reign, 27–28; plague in, 37–38

Marranos. *See* New Christians

Marseilles, 20, 23, 43, 104, 114, 128, 123, 126, 201–2*n*1

Mashisha, Moshe b., 34

Massaʾ Baʿrav (Romanelli), 18–19

Matra, James, 48, 52, 54

Mawsim. See Sidi Ahmad U Musa

Mayhew, Henry, 67

Mazagan. *See* El Jadida

Mead, Richard, 49

Mecca, 126

Mediterranean trade, 39–43, 46. *See also* Sephardim

Meknes, 27, 38, 75, 90, 112

Meldola, David, 74

Meldola, Raphael, 69, 74

Mellah (Jewish Quarter/Jewry), 27–29, 90–95, 108, 141, 150; foundation in Essaouira, 90–92; foundation in Fez; 17; foundation in Marrakesh, 16–17; Sulayman's creation of, 90–92

Merchants: Central European Jews as, 3; Christian and European, in Morocco, 17, 22–23, 30, 53, 78–79, 80–81, 85, 108, 114–15, 119, 176*n*109; English Jews as, 62, 66, 69, 76; and Jews and capitalism, 3, 26, 147, 157–58; Muslims as, 70, 79–80, 86, 96, 111, 126; and *tujjar* (sing. *tajir*) *al-sultan* (royal merchants), 34, 51, 54, 84–87, 109, 115, 126, 148–51, 153, 154–55. *See also individual merchants*

Merchants, Jewish. *See* Sephardim; *and individual merchants*

Millenarianism in England, 61, 186*n*9

Miramir, 82

Miran, Mordekhai, 81, 82

Mithqal. See Coins and currency

Mitzvah (pl. *mitzvot*), 95, 96, 138

Mocatta, Isaac, 75

Mogador. *See* Essaouira

Monopolies, of Jews with exclusive export rights, 17, 105–6, 115

Montefiore, Sir Moses, 68–69, 72–73, 144, 153

Montefiore family, xiii–xiv, 68–69, 72–73

Moroccan archives, xiii

Muhammad b. ʿAbdallah, Sidi (sultan), xi, 13, 17, 19, 22, 23–26, 29, 79, 87, 88, 108, 142; trade policies of, 13, 17, 22, 34

Mullowny, John (U.S. consul). *See* United States

Munitions trade, 23, 28, 54, 101, 104, 120

Munson, Henry, 10

Murabit, 15, 34

Nagid, 18, 169*n*21, 172*n*53

Naples, 126

Napoleonic Wars, xiii, 14, 43, 46, 51, 68, 78, 90, 99–100

Netherlands. *See* Holland

New Christians, 39, 60–61, 62, 65, 66

Nieto, David, 69

Nieto, Isaac, 69

Northumberland (ship). *See* Shipwrecks

Novo Cemetery. *See under* Spanish and Portuguese Jews' Congregation